Meaning and Translation

Meaning and Translation

Philosophical and Linguistic Approaches

edited by
F. Guenthner and
M. Guenthner-Reutter

New York · New York University Press · 1978

Library of Congress Catalog Card Number: 78–57003
ISBN 0–8147–2974–6

Manufactured in Great Britain

Contents

Introduction

A FRUITFUL PERSPECTIVE on recent work in the philosophy of language as well as in linguistics is provided by the way both disciplines have attempted to deal with the notion of *translation* and its relations to semantic theory. Above all two works in the last twenty years have been fundamental in relating the theory of meaning and the theory of translation: Quine's 'Meaning and Translation' (1959), later incorporated in an expanded form into Chapter II of *Word and Object*, and Montague's 'Universal Grammar' (1970). It is not an exaggerated claim to assert that these two papers not only contain the central principles with respect to which any preoccupation with translation has to be evaluated, but also that they represent two fundamentally different views about the role of translation as a part of a theory of language. From Quine's work it would follow that translation is essentially an *object of analysis*; from Montague's, on the other hand, that it is a *method of analysis*. One of the aims of this collection is to clarify the basic features of these two approaches to translation.

By translation as object we mean essentially the analysis of existing or purported translations as well as the problem of producing translations (or translation relations) for expressions or languages. Philosophers and linguists have approached translation in this sense by raising quite different questions. The former have tended to ask to which extent translations are possible at all or to which extent they are determinable, whereas the latter have been more concerned with studying the ways the different structures of natural languages (their lexical, syntactic and logical diversity) interfere with translatability and relative expressibility. An important recent development in this domain is the step beyond purely lexical analyses to the investigation of principles of universal grammar and it is likely that future research in the theory of translation will profit immensely from the results in this area.

Some of the essays in this volume can be regarded as direct or indirect attempts to revise or refute Quine's assumptions about the 'indeterminacy' of translation as well as attempts to understand the role of translation in theories of truth for natural language (Wheeler, Tymoczko, Wallace). Related to this is the other main concern under this heading, namely, the problem of reference and identity of reference and meaning as a possible criterion for the adequacy of translations (Cresswell, Wilson, Putnam). The difficulties involved in the translation of self-referential expressions and of expressions in indirect contexts, which have been central issues in earlier discussions of translatability and synonymity, are reconsidered in the contributions by Burge and Bigelow. From a linguistic point of view, three essays (Katz, Keenan, Givón) deal explicitly with the ways natural languages can differ in their expressive power and how such differences affect translations. Evidence for a theory of translations based on the notion of a 'degree of translation' is provided from a wide variety of the world's languages.

When translation is used as a method, it is usually with the purpose of reducing the analysis of a language to that of another, better understood, idiom. This is a common practice in 'formal philosophy' (of which Montague's work is an important example). In our opinion, translation should be viewed as a mediating tool between 'two points sometimes mistakenly supposed incompatible: there is philosophic interest in attempting to analyse ordinary English; and ordinary English is an inadequate vehicle for philosophy' (Montague, 1974a, 186).

In particular, translations from natural languages to languages of predicate logic, and more recently, of modal and intensional logic, are employed in representing the logical structure of ordinary languages and in stating the semantic interpretation of these indirectly via the interpretation of the formal languages into which they are translated in a precise way. Different methodologies based on techniques of translation are at present being explored in this area. There are two basic problems which have to be resolved here: first, the exact nature of the *rules of translation* has to be determined; i.e. whether translations are to be obtained on the basis of metalinguistic statements as in Montague's theory or in terms of definitional extensions of languages and definitional axioms. Second, there is the problem of constructing the logical languages in which the logical structure of natural languages can be represented in a maximal way. There is some evidence that predicate logic in its standard formulation is not quite adequate as a representing language for all natural languages. Even Montague, who ultimately reduces ordinary English to predicate logic (as far as the 'extensional' fragment of English is concerned), has to resort to a higher-order language with lambda-abstraction in order to provide appropriate translations for English sentences. More radically different formal languages will have to be constructed if the logic of natural languages is to be adequately captured. More likely still, it seems that no single formal language will do for the analysis of all natural languages if it is to possess any explanatory power as far as the syntactic and semantic facts of particular languages are concerned. Here again, there will be an important use for translations, for if we have different formal representing languages we can then attempt to translate these in turn into some extension of predicate logic (for the extensional fragments, for instance) and compare on the basis of such translations the expressive capacities of the natural languages in question.

The papers by Katz, Keenan and Givón amply demonstrate how complex such representing languages for natural languages will have to be. Kamp's paper is a detailed description of how translation relations between two languages can be constructed and evaluated; this paper as well as Cooper's are based on Montague's theory of grammar and both show that translations from a natural language into a formal language is a means of providing a semantics as well as a justification of the syntactic analyses for the natural language under consideration. The construction of new formal languages and their relation to natural languages on the one hand and to predicate logic on the other is exemplified in the area of the treatment of quantification in the paper by Åqvist and Guenthner.

With the exception of Putnam's essay (which has appeared in a somewhat different form elsewhere), all the papers in this collection were especially written for it. For diverse reasons we forego presenting detailed summaries of their contents and main results. A substantial introduction to the variety of approaches and the particular issues discussed would not only go far beyond the scope of an introduction of this sort, it would also imply shading the glasses of the reader with views that he or she can and should certainly do without.

Arranging the papers as we have done will give an indication of their general themes. Other groupings as well as many other topics could have been possible. As such, this collection is certainly not meant to be representative of *all* current work on translation. Quite a few different and sometimes conflicting theories of meaning and translation are proposed, but they can all be taken to show that the connections between translation and theories of meaning (theories of reference, possible world semantics, theories of truth or semantics within a particular linguistic framework) are still in need of elucidation. The evident bias has been towards logically oriented analyses and it is hoped that this volume reveals not only some aspects of the relations between its two subject matters, but also between the disciplines which deal with them.

We are very grateful to all the contributors for their interest in this collection and for their generous assistance; in particular, we would like to

1*

acknowledge the support and encouragement received from the publishers in preparing this volume.

F. Guenthner
M. Guenthner-Reutter
University of Stuttgart

Notes on the Contributors

M. J. Cresswell is a Professor of Philosophy at Victoria University in Wellington, New Zealand

T. Tymoczko is an Associate Professor of Philosophy at Smith College, Northampton, Mass.

J. Wallace is a Professor of Philosophy at the University of Minnesota, Minneapolis

H. Putnam is a Professor of Philosophy at Harvard University, Cambridge, Mass.

S. Wheeler is an Associate Professor of Philosophy at the University of Connecticut, Storrs, Conn.

N. L. Wilson is a Professor of Philosophy at McMasters University, Hamilton, Ont.

J. Bigelow is a Lecturer in Philosophy at Victoria University in Wellington, New Zealand

T. Burge is an Associate Professor of Philosophy at the University of California at Los Angeles

E. L. Keenan is a Professor of Linguistics at the University of California at Los Angeles

J. J. Katz is a Professor of Philosophy at the City University in New York

T. Givón is a Professor of Linguistics at the University of California at Los Angeles

H. Kamp is a Lecturer in Philosophy at Bedford College, London

R. Cooper is an Assistant Professor of Linguistics at the University of Massachusetts, Amherst, Mass.

L. Åqvist and F. Guenthner are researchers in a project on the formal semantics of natural language supported by the Deutsche Forschungsgemeinschaft at Stuttgart

M. Guenthner-Reutter is a *Lehrbeauftragte* in Linguistics at the University of Stuttgart

I

MEANING AND TRANSLATION

M. J. Cresswell

Semantic Competence

CHOMSKY'S DISTINCTION BETWEEN linguistic competence and linguistic performance (Chomsky, 1965, 3–15) is well known, widely discussed and contentious. For all its difficulties it seems to me a vital distinction and I want, in this paper, to show how an account of semantic competence can be given which links it directly with semantical theories of a truth-conditional kind.

I take it that the basic difference between competence and performance is that linguistic competence is an ability which underlies linguistic activity. In the area of syntax linguistic competence is concerned with the class of sentences a native speaker finds grammatically acceptable, linguistic performance with the sentences we find a speaker actually producing.[1] This paper is to be about *semantic* competence. I want to argue for an account of semantic competence which will favour truth-conditional semantics (whether of the possible-worlds variety or the Davidsonian variety) over, on the one hand, semantics of the Katz/Fodor/Postal type (henceforth KF semantics); and on the other hand over the 'speech act' type of Searle and Grice. KF semantics will be argued to be incomplete, rather than incorrect; and the speech-act theories will be revealed as theories of semantic performance rather than as theories of semantic competence.[2]

1. Truth Conditions

In a recent paper, Katz and Nagel (1974) list what they take to be the data of semantics. Semantic competence on their view explains the ability of

1. A great deal of the discussion of competence and performance has been focused on the role of the 'ideal speaker-hearer'. It may be that my construal of the distinction as one between the sentences a speaker accepts and the sentences he produces is itself a tendentious one but there nevertheless does seem to me an ability, which native speakers have, to distinguish between the sentences which are grammatically acceptable and those which are grammatically unacceptable. This ability is evidenced in part by what native speakers say they find acceptable or unacceptable although, as mentioned in section 4, only in part.

2. Any semantics which proposes a base in formal logic (e.g. McCawley, 1971; or Lakoff, 1972) is probably, even if without knowing it, coming down in favour of a truth-conditional view of semantic competence.

speakers to make judgments about the following kinds of property: synonymy, redundancy, contradictoriness, entailment, ambiguity, semantic anomaly, antonymy and superordination; and they give illustrations.[3]

Now certainly a theory of semantic competence ought to explain the native speaker's ability to make judgments of this kind, but surely Katz and Nagel have left out the crucial point that semantics is about the relation between language and the world? What I want to put forward as the semantic competence of a native speaker is nothing more nor less than his ability, when presented with a sentence and a situation, to tell whether the sentence, in that situation, is true or false.

Consider the sentence

(1)   John is married.

Our native speaker knows that he must judge (1) to be true in a circumstance in which John *is* married and false in a circumstance in which John is not married; i.e. he must judge that (1) is true iff John is married. This of course is little more than Tarski's definition of truth presented as an account of semantic competence. To be sure. Indeed I hope to show why it is that Tarski's theory seems at once so obvious and yet apparently so contentless.

Consider a child who does not know the meaning of the (English)[4] sentence

(2)   The cat is on the mat.

I am suggesting that coming to know the meaning of (2) is coming to know that when the child is in a situation in which the cat *is* on the mat he can describe (2) as 'true' and when the child is in a situation in which the cat is not on the mat he can describe it as 'false'.[5] Now of course in setting

3. Katz and Nagel, 1974, 313. Their main point is to show that a theory based on Carnapian meaning postulates is not adequate as a theory of semantics. This they do well, though the introduction to their paper gives the unfortunate impression that Carnap's is a 'most recent form of intensionalist theory'. They do not mention possible-worlds semantics.

4. I have to say 'the English sentence' in case it should happen that that same sentence has, in another language, a different meaning. (Or even e.g. that an eccentric English speaker uses the words 'cat' and 'mat' to mean what the rest of us mean by 'dog' and 'log'.)

5. A point which will emerge later, when we discuss theories of semantic performance, is that the description of this ability, makes no reference to the purpose of uttering (2). Why someone, the child, his teacher, or anyone else should choose to utter this sentence is not, in the view of this paper, involved in the notion of semantic competence.

up this case I have done so by using language. But the child's being in a situation in which the cat is on the mat is not a fact of language; so that in teaching the child to accept (2) as true when and only when he is in a situation in which the cat *is* on the mat, we really are matching up a sentence with the way the world is. (This has been put in such a way as to make it appear that a child cannot be said to know the meaning of (2) unless he can use the words 'true' and 'false'. What I really mean is that knowing the meaning of (2) amounts to recognising that relationship between (2) and the cat's being on the mat which we describe using the words 'true' and 'false', whether or not the child knows those words.)

Of course the situation is somewhat more complicated than I have described. Indeed from certain points of view I have chosen a bad example in (2). For in order to make plausible the talk of situations in which the child has been placed, and particularly to make plausible the idea that these have all been *actual* situations (for what other situations has the child *actually* been in?) I have had to choose a sentence which can change its truth value with the passage of time. Such sentences are sometimes called *context-dependent* or *indexical* sentences. In this case to know whether to judge the sentence to be true or false we must know what time reference is being understood (and we must also know which cat is intended).

The proper way to represent indexicality can be and is frequently disputed.[6] It is certainly an important topic, but the points I am trying to make in this paper can be made equally well by choosing a sentence which is not context dependent. Consider the sentence

(3) There is a cat on the smallest table in the seminar room of 22 Kelburn Parade, Wellington, New Zealand, at 1.30 p.m. NZDT on 15 November 1974.

This sentence is false. And since the time and place references have been incorporated into it there is no situation *in the actual world* in which it is true. But is this all that there is to be grasped about the meaning of (3)?

6. One approach is to treat each contextual feature such as e.g. time, place, utterer . . . etc. as an 'index' (Montague, 1974a; Scott, 1970, 143ff; Lewis, 1972, 174–6) and say that each sentence determines a set of possible worlds only with respect to a complete assignment of contextual indices. The possible world itself can also be regarded as an index and in that case what a sentence determines when the complete context is supplied is simply a truth value. I have suggested (Cresswell, 1973, 114) that contexts of use should be construed as properties of utterances. A quite different analysis, which construes all sentences as embedded in performatives, has been advocated by Lakoff (1972) who claims (p. 569) that the need for contextual indices disappears. Still another approach, in the Davidson tradition, is advocated by Tyler Burge (1974).

Clearly not. Something more is needed. In brief we need to know not the truth *value* of (3) but rather the truth *conditions* of (3).

One approach is to say that knowing what (3) means is not a matter of knowing that it *is* false, but being able to say in what circumstances it would not be false; i.e. we must take into account not only the way the world *actually* is but all the ways the world might be. Putting the point in language which sounds metaphysically grander but which at bottom amounts to the same thing, we say that truth judgments must be evaluated not only with respect to the actual world but with respect to all possible worlds.[7]

Knowing the meaning of (3) then, is simply having the ability to distinguish between worlds in which it is true and worlds in which it is false. This idea leads directly to what is called *possible-worlds semantics*. In possible-worlds semantics a collection of possible worlds is taken as primitive and the meaning of every sentence is identified with the set of worlds in which it is true. A set of possible worlds therefore is sometimes called a *proposition*.

A word should be said here about a trap for the unwary. We have said that knowing the truth value of (3), in the actual world, is not sufficient for knowing its meaning. This suggests that knowing the meaning of (3) is something *more* than knowing its truth value. And this in turn suggests that we cannot, on the truth-conditional approach, know the meaning of any sentence until we know whether it is true or not. Obviously any account of semantic competence which entailed that we could not know the meaning of a sentence without knowing its truth value cannot be right. However a closer look will reveal that knowing the meaning of (3) does not entail knowing its truth value. Knowing the meaning of (3) is knowing, given any possible world, whether (3) is true or false in that world. In other words it is knowing, *given a complete and total situation*, whether (3) is true or false in it. Since we do not know in general which of the many possible worlds is the actual one, we can know whether (3) *would be true* in this or that possible world, because we know whether it would be true *if that world were actual*. Since we are not omniscient we will not know whether that world *is* actual.

7. The idea of a possible world has a long history in philosophy, but a word of explanation might be in order for those who have not met the notion before. A 'possible world' simply means a way that the world might be, when this is understood as a complete alternative to the actual world. The completeness of the alternative possible worlds means that it is a mistake to think of a possible world as in some way 'out there', a disconnected part of the actual world (much as a theological heaven or hell). Any world like that would of course be a part of the actual world. (For similar reasons it would be logically impossible to, actually, make a journey to a non-actual world.) Possible-worlds theorists have sometimes been spoken of as if they believed that possible worlds are actual, but of course they do not. (For the use of the word 'actual' in possible-worlds semantics *vide* footnote 8.)

In considering the semantic competence of a native speaker, the possible-worlds approach refers to an ability to make judgments about worlds other than the actual one, but of course the ability of a speaker which constitutes his semantic competence is an ability which he has in the actual world.[8] This ability can only be tested in that world. If he is to make a judgment about another possible world he must be offered something which represents that possible world in the actual world.[9] Typically this other world will be presented to him in language. This may give the impression that a judgment about a possible world is a judgment about a sentence. But this is a mistake. A possible world need not be represented linguistically. Paintings, motion pictures and television programmes need not rely on words, yet we may indeed wonder whether the world they portray is real or not.[10] The possible-worlds approach is that, however a possible world may be presented to the speaker, he is to be construed as judging whether or not his sentence is true or false in that world.

I think it is also a mistake to suppose that possible worlds, or sets of possible worlds, should be able to be represented in some kind of canonical notation. Possible worlds are theoretical entities. We could perhaps consider them as analogous to points of space-time. No physical theory has names for all points of space-time (there are too many) and the statement of the theory does not require it. It may be that some possible worlds, or sets of them, do have names but even if so it is almost certain that we will have to postulate unnamable possible worlds in order to unify data which involve worlds which are empirically recognisable. (In much the same way as we postulate the past in order to unify the evidence of the present.)

It seems to be a presupposition of a great deal of linguistic work in semantics that its goal is the discovery and justification of some kind of canonical notation for all possible meanings (Chomsky, 1971, 183; Katz, 1972, 32ff). It is then suggested that the task of semantics is the construction of an

8. The word 'actual' simply means the world the speaker is in. A speaker in another possible world who refers to the 'actual' world refers of course to his world, not ours.

9. It has been proposed (Morton, 1973) that instead of taking other possible worlds as theoretical entities on which to base semantics we take parts of the actual world which 'represent' these other possible worlds. My suspicion is that this will not make for as simple or general a theory, but nothing in this paper would be incompatible with such an approach.

10. Some of Jackendoff's work on picturing (1975) seems to have links with possible-worlds semantics, at least for the syntactic category of sentence. It is a bit harder to see how to picture a functor like e.g. negation. One difficulty with the picture theory of meaning is of course to find something that a false sentence could be a picture of. Possible-worlds semantics can at least solve *that* problem since a false sentence is a picture of worlds other than the actual world.

axiomatic system from which may be derived as theorems all truths of the form

A means B

where A is the name of an expression and B is the name (in canonical notation) of the meaning of that expression. I do not in this paper wish to suggest that this cannot be done. (Although I am inclined to think that it cannot be done.) But I want to suggest first that it is at best not an analysis of what meaning *is* but only an account of how to represent it, and second that an account of what meanings are may still be correct even if we do not have a way of representing all of them.

A consequence of what I have just been saying is of course that it is not the business of semantics to provide an axiomatic system to prove, say, all analytic sentences, or all true entailments of some natural language. If this is the business of Lakoff's 'natural logic' (Lakoff, 1972) then I think what lies behind it is misguided. The search for axiomatisability in logic has long been recognised as fruitless in many cases. E.g. we have a perfectly well-defined account of validity for second-order logic, yet a perfectly rigorous proof that its set of valid sentences cannot be generated by an axiomatic system (Hermes, 1965, 171–5).

There is an alternative version of truth-conditional semantics which eschews explicit reference to possible worlds. This version says that knowing the truth value of (3) is indeed not sufficient, nor even necessary, for knowing its meaning; but not because there is something more to know about (3), as the possible-worlds approach claims, but rather because we need to know the truth values of various *other* sentences. E.g. we must know the (actual) truth value of sentences like

(4) (3) is true iff there is a cat on the smallest table of the seminar room of 22 Kelburn Parade at 1.30 p.m. NZDT on 15 November 1974.

This approach has been championed by Donald Davidson (1967) and by John Wallace (1972a) who see the task of semantics as being the creation of an axiomatic theory in which formal versions of sentences like (4) come out as theorems.

This paper is not concerned with the relative merits of the possible-worlds option and the Davidson option. My own work has been in the former field and in the remainder of the paper I shall be putting my points with the aid of the possible-worlds version. The thing which we notice about sentence (4) is that it can be regarded as a metalinguistic statement of the truth conditions of (3). In order for (4) to tell us anything we must understand its meaning. The Davidson theory simply invites us to understand (4) without saying too much about how the meaning of (4) is arrived at. It is thus at this point more neutral in its ontological commitment than the possible-worlds framework.[11] I mention the Davidson option so that those whom David Lewis refers to as the 'ontologically parsimonious' (Lewis, 1972, 190) can take the possible-worlds talk which follows as theoretically dispensable and not necessary to the main point of the paper.

2. *Possible worlds and semantic judgments*

I shall briefly set out the essential features of a possible-worlds approach to formal semantics. It should be pointed out that a great deal of very detailed work has been done within this framework[12] and the rather vague generalities in which I am about to indulge can be backed up by more solid writings.

Possible-worlds semantics is developed within the framework of set theory, and of particular importance is the set-theoretical notion of a function. A function (or mapping) is simply something which associates with an entity (called the argument of the function) another entity (called the value of the function for that argument). If ω is a function then $\omega(a)$ denotes the value of ω for the argument a. Those as which the function will accept as arguments form the *domain* of the function. Ignoring for the moment that sentences like (1) and (2) depend on a context of use, and concerning ourselves only with sentences like (3) we can say that the meaning of a sentence is a set of possible worlds. If the sentence is a simple subject-predicate sentence and if the subject is the proper name of an entity[13] then the mean-

11. Of course the possible-worlds theorist will argue that a truth theory of the Davidson kind will need, in order to give an adequate analysis of such intensional constructions as modals and counterfactual conditionals, to have recourse to things which will turn out to look so like possible worlds that the smaller ontological commitment will be shown to have been superficial only.

12. It is becoming best known to linguists in the form of 'Montague Grammar'. This term can be said to have a wide use, in which it means any formal representation of a natural language which makes use of possible-worlds semantics; and a more restricted use, in which it refers either to Montague's own work or to papers which have explicitly regarded themselves as extending it. Montague's papers on the philosophy of language have been collected (Montague, 1974a). Subsequent work by others has been collected by Barbara Partee (1975). A good short introduction to possible-worlds semantics is found in Lewis (1972), though for obvious reasons I tend to have at the back of my own mind the framework I set out in Cresswell (1973).

13. It is one of the contentions of Cresswell (1973) that very few subject terms are names of entities, even those which, like definite descriptions, have been thought to be names. It is even suggested (pp. 131ff) that cases like 'Fido' could also be construed as like definite descriptions. However that question does not affect the present discussion.

ing of a predicate is simply a function from things of the kind denoted by the subject term to sets of possible worlds; i.e. in a sentence like

(5)　Fido runs

we can say that (ignoring tense) the word 'Fido' is the name of Fido and the meaning of 'runs' is the function ω such that its domain consists of animate objects, and for any such a, $\omega(a)$ is the set of worlds in which a is running. In (5) a is Fido so that (5) is the set of worlds in which Fido is running.

This type of semantics obviously makes it possible to show how the truth conditions of whole sentences depend on the meanings of the words in the sentences together with the syntax of the sentences. Another point to note is that the use of functions enables the explanation of semantic anomalies. For instance the account given above of the meaning ω of the word 'runs' makes it clear that the number 27 is not in its domain. This means that if 'twenty-seven' is treated as the proper name of 27 then the sentence

(6)　twenty-seven runs

would be semantically anomalous, in that there would be no set of worlds which was its meaning.[14]

We can now show how a semantics based on possible worlds together with the truth-conditional view of semantic competence enables us to predict that a native speaker will have all the abilities listed by Katz and Nagel.

If a speaker can distinguish between the possible worlds in which a sentence is true and those in which it is false then he can know, of two sentences A and B

(i) whether A and B are true in precisely the same worlds, i.e. whether they are synonymous, or at least logically equivalent;[15]

(ii) whether B is true in all the worlds in which A is, i.e. whether A entails B;

14. I discuss this example a little more fully in Cresswell (1975a). One problem for any discussion of semantic deviance is to recognise the difficulties produced by the existence of metaphor (Harrison, 1974, 600). Whether the semantic anomaly is explained as in Cresswell (1975a) by domains of functions or by the KF device of 'selectional restrictions' there will always be cases in which anomalous sentences are deliberately used for some stylistic effect. All I want to say here is that a formal analysis of metaphor is something we need as much as we lack.

15. Synonymy is a stronger relation than logical equivalence. We make some observations about this (both in the text and in footnote 20) when discussing some remarks made by Katz (1972).

(iii) whether there is no world in which A is true, i.e. whether A is contradictory.[16]

This covers three of the judgments listed by Katz and Nagel concerning semantic relations between sentences. The two other properties of sentences they list are ambiguity and semantic anomaly. We have already seen how the function and argument approach of possible-worlds semantics can entail that a sentence may not express a proposition (because in obtaining its meaning from the meanings of its parts we may reach a point at which a function is presented with an argument which is not in its domain). This means that possible-worlds semantics gives an explanation of deviant sentences.

Ambiguity requires a little more to be said. In the case of structural ambiguity what happens is that in the representing formal language (which may be thought of perhaps as a representation of the 'deep structure' of the sentence) there will be two expressions for the same surface sentence. This is rather like the situation in logic where we can represent

(7) everyone loves someone

as either

(8) (everyone x)((someone y)(x loves y))

or

(9) (someone y)((everyone x)(x loves y)).[17]

Lexical ambiguity can be treated in a similar way. We assume that there are several distinct symbols in the deep structure which have a common surface realisation (Cresswell, 1973, 215ff). This approach is a little different from the one found in KF semantics where each dictionary entry is accompanied by a list of the various senses of the word. Nevertheless it can hardly be seen as much more than a notational difference whether we speak of a single surface realisation of several distinct items, or a multiplicity of senses for a single item. In any case whichever of these two ways the game is

16. To say that A and B are contraries is just to say that there is no world in which they are both true; to say that they are contradictories is just to say that the worlds in which A is true are precisely those in which B is not.

17. Writing 'everyone' as $\forall$, 'someone' as $\exists$ and 'loves' as F we get versions more familiar to logicians: $(\forall x)(\exists y)Fxy$ and $(\exists y)(\forall x)Fxy$. More sophisticated ways of representing these sentences are given in Cresswell (1973, 90ff).

played is strictly independent of whether one is working with a truth-conditional type of semantics or a KF-semantics.

The other judgments which Katz and Nagel list as involved in semantics are not about whole sentences. They are: redundancy, antonymy and super-ordination. Their example for redundancy is 'naked nudes'. In possible-worlds semantics a noun like 'nude' would be represented by the predicate 'x is a nude', and the complex phrase 'naked nude' by the predicate 'x is a naked nude'. In this case the native speaker who knows, of any given x which are the worlds where 'x is a nude' and 'x is a naked nude' respectively are true, knows that they are exactly the same worlds and so knows that the addition of the word 'naked' is redundant.

The speaker who knows the worlds in which respectively 'x is red' and 'x is green' are true, knows that they are disjoint and so knows that 'red' and 'green' are antonyms. The speaker who knows the worlds in which 'x is red' and 'x is coloured' respectively, are true, knows also that the former set is contained in the latter, and so knows that the relation of super-ordination holds.

3. *KF Semantics*

In the previous section we have seen that truth-conditional semantics explains all the semantic abilities Katz and Nagel list. It is important to realise of course that truth-conditional semantics, at least in its possible-worlds version, is not incompatible in principle with a KF type of semantics. Katz regards meanings as theoretical constructs and so there is no reason why they should not be themselves constructed out of theoretically more basic entities. Possible-worlds semantics gives an analysis of the kinds of things which the entities of the KF semantics would have to be if the view of semantic competence argued for in this paper is correct. Consider the reading for 'chair' on page 40 of Katz (1972). 'chair' is decomposed into

(10) (Object), (Physical), (Non-living), (Artifact), (Furniture), (Portable), (Something with legs), (Something with a back), (Something with a seat), (Seat for one).

A certain amount of confusion has been generated as a result of Katz's refusal to say what e.g. (Object) is. Even as recently as Harrison (1974, 601ff) we find them construed as English words. Katz of course has said that they are theoretical constructs but without saying what they are. There is nothing illegitimate about this, except that we have to regard something like (Seat for one)[18] as akin to an electron in a physical theory. It is therefore an improvement if we can produce a theory within which all these constructs can be accounted for on the basis of entities of a more uniform kind.

On a possible-worlds approach to semantics the noun 'chair' would be represented semantically by the function ω such that for any world w and thing a, $w \in \omega(a)$ iff a is a chair in w.[19] To accommodate a Katz-type approach what we would do would be to represent the word 'chair' not as a single symbol whose meaning is ω but as a complex expression of the form

$$(x \text{ is an object}) \& \ldots \& (x \text{ is a seat for one}).$$

If the meanings of the ten predicates in (10) are, respectively, $\omega_1, \ldots, \omega_{10}$ then for any world w and any a in the domain of ω:

$$w \in \omega(a) \equiv (w \in \omega_1(a) \& w \in \omega_2(a) \& \ldots \& w \in \omega_{10}(a)).$$

On a possible-worlds approach lexical decomposition is not necessary to explain such semantic relations as entailment. E.g. suppose we have two lexical items 'bachelor' and 'man'. The meaning of 'bachelor' will be the function ω such that for any a, and possible world w, $w \in \omega(a)$ iff a is a bachelor in w. The meaning of 'man' will be the function ω' such that $w \in \omega'(a)$ iff a is a man in w. On the truth-conditional view of semantic competence knowing the meanings of 'bachelor' and 'man' respectively simply means knowing for any a which worlds are in $\omega(a)$ and which are in $\omega'(a)$. The native speaker's knowledge that being a bachelor entails being a man simply amounts to his knowledge that any world in $\omega(a)$ is also in

18. That is assuming that (Seat for one) cannot be further decomposed. One of the difficulties with the marriage of lexical decomposition and Katz's view of the basis of semantics in terms of theoretical entities is that until we have some guarantee that lexical decomposition has gone as far as it can we have no idea of what the basic theoretical entities might be. In this respect the analogy with sub-atomic physics certainly breaks down; and so does the analogy with possible-worlds semantics. For in the latter cases we *do* know what the primitive entities of the theory are.

19. This is not quite accurate enough. As well as a reference to a possible world there ought to be reference to a moment of time since the same thing can undoubtedly be a chair at one time but not at another. Context-dependence of a temporal sort for the predicates which represent common names has been recognised both in possible-worlds semantics, e.g. Cresswell (1973, 180), and in KF semantics, Katz (1972, 303ff). I hope that in the light of what has already been said it should be clear that the circularity here is only apparent. In using the word 'chair' in my English metalanguage I have of course been trading on my reader's knowledge of that metalanguage. Thus the manner in which the set of worlds in which x is a chair has been presented to him has used the word 'chair'. Nevertheless it is that set of worlds, however presented, which constitutes $\omega(a)$.

$\omega'(a)$. Obviously this knowledge is a direct consequence of his semantic competence and does not require any lexical decomposition.

A point worth noting about lexical decomposition is that the decomposition of 'chair' in (10) requires us to treat its meaning as a conjunction of the ten features Katz lists. This means that, although Katz does not make it explicit, his semantics makes essential use of such logical operations as conjunction in the representation of meanings. This is seen even more clearly in such constructs as $\langle$(Human) v (Animal)$\rangle$ and $\langle$(Human) & $\overline{\text{(Infant)}}\rangle$ (pp. 106ff). What is interesting about this is that one of Katz's major criticisms of the application of logic to linguistics is that it makes a distinction between 'logical' and 'descriptive' words, and decides to call valid those arguments which depend only on the meanings of the logical words. On page xix he says: 'But there is no nonarbitrary basis for making such a decision in a way that divides the words of language into the familiar logical particles and everything else.' With this I wholeheartedly agree and have made the point myself in several places (Cresswell, 1972, 5–7; 1973, 28; 1974, Sect. 6). What Katz seems to fail to realise is that the idea of lexical decomposition, which is the cornerstone of his semantic theory, is itself founded on just such a distinction as he professes to reject.

Nevertheless possible-worlds semantics is not incompatible with lexical decomposition and if there are compelling reasons for accepting it then it can be accommodated.[20] One way of accommodating it is to suppose as in

---

20. For instance, suppose Katz's (1972, 50) definition of analyticity is accepted and we agree to distinguish between analyticity and necessary truth (182–4). Then lexical decomposition may be necessary to the definition of analyticity. Another motivation is, I think, the belief that e.g. we are more certain that 'x is a bachelor' entails 'x is male' than we are of just which worlds are included in each proposition. My own inclination in this latter case is to link it with an explanation of vagueness in terms of a 'communication class' (Cresswell, 1973, 59) and say that although different sets of worlds may be assigned to 'x is a bachelor' and 'x is male' in each member of the communication class of English (i.e. in each way of making precise all the meanings of all words), yet in each of these (different) precise evaluations the set assigned to 'x is a bachelor' will be a subset of the set assigned to 'x is male'. The notion of a 'communication class' (called by van Fraassen a 'supervaluation': van Fraassen, 1971, 94–6) has, I believe, a link with meaning postulates of a Carnapian kind. A Carnapian meaning postulate may be regarded as a meta-linguistic statement of certain relations between symbols which hold in every member of the communication class of (say) English. It is important however to realise that meaning postulates are not theoretically necessary to the existence of the communication class, and also that they are not, in possible-worlds semantics, necessary to the definition of such notions as necessary truth or entailment.

Another motive for lexical decomposition has been the need to give a truth-conditional semantics for propositional attitudes. Since any two logically-equivalent propositions are true in exactly the same possible worlds, then if we *identify* a proposition with a set of possible worlds we cannot admit distinct but logically equivalent propositions. One way

Cresswell (1973, 210–13), that a single surface symbol realises a complex expression in the deep structure. David Lewis (1972, 182–6) makes a distinction between meanings and intensions. Essentially a meaning is a complex set-theoretical structure which reflects both the meanings of the simplest units of the sentence and the way the sentence is made up. These meanings have the crucial property that each meaning determines an *intension* (as e.g. $\omega_1, \ldots, \omega_{10}$ above determine ω). Thus lexical decomposition in a possible-worlds framework has all the advantages of a KF semantics with, in addition, a property that KF semantics conspicuously lacks; viz. an explicit procedure for obtaining the truth conditions of a sentence from its meaning. This is what is meant by saying that KF semantics is not so much wrong as incomplete.

Katz does have some comments on truth conditions but they seem not uniform. In some places (Katz, 1972, 239ff) he seems to welcome the attempt to relate semantics to truth conditions and claims that this is part of his own programme. In other places (page 182) he seems to think that truth conditions have little to do with semantics. Since this is in part no more than a matter of the definition of the scope of 'semantics' it need not detain us. The aim of this paper is to link a truth-conditional view of semantics with an empirically observable ability of native speakers.

4. *Semantic performance*

I should like now to say a little about the relation between semantic competence and semantic performance. I am taking it that examples of theories of semantic performance are theories of the kind offered e.g. by Grice or Searle.

I have linked a certain view of semantic competence fairly closely with truth-conditional semantics. The link is I believe of a kind which cannot be made with semantic performance. Almost the only author I am aware of who has tried to make it is David Lewis (1969, and more explicitly in 1975). Lewis has to postulate that a large amount of use, indeed it would appear that the central use, of a language $\mathscr{L}$ is based on a 'convention of truthfulness and trust in $\mathscr{L}$'. $\mathscr{L}$ will in fact be a semantic structure which specifies the truth conditions for all the sentences of the language it represents; and the

---

of dealing with this problem is to follow Lewis's lead and say that propositions are structured entities which reflect the way they are made up from simple meaning units. This idea is applied to propositional attitudes in Cresswell (1975b) and Bigelow (this volume). There is obviously a link between this view and the lexical decomposition hypothesis although its outworkings seem to be very difficult and baffling.

convention of truthfulness and trust will obtain if the speakers of $\mathscr{L}$ try themselves to utter true sentences and expect others to do the same.

Now it may indeed be that, as Lewis tries to argue, this convention is a central one to the use of language, but to me at least it seems a matter for empirical investigation rather than of definition that this should be so.[21] And even if there did turn out to be a logical connection between the use of a language and a convention of truthfulness and trust in it, it seems to me better at the beginning not to have to build this into a theory of semantics. At any rate it is one of the arguments of the present paper that there is no need for semantics to establish a link between competence and performance. The reason for this is that the ability which I have labelled semantic competence is an empirical phenomenon. It is an ability which native speakers have and so an explanation of how they have it is a well-determined problem. One can therefore simply *define* semantics as the formal account of how a native speaker has the ability to match up sentences with sets of possible worlds (or more neutrally, of how he is able to recognise their truth conditions).

Of course one can define anything as anything, so that something needs to be said to show that this ability has a right to be called the basic semantic ability. Calling anything a semantic ability does impose certain constraints on the kind of thing it is. In particular the ability must be such as to enable a person to recognise the meanings of whole new sentences on the basis of meanings of their parts. This at once shows that the ability must be defined in terms of linguistic expressions (i.e. expression types) rather than occurrences of them (i.e. expression tokens). In particular, because it is sentences which are embedded in sentences, not utterances in utterances, linguistic meaning must be a property of sentences.

This has certain consequences for any theory of meaning which might try to say that the meaning of a sentence is, say, its illocutionary force.[22] For on any reasonable account of illocutionary force it must be possible for the same sentence to occur with a different illocutionary force, and for a sentence which normally has one illocutionary force to be embedded in a sentence which has another illocutionary force. The best that could be done along this line would be to say that the meaning of a sentence is a function

21. E.g. I have been told (by John Bigelow) that one of the earliest functions of language was in story-telling. Whether this is wrong or right it seems to me at least plausible to suggest that it is in the development of the imaginative faculty rather than in the necessity for day-to-day communication that we must seek the central role of language.

22. The notion of illocutionary force is based on Austin's notion of an illocutionary act. It is used by Searle (e.g. 1969, 30).

from contexts of use to the force the sentence would have if uttered in that context. This in itself is not of course an insuperable objection to a 'force-based' semantics. Even a truth-conditional semantics has to recognise context dependence and has to make the meanings of sentences functions from contexts of use. But in my experience it is only a truth-conditionally-based semantics[23] which has taken the problem of embedded constructions seriously.

Truth-conditional semantics takes into account everything necessary to determine the truth conditions of whole sentences. It has to take into account more than truth values, more even than truth conditions, but so far as we can tell, it is not necessary, in order to obtain the truth conditions of a large sentence, to know anything about the possible illocutionary force of any of its embedded sentences. What this means of course is that our definition of semantic competence marks out an area of linguistic study which seems to square with the intuitive formal requirements for a theory of linguistic meaning.

Can we then say any more? Having seen that facts of semantic performance need not be involved in a theory of semantic competence can we show that, by contrast, semantic competence plays an essential role in any theory of semantic performance? I do not know how to show this in general, but what I can do is to take several influential theories of semantic performance and show that either semantic competence is involved in them, or that they are defective just to the extent that it is not.

As an example take Searle's analysis of the speech act of promising (Searle, 1969, 63). An essential part of S's promising H to do A is that the promising occurs in a sentence 'the utterance of which predicates some future act A of the speaker S'. Now the only point I want to make about this is that it involves semantic competence of a truth-conditional kind. I am not concerned with the details of Searle's analysis of predication (e.g. with the fact that he always treats it as a speech act) except that its crucial feature is its link with truth. Searle says (p. 124): 'To predicate an expression "P" of an object R is to raise the question of the truth of the predicate expression of the object referred to.' It is surely clear that this question could only be raised by one who knew the truth conditions of sentences containing 'P'. Searle recognises a 'propositional act' as what is common to speech acts of many different kinds. In so doing he can, it seems to me, be construed as constructing a theory of semantic performance in which semantic competence of a truth-conditional kind is essentially involved.

23. With the exception of course of KF semantics which is certainly compositional. However, as I have said, I do not regard KF semantics as in competition with truth-conditional semantics; I regard the latter as a way of giving content to the former.

The other influential theory of semantic performance has been that of
H. P. Grice (1968). Grice's theory takes as basic the idea of what an *utterer*
means by an *utterance*. This in turn is explicated in terms of the intention on
the part of the utterer to produce in the hearer a certain state of mind. The
details of the analysis are complicated and debated but, for our purposes,
are somewhat beside the point because, although Grice's theory of meaning
does not involve reference to truth conditions, neither does it have anything to say about how a hearer can predict, on the basis of his linguistic
competence, the meanings of sentences he has not come across before. The
only place I am aware of at which this problem has been discussed in a
Gricean framework is at the end of Schiffer's book on meaning (1972).
On page 162 Schiffer offers, in answer to the problem of how the
meanings of sentences we have never met before are to be obtained, an
approach 'which makes use of the Tarskian conception of a semantic definition of truth and adds an intensional element to it'. On page 164 he
proposes, in effect, something very like Lewis's conventions of truthfulness
and trust. As I have already said I am a little suspicious of a direct link of
this kind, but it is interesting to see that a Gricean approach too, seems, in
the end, to lead to truth-conditional semantics.

Why is it that the truth-conditional theory of meaning has had a hard
time in so much recent philosophy? One misconception I think seems to
have been the view that 'true' is a 'success word' used to commend an
utterance of a certain kind. I am not so much interested in a detailed analysis
of how 'true' is used in English but rather I am thinking of the view that the
point of describing an utterance as true is to commend it, because the aim
of a certain kind of discourse is to say what is true. I hope it is clear that the
truth-conditional account of semantic competence does not involve any judgments about whether or not one ought to say what is true. It may of course
turn out that an important fragment of language involves the convention
that we try to say what is true but it is, I hope, clear that the more basic
ability is to recognise that what is true *is* true and that what is not is not.

The way we obtain evidence of semantic competence from a native
speaker must not of course be capricious. For a native speaker might well
misdescribe his own ability (*vide* Bar-Hillel, 1971, 404; Weydt, 1973, 578).
In a standard occurrence of the sentence

(11)   I promise to pay you five dollars

the question of truth and falsity might be thought by the speaker inappropriate. If we say to him 'Is (11) true or false?' he might say 'Neither,

I was making a promise'. The first point is that the question of the truth or falsity of (11) has nothing to do with the purpose of making the utterance. Nevertheless the speaker might be unwilling, for whatever reason, to describe (11) as true. How might we convince him that still he does accept it as such? What we can do I believe is to show him that the semantical analysis of the meanings of the words in (11) which is required to deal with cases in which his judgment *is* clear necessitates that (11) has a definite truth value. E.g. if the meaning of 'I' in (11) is to be the same as it is in

(12)   if I come I will bring a friend

or

(13)   he asked whether I was sick

and the meaning of 'promise' the same as in

(14)   wherever we promise to play our mother will not let us keep that promise

and so on, then it will be clear that (11) will be true iff the speaker does promise to pay the hearer five dollars. Since, in felicitous circumstances, an utterance of (11) counts as the speaker's promising to pay the hearer five dollars then we may say that in felicitous circumstances utterances of (11) are true.[24] Of course that (11) should be true by no means entails that an utterance of it can be counted as an *assertion* of its truth. Probably most utterances of (11) are not assertions of its truth. This is where the view that 'true' is a success word is so misleading.

5. Conclusions

In this paper I have tried to show that a truth-conditional view of semantic competence is sufficient to account for any feature of semantics necessary

24. It seems to me that the idea that performatives have no truth value may have been counterproductive in their analysis. For surely what distinguishes performatives from other sentences is simply that their utterance, in felicitous circumstances, is what creates the fact that makes them true; i.e. it seems that, in human affairs, there is a large number of institutional relationships (e.g. the relationship of being under a promissory obligation) which require a convention for their creation, but a convention whose precise nature is somewhat arbitrary. In such a case what better way to create the relationship than by saying that it exists or that it has been created? But of course *this* analysis of performatives requires that the sentences which create the relationship can have a truth value.

for linguistic meaning. I have claimed that the only other detailed attempt at linguistic semantics, viz. that inspired by Katz, Fodor and Postal can be seen as a partial answer which can be completed and given content by a truth-conditional approach. I have also claimed that theories which appear to offer more than a truth-conditional analysis are best seen as theories of semantic performance.

Can one however say anything more direct? For I have offered no argument to show that any semantic theory must be linked with truth conditions. To be sure I have claimed that native speakers do have an ability which I have described as semantic competence, that this ability enables the prediction of judgments which are clearly semantic judgments, and that this ability gives a semantical theory which shows how we understand new sentences. All this is indirect in that I have not deduced the ability from any defining characteristic of language.

But perhaps after all linguistic ability and the idea of a possible world are intimately connected. Perhaps the ability which has caused man to invent language is the ability to represent situations which are not actually present to him. Perhaps it is this feature which marks the development of consciousness. For animals perhaps there is only the way the world is. Since man can represent to himself the way the world is he can represent to himself the way the world might be but isn't. So a formal theory of what is going on leads naturally to the postulation of entities which are these 'ways the world might be'; these are the possible worlds. Language then becomes a rule-governed device for putting into the mind of another a representation of the same set of possible worlds which is in the mind of the speaker. If this is so then the notion of a possible world is at the heart of semantics, and is even more basic than the notion of truth. For when we identify a proposition as a set of possible worlds then we can define a proposition as true in a world iff it contains that world as a member.

If this story of the essential nature of language is correct then it is not surprising that semantic competence is truth-conditional in character. That the story is correct has not of course been shown or argued for in this paper. My aim has been to show merely that speakers do have the ability to match up sentences with situations, and that this ability has enough of the required formal properties to underlie a theory of semantic competence.

6. *Appendix on the theory of translation*

It is I hope obvious that the theory of semantic competence outlined in this paper imposes very strong constraints on any theory of translation. Let us say that α and β (in different languages) are correct translations, each of the other, iff they have the same meaning.[25] For this definition to be viable we require language-independent entities to be the meanings of α and β, so that we can say that the entity which is α's meaning in its language is the same entity as that which is β's meaning in its language.

Our theory of semantic competence enables a speaker to match up α and β with sets of possible worlds. Since possible worlds are language-independent he has the ability to tell whether α and β are logically equivalent, and it will be a necessary, though not in general a sufficient, condition for a sentence α and a sentence β to be (correctly) intertranslatable that they be true in precisely the same set of possible worlds.

Moreover, an adequate truth-conditional semantics for a single language will require a treatment of such contexts as indirect discourse and propositional attitudes—contexts I have labelled 'hyperintensional' (Cresswell, 1975b). I have already referred (footnote 20) to some of the problems which arise in this area. What seems likely is that an adequate treatment of these problems in possible-worlds semantics will require the use of theoretical entities which can represent distinct, though logically equivalent, propositions. If these entities are language-independent (as sets of possible worlds are language-independent) then, by treating them as the meanings of sentences in any language, we can say that α and β, in different languages, are correct translations of each other iff they have the same meaning.

Since an adequate truth-conditional semantics will have to account for expressions like 'means the same as' it follows that, in order to solve its own internal problems, a theory of meaning based on the truth-conditional view of semantic competence offered in this paper will be sufficiently constrained to test the correctness of any synonymy claim in a single language; and granted the use of language-independent meanings, will therefore be able to test the correctness of any translation between one language and another.

---

25. To say that a translation is correct is not the same as saying that it is appropriate. E.g. it is appropriate, for many purposes, to translate direct quotations even though it is not correct to translate them.

T. Tymoczko

Translation and Meaning

THE SUBJECT OF translation is an interdisciplinary topic. Naturally, in the investigation of translations one utilises such linguistic theories as phonology (or graphology), syntax, semantics and pragmatics. However, there are also extralinguistic factors involved in translation and to accommodate these factors, the translation theorist must draw on additional theories of the language speakers, their environment, culture and beliefs. The point that translation involves such extralinguistic factors has been made in different ways by Nida (1945) and Quine (1960). Yet it is a point not always appreciated.

One reason for this lack of appreciation stems from the belief that translation is essentially a semantic affair. It might be argued that a translation of a sentence in one language is, by definition, a sentence in a second language which means the same as the original. Under this conception a translator begins with sentences which have meaning in the semantic structure of one language and attempts to construct equivalent sentences using the semantic devices of the second language. Hence semantic theory, built upon syntax and phonology, is sufficient to provide an adequate theory of translation. Translation theory is applied semantics; it is not interdisciplinary.

This argument turns on a false contrast between semantics (including syntax and phonology-graphology) and other sciences. Semantics is already an interdisciplinary theory dependent on theories of environment and culture. Hence, since translation theory depends on semantics, it must depend on other non-linguistic theories as well.

This essay will explore the non-linguistic factors involved in semantic theory. Such an exploration is fruitless under the assumption that semantic theory is a foundational discipline constructible on the basis of speaker's intuitions without the aid of special sciences. The point I wish to make, of course, is that semantic theory does not lie at the foundations of our conceptual framework but is a rather high level theory dependent on a number of special sciences. The approach of the essay will be to consider what is involved in the process of assigning meanings to a body of discourse in a language. The intuitive idea of assigning meanings to sentences will be represented by the technical notion of a meaning assignment. After defining meaning assignments, I will argue that for any meaning assignment, M_1, to a language, there is another meaning assignment, M_2, to that language with the following characteristics. To various sentences in the language—which sentences can often be settled beforehand—M_2 provides a different semantic interpretation from M_1. Indeed the interpretations can differ to such an extent that sentences are assigned different truth values by M_1 and M_2. Moreover, semantic theory proper is incapable of deciding whether M_1 or M_2 best represents the actual structure of the language's meaning. The relativity of meaning assignments resides in this fact; that whatever evidence we have for the choice of a class of 'correct' meaning assignments to a language is drawn not merely from semantical considerations, but also from other facets of our body of knowledge. The arguments for the thesis of the relativity of meaning assignments will show the dependency of meaning assignments on the scientific theories of the semantic theorist, most especially on those classified as social sciences.

A meaning assignment is a model—or metaphor, albeit a technical one—for the actual meaning of a body of discourse. Although it is not without drawbacks, it is one of the better models that our present science and mathematics can offer. This suggests that the relativity of meaning assignments carries over to meanings themselves. The relation between a body of discourse and the meanings expressed by its sentences is not exclusively a formal semantical relation. It obtains only relative to other facts or theories about the world, particularly about the language users' environment and about the language users' relations to that environment and to each other. Meanings, as it were, are relative to the speakers and their environments. Hence, the distinction between a semantical account of translation and a broader account which brings to bear ethnological considerations is illusory. The semantic account of a language includes ethnological analyses of the linguistic community. A fortiori, translation theory itself must include such analyses.

A meaning assignment to a language or body of discourse consists of a formal language, a Tarskian interpretation or truth definition of that formal language and a mapping from each sentence in the language or body of discourse to a formula of the formal language.[1] Symbolically, we can represent meaning assignments as a function, $M_{L,D}(x)$, where the subscripts indicate the formal language L and the interpretation D of that language

---

1. The interposition of a formal language between the natural language and the truth definition should not be taken as an absolute requirement. My intention is to allow for the possibility of this step in the analysis.

which is to be employed. The domain of the function is the set of sentences to be analysed and the range is included in the set of formulae of L. The semantic means at our disposal enable us to say, in a mathematically precise way, under which conditions the formulae of L are true. Consequently, for a large subset of sentences in the body of discourse, the meaning assignment, $M_{L,D}(x)$, gives us a way of determining the conditions under which *they* are true or false. To the indefinite sentences in the body of discourse, those involving indexical expressions like 'I', 'you', 'now', the meaning assignment provides the means to determine the conditions of their satisfaction along familiar lines, e.g. 'P(I)' as spoken by *a* is true if and only if P(*a*). When for any sentence in a body of discourse we know the truth conditions or conditions of satisfaction for that sentence, we can be said to know the meaning of that body of discourse. The thesis that an account of meaning must involve a theory of truth was made early by Frege and Wittgenstein. It has been stressed recently in the work of Davidson (1967). The term 'meaning assignment' is, then, an appropriate designation of a process of determining truth conditions of sentences.

This definition of meaning assignment omits much that could be included in semantic theory: modal logic, tensed logic, deontic logic, transformational grammar and generative semantics. For semantical investigation it would be wise to broaden the notion of meaning assignment to include the commonly recognised results in these areas. For the purposes of this paper, such a complication is unnecessary. The philosophical theses about meaning assignments narrowly defined quite clearly carry over to meaning assignments with a broader definition. Moreover, even if quite different definitions of meaning assignment were given, say in terms of verification rather than truth, I believe that the thesis of this essay would carry through. Following Quine, I would argue that to a large extent it is the complexity of a satisfactory meaning assignment that permits the sort of gerrymandering that gives rise to the relativity of meaning assignments.

It is clear how meaning assignments figure in the analysis of language. Suppose, as our formal language, a first order language of the type used in predicate logic. Suppose it contains the 2-place relation symbol $R(x, y)$ and the constant letter *a*. Let the interpretation count $R(d_1, d_2)$ as true if and only if d_1 is in (spatially) d_2 and let the interpretation assign to *a*, as its referent, a certain abandoned farmhouse in Maine—called 'Matt's Place' by natives. Then a meaning assignment to English might assign to the sentence 'There's no one in Matt's Place' the formula of the formal language '$\sim(\exists x)R(x, a)$' where the domain of quantification is the set of all people. This interpreted formula is the value of $M_{L,D}$ applied to the sentence 'There's no one in Matt's Place'. In the context of the language and interpretation the formula says, very precisely, 'It is not the case that there is a person who is in that certain farmhouse in Maine'. But the formula '$\sim(\exists\, x)R(x,\, a)$' should not be thought of as the meaning of 'There's no one in Matt's Place'. It is only because that formula is embedded in the context of a formal language with an interpretation that we have some justification for speaking of meaning in this connection.

The process of constructing a meaning assignment to a language or body of discourse reveals the semantic structure of the sentences involved and their semantic interrelation. When we feel quite confident of our knowledge of the meaning of the relevant discourse, the construction of a meaning assignment might appear to be a merely formal exercise. When we are uncertain of the meaning, the construction of a meaning assignment can actually provide enlightenment—of the semantic sort.

Probably the most significant contribution to human knowledge that a meaning assignment can make is to facilitate the explanation of the activities or behaviour of language users. Imagine that a posse has pursued a desperado to the vicinity of Matt's Place, an abandoned farmhouse in Maine. Upon reaching the farmhouse, the members of the posse dismount and surround the structure firing random shots into it. They are obviously agitated: both excited and afraid. And their behaviour has a certain rational coherence to it. For instance they provide covering fire for one of their number, who succeeds in reaching the farmhouse. After a few minutes of silence, that fellow comes to the door and delivers a verbal message to his colleagues: 'There's no one in Matt's Place'. This vocal activity has a rather startling effect on the behaviour and plans of the posse. Its members cease firing, become calmer and advance to the farmhouse—carefully. (A naïve behaviourist might wonder why the scout did not give this signal to his colleagues *before* they dismounted thereby saving them all that worry and lead!) There is a legitimate scientific question to be asked here: how did the utterance achieve its effect? Part of the answer must be given in terms of a meaning assignment which assigns to the utterance truth conditions hypothetically available to all members of the linguistic community. As rational agents carrying out a plan, the members of the posse respond to the signalled truth conditions by altering their beliefs and actions in relevant ways. The details of this account wait less on developments in pure semantic theory than on developments in the science of human behaviour, especially rational psychology.

The nervous posse presented a contrived example of a commonplace truth: words matter. Our sophisticated verbal interchanges produce dramatic effects on our behaviour and on our material environment. If there is meaning to these verbal interchanges, and if a meaning assignment can represent it, then the meaning assignment must function in the overall behaviour patterns of language users.

Meaning assignments are functions from the sentences of a language to the formulae in some interpreted formal language. Briefly, meaning assignments assign truth conditions to sentences. They represent the semantical aspect of linguistic behaviour and, as such, play an important role in the explanation of the behaviour of any linguistically sophisticated society.

The notion of a meaning assignment or semantic interpretation is currently being refined by researchers in semantic theory. But these technical developments need not concern us in this essay. Meaning assignments, as defined, are good models of one current trend in semantics—and I personally think that they are among the best models. As such, they can be taken as a basis for philosophical reflection about meaning.

Meaning assignments are relatively indeterminate. There are alternative meaning assignments that give very different semantic interpretations to particular sentences in the language. Yet each of the alternatives is cogent from the viewpoint of semantic theory and can be made out to be consistent with much empirical data such as actual contexts of utterances. It is not claimed that divergent meaning assignments can agree with *all* empirical data. That claim, which might be called the 'absolute indeterminacy of meaning assignments', suggests there is, in principle, no right or wrong in semantic matters. Logically it is equivalent to Quine's thesis of indeterminacy of translation. Relativity of meaning assignments does not deny that there is such a thing as a correct meaning assignment. It claims only that important evidence necessary to differentiate among meaning assignments is not properly semantical and further that such evidence can be typified in a coherent fashion. As the argument proceeds there will emerge a certain picture of the relationship between the investigation of meaning assignments (read 'semantic theory') and the special sciences.

The thesis of relativity of meaning assignments states that for any given meaning assignment M_1 to a language or body of discourse there is another M_2 and that this pair has the characteristics:

(i) for certain sentences s under consideration, $M_1(s)$ and $M_2(s)$ are different semantic structures;
(ii) the correctness or incorrectness of these meaning assignments cannot be judged on semantic grounds alone.

The most extreme semantic difference between $M_1(s)$ and $M_2(s)$ is that they disagree in truth value. A less extreme and more common difference is that M_1 and M_2 describe s in terms of different semantica lunits. For instance M_1 might attribute the form 'F(a)' to s while M_2 formalises s as '$(\exists x)(G(x) \,\&\, (y)(G(y) \supset y = x) \,\&\, F(x))$'. Such divergence would be of little significance were it not for the second characteristic: that M_2 can be chosen to be semantically cogent and as compatible with a normal range of semantical data as M_1. This suggests that crucial evidence for one meaning assignment's being more 'correct' than the other is non-semantical. Indeed, in any given case it can be made more perspicuous: physical, environmental, economic, psychological, etc. In the following section of this essay, I will attempt to sketch the general structure of the dependence of semantic theory on non-semantical considerations.

The two crucial features of meaning assignments that will be exploited in the arguments are that they depend both upon the domains available to supply interpretations to a language and upon the community of language users whose practice involves non-semantical relations with their environment or domain of discourse. The first feature generates the conclusion that meaning assignments are dependent on the sciences, including the social sciences, as sources of potential domains of discourse. The second feature suggests that there is another kind of dependence special to the social sciences as the study of conscious rational beings. Simply put, a meaning assignment to a language depends upon the environment of the language users and upon their perspective on that environment. That semantic theory yields models with these features was emphasised by Quine in his arguments for the (absolute) indeterminacy of translation.

Meaning assignments involve interpretations which in turn involve domains of discourse. The potential domains of discourse available to a semantic theorist are determined by the special sciences to which the semantic theorist has access. The special sciences provide him with the mathematical, physical and psychological constructs with which to construct semantic theory. Therefore he can judge the appropriateness of a meaning assignment only relative to his general scientific knowledge. It is in virtue of the knowledge of the language users' environment that one can hope to assign conditions of truth and falsity to the sentences of their language.

Let us try exemplifying this point in a fanciful way. Suppose that an occult semanticist actually constructs a meaning assignment for that body of English discourse involving 'poltergeist' in an essential way. I don't believe in poltergeists but I can imagine that someone could make a serious attempt at such a project. (Something like this must have once been done, in a primitive way, for words like 'ether' or 'phlogiston'.) Those of us who do not believe poltergeists exist will prefer a different meaning assignment. Perhaps we will choose one whose interpretation involves certain physical phenomena— small movements of objects produced by subsonic waves. Or maybe we'll choose one that utilises psychological constructs—ideas, perhaps polter- geist ideas. One meaning assignment construes the discourse as being about poltergeist, another as being about physical phenomena, a third, as being about nothing, but explicable in terms of psychological constructs of the speakers. Surely one cannot evaluate these meaning assignments on semantic grounds alone without appealing to theories of poltergeists, physical phe- nomena and psychological constructs. No doubt that semantical features of the assignments will play a role in this evaluation. But no matter how elegant and workable is the meaning assignment which posits poltergeists, we cannot accept it without first altering our science to include poltergeists as objects of investigation.

The example can be made less fanciful by imagining the term 'poltergeist' replaced by a more common, if more sombre, term such as 'spirit'—or by a network of terms such as 'soul', 'grace', 'temptation', and so on. If in a body of discourse, 'spirit', or a word we want to translate as 'spirit', frequently occurs, then the range of meaning assignments available to us depends upon our attitude towards the reality of spirit. This point is obvious from the definition of meaning assignments; the set of potential domains varies accord- ing to the state of the special sciences which are our workable theories of what exists.[2]

But what of meanings themselves? One is tempted to believe that meaning can be fixed independently of what exists, that the meaning of discourse related to 'spirit' could be fixed independently of whether spirits exist or not. The temptation is misleading as can be seen by reflecting on a basic principle of meaning; the significance of a meaning assignment to a body of discourse is that it helps explain those kinds of social behaviour in which the body of discourse is utilised. 'Those kinds of social behaviour' is the rub. The relevant social behaviour will be construed one way by a person who believes in the reality of spirit and can take the behaviour to centre on human relations with spirit. It will be construed very differently by one who denies spirit; for in that case, whatever the behaviour is, it can

2. A more striking example might be the case of belief. If the capacity for belief is a natural capacity of human beings, then this fact lays down the framework for a semantic analysis of belief sentences. On the other hand, if belief is a parochial construct of a particular tradition, then the semantic analysis of belief sentences must develop along totally different lines. This point is argued in detail by Needham (1972) who makes clear its relevance to translation.

2*

have nothing to do with spirit. The contexts into which meanings—or meaning assignments—must fit differ significantly in the two cases. We can no more expect a 'neutral' assignment of meaning to fit into the two very different contexts, than we can expect a single jigsaw puzzle piece to fit into two different places on the puzzle.

Our conclusion, then, must be that the states of the special sciences directly influence our choice of meaning assignments to a language. What a language can mean depends upon the environment of the language users—and what that environment is like is a question to be settled, by and large, by the sciences.

A corollary to this thesis is that the social sciences must be especially significant to the choice of meaning assignments to a language. This is so, in part, because so much of a people's discourse is directed towards their social environment. Here 'social environment' is a non-technical term intended to cover such things as the available roles in a society, its modes of personal interaction, its institutions and institutional obligations, etc.

Just as the semanticist must know the physical environment of a society in order to assign meanings to the linguistic vocabulary related to weather, so the semanticist must know their economic environment in order to assign meanings to their pronouncements on economics. Are the speakers talking about and interacting with a society that maximises individual choice or a society that exploits the majority of workers? (These are not mutually exclusive alternatives but reconciling them requires a suitable psychological theory of the workers.) The semanticist answers this question by choosing a theory of capitalism or a theory of communism in which to frame his sociological analysis. And each choice provides him with a different set of tools for his semantic analysis. The meaning of economic discourse in a society can be explicated in terms of such concepts as private enterprise, free market, supply and demand or such concepts as working class, capitalist class, class struggle. I suggest that a theorist who chooses the second framework will find, for example, the pair of expressions 'capitalist-worker' are marked by a greater semantic contrast than will a theorist who chooses the first framework.

Obviously, communists and capitalists disagree. What I am arguing is that such disagreement can effect semantic analysis. Truth and meaning are not separate topics. The actual economic practices of a society play a crucial role in the determination of a correct assignment of meanings to its economic discourse.

This point is not confined to economics. The semanticist needs to know a great deal about social structure such as the interaction of its racial or sexual groups. The semantic analyst is forced to choose between a feminist analysis of sexual interaction or a male supremacist analysis (or some third alternative, of course). Each analysis provides a context in which a meaning assignment is to operate. These contexts are so very different that only very different meaning assignments could operate in each with any degree of plausibility. It is no wonder that the protagonists in the debates about the actual economic, racial or sexual structures of a contemporary society focus so insistently on language—as in the feminists' concern with the semantics of 'he' and 'she'. In principle one meaning assignment might be correct and another simply wrong. But we cannot accept it as correct without simultaneously accepting certain theses in social science.

Meaning assignments, and meanings, are relative to the sciences, especially the social sciences. The natural and social environments in which a language is used lay down the limits of acceptable meaning assignments. (To paraphrase Wittgenstein: 'the limits of my world are the limits of my language'.) We have demonstrated this by reflecting on possible macroscopic changes in the interpretation of a language. In fact, rather minor changes in the interpretation—changes of a technical nature—can engender significantly different meaning assignments. The reason for this is that semantic theory, including mathematical logic, is rich in its resources for formal construction. Two sets of constructions might be employed to gain the same overall effect while nevertheless diverging on their results for some specific sentences. Their difference on these sentences often can be accommodated by relatively minor shifts in our theory of pragmatics.

Propositional logic alone affords many examples of this such as the familiar problem of the English conditional sentences of the form 'If p, then q'. Do such sentences exhibit truth value 'gaps'? According to a standard meaning assignment, they do when the antecedent, p is false; and sentences like 'If Bertrand Russell is president of the United States, I'm a monkey's uncle' have no truth value. Perhaps such sentences are, strictly speaking, meaningless—they make no statement. On another common meaning assignment, this type of conditional is accorded a full truth value analysis so that the sentence mentioning Russell comes out to be true. Now is that aforementioned sentence true or not? I suggest that the semantics needed to answer this question are well understood. What is not yet clearly understood is the theory of language use—pragmatics—in which the semantical structures are to be imbedded. It is relative to what results from taking people to speak truly in certain contexts as opposed to speaking 'truth value gappily' in those contexts that we frame our detailed semantic analysis of 'If p, then q'.

An example drawn from quantification theory will help us appreciate the importance of pragmatics to semantic theory. Pragmatics, in part, investigates the tone of discourse, what linguistic activities people perform with words, e.g. reporting, predicting, hypothesising, bantering, lying, joking, and so on. Our theory of what a language *means* is dependent upon our theory of what the language users are doing with their language. Here is a hypothetical case.[3]

Consider the English sentence 'All crows are black'. Under a typical meaning assignment, it might be analysed as $(x)(Cx \supset Bx)$ in some formal language where $Cx(Bx)$ is true of x if and only if x is a crow (is black) and the domain of quantification is, perhaps, a set of birds. Grant as hypothesis of the example that there are albino crows. This hypothesis generates the following puzzle. The sentence 'All crows are black' typically occurs in certain contexts (such as discussions of induction) and in these contexts appears to function as a true sentence. Yet if there are albino crows, the sentence is assigned the truth value false by the natural meaning assignment. This situation arises frequently. For example, a student who gives the distance between earth and sun as 93 million miles usually is said to speak correctly, although the distance is not exactly 93 million miles.

How shall we resolve this puzzle? Well, we can keep the meaning assignment if we assume that the language users are making a lot of *mistakes* about crows. But will our assumption always be justified? What if their supposed mistakes don't seem to hamper their practice? Another plausible resolution of the puzzle is to recognise in their use of language a variety of tones, or different linguistic acts. In addition to, say, 'straight reporting' there is a practice of 'approximating truth when sufficient'—useful exaggeration, as it were. 'All crows are black' remains false, but the language users do not make frequent mistakes with it, since they come to be seen as using it in contexts of 'approximating truth' rather than 'straight reporting' where truth is necessary to avoid error. But perhaps a simpler resolution can be achieved by abandoning the meaning assignment with which we began. Perhaps 'Cx' is the kind of predicate that is true of certain subsets of natural birds, the normal ones—freaks excluded. Since the domain now includes only normal crows, albinos are excluded and 'All crows are black' really is true under the meaning assignment, just as the speaker seems to assume. The pragmatics, or theory of language use, remains simple—at the price of complicating the semantics!

All this to illustrate what can be regarded as a self-evident point. The

3. Pragmatics overlaps considerably with what Dummett calls the theory of force. In Dummett (1976) he argues, in effect, that a theory of force as well as a theory of sense are required to relate a meaning assignment to an overall theory of language use.

precise details of the patterns of a meaning assignment vary with the patterns of the theory of pragmatics—the analysis of the socio-linguistic contexts in which that body of discourse is rooted. Two equally plausible meaning assignments may assign different truth values to a sentence as long as this is compensated for by different theories of pragmatics. Both in the illustration and in general one meaning assignment might actually be correct and we might actually know it is correct. This possibility is not being denied. What is being asserted is that the decisive evidence for the correctness of a meaning assignment might be its coherence with a correct theory of pragmatics.[4]

Meanings are expressed in contexts, and meaning assignments are assigned to sentences used in contexts. The general shape of these contexts is inter-dependent with the general shape of semantic theory. This remains true whether we take 'contexts' in the broadest sense of the total environment of the speaker, whether we focus our attention on the social contexts in which the speaker operates, or whether we narrow the context to include the linguistic operations that can be performed with sentences—such as asserting, ordering, exaggerating and so on. We have called this principle the relativity of meaning assignments.

There is an aspect of this relativity that deserves more attention than it has yet received in this essay. The arguments have, until now, stressed the *environment* in which a language operates. But if we assume that the users of a language are conscious rational agents, beings who can adopt articulate plans, then it would seem that the environment must include the individual and social consciousness of the language users. Or to put the matter in other words, in giving an account of human behaviour in the world we must refer not only to the environment in which humans operate, but also to their *perspectives* on that environment. To determine a correct meaning assignment for a language we must have at our disposal theories of the language users' environment and theories of how that environment appears to them —theories of what they believe. The theory of perspectives might be labelled 'rational psychology' in deference to the assumption of human rationality on which it is based. But in this case it probably should be thought of as forming an integral part of all the social sciences, not just psychology. We might also call it a 'theory of belief' since philosophers and social scientists often refer to the *beliefs* of an individual or society in articulating the per-spective held by the individual or society.[5] In the latter vein we could say

4. Hilary Putnam stresses the importance of such coherence in Putnam (1975)

5. This is to assume that the traditional view according to which humans have a natural capacity for belief is correct. If Needham is correct and they have no such capacity (see footnote 2), then the theory of perspectives would have to be developed without appeal to the concept of belief.

that the relativity thesis included the relativity of meanings to beliefs. Nida uses the term 'material culture' for the topics falling under a theory of perspective. The distinction between a theory of environment and a theory of perspective might be put simply as follows. Biology can tell us what has nutritional value in a culture's environment. But the concept of food—what the culture perceives as edible—belongs to the theory of perspective.

All of the earlier arguments showing the relativity of meanings to the various environments of the language users can be recast to bring out the relativity of meaning assignments to beliefs. Even after semantic investigators have decided upon the reality of spirits, the meaning assignment given to a body of discourse involving 'spirit' must depend on whether the language users do or do not believe in spirit.

A communist's semantic analysis of discourse depends on what he takes the capitalists to believe about the economic reality in which they participate, as well as on what he takes that reality to be. Do capitalists believe a restriction on the profits of corporations will have disastrous effects on the well-being of society's members or do they believe such a restriction is a disaster in itself? The right answer will influence even a communist's semantic analysis of statements about 'the economy', for example.

How one interprets the meaning of 'All crows are black' depends uodn what he takes the speaker of that sentence to believe about crows and about linguistic acts. The point has been made by Quine and Putnam, of late, perhaps originally by Brentano. Different meaning assignments to a language cohere with different theories of the speakers' beliefs.

There's a special dependence, then, that meaning assignments have on those social sciences which involve theories of perspective. A language spoken by humans has a correct meaning assignment relative to the environment of its speaker: this is the general relativity of meaning assignments to the special sciences. But if the speakers are rational it has a correct meaning assignment relative to how the speakers collectively perceive that environment, what they believe. This is the special relativity of meaning assignments to the social sciences. Let us pause now to recapitulate the argument.

We introduced the idea of assigning meaning to a language or body of discourse through the technical notion of 'meaning assignments'. We observed that a crucial value of assigning meanings to a language is that this assignment can play a role in the theories of behaviour of the language user.

At this point we should remember that meaning assignments are represented with fairly abstract formal concepts. As such their use is governed by two practical principles; in general it is difficult to find one meaning assignment which is roughly satisfactory for any extended body of discourse; and if it is possible to find one, it is, in general, possible to find several interesting variants which are roughly satisfactory. Our examples tried to suggest some possibilities in more detail. Now, not every formal invention can be the correct meaning assignment to a body of discourse. The very abstractness of meaning assignments, which is so essential to their function, allows us to gerrymander the constructions so as to make particular samples from the discourse come out to be true, false or even semantic nonsense. What about the notion of a correct meaning assignment? It corresponds, intuitively, to what a collection of speakers actually said, what statements they made, in a series of contexts. We have discovered that it makes sense to speak of correct meaning assignments to statements actually made by speakers only relative to certain background theories. The concept of meaning is not absolute, it is not an *a priori* foundation of one's conceptual system. The concept of meaning is relative to other theories in his conceptual framework.

Any special science, or for that matter any reputable body of knowledge, can be called into play when assessing meaning assignments. When the body of discourse is set in contexts involving certain aspects of the environment, our scientific theories about those aspects of the environment and the speaker's interaction with them will shape our assessment of meaning assignments.

The social sciences—our theories of social organisation and interrelations—will be especially utilised since the society is a prime topic of concern to its participants.

Of course, the actual employment of semantic structures in 'real life' contexts—as it is given by our theory of pragmatics or 'semantical engineering'—will have a significant impact on the concept of correct meaning assignments. We have to learn to recognise the jokes of a language in order to proceed confidently with a theory of meaning.

But a sound theory of pragmatics goes hand in glove with an appropriate psychological theory of the speakers as conscious rational agents. It is to their perspectives on their environment that meanings will be especially keyed.

These results we have subsumed under the heading 'the relativity of meaning assignments'. Philosophically speaking, I think that we are entitled to assume that the meanings of sentences—in one of our ordinary senses of 'meaning'—are similarly relative. For meaning assignments are, in their main parts, the best models of meaning that we now have. Moreover, it is clear that most of our considerations apply directly, if less precisely, to the less precise concept of meaning, itself.

These results have been noted by Quine in his arguments for the thesis of indeterminacy of translation. Nevertheless, Quine's thesis differs from the relativity thesis elaborated here in a number of ways. The most obvious is that the thesis of indeterminacy deals directly with translation, whereas the relativity of meaning assignments deals immediately with the semantic structure of a language. Of course, the principle of relativity of meanings has consequences for translation theory, just as the indeterminacy thesis has consequences for semantics.

A more significant difference is that Quine tends to characterise the relativity of meanings (in his case, translations) using fewer categories. He cites the dependence of meaning on physical theories, which he attempts to incorporate under the notions of 'stimulation' and 'stimulus meaning.' Any further relativity is treated as a dependence of meanings on mentalistic theories. Thus Quine analyses the relativity of meanings into two components:

(i) physical   (stimulus meanings)
(ii) mental   (analytical hypotheses).

I have attempted to characterise the relativity in a more complex fashion by drawing attention to the dependence of meanings on

(i) the special sciences
(ii) the social sciences
(iii) pragmatics
(iv) the theory of perspectives or theory of belief.

This difference is especially important because Quine, for independent reasons, believes that mentalistic ideas are generally incoherent. His argument presupposes, at least, that there are no correct mental theories in anything like the sense in which there are correct physical theories. But assigning meaning to a language, correctly, is relative to assigning correct beliefs to its speakers, for example. Since the latter task cannot be accomplished, the former cannot. Meanings are not merely relative, they are absolutely indeterminate with respect to our system of rational knowledge which is exhausted by physics and mathematics. Meanings don't exist. Such is the sense of Quine's thesis of indeterminacy of translation, a thesis of absolute indeterminacy. Clearly it goes far beyond the thesis of relativity of meanings. It seems that the absolute thesis of indeterminacy would follow from the relativity thesis together with a doctrine of materialism or physicalism. I suspect that the actual argument requires some general principles of a reductionist sort as well (e.g. 'atomic physics is the fundamental science, all others are in principle reducible to it'). In any case, the two theses are not equivalent.

A theory of translation for two languages includes a general account of the possibilities and limitations for translating sentences of each language into sentences of the other. To give such an account with any degree of scientific precision, one needs to know the semantic structures of each language. Knowing the semantic structure of a language, I have argued, depends upon knowing about the speakers, their environment, their society and their beliefs. Progress in translation theory depends on progress in linguistics; indeed, a relatively autonomous linguistic theory of translation might be possible. But such a linguistic theory would be only a part of translation theory, not all of it.

J. Wallace

Logical Form, Meaning, Translation

WHAT IS A theory of meaning for a language? At least this: a theory such that anyone who knows it is in a position to understand every sentence of the language. Thus in seeking a theory of meaning for, say, German, we are trying to solve for 'p' the following expression:

(1) For all persons, x, if x knew that p, then x would be in a position to understand every sentence of German.

Here to solve for 'p' is to find a sentence which when substituted for 'p' in (1) yields a true sentence. Sentences, not names or descriptions of sentences, are in point; substituting a name or description, no matter of what, for p in (1) yields an ungrammatical expression. We are, if you like, using a substitution interpretation of (1); in solving for 'p', we make no assignment of an entity to 'p', but a substitution for it.

It is hard to imagine on what grounds anyone could object to this condition on theories of meaning. One might demand more of a theory of meaning, e.g. that it also be true or that it also be learnable by creatures with no more than human powers. But the condition is proposed only as necessary, not as sufficient, for adequacy. One might complain that the idea of understanding a sentence, which (1) uses, is vague. So it is, in several ways; but here one should hold one's fire until one sees that the vaguenesses affect the points the condition is used to make. I believe that the points to follow steer well clear of the areas of vagueness.

The condition rules out some otherwise plausible and attractive approaches to the theory of meaning. A translation manual cannot be a theory of meaning; neither can a theory of truth.

If Gerald Ford knew that 'Die Erde ist rund' translates from German to English as 'The earth is round', then he would understand the German sentence 'Die Erde ist rund'. And if he had a rule for passing from any German sentence to its English translation, and knew that the rule had this character, he would thereby be in a position to understand every German sentence. Reflections of this sort might lead one to suppose that a translation manual could be a theory of meaning for German. But the truth of the first sentence of this paragraph depends on the fact that Gerald Ford speaks English. The general statement

> (2) For all persons, x, if x knew that 'Die Erde ist rund' translates from German to English as 'The earth is round', then x would be in a position to understand 'Die Erde ist rund' as a sentence of German

is false; anyone who knows neither German nor English is a counter-example. What is true in general is the statement

> For all persons, x, if x knew that 'Die Erde ist rund' translates from German to English as 'The earth is round' and x understood 'The earth is round' as a sentence of English, then x would be in a position to understand 'Die Erde ist rund' as a sentence of German.

In short, the ability to translate does not by itself generate understanding; it can only transfer understanding from one language to another. Thus a translation manual cannot pass our test for a theory of meaning.

A closely related point is made by C. I. Lewis (1946, 132):

> One who tried to learn the meaning of an Arabic word with only an Arabic dictionary at hand, might—if his acquaintance with Arabic be slight—be obliged to look up also words used in defining the one whose meaning he sought, and the further words defining these, and so on. (It would improve the illustration if we should suppose that while all words defined, and all which define them, are in Arabic, the relations between these are expressed in English; that is, that the 'syntactic language' is one already understood.) He might thus eventually determine an extended pattern of linguistic relations of the word in question to other Arabic expressions. If the process of this example could, by some miracle, be carried to its logical limit, a person might thus come to grasp completely and with complete accuracy the linguistic pattern relating the term in question to all other terms in Arabic with which it had any essential or analytic relationship. But—supposing the person in question to be also lacking in wit, so that he learned nothing through his investigation excepting that of which the dictionary informed him—he might still fail to understand, in a sense which will be obvious, what any one of these words *meant*.

This is fine up to the last sentence. But how could wit, however copious and intense, help Lewis's man derive from his study of the dictionary understanding of even a single Arabic word?

So much for translation. Let us turn to truth. Is the following true?

(3) If Gerald Ford knew that 'Die Erde ist rund' is true in German if and only if the earth is round, then he would be in a position to understand 'Die Erde ist rund' as a sentence of German.

Knowing a biconditional of the form 's is true in German if and only if p' has the advantage over knowing a translation that it connects the sentence with a condition in the world and not just with another sentence. Even so, (3) is false. Knowing that 'Die Erde ist rund' is true in German if and only if the earth is round is compatible with not knowing that 'Die Erde ist rund' means in German that the earth is round; it is compatible, indeed, with believing that 'Die Erde ist rund' does *not* mean in German that the earth is round. These remarks extend to the general case. Knowing a recursive truth definition which turns out consequences of the form 's is true in German if and only if p' when and only when in fact 's means in German that p' also holds, i.e. the truth biconditionals turned out invariably reflect meaning, is compatible with believing that the truth biconditionals turned out fail to reflect meaning in countless cases not predictable in advance. Knowing a recursive truth definition for German is compatible with not understanding a single German sentence. Thus such a theory does not pass our test for a theory of meaning.

As Gareth Evans (1975, 343) has well said, 'a theory of meaning . . . entails, for each sentence of the language under study, a statement of what it means'. The point to be driven home is that

(4) 'Die Erde ist rund' is true in German if and only if the earth is round

is no more a statement of what the German sentence means than is

(5) 'Die Erde ist rund' is true in German if and only if snow is white

or even

(6) 'Die Erde ist rund' contains fourteen letters if and only if the earth is round.

To be sure, (4) is distinguished from (5) by the fact that it follows from a true statement about meaning by way of the general truth that s is true in German if and only if *p*

is entailed by

s means in German that *p*.

But the converse entailment does not hold. The distinction between knowing a proposition and knowing premises from which the proposition follows is one we must respect in this case as in others. Compare 'A caused B' and 'A was temporally prior or contiguous to B'. The first may entail the second and may even be connected with it in some more intimate way; no one would say that knowing the second is tantamount to knowing the first.

When it comes to the theory of meaning, it appears, there is nothing— not 'translates', not 'is true if and only if'—quite like 'means'. Anyone who knows that 'Die Erde ist rund' means in German that the earth is round understands one German sentence. If he also knows that 'Der Schnee ist weiss' is true in German if and only if snow is white, he understands two. But what could he know that would give him understanding of every German sentence? Clearly something that implied every relevant instance of

s means in German that *p*

would do. But what would do this? We may articulate the difference between (4) on the one hand and (5) and (6) on the other by calling on a modal operator, 'it is a matter of meaning alone that'. It is a matter of meaning alone that 'Die Erde ist rund' is true in German if and only if the earth is round; it is true, but not a matter of meaning alone, that the sentence is true if and only if snow is white; it is true, but not a matter of meaning alone, that the sentence has fourteen letters if and only if the earth is round. Now I propose, first, that we prefix this modal operator to the usual laws of a Tarski-type theory of truth. In a slightly simplified form, sample laws would be (here I suppress a relativity of satisfaction and truth to English):

It is a matter of meaning alone that for all objects, *x*, *x* satisfies 'heart' if and only if *x* is a heart.
It is a matter of meaning alone that for all objects, *x*, *x* satisfies 'two-chambered' if and only if *x* has two chambers.
It is a matter of meaning alone that for all objects, *x*, and all expressions, *y* and *z*, *x* satisfies conj(*y*, *z*) if and only if *x* satisfies *y* and *x* satisfies *z*.

It is a matter of meaning alone that for all expressions, y, exquant(y) is true if and only if there is an object, x, such that x satisfies y.

Next we would need to state principles licensing us to make within the scope of the modal operator the standard logical moves which issue in proofs of sentences of the form

s is true if and only if p

from the laws of a truth theory. Only now the things we prove, leaving the modal operator in place, have the form

It is a matter of meaning alone that s is true if and only if p.

To see what sorts of principles would be needed one should try proving from the sample theory

It is a matter of meaning alone that equant(conj('heart', 'two-chambered')) is true if and only if there is an object, x, such that x is a heart and x has two chambers.

This exercise should convince anyone that the needed principles are extremely plausible.

Notice that

It is a matter of meaning alone that s is true if and only if p

is not equivalent to

s means that p.

For example, we have

It is a matter of meaning alone that exquant(conj('heart', 'two-chambered')) is true if and only if there is an object, x, such that x satisfies 'heart' and x satisfies 'two-chambered'.

But we should reject

Exquant(conj('heart', 'two-chambered')) means that there is an object, x, such that x satisfies 'heart' and x satisfies 'two-chambered'.

We can, however, explain 'means that' in terms of our modal operator; *s* means that *p* is defined as follows:

> It is a matter of meaning alone that *s* is true if and only if *p* and for all *q*, if it is a matter of meaning alone that *s* is true if and only if *q*, then it is a matter of the laws of meaning applied in the left–right direction only that if *q*, then *p*.

Here the idea is that (i) (*s* is true if and only if *p*) falls out of the laws and (ii) *p* is either to the right of (from the point of view of the laws) or coincides with any *q* for which (*s* is true if and only if *q*) falls out of the laws. Here we have called on a further modal operator, expressed by the phrase, 'it is a matter of the laws of meaning applied in the left–right direction only that'. The intelligibility of this operator rests on the intuition that the familiar semantical laws have a direction; they engineer a step by step shift from words and structures *mentioned* on the left side of a biconditional to words and structures used on the right. This intuition seems quite firm and to have unambiguous application in concrete cases.

As far as I can see, anyone who knows the Tarski-type laws with the modal operator attached and knows the connection between the modal operator and the idea of meaning *that*, is in a position to understand every sentence which falls within the scope of the theory. It is important to notice that enriching a Tarski-type theory with a modal operator in the way I suggest opens the way for a new type of semantical law for dealing with non-extensional constructions. Thus for one class of belief sentences we have the law:

> It is a matter of meaning alone that for all sentences, *s*, 'Jones believes' $\frown$ *s* is true if and only if Jones believes what *s* means.

Adding this law to the sample theory we have a straightforward intuitive consequence

> 'Jones believes' $\frown$ exquant(conj('heart', 'two-chambered')) means that Jones believes that there is an object, *x*, such that *x* is a heart and *x* has two chambers.

We have now found a type of theory, the essential feature of which is that in it a special modal operator works interdependently with the standard notions of a Tarski-type truth theory, which solves the problem with which we began, if not for any whole natural language, at least for fragments of a natural language containing an infinite number of sentences, involving non-extensional constructions. Most important, the type of theory sketched overcomes the difficulties which were seen to face theories based on translation and theories based on unsupplemented Tarski-type truth theory. The position we have reached calls for several comments.

A.   A person who has mastered a natural language is in a position to understand, on a first hearing, an infinite number of sentences of that language. How is such mastery possible? A theory which passes our test for a theory of meaning partially answers this question, for it articulates something which, if known, would produce the mastery. The answer thus provided is so far only partial; to complete it we need to persuade ourselves that the theory is true and that it is possible for a person to acquire the theory. But finding a theory which meets our test seems an essential part of a satisfying analysis of our linguistic creativity; for the test demands simply that the meanings of all sentences be seen as generated from a finite number of words by a finite number of rules of composition.

B.   Difficulties parallel to those I noted for the idea that a theory of truth is a theory of meaning have been noted by Davidson for the idea that knowing that a theory of truth for a language is true enables one to understand every sentence of the language (Davidson, 1973; see especially pp. 325–7). It is important to see that Davidson's discussion goes off on a wrong track from the beginning. If Brezhnev knows that a certain English sentence is both true and a theory of truth for German, he may know nothing about the conditions under which any German sentence is true, not because anything is queer about the truth theory, but because he does not understand English. Knowing that some English sentences are true and that they meet appropriate formal constraints and that they are grounded on evidence in the right sort of way—these last two being requirements Davidson suggests for overcoming the difficulties on which he is trying to focus—get Brezhnev nowhere unless he understands English.

Going off on this wrong track does not damage Davidson's main idea for overcoming the difficulties in the way of taking a theory of truth to be a theory of meaning. Before turning to this idea, it will be worthwhile to point up the slip that leads to the wrong track by taking up a suggestion of Fodor's. Fodor writes (1970, 299):

> Actually it remains to be shown that a truth definition must, *ipso facto*, reveal logical form. Say S is a syntax of L iff S recursively enumerates all and only the well-formed formulae (the grammatical sentences) of L. Every sentence in the range of S will be identifiable with an ordered sequence of markers

(say, for the sake of simplicity, words) and every such sequence will, presumably, be of finite length. It is trivial, given a well-formed formula $F(= w_1, w_2, \ldots, w_n)$ to define a function which maps that formula onto a formula of the form ' "$w_1, w_2, \ldots, w_n$" iff $w_1, w_2, \ldots, w_n$'. If we now want a theory which entails all formulae of this latter form, we need only adopt the postulate that every well-formed formula of that form is an axiom.

The crucial point here is that we can give a finite description of a certain infinite set of sentences: 'the set of sentences formed by such-and-such rule'. But how does this help solve for 'p' the crucial expression (1)? If we put for 'p' the description itself we get:

> For all persons, x, if x knew the set of sentences formed by such and such a rule, he would be in a position to understand every sentence of German.

This is not even a grammatical expression, unless it is regarded as shorthand for:

> For all persons, x, if x knew that every sentence in the set of sentences formed by such and such a rule is true, he would be in a position to understand every sentence of German.

This last is grammatical, but false; a person might know that all the sentences in a certain collection are true without knowing what any of them mean. So even if knowing what they all mean would enable him to interpret sentences in some further collection, that is no help to him; his understanding is blocked at an earlier stage. The upshot is that when the test for a theory of meaning is cast in form (1), the requirement that a theory of meaning be finite is not an additional requirement; it is already implicit in the test.

Let us return now to Davidson's idea for overcoming the difficulties which prevented truth theories from passing our test for a theory of meaning. The idea is that

> (7) 'Die Erde ist rund' is true in German if and only if the earth is round

and

> (8) 'Die Erde ist rund' is true in German if **and only** if snow is white

differ not in how well they are confirmed—both are as well confirmed as can be—but in how they are confirmed; roughly speaking, (7) is confirmed by one process while (8) is confirmed by compounding that process with a process which confirms that the earth is round if and only if snow is white. The special light in which we view confirmation of (7) when we have meaning on our minds can be elucidated by means of examples designed to bring out how we do, or how we would, proceed with interpretation of another in actual situations. But as far as I can see, the effect of this 'semantical' process of confirmation on what is known, when one knows the meaning, is reflected in a modal operator not analysable in more basic terms. For this modal operator I use the words 'it is a matter of meaning alone that'.

C. My point about belief sentences is that once we introduce the modal operator we can use it also to articulate how the meanings of belief sentences depend on the meanings of their parts. It is important to notice that the modal operator was not brought in to deal with belief sentences. It was brought in to articulate what knowledge is involved in understanding even the simplest sentences. But once in place it has another application. The resulting theory of belief sentences is extremely natural. All other theories of belief sentences known to me make some strained use of the notion of reference. In 'x believes that s' what fills in for 's' refers conventionally to a proposition (Frege); the utterer of the belief sentence refers demonstratively to a speech act he makes using 's' (Davidson); the 's' in surface structure hides elaborate reference to possible worlds related somehow to the believer, and there is complicated cross-reference between variables ranging over these and 'x'. The theory I propose avoids all such uses of reference; to grasp the meaning of 'x believes s' it is sufficient to grasp what the sentence in the 's' position means.

D. It might be objected that the use of the modal operator 'it is a matter of meaning alone that' is question-begging. But what question is begged? Not the question 'What general theory could we know which would generate understanding of all the sentences of our language?' Answering this question requires a general theory, but not a theory whose vocabulary is restricted in some pre-assigned way. A demand to reduce the notion of meaning to simpler notions would of course not be met by the sort of theory I have advocated. I am inclined to doubt that the demand for reduction can be met. In any case, it is important to see that there are substantial questions about language which can be answered without meeting it. It is worth remarking also that the role we have set for the meaning modal operator is exhausted in connecting expressions with what they mean, so that there is no occasion to posit an analytic sentence, i.e. a sentence s such that it is a matter of meaning alone that *s* is true. It is compatible with present purposes that there be no such sentences.

E.   Seeing the need for the meaning modal operator has helped me straighten out something that has long puzzled me in Church's semantical theory. Having distinguished rules of denotation from rules of sense and given a careful sketch of how the two kinds of rules operate, Church goes on to say that, from one point of view at least, the rules of sense are superfluous; they can be seen as already implicit in the rules of denotation. He writes (1951a, 102):

> The . . . intensional part of the semantics does not follow from the extensional part. For the sense of a name is not uniquely determined by its denotation, and thus a particular rule of denotation does not of itself have as a consequence the corresponding rule of sense. On the other hand, because the meta-linguistic phrase which is used in the rule of denotation must itself have a sense, there is a certain sense (though not that of logical consequence) in which the rule of denotation, by being given as a primitive rule of denotation, uniquely determines the corresponding rule of sense. Since the like is true of the rules of range and rules of value, it is permissible to say that we have fixed an interpretation of a given logistic system, and thus a formalized language, if we have stated only the extensional part of the semantics.

What puzzled me about this was (a) it seemed right, and for the deep reason, which Church mentions, that the words we use in giving a rule of denotation have sense as well as reference but (b) it seemed that if it were true, one should be able to go ahead and give the extensional (and thus, implicitly, the intensional) semantics for belief sentences without ever explicitly stating the intensional semantical rules. This last I could not see how to do. I suggest that what is right about what Church says is that e.g. not only is the rule of denotation

'the world' denotes the world

correct, but the stronger statement

it is a matter of meaning alone that 'the world' denotes the world

or, as we might as well put it, echoing Church's words,

it is a rule of denotation that 'the world' denotes the world

is also correct. When this modal element is explicitly incorporated in the theory, one can give semantics for belief sentences without ever explicitly assigning senses to their parts.

F.   The line of argument used at the beginning of the paper to show that a translation manual cannot be a theory of meaning seems to me extremely important in the theory of meaning and the theory of knowledge. It is involved, I think, in the early pages of Wittgenstein's *Blue Book*; he writes, for example (1965, 5):

> One is tempted to imagine that which gives the sentence life as something in an occult sphere, accompanying the sentence. But whatever accompanied it would for us just be another sign.

If translation were fundamental in the theory of meaning, one could in a curious way dissociate oneself from one's own language; understanding another person's language might then be a matter of viewing his use of language as a pattern of stimuli and responses, viewing one's own use of language in the same distanced way, and finding a mapping between the two sets of sentences which preserves structure in the patterns. But our test for a theory of meaning shows that it is not so. Understanding involves using one's own language, and potentially all of one's own language, not just a part concerned with stimulation and response, to construct what the other person means by his words.

G.   This outcome has important implications for the idea of logical form. We may regard as logical that form which we read into the sentences of a language in order to see their meanings as projected by a finite number of rules, i.e. that form which a theory satisfying our test finds in sentences. From this point of view, if a translation manual were a theory of meaning, logical form would be widely indeterminate. A translation manual is a recursive device, so each translation manual somehow breaks the sentences of the languages with which it deals into a finite number of bits. But how the breaks are made is largely arbitrary, largely a matter of convenience; any correlation between sentences which can be recursively generated at all can be recursively generated on the basis of countably many analyses of sentences into bits. Considerations of simplicity may rule out many or even most of these, but it seems inevitable that a large degree of arbitrariness would remain. As we have seen, a translation manual is not a theory of meaning, so such indeterminacy of logical form is not a real worry. There is no proof, but if a theory of meaning follows the lines of the one I have sketched, that is, an interweaving of a Tarski-type theory of truth and the modal operator 'it is a matter of meaning alone that', leeway in assignment of logical forms is very slight. If these are the lines a theory of meaning must follow, and I know of no alternatives, then the catalogue of forms will be the familiar ones, predication, quantification, truth-functional combination, plus the attachment of a non-extensional operator, such as 'believes that', to a sentence.

H. It would be natural to conjecture that fresh theories of meaning which pass our test would be found in, or at least suggested by, the writings of transformational grammarians. I cannot claim to have studied the very extensive writings of these scholars with the care which would be needed to be certain that the conjecture is false. I would like to point out, however, that some things they write indicate that they have not had our problem in mind. Thus Chomsky writes (1968a, 25):

> As I indicated in the first lecture, I believe that the most appropriate general framework for the study of problems of language and mind is the system of ideas developed as part of the rationalist psychology of the seventeenth and and eighteenth centuries, elaborated in important respects by the romantics and then largely forgotten as attention shifted to other matters. According to this traditional conception, a system of propositions expressing the meaning of a sentence is produced in the mind as the sentence is realized as a physical signal, the two being related by certain formal operations that, in current terminology, we may call *grammatical transformations*. Continuing with current terminology, we can thus distinguish the *surface structure* of the sentence, the organization into categories and phrases that is directly associated with the physical signal, from the underlying *deep structure*, also a system of categories and phrases, but with a more abstract character. Thus, the surface structure of the sentence 'A wise man is honest' might analyze it into the subject 'a wise man' and the predicate 'is honest'. The deep structure, however, will be rather different. It will, in particular, extract from the complex idea that constitutes the subject of the surface structure an underlying proposition with the subject 'man' and the predicate 'be wise'. In fact, the deep structure, in the traditional view, is a system of two propositions, neither of which is asserted, but which interrelate in such a way as to express the meaning of the sentence 'A wise man is honest'.

A bit further on he writes (p. 26):

> Knowledge of a language involves the ability to assign deep and surface structures to an infinite range of sentences, to relate these structures appropriately, and to assign a semantic interpretation and a phonetic interpretation to the paired deep and surface structures. This outline of the nature of grammar seems to be quite accurate as a first approximation to the characterization of 'knowledge of a language'.

And earlier in the book he writes (p. 15):

If I say that a wise man is honest, I am not asserting that men are wise or honest, even though in the Port-Royal theory the propositions 'a man is wise' and 'a man is honest' enter into the deep structure. Rather, these propositions into the complex ideas that are present to the mind, though rarely articulated in the signal, when the sentence is uttered.

Now the question is: what is or could be known about these expressions and propositions and structures and the connections between them that would enable us to understand the sentence 'a wise man is honest'? We are not told. If it is a matter of mapping one arrangement of expressions on to another, it leaves us in the same bind as Lewis's man with the Arabic dictionary. If it is a matter of mapping arrangements of expressions into meanings, we need some explanation of what these meanings are; why are they not for us, in Wittgenstein's image, just more (dead) signs? Apparently the sentence 'a wise man is honest' is to be regarded as built semantically out of the sentence 'a man is wise' and 'a man is honest'. The latter two are parts of the former. But what does 'part' mean here? Is there a rule which projects semantical properties of the simpler sentences into semantical properties of the more complex sentence? No such rule is hinted at. We are not told even what semantical properties might be involved. In these circumstances the idea of 'part' is pale metaphor, indeed. Details aside, the overall project which seems to surround this example is extremely puzzling. The project seems to be to analyse general sentences into a finite number of sentence parts. I should think that if we have learned anything from the Frege–Russell–Tarski analysis of generality, it is that this project must fail; the idea of a predicate as a sub-sentential fragment to which variables or some equivalent device may be applied to produce open sentences is essential if general sentences are to be analysed into a finite number of parts. I do not say that there is nothing in the ideas which Chomsky expresses so provocatively in the passages I have quoted; I do not think he says enough to see that he is suggesting anything to the purpose of the theory of meaning, as I have advocated we understand that phrase.

I.   Finally, a word about the concept of logical consequence. Any general theory of linguistic interpretation must give a central position to a distinction between speakers being right and their being reasonable. The concept of truth is a natural foundation for one side of this distinction; the concept of logical consequence is a natural foundation for the other. Now in the classical Tarskian theory there is a remarkable connection between these two concepts. Starting from the side of the theory of truth, we have assigned sentences a recursive structure and have gone on to give a recursive definition, with the standard basis and recursion clauses. This process defines truth. Now turn to the idea of logical consequence. Consider all structurally truth-like properties, that is, all properties of sentences which have a recursive definition whose recursions are like those in the definition of truth except that basis clauses are allowed to differ *ad lib* from those in the definition of truth (we also allow the range of variables to vary *ad lib*, so long as it is non-empty). We find that if we define logical consequence in terms of preservation of all structurally truth-like properties—sentence S is a logical consequence of a sentence U if and only if S has every structurally truth-like property which U has—we get a relationship which serves well as a foundation for the criticism of reasonableness. On this scheme, being right and being reasonable have a fundamental link; it is manifest from the definition that the relation of logical consequence is truth preserving. This classical scheme transfers without a hitch to the semantical approach I have advocated in this paper. The approach interweaves truth and satisfaction with the meaning modal operator. The resulting theory still has a recursive structure, and the idea of a structurally truth-like property still has application. There is the question now whether to treat the interpretation of 'believes' as fixed or as something which is allowed to vary. It seems to me that the theory's clause for treating 'believes' is more like a basis clause than a recursion clause; it therefore seems to me that in defining structurally truth-like properties its interpretation should be allowed to vary. Nothing much hinges on this, as far as I can see; it seems to be a genuine case in which the decision whether or not to regard a word as a logical constant is a matter of taste. What does seem important is that, whatever the decision on this point, the resulting account of logical consequence covers belief sentences and makes it manifest, as in Tarski's classical theory for extensional languages, that logical consequence preserves truth. And either way, it is clear that there is a structurally truth-like property which the sentence 'Jones believes that the morning star is identical with the morning star' and the sentence 'the morning star is identical with the evening star' both have but which the sentence 'Jones believes that the morning star is identical with the evening star' lacks; choose the right Jones, and truth is itself such a property.

II

THEORIES OF REFERENCE
AND TRANSLATION

H. Putnam

Meaning, Reference and Stereotypes*

UNCLEAR AS IT is, the traditional doctrine that the notion 'meaning' possesses the extension/intension ambiguity has certain typical consequences. The doctrine that the meaning of a term is a concept carried the implication that meanings are mental entities. Frege, however, rebelled against this 'psychologism'. Feeling that meanings are *public* property—that the same meaning can be 'grasped' by more than one person and by persons at different times—he identified concepts (and hence 'intensions' or meanings) with abstract entities rather than mental entities. However, 'grasping' these abstract entities was still an individual psychological act. None of these philosophers doubted that understanding a word (knowing its intension) was just a matter of being in a certain psychological state (somewhat in the way in which knowing how to factor numbers in one's head is just a matter of being in a certain very complex psychological state).

Secondly, the timeworn example of the two terms 'creature with a kidney' and 'creature with a heart' does show that two terms can have the same extension and yet differ in intension. But it was taken to be obvious that the reverse is impossible (two terms cannot differ in extension and have the same intension). Interestingly, no argument for this impossibility was ever offered. Probably it reflects the tradition of the ancient and medieval philosophers, who assumed that the concept corresponding to a term was just a conjunction of predicates, and hence that the concept corresponding to a term must *always* provide a necessary and sufficient condition for falling into the extension of the term. For philosophers, like Carnap, who accepted the verifiability theory of meaning, the concept corresponding to a term provided (in the ideal case, where the term had 'complete meaning') a criterion for belonging to the extension (not just in the sense of 'necessary and sufficient condition', but in the strong sense of *way of recognising* whether a given thing falls into the extension or not). So theory of meaning came to rest on two unchallenged assumptions:

* A very much expanded version of this paper will appear in volume 7 of Minnesota Studies in the Philosophy of Science (edited by Keith Gunderson), under the title 'The Meaning of "Meaning" '.

(1) That knowing the meaning of a term is just a matter of being in a certain psychological state (in the sense of 'psychological state', in which states of memory and belief are 'psychological states', no one thought that knowing the meaning of a word was a continuous state of consciousness, of course).

(2) That the meaning of a term determines its extension (in the sense that sameness of intension entails sameness of extension).

I shall argue that these two assumptions are not jointly satisfied by any notion, let alone any notion of meaning. The traditional concept of meaning is a concept which rests on a false theory.

Are meanings in the head?

For the purpose of the following science-fiction examples, we shall suppose that somewhere there is a planet we shall call Twin Earth. Twin Earth is very much like Earth: in fact, people on Twin Earth even speak English. In fact, apart from the differences we shall specify in our science-fiction examples, the reader may suppose that Twin Earth is *exactly* like Earth. He may even suppose that he has a *Doppelgänger*—an identical copy—on Twin Earth, if he wishes, although my stories will not depend on this.

Although some of the people on Twin Earth (say, those who call themselves 'Americans' and those who call themselves 'Canadians' and those who call themselves 'Englishmen', etc.) speak English, there are, not surprisingly, a few tiny differences between the dialects of English spoken on Twin Earth and standard English.

One of the peculiarities of Twin Earth is that the liquid called 'water' is not H_2O but a different liquid whose chemical formula is very long and complicated. I shall abbreviate this chemical formula simply as XYZ. I shall suppose that XYZ is indistinguishable from water at normal temperatures and pressures. Also, I shall suppose that the oceans and lakes and seas of Twin Earth contain XYZ and not water, that it rains XYZ on Twin Earth and not water, etc.

If a space ship from Earth ever visits Twin Earth, then the supposition at first will be that 'water' has the same meaning on Earth and on Twin Earth. This supposition will be corrected when it is discovered that 'water' on Twin Earth is XYZ, and the Earthian space ship will report somewhat as follows: 'On Twin Earth the word "water" means XYZ'.

Symmetrically, if a space ship from Twin Earth ever visits Earth, then the supposition at first will be that the word 'water' has the same meaning on

Twin Earth and on Earth. This supposition will be corrected when it is discovered that 'water' on Earth is H_2O and the Twin Earthian space ship will report: 'On Earth the word "water" means H_2O'.

Note that there is no problem about the extension of the term 'water': the word simply has two different meanings (as we say): in the sense in which it is used on Twin Earth, the sense of water$_{TE}$, what we call 'water' simply isn't water, while in the sense in which it is used on Earth, the sense of water$_E$, what the Twin Earthians call 'water' simply isn't water. The extension of 'water' in the sense of water$_E$ is the set of all wholes consisting of H_2O molecules, or something like that; the extension of water in the sense of water$_{TE}$ is the set of all wholes consisting of XYZ molecules or something like that.

Now let us roll the time back to about 1750. The typical Earthian speaker of English did not know that water consisted of hydrogen and oxygen, and the typical Twin-Earthian speaker of English did not know that 'water' consisted of XYZ. Let Oscar$_1$ be such a typical Earthian English speaker, and let Oscar$_2$ be his counterpart on Twin Earth. You may suppose that there is no belief that Oscar$_1$ had about water that Oscar$_2$ did not have about 'water'. If you like, you may even suppose that Oscar$_1$ and Oscar$_2$ were exact duplicates in appearance, feelings, thought, interior monologue, etc. Yet the extension of the term 'water' was just as much H_2O on Earth in 1750 as in 1950; and the extension of the term 'water' was just as much XYZ on Twin Earth in 1750 as in 1950. Oscar$_1$ and Oscar$_2$ understood the term 'water' differently in 1750 although they were in the same psychological state, and although, given the state of science at the time, it would have taken their scientific communities about fifty years to discover that they understood the term 'water' differently. Thus the extension of the term 'water' (and, in fact, its meaning, in the intuitive pre-analytical usage of that term) is *not* a function of the psychological state of the speaker by itself.[1]

But, it might be objected, why should we accept it that the term 'water' had the same extension in 1750 and in 1950 (on both Earths)? Suppose I point to a glass of water and say 'this liquid is called water'. 'My 'ostensive definition' of water has the following empirical presupposition: that the body of liquid I am pointing to bears a certain sameness relation (say, *x is the same liquid as y*, or *x is the same$_L$ as y*) to most of the stuff I and other speakers in my linguistic community have on other occasions called 'water'. If this presupposition is false because, say, I am—unknown to me—pointing to a glass of gin and not a glass of water, then I do not intend my ostensive definition to be accepted. Thus the ostensive definition conveys what might

---

1. See footnote 2, below, and the corresponding text.

be called a 'defeasible' necessary and sufficient condition; the necessary and sufficient condition for being water is bearing the relation $same_L$ to the stuff in the glass; but this is the necessary and sufficient condition only if the empirical presupposition is satisfied. If it is not satisfied, then one of a series of, so to speak, 'fallback' conditions becomes activated.

The key point is that the relation $same_L$ is a theoretical relation: whether something is or is not the same liquid as *this* may take an indeterminate amount of scientific investigation to determine. Thus, the fact that an English speaker in 1750 might have called XYZ 'water', whereas he or his successors would not have called XYZ water in 1800 or 1850 does not mean that the 'meaning' of 'water' changed for the average speaker in the interval. In 1750 or in 1850 or in 1950 one might have pointed to, say, the liquid in Lake Michigan as an example of 'water'. What changed was that in 1750 we would have mistakenly thought that XYZ bore the relation $same_L$ to the liquid in Lake Michigan, whereas in 1800 or 1850 we would have known that it did not.

Let us now modify our science-fiction story. I shall suppose that molybdenum pots and pans cannot be distinguished from aluminium pots and pans save by an expert. (This could be true for all I know, and, *a fortiori*, it could be true for all I know by virtue of 'knowing the meaning' of the words aluminium and molybdenum.) We will now suppose that molybdenum is as common on Twin Earth as aluminium is on Earth, and that aluminium is as rare on Twin Earth as molybdenum is on Earth. In particular, we shall assume that 'aluminium' pots and pans are made of molybdenum on Twin Earth. Finally, we shall assume that the words 'aluminium' and 'molybdenum' are switched on Twin Earth: 'aluminium' is the name of molybdenum, and 'molybdenum' is the name of aluminium. If a space ship from Earth visited Twin Earth, the visitors from Earth probably would not suspect that the 'aluminium' pots and pans on Twin Earth were not made of aluminium, especially when the Twin Earthians said they were. But there is one important difference between the two cases. An Earthian metallurgist could tell very easily that 'aluminium' was molybdenum, and a Twin Earthian metallurgist could tell equally easily that aluminium was 'molybdenum'. (The shudder quotes in the preceding sentence indicate Twin Earthian usages.) Whereas in 1750 no one on either Earth or Twin Earth could have distinguished water from 'water', the confusion of aluminium with 'aluminium' involves only a part of the linguistic communities involved.

This example makes the same point as the preceding example. If Oscar$_1$ and Oscar$_2$ are standard speakers of Earthian English and Twin Earthian English, respectively, and neither is chemically or metallurgically sophisticated, then there may be no difference at all in their psychological states when they use the word 'aluminium'; nevertheless, we have to say that 'aluminium' has the extension *aluminium* in the idiolect of Oscar$_1$ and the extension *molybdenum* in the idiolect of Oscar$_2$. (Also we have to say that Oscar$_1$ and Oscar$_2$ mean different things by 'aluminium'; that 'aluminium' has a different meaning on Earth than it does on Twin Earth, etc.) Again we see that the psychological state of the speaker does *not* determine the extension (*or* the 'meaning' speaking pre-analytically) of the word.

Before discussing this example further, let me introduce a non-science-fiction example. Suppose you are like me and cannot tell an elm from a beech tree. We still say that the extension of 'elm' in my idiolect is the same as the extension of 'elm' in anyone else's, viz. the set of all elm trees, and that the set of all beech trees is the extension of 'beech' in *both* of our idiolects. Thus 'elm' in my idiolect has a different extension from 'beech' in your idiolect (as it should). Is it really credible that this difference in extension is brought about by some difference in our concepts? My concept of an elm tree is exactly the same as my concept of a beech tree (I blush to confess). If someone heroically attempts to maintain that the difference between the extension of 'elm' and the extension of 'beech' in *my* idiolect is explained by a difference in my psychological state, then we can always refute him by constructing a 'Twin Earth' example—must let the words 'elm' and 'beech' be switched on Twin Earth (the way 'aluminium' and 'molybdenum' were in the previous example). Moreover, suppose I have a *Doppelgänger* on Twin Earth who is molecule for molecule 'identical' with me. If you are a dualist, then also suppose my *Doppelgänger* thinks the same verbalised thoughts I do, has the same sense data, the same dispositions, etc. It is absurd to think his psychological state is one bit different from mine: yet he 'means' beech when he says 'elm', and *I* 'mean' elm when I say 'elm'. Cut the pie any way you like, 'meanings' just ain't in the head!

A socio-linguistic hypothesis

The last two examples depend upon a fact about language that seems, surprisingly, never to have been pointed out: that there is *division of linguistic labour*. We could hardly use such words as 'elm' and 'aluminium' if no one possessed a way of recognising elm trees and aluminium metal; but not everyone to whom the distinction is important has to be able to make the distinction. Let us shift the example; consider gold. Gold is important for many reasons: it is a precious metal; it is a monetary metal; it has symbolic value (it is important to most people that the 'gold' wedding ring they wear really consist of gold and not just look gold); etc. Consider our community as a 'factory': in this 'factory' some people have the 'job' of wearing gold wedding rings; other people have the 'job' of selling gold wedding rings; still other people have the job of telling whether or not something is really gold. It is not at all necessary or efficient that everyone who wears a gold ring (or a gold cufflink, etc.), or discusses the 'gold standard', etc., engage in buying and selling gold. Nor is it necessary or efficient that everyone who buys and sells gold be able to tell whether or not something is really gold in a society where this form of dishonesty is uncommon (selling fake gold) and in which one can easily consult an expert in case of doubt. And it is certainly not necessary or efficient that everyone who has occasion to buy or wear gold be able to tell with any reliability whether or not something is really gold.

The foregoing facts are just examples of mundane division of labour (in a wide sense). But they engender a division of linguistic labour: every one to whom gold is important for any reason has to acquire the word 'gold'; but he does not have to acquire the method of recognising whether something is or is not gold. He can rely on a special subclass of speakers. The features that are generally thought to be present in connection with a general name— necessary and sufficient conditions for membership in the extension, ways of recognising whether something is in the extension, etc.—are all present in the linguistic community *considered as a collective body*; but that collective body divides the 'labour' of knowing and employing these various parts of the 'meaning' of 'gold'.

This division of linguistic labour rests upon and presupposes the division of *non*-linguistic labour, of course. If only the people who know how to tell whether some metal is really gold or not have any reason to have the word 'gold' in their vocabulary, then the word 'gold' will be as the word 'water' was in 1750 with respect to that subclass of speakers, and the other speakers just won't acquire it at all. And some words do not exhibit any division of linguistic labour: 'chair', for example. But with the increase of division of labour in the society and the rise of science, more and more words begin to exhibit this kind of division of labour. 'Water', for example, did not exhibit it at all before the rise of chemistry. Today it is obviously necessary for every speaker to be able to recognise water (reliably under normal conditions), and probably most adult speakers even know the necessary and sufficient condition 'water is H_2O' but only a few adult speakers could distinguish water from liquids that superficially resembled water. In case of doubt, other speakers would rely on the judgment of these 'expert' speakers. Thus the way of recognising possessed by these 'expert' speakers is also, through them, possessed by the collective linguistic body, even though it is not possessed by each individual member of the body, and in this way the most *recherché* fact about water may become part of the *social* meaning of the word although unknown to almost all speakers who acquire the word.

It seems to me that this phenomenon of division of linguistic labour is one that it will be very important for socio-linguistics to investigate. In connection with it, I should like to propose the following hypothesis:

Hypothesis of the universality of the division of linguistic labour:

Every linguistic community exemplifies the sort of division of linguistic labour just described; that is, it possesses at least some terms whose associated 'criteria' are known only to a subset of the speakers who acquire the terms, and whose use by the other speakers depends upon a structured cooperation between them and the speakers in the relevant subsets.

It is easy to see how this phenomenon accounts for some of the examples given above of the failure of the assumptions (1) and (2). When a term is subject to the division of linguistic labour, the 'average' speaker who acquires it does not acquire anything that fixes its extension. In particular, his individual psychological state *certainly* does not fix its extension; it is only the socio-linguistic state of the collective linguistic body to which the speaker belongs that fixes the extension.

We may summarise this discussion by pointing out that there are two sorts of tools in the world: there are tools like a hammer or a screwdriver which can be used by one person; and there are tools like a steamship which requires the cooperative activity of a number of persons to use. Words have been thought of too much on the model of the first sort of tool.

Indexicality and rigidity

The first of our science-fiction examples—'water' on Earth and on Twin Earth in 1750—does not involve division of linguistic labour, or at least does not involve it in the same way the examples of 'aluminium' and 'elm' do. There were not (in our story, anyway) any 'experts' on water on Earth in 1750, nor any experts on 'water' on Twin Earth. The example does involve things which are of fundamental importance to the theory of reference and also to the theory of necessary truth, which we shall now discuss.

Let W_1 and W_2 be two possible worlds in which I exist and in which this glass exists and in which I am giving a meaning explanation by pointing to this glass and saying 'This is water'. Let us suppose that in W_1 the glass is full of H_2O and in W_2 the glass is full of XYZ. We shall also suppose that W_1 is the actual world, and that XYZ is the stuff typically called 'water' in the world W_2 (so that the relation between English speakers in W_1 and English speakers in W_2 is exactly the same as the relation between English speakers on Earth and English speakers on Twin Earth). Then there are two theories one might have concerning the meaning of 'water':

(1) One might hold that 'water' was world-relative but constant in meaning (i.e. the word has a constant relative meaning).

On this theory, 'water' means the same in W_1 and W_2; it is just that water is H_2O in W_1 and water is XYZ in W_2.

(2) One might hold that water is H_2O in all worlds (the stuff called 'water' in W_2 is not water), but 'water' does not have the same meaning in W_1 and W_2.

If what was said before about the Twin Earth case was correct, then (2) is clearly the correct theory. When I say 'this (liquid) is water', the 'this' is, so to speak, a *de re* 'this'—i.e. the force of my explanation is that 'water' is whatever bears a certain equivalence relation (the relation we called '$same_L$' above) to the piece of liquid referred to as 'this' in the actual world.

We might symbolise the difference between the two theories as a 'scope' difference in the following way. On theory (1), the following is true:

(1') (For every world W) (For every x in W) (x is water $\equiv$ x bears $same_L$ to the entity referred to as 'this' in W)

while on theory (2)

(2') (For every world W) (For every x in W) (x is water $\equiv$ x bears $same_L$ to the entity referred to as 'this' *in the actual world* W_1)

I call this a 'scope' difference because in (1') the entity referred to as 'this' is within the scope of 'For every world W'—as the qualifying phrase 'in W' makes explicit—whereas in (2') the entity referred to as 'this' means 'the entity referred to as "this" *in the actual world*', and has thus a reference *independent* of the bound variable 'W'.

Kripke calls a designator 'rigid' (in a given sentence) if (in that sentence) it refers to the same individual in every possible world in which the designator designates. If we extend this notion of rigidity to substance names, then we may express Kripke's theory and mine by saying that the term 'water' is rigid.

The rigidity of the term 'water' follows from the fact that when I give the 'ostensive definition': 'this (liquid) is water', I intend (2') and not (1').

We may also say, following Kripke, that when I give the ostensive definition 'this (liquid) is water', the demonstrative 'this' is rigid.

What Kripke was the first to observe is that this theory of the meaning (or 'use', or whatever) of the word 'water' (and other natural-kind terms as well) has startling consequences for the theory of necessary truth.

To explain this, let me introduce the notion of a cross-world relation. A two-term relation R will be called cross-world when it is understood in such a way that its extension is a set of ordered pairs of individuals not all in the same possible world. For example, it is easy to understand the relation *same height as* as a cross-world relation: just understand it so that, e.g. if x is an individual in a world W_1 who is 5 feet tall (in W_1) and y is an individual in W_2 who is 5 feet tall (in W_2), then the ordered pair x,y belongs to the extension of *same height as*. (Since an individual may have different heights in different possible worlds in which that same individual exists, strictly speaking, it is not the ordered pair x,y that constitutes an element of the extension of *same height as*, but rather the ordered pair x-*in-world-*W_1, y-*in-world-*W_2.)

Similarly, we can understand the relation *same*$_L$ (same liquid as) as a cross-world relation by understanding it so that a liquid in world W_1 which has the same important physical properties (in W_1) that a liquid in W_2 possesses (in W_2) bears *same*$_L$ to the latter liquid.

Then the theory we have been presenting may be summarised by saying that an entity x, in an arbitrary possible world, is water if and only if it bears the relation *same*$_L$ (construed as a cross-world relation) to the stuff we call 'water' in the actual world.

Suppose, now, that I have not yet discovered what the important physical properties of water are (in the actual world)—i.e. I don't yet know that water is H_2O. I may have ways of recognising water that are successful (of course, I may make a small number of mistakes that I will not be able to detect until a later stage in our scientific development), but not know the microstructure of water. If I agree that a liquid with the superficial properties of 'water' but a different microstructure isn't really water, then my ways of recognising water cannot be regarded as an analytical specification of what it is to be water. Rather, the operational definition, like the ostensive one, is simply a way of pointing out a standard—pointing out the stuff in the actual world such that, for x to be water, in any world, is for x to bear the relation *same*$_L$ to the normal members of the class of local entities that satisfy the operational definition. 'Water' on Twin Earth is not water, even if it satisfies the operational definition, because it doesn't bear *same*$_L$ to the local stuff that satisfies the operational definition, and local stuff that satisfies the operational definition but has a microstructure different from the rest of the local stuff that satisfies the operational definition is not water either, because it doesn't bear *same*$_L$ to the normal examples of the local 'water'.

Suppose, now, that I discover the microstructure of water—that water is H_2O. At this point I will be able to say that the stuff on Twin Earth that I earlier mistook for water is not really water. In the same way, if you describe, not another planet in the actual universe, but another possible universe in which there is stuff with the chemical formula XYZ which passes the 'operational test' for water, we shall have to say that that stuff isn't water but merely XYZ. You will not have described a possible world in which 'water is XYZ', but merely a possible world in which there are lakes of XYZ, people drink XYZ (and not water), or whatever. In fact, once we have discovered the nature of water, nothing counts as a possible world in which water does not have that nature. Once we have discovered that water (in the actual world) is H_2O, nothing counts as a possible world in which water is not H_2O.

On the other hand, we can perfectly well imagine having experiences that would convince us (and that would make it rational to believe that) water isn't H_2O. In that sense, it is conceivable that water is not H_2O. It is conceivable but it is not possible! Conceivability is no proof of possibility.

Kripke refers to statements that are rationally unrevisable (assuming there are such) as *epistemically necessary*. Statements that are true in all possible worlds he refers to simply as necessary (or sometimes as 'metaphysically necessary'). In this terminology, the point just made can be restated as: a statement can be (metaphysically) necessary and epistemically contingent. Human intuition has no privileged access to metaphysical necessity.

In this paper, our interest is in theory of meaning, however, and not in theory of necessary truth. Words like 'now', 'this', 'here' have long been recognised to be indexical, or token–reflexive—i.e. to have an extension which varies from context to context or token to token. For these words, no one has ever suggested the traditional theory that 'intension determines extension'. To take our Twin Earth example: if I have a *Doppelgänger* on Twin Earth, then when I think 'I have a headache', *he* thinks 'I have a headache'. But the extension of the particular token of 'I' in his verbalised thought is himself (or his unit class, to be precise), while the extension of the token of 'I' in my verbalised thought is me (or my unit class, to be precise). So the same word, 'I', has two different extensions in two different idiolects; but it does not follow that the concept I have of myself is in any way different from the concept my *Doppelgänger* has of himself.

Now then, we have maintained that indexicality extends beyond the obviously indexical words and morphemes (e.g. the tenses of verbs). Our theory can be summarised as saying that words like 'water' have an unnoticed indexical component: 'water' is stuff that bears a certain similarity relation to the water around here. Water at another time or in another place or even in another possible world has to bear the relation *same*$_L$ to our 'water' in order to be water. Thus the theory that (1) words have 'intensions', which are something like concepts associated with the words by speakers; and (2) intension determines extension—cannot be true of natural-kind words like 'water' for the same reason it cannot be true of obviously indexical words like 'I'.

The theory that natural-kind words like 'water' are indexical leaves it open, however, whether to say that 'water' in the Twin Earth dialect of English has the same meaning as 'water' in the Earth dialect and a different extension—which is what we normally say about 'I' in different idiolects—thereby giving up the doctrine that 'meaning (intension) determines extension', or to say, as we have chosen to do, that difference in extension is *ipso facto* a difference in meaning for natural-kind words, thereby giving up the doctrine that meanings are concepts, or, indeed, mental entities of any kind.[2]

It should be clear, however, that Kripke's doctrine that natural-kind words are rigid designators and our doctrine that they are indexical are but two ways of making the same point.

Meaning

Let us now see where we are with respect to the notion of meaning. We have now seen that the extension of a term is not fixed by a concept that the individual speaker has in his head, and this is true both because extension is, in

2. Our reasons for rejecting the first option—to say that 'water' has the same meaning on Earth and on Twin Earth, while giving up the doctrine that meaning determines reference—are presented in 'The Meaning of "Meaning"'. They may be illustrated thus: suppose 'water' has the same meaning on Earth and on Twin Earth. Now, let the word 'water' become phonemically different on Twin Earth—say, it becomes 'quaxel'. Presumably, this is not a change in meaning *per se*, on any view. So 'water' and 'quaxel' have the same meaning (although they refer to different liquids). But this is highly counterintuitive. Why not say, then, that 'elm' in my idiolect has the same meaning as 'beech' in your idiolect, although they refer to different trees?

general, determined socially—there is division of linguistic labour as much as of 'real' labour—and because extension is, in part, determined indexically. The extension of our terms depends upon the actual nature of the particular things that serve as paradigms, and this actual nature is not, in general, fully known to the speaker. Traditional semantic theory leaves out only two contributions to the determination of extension—the contribution of society and the contribution of the real world!

We saw at the outset that meaning cannot be identified with extension. Yet it cannot be identified with 'intension' either, if intension is something like an individual speaker's concept. What are we to do?

There are two plausible routes that we might take. One route would be to retain the identification of meaning with concept and pay the price of giving up the idea that meaning determines extension. If we followed this route, we might say that 'water' has the same meaning on Earth and on Twin Earth, but a different extension. (Not just a different local extension but a different global extension. The XYZ on Twin Earth is not in the extension of the tokens of 'water' that I utter, but it is in the extension of the tokens of 'water' that my *Doppelgänger* utters, and this is not just because Twin Earth is far away from me, since molecules of H_2O are in the extension of the tokens of 'water' that I utter no matter how far away from me they are in space and time. Also, what I can counterfactually suppose water to be is different from what my *Doppelgänger* can counterfactually suppose 'water' to be.) While this is the correct route to take for an absolutely indexical word like 'I', it seems incorrect for the words we have been discussing. Consider 'elm' and 'beech', for example. If these are 'switched' on Twin Earth, then surely we would *not* say that 'elm' has the same meaning on Earth and Twin Earth, even if my *Doppelgänger*'s stereotype of a beech (or an 'elm', as he calls it) is identical with my stereotype of an elm. Rather, we would say that 'elm' in my *Doppelgänger*'s idiolect means beech. For this reason, it seems preferable to take a different route, and identify 'meaning' with an ordered pair (or possibly an ordered *n*-tuple) of entities, one of which is the extension (the other components of the, so to speak, 'meaning vector' will be specified later). Doing this makes it trivially true that meaning determines extension (i.e. difference in extension is *ipso facto* difference in meaning), but totally abandons the idea that if there is a difference in the meaning my *Doppelgänger* and I assign to a word, then there must be some difference in our concepts (or in our psychological state). Following this route, we can say that my *Doppelgänger* and I mean something different when we say 'elm', but this will not be an assertion about our psychological states. All this means is that the tokens of the word he utters have a different extension than the tokens of the word I utter; but this difference in extension is not a reflection of any difference in our individual linguistic competence considered in isolation.

If this is correct, and I think it is, then the traditional problem of meaning splits into two problems. The first problem is to account for the *determination of extension*. Since, in many cases, extension is determined socially and not individually, owing to the division of linguistic labour, I believe that this problem is properly a problem for socio-linguistics. Solving it would involve spelling out in detail exactly how the division of linguistic labour works. The so-called 'causal theory of reference' introduced by Kripke for proper names, and extended by us to natural kind words and physical magnitude terms, falls into this province. For the fact that, in many contexts, we assign to the tokens of a name that I utter whatever reference we assign to the tokens of the same name uttered by the person from whom I acquired the name (so that the reference is transmitted from speaker to speaker, starting from the speakers who were present at the 'naming ceremony', even though no fixed description is transmitted) is simply a special case of social cooperation in the determination of reference.

The other problem is to describe individual competence. Extension may be determined socially, in many cases, but we do not assign the standard extension to the tokens of a word W uttered by Jones no matter how Jones uses W. Jones has to have some particular ideas and skills in connection with W in order to play his part in the linguistic division of labour. Once we give up the idea that individual competence has to be so strong as to actually determine extension, we can begin to study it in a fresh frame of mind.

In this connection, it is constructive to observe that nouns like 'tiger' or 'water' are very different from proper names. One can use the proper name 'Sanders' correctly without knowing anything about the referent except that he is called 'Sanders'—and even that may not be correct. ('Once upon a time, a very long time ago now, about last Friday, Winnie-the-Pooh lived in a forest all by himself under the name Sanders.') But one cannot use the word tigers correctly, save *per accidans*, without knowing a good deal about tigers, or at least about a certain conception of tigers. In this sense, concepts *do* have a lot to do with meaning.

Just as the study of the first problem is properly a topic in socio-linguistics, so the study of the second problem is properly a topic in psycho-linguistics. To this topic we now turn.

Stereotypes and communication

Suppose a speaker knows that 'tiger' has a set of physical objects as its extension, but no more. If he possesses normal linguistic competence in other respects, then he could use 'tiger' in some sentences: for example, 'tigers have mass', 'tigers take up space', 'give me a tiger', 'is that a tiger?', etc. Moreover, the socially determined extension of 'tiger' in these sentences would be the standard one, i.e. the set of tigers. Yet we would not count such a speaker as 'knowing the meaning' of the word tiger. Why not?

Before attempting to answer this question, let us reformulate it a bit. We shall speak of someone as having acquired the word 'tiger' if (1) he is able to use it in such a way that his use passes muster (i.e. people don't say of him such things as 'he doesn't know what a tiger is', 'he doesn't know the meaning of the word "tiger" ', etc.); and (2) his total way of being situated in the world and in his linguistic community is such that the socially determined extension of the word 'tiger' in his idiolect is the set of tigers. Clause (1) means, roughly, that speakers like the one hypothesised in the preceding paragraph do not count as having acquired the word 'tiger' (or whichever). We might speak of them, in some cases, as having partially acquired the word; but let us defer this for the moment. Clause (2) means that speakers on Twin Earth who have the same linguistic habits as we do, count as having acquired the word 'tiger' only if the extension of 'tiger' in their idiolect is the set of tigers. The burden of the preceding sections of this paper is that it does *not* follow that the extension of 'tiger' in Twin Earth dialect (or idiolects) is the set of tigers merely because their linguistic habits are the same as ours: the nature of Twin Earth 'tigers' is also relevant. (If Twin Earth organisms have a silicon chemistry, for example, then their 'tigers' are not really tigers, even if they look like tigers, although the linguistic habits of the lay Twin Earth speaker exactly correspond to those of Earth speakers.) Thus, clause (2) means that in this case we have decided to say that Twin Earth speakers have not acquired our word 'tiger' (although they have acquired another word with the same spelling and pronunciation).

Our reason for introducing this way of speaking is that the question 'does he know the meaning of the word "tiger"?' is biased in favour of the theory that acquiring a word is coming to possess a thing called its 'meaning'. Identify this thing with a concept, and we are back at the theory that a sufficient condition for acquiring a word is associating it with the right concept (or, more generally, being in the right psychological state with respect to it)—the very theory we have spent all this time refuting. So, henceforth, we will 'acquire' words, rather than 'learn their meaning'.

We can now reformulate the question with which this section began. The use of the speaker we described does not pass muster, although it is not such as to cause us to assign a non-standard extension to the word 'tiger' in his idiolect. Why does it not pass muster?

Suppose our hypothetical speaker points to a snowball and asks 'is that a tiger?'. Clearly there is not much point in talking tigers with *him*. Significant communication requires that people know something of what they are talking about: but the sense in which the man who points to a snowball and asks 'is that a tiger?' knows nothing about tigers is so far beyond the sense in which the man who thinks that Vancouver is going to win the Stanley Cup knows nothing about Vancouver, or the man who thinks that the Vietnam war was fought to help the South Vietnamese knows nothing about the Vietnam war, that one obviously cannot remedy it by the adoption of linguistic conventions; but not knowing what one is talking about in the first, mind-boggling sense can be and is prevented, near enough, by our conventions of language. What I contend is that speakers are required to know something about (stereotypical) tigers in order to count as having acquired the word 'tiger'; something about elm trees (or, anyway, about the stereotype thereof) to count as having acquired the word 'elm'; etc.

This idea should not seem too surprising. After all, we do not permit people to drive on the highways without first passing some tests to determine that they have a *minimum* level of competence; and we do not dine with people who have not learned to use a knife and fork. The linguistic community too has its minimum standards, both with respect to syntax and 'semantics'.

The nature of the required minimum level of competence depends heavily upon both the culture and the topic, however. In our culture, speakers are required to know what tigers look like (if they acquire the word 'tiger', and this is virtually obligatory); they are not required to know the fine details (such as leaf shape) of what an elm tree looks like. English speakers are required by their language to be able to tell tigers from leopards; they are not required to be able to tell elm trees from beech trees.

This could easily have been different. Imagine an Indian tribe, call it the Cheroquoi, who have words, say *uhaba'* and *wa'arabi*, for elm trees and beech trees respectively, and who make it obligatory to know the difference. A Cheroquoi who could not recognise an elm would be said not to know what an *uhaba'* is, not to know the meaning of the word '*uhaba'* ' (perhaps, not to know the word, or not to *have* the word); just as an English speaker who had no idea that tigers are striped would be said not to know what a tiger is, not to know the meaning of the word 'tiger' (of course, if he at least knows that tigers are large felines we might say he knows part of the meaning, or partially knows the meaning), etc. Then the translation of *uhaba'* as 'elm' and *wa'arabi* as 'beech' would, in our view, be only *approximately* correct. In this sense, there is a real difficulty with radical translation; but this is not the abstract difficulty that Quine is talking about, and which in our view is no difficulty at all, but a sceptical conundrum.

What stereotypes are

In ordinary parlance, a 'stereotype' is a conventional (frequently malicious) idea (which may be wildly inaccurate) of what an X looks like or acts like or is. Obviously, I am trading on some features of the ordinary parlance. I am not concerned with malicious stereotypes (save where the language itself is malicious); but I am concerned with conventional ideas, which may be inaccurate. I am suggesting that just such a conventional idea is associated with 'tiger', with 'gold', etc., and, moreover, that this is the sole element of truth in the 'concept' theory.

On this view, someone who knows what 'tiger' means (or, as we have decided to say instead, has acquired the word 'tiger'), is required to know that stereotypical tigers are striped. More precisely, there is one stereotype of tigers (he may have others) which is required by the linguistic community as such: he is required to have this stereotype, and to know (implicitly) that it is obligatory. This stereotype must include the feature of stripes if his acquisition is to count as successful.

The fact that a feature (e.g. stripes) is included in the stereotype associated with a word X does not mean that it is an analytic truth that all Xs have that feature, nor that most Xs have that feature, nor that all normal Xs have that feature, nor that some Xs have that feature. Three-legged tigers and albino tigers are not logically contradictory entities. Discovering that our stereotype has been based on non-normal or unrepresentative members of a natural kind is not discovering a logical contradiction. If tigers lost their stripes they would not necessarily cease to be tigers, nor would butterflies necessarily cease to be butterflies if they lost their wings.

(Strictly speaking, the situation is more complicated than this. It is impossible to give a word like 'butterfly' a sense in which butterflies would cease to be butterflies if they lost their wings—through mutation, say. Thus one can find *a* sense of 'butterfly' in which it is analytic that 'butterflies have wings'. But the most important sense of the term, I believe, is the one in which the wingless butterflies would still be butterflies.)

At this point the reader may wonder what the value to the linguistic com-

munity of having stereotypes is, if the 'information' contained in the stereotype is not necessarily correct. But this is not really such a mystery. Most
stereotypes do, in fact, capture features possessed by paradigmatic members
of the class in question. Even where stereotypes go wrong, the way in which
they go wrong sheds light on the contribution normally made by stereotypes
to communication. The stereotype for gold, for example, contains the
feature *yellow* even though chemically pure gold is nearly white. But the
gold we see in jewellery is typically yellow (due to the presence of copper),
so the presence of this feature in the stereotype is even useful in lay contexts.
And the fact that our language has *some* stereotypes which impede rather than
facilitate our dealings with the world and each other only points to the fact
that we are not infallible beings, and how could we be? The fact is, that we
could hardly communicate successfully if most of our stereotypes were not
pretty accurate as far as they go.

Semantic markers

If the approach suggested here is correct, then there is a great deal of
scientific work to be done in (1) finding out what sorts of items can appear
in stereotypes; (2) working out a convenient system for representing
stereotypes; etc. This work is not work that can be done by philosophical
discussion, however. It is rather the province of linguistics and psycho-
linguistics. One idea that can, I believe, be of value is the idea of a semantic
marker. The idea comes from the work of Jerrold Katz and Jerry Fodor;
we shall modify it somewhat here.

Consider the stereotype of 'tiger' for a moment. This includes such
features as being an animal; being big-cat-like; having black stripes on a
yellow ground (yellow stripes on a black ground?); etc. Now, there is
something very special about the feature *animal*. In terms of Quine's notion
of centrality or unrevisability, it is qualitatively different from the others
listed. It is not impossible to imagine that tigers might not be animals (they
might be robots). But spelling this out (they must always have been robots;
we do not want to tell a story about the tigers being replaced by robots,
because then the robots wouldn't be tigers. Or, if they were not always
robots, they must have become robots, which is even harder to imagine. If
tigers are and always were robots, these robots must not be too 'intelligent', or
else we may not have a case in which tigers are not animals—we may, rather,
have described a case in which some robots are animals. Best make them
'other directed' robots—say, have an operator on Mars controlling each
motion remotely)—spelling this out, I repeat, is difficult, and it is curiously

hard to think of the case to begin with, which is why it is easy to make the mistake of thinking that it is 'logically impossible' for a tiger *not* to be an animal. On the other hand, there is no difficulty in imagining an individual tiger that is not striped; it might be an albino. Nor is it difficult to imagine an individual tiger that does not look like a big cat; it might be horribly deformed. We can even imagine the whole species losing its stripes or becoming horribly deformed. But tigers ceasing to be animals? Great difficulty again!

Notice that we are not making the mistake that Quine rightly criticised, of attributing an absolute unrevisability to such statements as 'tigers are animals', 'tigers could not change from animals into something else and still be tigers'. Indeed, we can describe far-fetched cases in which these statements would be given up. But we maintain that it is qualitatively harder to revise 'all tigers are animals' than 'all tigers have stripes'—indeed, the latter statement is not even true.

Not only do such features as 'animal', 'living thing', 'artifact', 'day of the week', 'period of time', attach with enormous centrality to the words 'tiger', 'clam', 'chair', 'Tuesday', 'hour'; but they also form part of a widely used and important system of classification. The centrality guarantees that items classified under these headings virtually never have to be *re*classified; thus these headings are the natural ones to use as category-indicators in a host of contexts. It seems to me reasonable that, just as in syntax we use such markers as 'noun', 'adjective', and, more narrowly, 'concrete noun', 'verb taking a person as subject and an abstract object', etc., to classify words, so in semantics these category-indicators should be used as markers.

It is interesting that when Katz and Fodor originally introduced the idea of a semantic marker, they did not propose to exhaust the meaning—what we call the stereotype—by a list of such markers. Rather, the markers were restricted to just the category-indicators of high centrality, which is what we propose. The remaining features were simply listed as a 'distinguisher'. Their scheme is not easily comparable with ours, because they wanted the semantic markers *plus* the distinguisher always to give a necessary and sufficient condition for membership in the extension of the term. Since the whole thing—markers and distinguisher—was supposed to represent what every speaker implicitly knows, they were committed to the idea that every speaker implicitly knows of a necessary and sufficient condition for membership in the extension of 'gold', 'aluminium', 'elm'—which, as we have pointed out, is not the case. Later Katz went further, and demanded that all the features constitute an analytically necessary and sufficient condition for membership in the extension. At this point, he dropped the distinction between markers and distinguishers; if all the features have, so to speak, the infinite degree of centrality why call some 'markers' and some 'distinguishers'? From our point of view, their original distinction between 'markers' and 'distinguisher' was sound—provided one drop the idea that the distinguisher provides (together with the markers) a necessary and sufficient condition, and the idea that any of this is a theory of analyticity. We suggest that the idea of a semantic marker is an important contribution, when taken as suggested here.

The meaning of 'meaning'

We may now summarise what has been said in the form of a proposal concerning how one might reconstruct the notion of 'meaning'. Our proposal is not the only one that might be advanced on the basis of these ideas, but it may serve to encapsulate some of the major points. In addition, I feel that it recovers as much of ordinary usage in common sense talk and in linguistics as one is likely to be able to preserve conveniently. Since, in my view, something like the assumptions (1) and (2) listed in the first part of this paper are deeply embedded in ordinary meaning talk, and these assumptions are jointly inconsistent with the facts, no reconstruction is going to be without some counter-intuitive consequences.

Briefly, my proposal is to define 'meaning' not by picking out an object which will be identified with the meaning (although that might be done in the usual set theoretic style if one insists), but by specifying a normal form (or, rather, a type of normal form) for the description of meaning. If we know what a 'normal form description' of the meaning of a word should be, then, as far as I am concerned, we know what meaning *is* in any scientifically interesting sense.

My proposal is that the normal form description of the meaning of a word should be a finite sequence, or 'vector', whose components should certainly include the following (it might be desirable to have other types of components as well): (1) the syntactic markers that apply to the word, e.g. 'noun'; (2) the semantic markers that apply to the word, e.g., 'animal', 'period of time'; (3) a description of the additional features of the stereotype, if any; (4) a description of the extension.

The following convention is a part of this proposal: the components of the vector all represent a hypothesis about the individual speaker's competence, *except the extension*. Thus the normal form description for 'water' might be, in part:

Syntactic markers	Semantic markers	Stereotype	Extension
mass noun, concrete	natural kind; liquid	colourless; transparent; tasteless; thirst-quenching; etc.	H_2O (give or take impurities)

This does *not* mean that knowledge of the fact that water is H_2O is being imputed to the individual speaker or even to the society. It means that (*we* say) the extension of the term 'water' as *they* (the speakers in question) use it is in fact H_2O. The objection 'who are *we* to say what the extension of *their* term is in fact' has been discussed above. Note that this is fundamentally an objection to the notion of truth, and that extension is a relative of truth, and inherits the family problems.

Let us call two descriptions equivalent if they are the same except for the description of the extension, and the two descriptions are coextensive. Then, if the set variously described in the two descriptions is, in fact, the extension of the word in question, and the other components in the description are correct characterisations of the various aspects of competence they represent, both descriptions count as correct. Equivalent descriptions are both correct or both incorrect. This is another way of making the point that, although we have to use a description of the extension to give the extension, we think of the component in question as being the extension (the set), not the description of the extension.

In particular, the representations of the words 'water' in Earth dialect and 'water' in Twin Earth dialect would be the same except that in the last column the normal form description of the Twin Earth word 'water' would have XYZ and not H_2O. This means, in view of what has just been said, that we are ascribing the same linguistic competence to the typical Earthian/ Twin Earthian speaker, but none the less a different extension to the word.

This proposal means that we keep assumption (2) of our early discussion. Meaning determines extension—by construction, so to speak. But (1) is given up; the psychological state of the individual speaker does not determine 'what he means'.

In most contexts this will agree with the way we speak, I believe. But one paradox: suppose Oscar is a German–English bilingual. In our view, in his total collection of dialects, the words *beech* and *Buche* are *exact synonyms*. The normal form descriptions of their meanings would be identical. But he might very well not know that they are synonyms. A speaker can have two synonyms in his vocabulary and not know that they are synonyms!

The amazing thing about the theory of meaning is how long the subject has been in the grip of philosophical misconceptions, and how strong these misconceptions are. Meaning has been identified with a necessary and sufficient condition by philosopher after philosopher. Nor have these misconceptions had the virtue of exclusiveness; not a few philosophers have held that meaning = method of verification = necessary and sufficient condition.

On the other side, it is amazing how weak the grip of the facts has been. After all, what have been pointed out in this essay are little more than home truths about the way we use words and how much (or rather, how little) we actually know when we use them. My own reflection on these matters began after I published a paper in which I confidently maintained that the meaning of a word was 'a battery of semantical rules', and then began to wonder how the meaning of the common word 'gold' could be accounted for in this way. And it is not that philosophers had never considered such examples: Locke, for example, uses this word as an example, and is not troubled by the idea that its meaning is a necessary and sufficient condition!

If there is a reason for both learned and lay opinion having gone so far astray with respect to a topic which deals, after all, with matters which are in everyone's experience, matters concerning which we all have more data than we know what to do with, matters concerning which we have, if we shed preconceptions, pretty clear intuitions, it must be connected to the fact that the grotesquely mistaken views of language which are and always have been current reflect two specific and very central philosophical tendencies; the tendency to treat cognition as a purely individual matter, and the tendency to ignore the world, insofar as it consists of more than the individual's 'observations'. Ignoring the division of linguistic labour is ignoring the social dimension of cognition; ignoring what we have called the indexicality of most words is ignoring the contribution of the environment. Traditional philosophy of language, like much traditional philosophy, leaves out other people and the world; a better philosophy and a better science of language must encompass both.

S. C. Wheeler

Indeterminacy of Radical Interpretation and the Causal Theory of Reference

1. *Radical interpretation*

DAVIDSON'S THEORY OF radical interpretation is an account of how, from observation of what members of a culture say when, a theory of truth for that culture can be constructed. I take as example Davidson's theory rather than Quine's because the thesis of the indeterminacy of radical interpretation Davidson arrives at is weaker than Quine's thesis of indeterminacy of translation and depends on fewer controversial premises. Moreover the premises Davidson uses are shared by Quine and are sufficient to yield the indeterminacy of translation.

This paper will draw out these central premises, show how they lead to the indeterminacy theses, and show that the causal theory of reference is inconsistent with these premises. After saying a few things in favour of the causal theory of reference and its presuppositions, it will argue that, whether or not a causal theory of reference is right, the theory of reference which leads Davidson and Quine to accept indeterminacy is wrong. It is further argued that, given reasonable suppositions about causation, Kripke is himself very probably wrong about the details of the causal theory of reference, since 'reference' must name a real physical relation between persons and kinds. Finally, it is argued that translation and interpretation are indeterminate for the large body of ordinary language where 'reference', strictly understood, cannot apply.

The central premises needed for a theory of interpretation which will lead to an indeterminacy thesis are the following:

Premise (1): The resemblance theory of reference
An interpretation of a term T_1 in the object language by term T_2 in the metalanguage is optimal, *ceteris paribus*, if such an interpretation induces as much agreement in accepted sentences between the speakers of the metalanguage and the speakers of the object language as any other. As Davidson remarks, this would be expanded to cover all sentential attitudes, not just

'believes-true'. This principle of interpretation amounts to the principle that, other things being equal, a term T_1 is correctly interpreted as term T_2 if the speakers of the interpreting culture hold most of the same sentential attitudes towards sentences in which T_2 occurs which speakers of the interpreted culture hold towards similarly interpreted sentences in which T_1 occurs.

Since interpreting a term T_1 by a term T_2 is just deciding that the extension of T_1 is the set of objects we call T_2s, and since the above criterion of interpretation in effect identifies the 'meaning' or 'sense' of a term with the set of propositional attitudes speakers hold with respect to sentences using that term, the criterion of interpretation amounts to the (qualified) thesis that a term has as its extension a certain set if and only if features of the term's meaning match features of the items in the set. That is, if the speakers of the language hold attitudes with respect to a term which are more or less appropriate to a certain kind of object that term has as its reference that kind of object. 'Appropriate', of course, means 'appropriate according to us'.

Radical interpretation, then, proceeds by seeing what people say in what circumstances, that is, by adopting a version of the 'meaning is use' doctrine. It interprets their speech acts as being as much as possible like the ones we would make in similar circumstances, the speech acts of the other reflect the sentential attitudes our act in those circumstances would reflect. Their wants, beliefs and perceptual attitudes are thus interpreted as being the wants, beliefs and perceptual attitudes we would have in similar situations. The contents of such attitudes are then used to interpret the sentences that occur in speech acts which express them. The constraint of 'charity of radical translation', for Davidson, amounts to making any agent as much like us as possible, consistent with a reasonably simple interpretive theory. Maximising agreement is really maximising the rationality of the other. This constraint, as we have indicated, makes the interpretation of a term depend on the degree of match between 'internal' features of the term for the person and features of objects in the (our) world. Among expressions of this constraint in Davidson's writings are the following:

Charity is forced on us;—whether we like it or not, if we want to understand others, we must count them right in most matters. (1974a, 19)

What matters is this: If all we know is what sentences a speaker holds true . . ., then we cannot take even a first step towards interpretation without knowing or assuming a great deal about the speaker's beliefs. Since knowledge of beliefs comes only with the ability to interpret words, the only possibility at the start is to assume general agreement on beliefs. (1974a, 18)

The general policy, however, is to choose truth-conditions that do as well as possible in making speakers hold sentences true when (according to the theory and the theory builder's view of the facts) those sentences are true. (1974b, 320)

Each interpretation and attribution of attitude is a move within a holistic theory, a theory necessarily governed by concern for consistency and general concern for the truth, and it is this that sets these theories forever apart from those that describe mindless objects, or describe objects as mindless. (1974b, 322)

Such a theory of meaning and reference is a very sophisticated and pure version of what I call a 'resemblance' theory of meaning. The interpretation of a term depends on what in the world fits the theory associated with the term. In a way, Davidson's theory of meaning is what a theorist arrives at who adopts Frege's view that reference is a function of sense, but who has rightly abandoned the idea that the sense of an expression can be separated from the theory associated with that expression. That is, if the analytic/synthetic distinction cannot be made, then all beliefs in which a term occurs are part of its sense. And if Frege is right that reference is a function of sense, then a Davidsonian resemblance theory of reference is correct.

The above characterisation of Davidsonian interpretation-theory needs to be qualified to a certain extent by noting that radical interpretation is holistic. General agreement for the most part in propositional attitudes is something that is required as a background which makes disagreement on particular cases possible. That is, interpretation proceeds in the first instance by maximising agreement. Only when a significant complication of the truth-theory would be required is disagreement, i.e. some kind of irrationality, contemplated. (By adjusting extensions of terms, of course, any culture can be made absolutely correct about everything. Thus an unfettered application of the charity constraint would make belief and meaning match totally, so that nothing the culture generally agrees on could be false. This and other such degenerations are controlled by such constraints as that of requiring that most of the predicates of the other have extensions which fit the extensions of simple terms of ours, i.e. by requiring that the truth-theory be reasonably simple.)

What are the supports for the resemblance theory of meaning, which makes meaning and truth simultaneously determined? Why could there not be a culture which differed enormously in the beliefs and desires they held, which behaved irrationally, by our lights, most of the time so that maximising resemblance to us got meaning wrong? Davidson's answer is that such a putative person or culture would be so unlike what we take persons and cultures to be that it would make no sense to call events in which they participate speech acts of persons in a culture. The features of our terms 'person', 'language', 'intentional act' would fit them so poorly that the terms wouldn't be true of those objects. For it to be rational to treat events as speech acts, the 'agents' must be such that our term 'person' correctly applies to them. But correct application of our concept is a matter of whether the objects fit that concept, i.e. whether they meet our criteria. But our criteria for personhood involve rationality, agency and the possession of wants and beliefs that each ascription entails. And the ascription to the other of irrational systems of belief and desire amounts to applying those terms to items which resemble our concepts too little to be correctly characterised by the terms.

The resemblance theory of meaning thus reinforces itself. The reason that any other must for the most part agree with us, and thus the reason that meaning and truth must be simultaneously determined, is that the resemblance theory of meaning is correct when applied to terms such as 'is a person', 'is a language' and 'is a belief'.

Premise (2): Statistical linguistic nominalism

A sophisticated version of a thesis resembling the thesis of linguistic nominalism is a corollary of the resemblance theory of meaning (this general thesis is stated in Davidson, 1974a). This is the view, crudely, that the kinds of things there are is for the most part, and holistically, determined by what extensions our language has predicated for. Since most of what any culture says must be true and most of the extensions of their terms must be extensions of some simple complexes of our terms, and since we are a culture, most of what we think must be true and most of the extensions of our predicates must be all right as far as getting 'real categories of the world' goes. It cannot be the case that most of our predicates somehow miss the real categories of the world. This is not because there is some Aristotelian affinity between our minds and the nature of things but rather because the supposition that we might be vastly mistaken does not make sense. And the reason Davidson claims it does not make sense is that meaning and truth are simultaneously determined for us as well as for anyone else.

Whatever we say is for the most part correct, because if we said anything very different, we would not be people, since we would not fit our concept of person. So these very different things we would say would not be sayings. Thus Davidson arrives at a conception of the world as depending on us in the sense that it has to resemble most of what we say about it, but not in the sense that there are other things we might say which would give us a different world. The adequation of concept and object is guaranteed a priori at least in a statistical way.

It may seem strange to apply Sellars' term 'linguistic nominalism' to such a view, since that term usually implies the possibility of 'alternative conceptual schemes' which Davidson denies. The essence of linguistic nominalism, though, is the claim that the idea of an external world with a division into kinds of its own, standing logically apart from our conceptions about it, does not make sense. Davidson is committed to this thesis statistically anyway as far as I can see. Some real kinds in the world are not extensions of any of our predicates, so 'the world' is a notion that makes some sense, but it is necessarily true that, for most of the extensions of our predicates, there is a kind which is that extension.

Premise (3): Irreducibility of mental to physical predicates

Davidson's argument for the thesis of the irreducibility of the mental to the physical (Davidson, 1970) proceeds from the motion that predicate-systems are shaped by synthetic a priori principles. This is, the application of a family of predicates is governed by overriding constraints which make the totality of applications of such predicates satisfy certain formal conditions. An example of such a principle for physical predicates is the transitivity of 'longer than'. If we observe that, prima facie $L(a, b)$, $L(b, c)$ and $L(c, a)$, either one of these observations is mistaken, or the objects have changed sizes in the interval between measurements or something else has gone wrong. In no case could we have a counter-example to '$(x)(y)(z)(L(x, y) \& L(y, z) \rightarrow -L(z, x))$'. Thus, the principle of transitivity of 'longer than' shapes the way our physical predicates get applied by, roughly, forcing whatever we say to abide by the principle. If we find too much difficulty in terms of complication of theory in holding to this principle in a particular type of situation, we will decide that our measure isn't a measure of length at all, for instance.

On Davidson's view, constraints on radical interpretation function in the intentional sphere analogously to the way transitivity principles and the like function in the physical sphere. We cannot have counter-examples to the principle that a person for the most part believes truths for the same reasons that we cannot have a counter-example to transitivity of 'longer than'. When the adjustments we have to make to observe this principle become too complicated, we similarly reasonably decide that we are not dealing with a language-user.

The important thing about these principles is that, by being held constant come what experience may, they force a particular kind of sorting of experience into extensions of predicates. Given the truth-constraint this sorting will be correct. (Strictly speaking, given Davidson's remarks about 'conceptual schemes', the notion of a set of experiences to be sorted misleads.) When two sets of synthetic *a priori* principles are applied to the same phenomena, the application of the predicates 'controlled' by each set will almost certainly yield mutually indefinable extensions. That is, unless the class of the physical phenomena identical with the class of particular cases of, for instance, obedience to the principle that short logical truths are assented to is also the class of cases of obedience to a principle like transitivity applied to some dimension of neurons, the application of both sets of constraints will lead to divergent and unrelated sorting of phenomena. This identity is very implausible, according to Davidson. Thus mental predicates and physical predicates, since they are governed by unrelated sets of constraints, are irreducible. The slack between the intensional and the extensional, and thus, since interpretation depends on ascriptions of intensional predicates, between interpretation of a speaker's language and the physical evidence for it, is therefore a consequence of the very way we ascribe such predicates.

What should be observed about this argument is its 'internalist' starting points. Davidson's synthetic *a priori* truths are principles governing the application of concepts, primarily, and principles which characterise the real world in virtue of the fact that the truth constraint makes most of what we believe correct. These constraints are, in fact, central features constitutive of our concepts 'physical object' and 'person' respectively. In terms of radical interpretation, no interpretation of a speaker's words could be correct which pictured him as speaking of physical objects and denying transitivity of 'longer than' or speaking of persons and refusing to maximise rationality in theorising about them.

The argument for irreducibility, then, requires a resemblance theory of reference. Only if what mental and physical predicates refer to is governed by internal features can a conclusion about irreducibility of phenomena be drawn from a premise about irreducibility of concepts.

The argument also seems to depend on Davidson's variety of linguistic nominalism, for much the same reason. Davidson seems not to be claiming, as Quine seems to (Quine, 1960, 221), that there are no intentional phenomena, since then the truth-constraint as it applies to us would be violated. Rather, mental phenomena are real and are as we think they are. The co-existence of unrelated kinds of phenomena is only a problem if one were to be a realist about kinds, i.e. only if one were to reject the idea that what we think is what there is. Indeterminacy does not reduce reality for Davidson, as far as I can see.

The above-mentioned slack between the mental and the physical leads to indeterminacy of interpretation whenever we get imperfect match between our propositional attitudes and the attitudes we ascribe to the other. When maximisation must be less than perfect, the adjustment can be made in any one of several places throughout the truth-theory for the person. Only if there were lawlike connections between mental and physical predicates could there be a way of deciding which adjustment which satisfied the constraints on the application of intensional predicates as well as any was correct.

Indeterminacy of translation arises from the fact that mental predicates are governed by maximisation constraints rather than by absolute constraints, as the application of physical predicates is. That is, the constraints on translation are not only holistic as physical constraints are, but also, in application to particular cases, statistical. They must be statistical, since there are several constraints which can apply to a particular case and come into conflict in that case. A simple case where indeterminacy arises is in conflicts between the truth-constraint and the constraint that the extensions of the predicates of the other be simply stated in our terms. Suppose a person being interpreted says things which, according to our preliminary interpretation, would mean that: (1) bactrians have one hump, that (2) dromedaries have two humps, that (3) bactrians are Arabian camels, and that (4) dromedaries appear on date packages. If these are all the relevant sentences he has attitudes towards using the terms we have interpreted as 'bactrian' and 'dromedary', we have the choice between making him mistaken about either dromedaries or bactrians, or making his predicates which we have interpreted as 'one' and 'two' mean 'one unless a bactrian hump, in which case two' and 'two unless a dromedary hump, in which case one'. (Adjustments in the interpretation of other predicates, we may suppose, creates even more messiness.) If we decide to ascribe error to the speaker, which sentences are in error is relative to our interpretive scheme. Either (1) and (2) can be false, retaining the interpretive scheme, or (3) and (4) can be false. The thesis of the indeterminacy of translation, then, follows from a theorist's acceptance of a resemblance theory of meaning and its corollaries.

2. *The causal theory of reference and its presuppositions*

The causal theory of reference is essentially the view that the reference of a term for a speaker is not in general a function of its sense, but is rather a matter of what real object in the world bears the appropriate relation to a term for a speaker. The 'causal' in 'causal theory of reference' is a general arm-waving towards a real relation which 'refers' names rather than any very specific idea about what the nature of the relation might be. According to the causal theory of reference, internal features of concepts do not determine what their extension is. A person can hold sentential attitudes with respect to a term which fit another object he has a concept of more accurately than they fit its referent. The 'objects' referred to can be kinds in the case of extensions of general terms as well as individuals in the case of names.

The evidence for the causal theory of reference is largely negative, consisting of examples which show that a resemblance theory of reference does not accord with our intuitions about 'refers'. The argument, as Kripke gives it, seems to demand that our intuitions about 'refers' give a conclusive positive demonstration that some causal social relation is part of the truth-conditions of 'refers'. The impression one gets is that mere examination of our intuitions would show us more precisely what the details of this causal relation are. This cannot be correct, since this examination of intuitions would demonstrably lead to a more accurate theory of reference only if the resemblance theory of meaning is correct. If the whole point of a causal theory of reference is to deny that 'conceptual analysis', i.e. *a priori* examination of our concepts, what we would say, is the way to find out about what those concepts are true of, then examination of intuitions cannot be the method for the causal theory of reference to clarify 'refers'. Concepts are true of objects not by fitting them, according to the causal theory, but by being in some causal relation with them. The content of a concept is, as it were, a theory of its referent. Conceptual analysis illuminates the referent only if the concept is a correct theory.

Kripke's arguments, then, should be taken as just reductions of resemblance theories of reference. The resemblance theory of reference, if applied to 'refers', predicts that the pairs people apply 'refers' to in various situations are pairs such that the object resembles the concept in the appropriate way. According to the theory also, whatever pairs people refer to by 'refers' is determined by their application of the predicate. Kripke's counter-examples, which show that the intuitive pairings in our concept of reference do not fit the resemblance criterion even statistically, thus show that, according to the resemblance theory of reference, the resemblance theory of reference says the wrong things about 'refers'. By the theory itself, the theory must be wrong. Thus the argument is not committed to intuitions being a reliable guide to reference. (Although proponents of the theory are often themselves so committed.)

If reference is not 'internal', then there is no reason to take intuitions about what would refer to what as data that any analysis must accommodate. It is only on a resemblance theory of reference that reflections about what we would say in various situations provide conclusive criteria for a theory of what a term's extension is. If such investigations are not *a priori*, in general, it is hard to see why they should be *a priori* in the case of the term 'refers'.

Since we have no *a priori* insight into what 'refers' asserts to obtain between the ordered pairs it is true of, the acceptance of a causal theory of reference amounts to the view that reference is a real relation between elements of the world and states of persons. If 'refers' refers, then there must be a kind of relation among the items of the world which is causally responsible for our term 'refers'. The causal theory of reference is a hypothesis that 'refers' names a kind of causal relation between persons and entities.

What sorts of things can be referred to if this hypothesis is correct? We can take what is probably true about causal relations in general and apply it to this particular case. Or any reasonable analysis of causation, a causal relation holds between a pair of events only if there are descriptions of the two events such that their conjunction is an instance of a causal law. Thus if the proper name 'John' for me names a certain individual, there is a causal relation of the sort 'refers' refers to between the word 'John' for me and that individual. For there to be a kind for 'refers' to refer to, it would further seem that the states of a person which are arguments of reference relations would have to constitute a kind about which there are real causal laws. That is, if reference is a special kind of causal relation, and there are descriptions of mental events and objects which fall under a causal law whenever 'refers' is true of a pair of them, then the states of persons which are caused must be elements of a real law-governed kind whose nature accounts for the fact that only these states are caused in the 'referential' way. The kinds and the laws that describe their interrelations must be culture-independent entities in the 'real world', since the a priorism that leads to positing culture-dependent kinds is denied on a causal theory of reference.

Reference to kinds by terms like 'gold' requires in a similar way that both the state of the person and the item involved in the event which is causally responsible for the state be describable so that their conjunction is an instance of a causal law. For the kind to be thus redescribable it must be a kind recognised in the terms in which real causal laws can be stated. Thus, the only kinds to which the causal theory will allow reference are genuine physical kinds. (A 'physical kind' here just means a kind about which strict laws of causal interaction with other physical kinds can be stated. Physical kinds may thus be as spiritual as you please, as long as they occur in some physical laws.)

The causal theory of reference, if taken seriously at all, requires person-independent language-independent kinds which can enter causal relations.

4

If reference is a real kind of relation, referring states which refer on several occasions to one entity in virtue of a single causal interaction must be a real kind of state of a person. If reference to gold is reference to a kind, furthermore, gold must be a kind in the sense of an object that can enter causal relations, just as persons are. In short a causal theory of reference requires that only real things can be referred to or refer, where 'real thing' means 'thing which is an element of a law-governed kind'. If causality requires real laws, and laws use only objectively projectible categories, not imaginary society-relative categories, then the causal theory of reference allows reference only to objects and kinds recognisable by physics (where physics is understood to be the theory of the kinds there are in the world). That is, only kinds which make physical sense, which can be specified and constructed from entities about which there are real laws, can be referred to. Obviously, also if 'refers' refers, reference itself must be a genuine physical relation.

If the above describes what a causal theory of reference is committed to, then, indeed, the basic assumptions needed to get indeterminacy of reference are in fact denied. Linguistic nominalism in any form is denied, since, if our conceptions are not a good guide to the extensions of our predicates, Davidson's arguments can't go through. We can both talk about the world and, for the most part, be wrong about it. Any culture which manages to refer will refer to kinds, but that does not guarantee that they will hold even approximately correct views about any of those kinds, given that their reference is a causal and not a resemblance relation.

The irreducibility of the mental to the physical is likewise denied on a causal view of reference. For causal relations literally to obtain between entities, persons and states of persons, persons must be a physical kind and some of their state-types must be physical kinds. A representation-type of Smith's which refers to Jones must be such that tokens of it for Smith are of the same physical kind, if reference is literally causal and terms such as 'Jones' refer on several occasions of use to the same person without continued causal interaction with Jones. The 'sameness' of various tokens of 'Jones' must be a matter of objective fact, if each of the tokens really refers to Jones in virtue of a causal relation between Jones and one of these tokens. Davidson's arguments about constraints on predicate-systems don't apply on a causal theory of reference.

If 'causal' is taken seriously in 'causal theory of reference' then, reference is a physically real relation between states of persons and entities in the world. In light of this, it seems very unlikely that the tangle of criteria Kripke hints at as constituting our intuitive theory of reference actually characterise reference. Rather it is more likely that our intuitive theory of reference is wrong, since a real physical relation seems unlikely to obtain or not to obtain in ways which will allow fame to matter, and 'Santa Claus' not to refer to an historical saint, while 'Jonah' refers to a whale-non-encountering prophet (Kripke, 1972, 301–2).

In fact, given that there must be a real physical relation between word and object, very likely much of what we take to be cases of reference are not so. Very many of our putative kind-terms probably do not refer to real kinds that can be causally responsible for our term. Terms for furniture kinds, automobile kinds, etc., probably have only nominal essences, that is, are culturally believed in fictional entities and can't refer in a causal way. I have argued elsewhere (Wheeler, 1975) that 'ontologically vague' terms with fuzzy borderlines cannot refer to kinds. On a causal theory of reference, then, reference is a fairly restricted phenomenon. Our basic intercourse with the world is referential, so that some of our terms, our proper names and selected kind-terms, do really refer. Very probably the majority of our terms, however, do not refer to anything. Sentences using such terms are literally false. If truth requires reference and reference requires causal relations and causal relations require relata which are physically real kinds and element of kinds, then, where a kind is lacking, a general term purporting to denote a kind lacks reference and cannot be used to state literal truths.

3. Radical interpretation revived

What can be made of such language, if the causal theory of reference is correct? A causal theory of translation, whose maxim would be 'Term A is correctly translated as term P if and only if the kind referred to by term A is the kind referred to by term B' clearly cannot apply to this kind of case, since there are no referents for the terms. For much of language, in particular whenever we have vague terms or terms which fail to denote a physical kind, translation or interpretation cannot function causally but must rather try to assign elements of one system of myths to elements of another mythical system of myths. It seems that, in the case of accepted mythology, a resemblance theory of myth-matching is in order.

Our procedure as radical interpreters, then, will be something like that of an enlightened Herodotus figuring out which Egyptian god is Apollo. Beyond proper names and references to real kinds of entity, then, radical interpretation operates by the resemblance theory of myth-matching. What Davidson describes as constraints on radical interpretation do apply as constraints on the interpretation of a large portion of any current natural language, just because large portions of current natural languages have kind-terms with only nominal essences. The extent of non-reference in a natural language is an empirical matter but it should be apparent that much of what Davidson says about the interpretation of language in general is true of interpretation of the parts of language that deals with fictional entities like the kinds cuspidor, the tall men, and red.

The constraints on interpretation will need to be modified to a certain extent, replacing reference to truth with reference to truth-according-to-a-system, but the essential outlines should stand. (The resemblance theory of reference leads to a mistaken view of reference but constitutes a correct theory of how we interpret the mythology of the other in terms of our mythology.) Indeterminacy of translation and interpretation then, can be generated for this part of the language by principles analogous to the principles Davidson applies to the whole language.

The analogue of the resemblance theory of reference, as we have said, is that an element A of the other myth is correctly interpreted as element A in our myth just in case that interpretation induces as much agreement between what we believe and what the other myth asserts under that interpretation, holistically, as any other interpretation.

The thesis of linguistic nominalism is obviously correct for mythical entities, since their essence is what we say about them. There is nothing to 'meaning' one fiction rather than another beyond the match of what we say with what someone else says about them. The analytic-synthetic distinction can no more plausibly be applied to terms for mythical entities than to terms for real ones, so there is no content to the motion that there could be a correct answer to what means what when we have optional matching of myths on two systems of interpretation.

The principle of the irreducibility of the intensional to the extensional will apply to this fictional part of the language just because Davidsonian constraints do govern the interpretation of the other's mythology in terms of our mythology. Briefly, what Davidson says about interpretation in general will hold of interpreting one mythology in terms of another, because there is no objective reference or 'aboutness' of beliefs whose matching can provide a sense to 'getting it right' in this case. Wherever language lacks objective ties to what is, the situation is as Davidson and Quine suppose it to be in general, and the indeterminacy of translation which they argue to apply in general, applies there.

N. L. Wilson

Concerning the Translation of Predicates

TRADITIONALLY, THERE HAS been a semantics of meaning and a semantics of reference. An adherent of this tradition would probably say that (qualifications aside)

(1) The predicate P_1 (in L_1) is a [correct] translation of P_2 (in L_2) just in case P_1 has the same meaning in L_1 as P_2 has in L_2.

By 'meaning' here one presumably means something like 'meaning in mind' or 'conceptual content' or 'semantic marker'. A meaning need not be construed as a mental entity. It is, however, something that can be *before* the mind and grasped by it. A fluently bilingual speaker of L_1 and L_2 need only inspect the meanings of P_1 and P_2 in order to determine whether or not they are the same. All this strikes me as quite mistaken, as does the whole tradition of meaning and reference which inspires it. The aim of this paper is to arrive at a more adequate account of translation.

Now obviously a correct translation statement such as

(2) P_1 in L_1 is a [correct] translation of P_2 in L_2

will *follow* from an adequate description of the two languages in question. On this account we shall have to spend some time dealing with the question of *describing* the semantics of a given language. And that will force us to spend some time on the matter of decipherment. For the most part I shall be concentrating on primitive predicates with some appeal, by way of analogical argument, to individual constants.

1. *Semantical rules and translation statements*

A language description will consist of (among other things) a lot of signification rules, e.g.:

(3) 'Köln' in German signifies[1] [the city of] Cologne.

Together with (4),

(4) Cologne = the third largest city in Germany,

statement (3) implies:

(5) 'Köln' in German signifies the third largest city in Germany.

This latter is true but is not a semantical rule. In certain cases, however, where the metalanguage has no name for what the object language expression signifies, we might have to make do with something like (5). But it should be noted that we do *not* have:

(6) 'Die drittgrösste Stadt in Deutschland' in German signifies Cologne.

Descriptions[2] do not signify any*thing*. They are significant by being composed in a syntactically significant way out of expressions that are, in one way or another, significant in their own right. The point is that 'signifies' is not to be taken as the same as 'refers'. In construing 'signifies' so that (6) is false, we are merely registering our desire *not* to have semantical rules for descriptions. We do, of course, want semantical rules for the *unitary designative parts* (names) of such descriptions.

Now suppose we have

(7) 'Cologne' in English signifies the city of Cologne.

It will follow from (7) and (3) that:

(8) 'Cologne' in English has the same significance as (*is a correct translation of*) 'Köln' in German.

1. In earlier papers and in Wilson (1959a) I used the term 'G-designates' in order to underscore the difference between the term in question and other terms then in common use, e.g. 'designates' and 'L-designates' (see Carnap's *Meaning and Necessity*). Provided we are careful, 'signifies' provides us with the most convenient and euphonious term not already pre-empted to a technical use.
2. The distinction between names and descriptions is roughly Kripke's distinction between rigid and non-rigid designators in Kripke (1972, 253–355).

This translation statement is one to which we would assent independently of any semantic theory. The point is that the two names in question are mutual intertranslations *just because they name the same thing* in their respective languages. That is why we take the significance of a proper name to be its nominatum. Note, too, that we would say: 'The third largest city in Germany' in English is *not* a correct translation of 'Köln' in German. It was in order to guarantee this that we stipulated that descriptions do not signify what they refer to (if anything).

The foregoing represents the pattern we shall continue to follow in the case of primitive predicates.

(9) 'Eisen' in German signifies [the property] *iron*.
(10) 'Iron' in English signifies [the property] *iron*.

Therefore

(11) 'Iron' in English has the same significance (is a correct translation of) 'Eisen' in German.

Now I think everyone would assent to (11)—at least in the sense of conceding that 'iron' and 'Eisen' are mutual translations. The disagreement will come with respect to the grounds. I want to say that they are mutual translations just because they name the same property (see (9) and (10)) and I would appeal to the parallel with (3), (7) and (8). One thing seems clear, independently of our construction: If there are properties and properties are named or signified by predicates, then if two predicates in different languages name the same property, they are mutual translations. After all, if one predicate failed to translate the other, in what could the failure consist?

The difficulty comes in the other direction. One might be put off by the platonism explicit in (9), (10) and (11) and seek for another account of the fact that 'iron' and 'Eisen' are mutual translations. Perhaps:

(12) 'Iron' and 'Eisen' are mutual translations because they have the same *meaning*.

But what are we to make of 'meaning' here? Either the meaning of a predicate is just the property (as Carnap said) in which case we are in effect back with a version of the theory just offered. (In a moment I shall show that a property cannot be a meaning.) Or else a meaning is something else again. But what else could it be? The main difficulty here is that in the case of primitive predicates, one cannot state what that meaning is. In the case of 'iron' for example, if it has a *meaning* distinct from the property, how is one to state what it is? Not by giving a synonymous phrase, for, 'iron' being primitive, there is no such synonymous phrase. The point is that ordinary language is unashamedly platonistic. It is full of direct references to properties ('iron') and indirect references by description ('the most commonly occurring metal'). But there are no direct references to meanings. The indirect references ('the meaning of "iron" ') are IOUs which cannot be cashed in.

There is perhaps a third possibility:

(13) 'Iron' and 'Eisen' (in English and German respectively) are mutual translations because they are *interlinguistically synonymous*.

This version at least does not appeal to *meanings*. But I do not see that an account of 'interlinguistically synonymous' is going to be available except perhaps in socio-linguistics. And the trouble with that is that we want a *purely semantical* account of language description and of translation. This third possible alternative will not give us that, whereas the original account, for all its unprepossessing platonism, does. I might mention that unless we have a satisfactory pure general semantics (and syntax and phonology) then we cannot hope for a satisfactory account of speech behaviour.

There is something else in the present account that will be bothersome: 'Granted that there are properties, you seem committed to something like: "pale" signifies the property paleness'. But as Quine has pointed out, ' "pale" is a general term and unlike the abstract singular "paleness", it never appears in an argument place and should not be taken as signifying (or naming) anything'. In reply I would point out that Quine's argument is a good one against the suggestion that we take every morpheme as signifying (or naming) something. Nevertheless once we *have* properties (once we *have* paleness to serve as nominatum of 'paleness') then there is no harm in allowing the corresponding general term to name also. We treat 'Socrates is pale' and 'Socrates has paleness' as mere typographical variants.

Actually, it is possible to accommodate the Quinian scruples mentioned. We have the semantical rule,

(14) 'Paleness' in English signifies *paleness*.

Then, assuming we have generalised truth conditions for a sentence $\ulcorner a$ has F-ness$\urcorner$, we can have another truth rule,

(15) ⌜*a* is F⌝ is true (in L) iff ⌜*a* has F-ness⌝ is true in L.

In this way we can 'state' the essential semantic properties of 'pale' (say) without assuming that 'pale' signifies any*thing*. The reason for shifting the example from 'iron' to 'pale' is that there are not two forms for 'iron' as there are 'pale' and 'paleness'.

It is important to realise that a property is not a meaning, as the following Frege-like argument makes clear. Let us consider the identity,

(16) Iron = the most strongly magnetisable metal.

The sentence is true. Therefore the two sides of the identity both refer to the same thing—the property, iron. Actually, iron is a *matter-kind*, but I am using the word 'property' broadly enough to cover both conventional attributes and matter-kinds, so that both count nouns and mass nouns will be taken as signifying properties. But our identity is not analytic, from which we may infer that the two sides differ in meaning (supposing that they have meanings). Furthermore, if we are to remain loyal to the traditional dualism between meaning and reference we would have to infer that the meanings are both distinct from the referent and that *iron* is not the meaning of anything. In general, properties are not meanings.

I have been arguing that we need properties in semantics. The semantic rule for a primitive predicate must mention the property that predicate signifies. For the most part, I have argued for properties as a case of *faute de mieux*. Nothing else will do. There is one final apparent alternative: that we use classes instead of properties. This would amount to having an extensional metalanguage. Thus we might have,

(17) 'Featherless biped' in English signifies the class of featherless bipeds.

(18) The class of humans = the class of featherless bipeds.

Therefore,

(19) 'Featherless biped' in English signifies the class of humans.

But

(20) 'Mensch' in German signifies the class of humans.

4*

Therefore,

(21) 'Featherless biped' in English has the same significance as (is a correct translation of) 'Mensch' in German.

But we would regard the latter as false. Therefore we cannot conjure with classes in semantics. As usual, we appeal to our intuitive judgments (e.g. that (21) is false) to discover the correct semantic methods.

In all the foregoing we assumed we were dealing with primitive predicates and we must now examine the reason for this restriction. What happens if we supposed that we have predicates defined with the help of the identity sign, connectives or quantifiers and that these signified logically complex properties? In the first place *if* the language description reports the definition as part of the language, then there would be a certain redundancy in also stating that the predicate in question signifies such and such a property.

There is a more serious objection, however. Consider the true identity,

(22) Blue = the colour of the sky.

Now define the predicate 'blee':

(23) x is blee $=_{df}$ ($\exists$ F)[x is F & (G)(G is a colour & the sky is G $\equiv$ G = F)].

The predicate 'blue' signifies one 'simple' property and 'blee' presumably signifies a different property, the logically complex property *determined*, as they say, by the RHS of (23). But blee = the colour of the sky (since 'x is the colour of the sky' expands as the RHS of (23)). So we have, from (22),

(24) Blue = blee (i.e. the colour of the sky).

If this is to be true (which it is) we cannot have 'blue' referring to the simple quality and blee referring to a different, logically complex property. The predicate 'blee' in fact is not a property name at all; it is a property description (of blue). It seems clear that we must dump all properties of the sort typified by *blee*. At this stage the earlier point about redundancy looks better than ever and so we make a clean sweep of all logically complex properties, which is to say, we do not suppose that predicates defined with the help of logical signs name or signify properties. Their 'significance' would be given via the definitions.

There are, as a matter of fact, certain technical considerations (which we leave out of account here; see Wilson, 1959a, section 17) which make it necessary to *retain* simple defined properties, such as *being shorter than Mt Everest*, which are defined *without* the aid of any logical signs. There is the redundancy problem but it is not a disaster.

What is much more serious is the apparent presupposition that there exists an objectively determinate stock of properties 'out there' and each language has predicates which jointly signify some or all of these properties, and that within each language there is a sharp distinction between defined or definable predicates and primitive ones. One senses, too, that the places where this presupposition breaks down will represent difficulties in the theory of translation. I myself regard the presupposition as a sort of working fiction or heuristic guide. It more or less fits many linguistic facts, especially the very simple ones we started off with, and we do our best to arrange the remaining facts so as to be consonant with it. But there are problems, and some of these will be dealt with in section 2.

Even in our own language, English, it would be very difficult to supply a general criterion for distinguishing primitive predicates (i.e. those which signify properties) and defined predicates (those which do not). The question here amounts to: what properties are there? For a start we should recognise sense qualities (red, green, smooth, rough, sour), natural species (tiger, goldenrod), matter kinds (water, wood, iron). On the other hand predicates derivative from other words (mower, musician, jurist) are clearly definable. Predicates not in any of the above classes might simply have to be dealt with case by case.

And a difficulty arises. We could regard 'brother' (say) as defined in terms of 'male' and 'sibling', the latter being taken as primitive. Or we might take 'brother' and 'sister' as primitive and take 'sibling' to be defined as 'brother or sister'. Either option will do. Here it seems more than likely that all the terms in question are definable in terms of other primitives. This would not be true if it were 'point' and 'line' that were in question. Here we would simply have to choose one option, and in choosing one over the other we are imposing more structure on the language than is really there, but this should not cause any problems.

But there is the following minor problem.

(25) 'Brother' in English is a translation of 'Bruder' in German.

This is true. If German contained the word 'Sibling' (it does have a Germanic ring to it, doesn't it?) then we could say that (25) is true because 'brother $=_{df}$

male sibling' is a definition of English, 'Bruder $=_{df}$ männlich Sibling' is a definition of German and 'male' in English is a translation of 'männlich' in German and 'sibling' in English is a translation of 'Sibling' in German. The trouble is that German contains no single morpheme that translates 'sibling'. So we adopt the somewhat devious procedure of introducing 'Sib' into German as an auxiliary term:

(26) 'Sib' in aux-German signifies *sibling*
(27) 'Bruder $=_{df}$ männlich Sib' is a definition of aux-German.

Then the grounding of (25) proceeds as before.

These remarks will have to suffice as an account of how to deal with the translation of defined or definable predicates.

2. *Decipherment and secondary semantics*

There are two things we need to do now. We need to consider where our signification rules (e.g. (3), (7), (9) and (10) above) come from and we need to consider certain problems of translation between unevenly matched languages, that is, languages that do not have the same ontology or domain.

Suppose somebody says to us, 'Aristocles was a Greek philosopher. He was the son of Ariston and brother of Adeimantus and Glaucon. He was married to Xantippe. Aristocles was a pupil of Cratylus and of Socrates. After Socrates' death he devoted himself to the writing of philosophical dialogues. He made three trips to Syracuse in the hopes of making a philosopher-king out of Dionysius II. When it turned out that Dionysius had no intention of getting his assignments in on time, Aristocles gave up in disgust' (I have already used this example in Wilson, 1973a and 1973b).

We would, I think, conclude that for our speaker, 'Aristocles' signifies Plato, even though his corpus contains at least one statement that is false of Plato. In order to decipher 'Aristocles' we get a sufficiently large corpus of utterances containing the word to be interpreted, we fall back on our knowledge of Greek philosophy and invoke the Principle of Charity whereby we select as signification the individual which will make more of the sentences of the corpus true than any other choice would.[3] We may use the term 'sense' to refer to the corpus or to the set of beliefs entertained by the speaker about the thing signified. 'Sense' will do some of the work traditionally done by the word 'meaning' and do so less mysteriously. The thing to note is that to understand the significance of a word like 'Aristocles' is just to know quite a

3. The Principle of Charity is dealt with in greater detail in Wilson (1959b and 1972).

lot about Aristocles (i.e. Plato), it is to know 'who he is'. This holds in general. The grasp of any language involves having quite a lot of factual knowledge about the entities in its domain. The idea that in principle one could grasp a language by knowing just its words and their 'meanings' without any knowledge of the world is simply false.

It is true that there will be a good deal of intersubjective variation in the sense of names. The sense of the word 'Plato' for the distinguished platonic scholar, Professor X, will be a good deal different from the sense for me, and that is because Professor X knows a great deal more about Plato than I do. But *sense* is not relevant to communication or to translation. For Professor X and I can intercommunicate about Plato provided we both use 'Plato' to *signify* the same individual. It is not required that the same *sense* attach to the name for each of us. (If it were required, we would almost never succeed in communicating.)

The decipherment of predicates is in much the same case. Suppose I say, 'Quicksilver is a silvery metal, liquid at room temperature. It is refined from cinnabar. Its specific gravity is 13'. Even if you had never heard of quicksilver, you would nevertheless infer that I was talking about mercury (assuming you know enough about mercury!) because mercury fits the description better than anything else does.

It might be mentioned that the theory of names (or theory of decipherment) offered here belongs in the group that Kripke calls 'cluster theories'. He finds fault with these theories and proposes in their place the Causal Theory of Names. According to this theory 'Aristocles' (above) deciphers as signifying Plato, not because this is indicated by the Principle of Charity, but because of a causal chain going from the speaker back to Plato. In almost all cases the two theories would yield the same answer (almost, that is, except for certain crazy counter-examples dreamed up by philosophers). This is not the place to discuss the relative merits of the two theories. It is worth pointing out, however, that Kripke's is a pragmatic theory. One deciphers the significance of a word *as used by so-and-so*. The present theory is semantic in the sense that we abstract from the speaker and deal simply with a corpus of statements. I call it *secondary* semantics because signification rules are dropped for the moment, the corpus taking their place. Decipherment is just a matter of passing from secondary to primary semantics. What we see in the process is precisely how a corpus of sentences can, *all by itself*, say something about the world.

The translation problem at hand is simply this. With certain plausible assumptions about the equality of English and German we were able in section 1 to give a rationale for translation statements. But what if it is a question of translating from English to Inuit, which, we may suppose, has a much smaller ontology?

First, let us look at what an English dictionary does with 'iron':

A silver-white metallic element, malleable and ductile, strongly attracted by magnets, readily oxidised (rusted) in moist air . . . At. no. 26; at. wt. 55.85 . . . sp. gr. 7.86 . . .

What we notice first of all is that this looks more like an encyclopaedia entry than like our naïve idea of a dictionary entry, and in fact it is. It gives the basic information about iron. One cannot maintain that it gives the 'meaning' of the word 'iron'. For on that view one would have to maintain that neither Shakespeare nor Dr Johnson understood the 'meaning' of 'iron', since neither of them knew anything about atomic numbers and atomic weights.[4] But this is absurd. Both knew enough so that *iron* fitted their beliefs better than anything else and that is all that is involved in 'understanding' the word 'iron'.

We can now appreciate the problem confronting the lexicographer. 'Iron' is *by nature* a primitive term. In primary semantics he would give us: ' "iron" in English signifies iron', which, though true enough, appears to be idle motion. So there is nothing for it but to go into secondary semantics and give us a corpus comprising the essential information about iron. Here it is not a question of the reader deciphering the corpus but rather simply appropriating the information so that he can have a sufficient stock of beliefs to qualify him as 'understanding' the word 'iron'.

Now we can see what is involved in translating from English to Inuit. For a starter, how about translating 'Bismarck' into Inuit? Obviously, the only thing one can do is supply a short history of Germany in the nineteenth century. At the very least the 'translation' will be of the form, 'the man who . . .', and we earlier noted that descriptions do not signify anything. (A description cannot qualify as a strict translation of a name.) If we suppose that the Inuit were unfamiliar with iron before the white man came and as a consequence had no word for *iron*, then, as in the Bismarck case, there would be no way of effecting a strict translation of 'iron' into Inuit. The best one could do would be to give a description of iron couched in terms that might be understood by the Inuit. (But don't tell them about atomic numbers.) They may coin a made-up term for it, just as 'fire-water' in the Indian dialects was presumably a term coined for the purpose of signifying whisky.

4. Johnson's *Dictionary* is interesting in that for a word like 'inevitable' he makes up the entry out of his head. But for 'iron', sensing his own lack of expertise, he falls back on an extract from John Hill's *History of Fossils*. (The entry is full of factual errors, incidentally.)

The problem of giving the Inuit a word for iron is something I shall leave to the missionaries, who know much more about this sort of thing than I do.

The conclusion of all this is that in general, there is what one might call the Impossibility of Strict Translation, a translation where one can say of the two terms: same significance. The reason is that a language is rooted in the environment of the language community and these environments may be quite different. You cannot translate 'snow' into the language of the Fiji Islanders and you cannot translate 'coconut' into Inuit. The situation here is quite the reverse from that of Quine's radical indeterminacy of translation. There it is a case of two *incompatible* candidates for translation being equally well supported by the field-worker's evidence. Here it is a case of *no* translation being available. One has to make do with a more or less loose paraphrase—along with a short course in history, metallurgy or whatever.

III

OBLIQUE CONTEXTS
AND TRANSLATION

J. Bigelow

Semantics of Thinking, Speaking and Translation

WHAT IS THE meaning of a sentence? It is something which determines the circumstances under which that sentence would be true. In other words, it is something which determines the set of possible worlds in which the sentence is true.[1] This set of possible worlds is called the *intension* of the sentence. A set of possible worlds is often called a *proposition*.

However, the meaning of a sentence must be something more than the intension it determines. Two logically equivalent sentences will have exactly the same intensions; yet clearly they may differ in meaning. Indeed, even if all we concern ourselves with are the intensions of sentences, we will still be forced to take account of differences in meaning over and above differences in intension. If two logically equivalent sentences α and β differ in meaning, then the sentences

    0.1   *x* believes that α
    0.2   *x* believes that β

will differ in intension. There will be possible worlds in which the person *x* is unaware that α and β are logically equivalent, and believes one but not the other.

What, then, is a meaning? David Lewis (1972) has recently proposed a very interesting answer to this question. In any language which we are likely to be interested in, the meanings of all the infinite number of sentences in the language will be determined by the meanings of the finite stock of symbols they contain. Each symbol in the language will be assigned as its value, or intension, a set-theoretical operation based on possible worlds and objects in possible worlds. By combining the operations corresponding to each symbol in a sentence, in the order in which the symbols in the sentence are concatenated, we will derive an intension for the whole sentence.

---

    1. The meaning of a sentence also determines which 'contexts of utterance' will make the sentence true. Many sentences will vary in truth value depending on who utters them, when they are uttered, and so on. Context-dependence is not, however, particularly relevant to the points at issue in this paper.

In such a language, the thing which 'determines' the intension of a sentence is the ordered sequence of the intensions of the symbols it contains. But, as we said above, the meaning of a sentence is the thing which determines its intension. Hence, Lewis suggests,[2] the meaning of a sentence is just the ordered sequence of the intensions of the symbols it contains: an ordered sequence of set-theoretical operations which jointly determine the set of possible worlds in which that sentence is true.

If meanings are what Lewis says they are, then it should be possible somehow to explain the difference in intension between 0.1 and 0.2, on the basis of the Lewis-meanings of α and β. A very promising start at such an explanation has been made by M. J. Cresswell in a paper, 'Hyperintensional Logic' (1975b). I wish to outline a number of extensions to Cresswell's system.

1. *Beliefs and objects*

Cresswell treats belief as a two-place relation between a person and the meaning of a sentence. I wish to generalise this treatment by broadening his conception of belief in a manner foreshadowed in Quine (1960, Sects. 30–2), and more explicitly urged in Wallace (1972b).

My contention will be that belief need not always be regarded as just a two-place relation between a person and a meaning, but may be a many-place relation between a person, several objects, and a meaning.

Suppose, for instance, that a person, Ralph, glimpses a man in a brown hat and conjectures that the man is a spy. So we have

    1.1   Ralph believes that the man in the brown hat is a spy.

As it happens, the man Ralph has seen is someone whom he knows quite well, Bernard J. Ortcutt, though he does not realise this. So we have,

    1.2   The man in the brown hat is Bernard J. Ortcutt.

Yet Ralph is firmly convinced that Ortcutt is not a spy. And so we have,

    1.3   Ralph believes that Ortcutt is not a spy,

and

---

2. My presentation differs from Lewis's in certain respects; but these differences in detail are not relevant to the points at issue in this paper. Lewis's 'meanings' are descendants of Carnap's 'intensional isomorphisms' (Carnap, 1947), but they differ crucially in being defined as language-independent entities.

1.4   Ralph does not believe that Ortcutt is a spy.

In such a case, Ralph stands in an important sort of relationship to Ortcutt. If Ortcutt knows he has been glimpsed by Ralph, he will realise that Ralph now stands in an important relationship to him, even if he did not recognise him at the time. This realisation may lead Ortcutt to actions which he would otherwise have no reason to perform. For instance, he may dispose of his brown hat.

However, neither 1.1 nor 1.2 by themselves serve to identify this important relationship between Ralph and Ortcutt, since 1.1 does not mention Ortcutt and 1.2 does not mention Ralph. And 1.3 and 1.4 also fail to identify the crucial relationship, since both were true before Ralph glimpsed Ortcutt —whereas the relationship we are after came into existence because of that glimpse.

Ralph believes that the man in the brown hat is a spy; and as it happens there is a man in a brown hat whose existence is responsible for Ralph's belief; and that man is someone Ralph knows, namely Ortcutt. The ensuing relationship between Ralph and Ortcutt is conveniently described in terminology suggested by Quine:

1.5   Ralph believes of Ortcutt that he is a spy.

This sentence is not intended to imply that Ralph realises that the man whom he believes to be a spy is in fact Ortcutt. It is meant to assert only that Ralph believes of someone who happens to be Ortcutt (namely, the man in the brown hat), that he is a spy.

It is worth noting that 1.5 can be inferred from 1.1 only given a number of complex assumptions about various causal relationships between Ralph and Ortcutt, and about Ralph's fairly robust mental representation of Ortcutt. To infer something of the form of 1.5 from something of the form of 1.1 is to indulge in what is known as *quantification into* an opaque context. See Kaplan (1968) for further details on the circumstances in which quantifying in will be admissible.

To see that quantification in is not always acceptable, consider certain other of Ralph's beliefs about spies. We may suppose for instance that, for no good reason at all,

1.6   Ralph believes that the shortest spy is a Russian.

Suppose that the shortest spy happens to be called Vladimir. Then, if we were to permit quantification in here, we could infer that

    1.7   Ralph believes of Vladimir that he is a Russian.

Yet Ralph has never seen or heard of Vladimir. So he does not stand to Vladimir in anything like the same sort of relationship as the one he stands in to Ortcutt after seeing him in the brown hat. Consequently we should regard 1.7 as false, despite the truth of 1.6. Whatever relationships may chance to hold between Ralph and Vladimir, they are all too remote and indiscriminate to justify quantifying in.

We should therefore allow for a concept of belief as a distinctive three-place relation between Ralph, Ortcutt, and the meaning of 'he is a spy'. This relation will be logically independent of any two-place belief relation between Ralph and a proposition. A three-place belief may or may not hold between Ralph, Ortcutt, and the meaning of 'he is a spy', whether or not a two-place belief holds between Ralph and the meaning of 'the man in the brown hat is a spy', or between Ralph and the meaning of 'Ortcutt is a spy'.

Belief, then, may be a relation between a person, an object, and a meaning. But what sort of a meaning is called for here? Not the meaning of a whole sentence. Ralph stands in a relation to Ortcutt and the meaning of 'he is a spy'; but in this context the words 'he is a spy' should not be taken as expressing a whole proposition. They do not represent the whole of Ralph's thought. Rather, they represent only the property which Ralph believes to be possessed by someone who happens to be Ortcutt. Such a property should be represented by a predicate, formed by abstraction from the whole content of Ralph's belief. From Ralph's belief that the man in the brown hat is a spy we abstract the property he ascribes to the man, the property of 'being a spy'. Or equivalently, but more conveniently from a formal point of view, we abstract the property of 'being a thing such that that thing is a spy'. This property will then be the meaning of a predicate: the meaning of the words 'he is a spy' in 1.5.

A three-place concept of belief can be generalised further. We can, for instance, introduce a five-place concept of belief, as in

    1.8   Cynthia believes of Ralph, of *Word and Object*, and of Ortcutt, that he gave it to him.

The arguments of 'believes' in this case include one meaning (the meaning of 'he gave it to him') and four individuals—but, it may be noted, no properties, relations, events, or entities of other categories. However, there is no reason why entities other than meanings and individuals might not be arguments for 'believes': as for instance in

> 1.9   Cynthia believes of wisdom, and of Socrates, that it characterises him.

Another point worth noting is that an expression within the scope of 'believes' may need to be replaced by a variable when the whole expression is embedded in a wider context. Thus we may wish to infer from 1.9 that

> 1.10   There is someone such that Cynthia believes of wisdom, and of him, that it characterises him.

The general representation of belief should therefore be by an $(n + 2)$-place operator which attaches to a variable or name referring to a person, n variables or names referring to entities of various categories, and an n-place predicate formed from a sentence by abstraction of n arguments of corresponding categories.

It may be noted that the concept of belief as a two-place relation between a person and a meaning will fall out as a special case of the wider concept of belief—the special case in which the argument of the belief-relation is the meaning of a zero-place predicate: a sentence.

2. *Variable-binding*

In order to formalise a relational concept of belief, we will have to specify Lewis-type meanings not only for closed sentences like 'the man in the brown hat is a spy', but also for n-place predicates formed by abstraction using variables and a variable-binding operator. It is imperative, therefore, to establish some account of the nature of variables and variable-binding and to define a kind of Lewis-meaning for abstracts.

One approach to variable-binding, adopted by Montague and Lewis, is to treat variables as something like context-dependent names, whose values are to be supplied by a contextual index (cf. Montague, 1974b). I have no strong arguments against this approach. I will, however, adopt a different approach to variable-binding, as developed by Cresswell (1973, especially Ch. 6).

One important function performed by variables is a purely logical one. Variables serve as place-markers, establishing logical and syntactic links between different expressions. This use of variables is closely analogous to use of the linear concatenation of symbols in order to weld them into a semantically structured sentence. Linear ordering needs to be supplemented by use of variables in order to overcome its two-dimensional limitations. For instance, a symbol a may need to be syntactically linked to b, and b to c; and we may establish these links by concatenation. But then in addition we may wish to represent a semantic link between a and c of much the same sort as that between a and b and between b and c. Not all the links we want can be represented by simple concatenation. So instead of concatenating a and c, we establish a syntactic link between them by concatenating them with the same variable.

Thus for instance in 1.8 we may wish to make it clearer that Cynthia believes of Ralph that he is the giver, of Ortcutt that he is the receiver, and of *Word and Object* that it is the given. We might do this by rewriting 1.8 as

> 2.1 Cynthia believes of Ralph, x, of *Word and Object*, y, and of Ortcutt, z, that he (x) gave it (y) to him (z).

Here the 'variables' x, y, and z serve only as place-markers: their role is very close to that of linear concatenation of symbols. And when one name is concatenated with another we do not treat the concatenation itself as yet a third name. Thus variables, in their role as place-markers, function quite differently from names.

If variables are treated as variable names, then their place-marking function will have to be superimposed on to their naming function. Montague and Lewis manage this by imposing a rigid and arbitrary ordering on to the set of objects which the variables name, so that the things the variables name can themselves serve as place-markers. Consequently, on this treatment variables are made to serve two functions at once.

On Cresswell's treatment, however, variables are analysed quite differently from names. Their logical, place-marking function is therefore revealed in isolation. The tasks which require context-dependent names are performed by symbols other than variables, separately introduced. There is, I think, something to be said for this division of labour.

For these reasons, in developing an analysis of belief-sentences I will opt for Cresswell's analysis of variable-binding. This approach will raise certain problems. If variables are just place-markers, then they will not have meanings in the way in which other symbols do. Yet we do need to represent the meanings of sentences containing variables; and we need to do so in a manner which reveals the structural features which the variables serve to establish in a sentence.

The solution I will adopt, suggested to me by Cresswell, is to take variables as their own meanings. This is a way of reflecting the fact that variables really have no meanings. The place-marking function they serve in a sentence is simply represented by a place-marker in the representation of that sentence's meaning.

3. *Opacity and quotation*

Geach (1963) has reminded us that whatever description, x, we may give to a rose, the sentence

x smells sweet

will remain true. Sentences of the form 'x smells sweet' are said for this reason to be 'referentially transparent'. Not all sentences are like this. Sometimes the truth of a sentence may be altered when we replace a name occurring in the sentence by another name of the same thing. In this case we say that the sentence is 'referentially opaque'.

One sort of opaque context is provided by quotation, as in

    3.1 'Cicero' has six letters
    3.2 Giorgione was so-called because of his size.

Some opaque contexts, however, appear not to be quotational, as for instance

    3.3 Ralph says his yacht is longer than it is
    3.4 My dog believes that the cat is on the roof.

On at least one reading, these sentences are referentially opaque. Ralph's yacht may be, for instance, the only yacht in Diamond Harbour, so that the words 'his yacht' in 3.3 have the same reference as the words 'the only yacht in Diamond Harbour'. Yet Ralph did not say that the only yacht in Diamond Harbour is longer than it is (though he did say *of* the only yacht in Diamond Harbour that it is a certain length). Similarly, the cat mentioned in 3.4 may chance to be the mangiest cat on the street; yet my dog does not believe that the mangiest cat on the street is on the roof (though he does believe *of* the mangiest cat on the street that *it* is on the roof).

Yet although 3.3 and 3.4 are referentially opaque, they appear not to be quotational. My dog said nothing: so clearly we cannot be quoting his words. And it is not clear what words Ralph used in saying his yacht is longer than it is: so the relationship between Ralph's words and the words in 3.3 cannot be one of direct quotation either.

In sentences like 3.3 and 3.4, unlike 3.1 and 3.2, what appears to be crucial is only the meanings of the words we use, and not the particular words themselves, or the language we choose to employ in expressing that meaning. For historical reasons, we may call opaque contexts of this sort Fregean contexts (Frege, 1960).

The way quotational contexts are handled formally is generally by the introduction of a quotation symbol which, when prefixed to any expression, or indeed to any object at all, creates a name of that expression or object. Cresswell's suggested analysis of Fregean contexts is structurally very similar to the usual treatment of quotation. In effect, he introduces a symbol, θ^+, which when prefixed to an expression creates a name of the *meaning* of that expression.[3] This analysis of Fregean contexts is, I think, sufficiently similar to the standard treatment of quotation to suggest the possibility of a unified analysis of both kinds of opaque context. Such an analysis may turn out in the end to be too cumbersome for standard use; but it may be instructive to see whether it can be done.

I will attempt a unified analysis by introducing an operator, θ^+, which does the job of both a quotation symbol and of Cresswell's θ^+. When my θ^+ is prefixed to any expression it will create a name of both the expression itself and the expression's Lewis-meaning. If α is any expression, the value of the sequence $\langle \theta^+, \alpha \rangle$ will be an ordered pair whose first member is the expression α itself, and whose second member is the Lewis-meaning of α.

An operator which includes within its domain such an ordered pair may then be more sensitive to one half of the pair than to the other. A purely quotational operator will be sensitive only to the first member of the pair. A purely Fregean operator will be sensitive only to the second member. There is also, however, the possibility of introducing an operator which is sensitive to both members of the pair. Such a semi-quotational operator will call for something which lies somewhere between direct quotation on the one hand, and free précis on the other. Something more like parody, perhaps.

Such semi-quotational operators may even be found in natural languages. An example might be,

3.5 Charles swore that by Jove he'd get to the top of that jolly old mountain if it was the last thing he did.

---

3. This step in Cresswell's analysis is somewhat obscured because the quotation-like operator, θ^+, is amalgamated with another operator, θ^-, to produce an operator, θ, which is no longer closely analogous to quotation. But see his footnote 11 in 'Hyperintensional Logic' for details on how θ can be decomposed to give θ^+.

B. H. Partee (1973) has suggested several similar examples. A unified analysis of opaque contexts, of the sort I will propose, may therefore provide us as a bonus with a natural method of representing the logical form of some semantically anomalous sentences in natural language.

4. *Categorical languages*

I shall now set out the above suggestions within the framework of the formal philosophy of language of Cresswell's *Logics and Languages*.

Where Nat is the set of natural numbers 0, 1, 2,... etc., the set Syn of *syntactic categories* is the smallest set such that

4.1   Nat $\subseteq$ Syn

4.2   If $\tau, \sigma_1, \ldots, \sigma_n \in$ Syn then $\langle \tau, \sigma_1, \ldots, \sigma_n \rangle \in$ Syn.

A λ-categorial language $\mathscr{L}^\lambda$ is an ordered quadruple $\langle F, X, \lambda, E \rangle$, where

(i) F is a function from Syn whose range is a set of pairwise disjoint sets, all of which are finite, and all but finitely many of which are empty. Where $\sigma \in$ Syn, F_σ is the set of *constants* of category σ. The union of all sets F_σ, $\sigma \in$ Syn, is denoted by F$^+$.

(ii) X is a function from Syn whose range is a set of pairwise disjoint, denumerably infinite sets. Where $\sigma \in$ Syn, X_σ is the denumerably infinite set of *variables* of syntactic category σ. The union of all sets X_σ, $\sigma \in$ Syn, is denoted by X$^+$. The set X$^+$ should be disjoint from any set made up out of members of F$^+$.

(iii) λ is a symbol, called an *abstraction operator*, which is distinct from any symbol in F$^+$ or X$^+$, and which is not constructed out of any set of members of F$^+$ and X$^+$.

(iv) E is that function from Syn whose range is the smallest system of sets, E_σ, of the well-formed *expressions* of syntactic category σ, these sets E_σ satisfying the following conditions: For any $\sigma, \tau, \sigma_1, \ldots, \sigma_n \in$ Syn,

4.3 $F_\sigma \subseteq E_\sigma$

4.4 $X_\sigma \subseteq E_\sigma$

4.5   If $\alpha_1, \ldots, \alpha_n \in E_{\sigma_1}, \ldots, E_{\sigma_n}$ and $\delta \in E_{\langle \tau, \sigma_1, \ldots, \sigma_n \rangle}$ then $\langle \delta, \alpha_1, \ldots, \alpha_n \rangle \in E_\tau$

4.6   If $\alpha \in E_\tau$ and $x \in X_\sigma$ then $\langle \lambda, x, \alpha \rangle \in E_{\langle \tau, \sigma \rangle}$

4.7   If $\alpha_1, \ldots, \alpha_n \in E^+$ then $\langle \alpha_1, \ldots, \alpha_n \rangle \notin F^+$; and if $\alpha \in E^+$, $x \in X^+$, then $\langle \lambda, x, \alpha \rangle \notin F^+$.

Condition 4.7 ensures that no symbol is in more than one syntactic category, and that there is no expression which is both a simple symbol and a complex expression. When this condition is met, $\mathscr{L}^\lambda$ is said to be *grounded*.

A system D^+ of intensional domains for a λ-categorial language is defined as follows. D is a function from Syn such that, where $\sigma = \langle \tau, \sigma_1, \ldots, \sigma_n \rangle$, D_σ is a set of partial functions from $D_{\sigma_1} \text{X} \ldots \text{X} D_{\sigma_n}$ into D_τ.

D_1 is a domain of things; and D_0 is the domain of propositions. A proposition is to be regarded as a set of possible worlds; so that where W is the set of all possible worlds, and $\mathscr{P}W$ is the set of all sets of possible worlds, $D_0 \subseteq \mathscr{P}W$. D^+ is then the union of all sets D_σ, $\sigma \in$ Syn.

An interpretation for a λ-categorial language $\mathscr{L}^\lambda$ is a function V_ν from the symbols of $\mathscr{L}^\lambda$ into D^+. An interpretation V_ν is induced by two functions, V and ν. V is an assignment of values to the constants of $\mathscr{L}^\lambda$, that is, to the members of F^+; and ν is an assignment of values to the variables, that is, to the members of X^+.

An assignment, V, is a function from F^+ into D^+ such that

> 4.8 For any $\sigma \in$ Syn, if $\alpha \in F_\sigma$ then $V(\alpha) \in D_\sigma$.

An assignment to variables, ν, is a function from X^+ into D^+ such that

> 4.9 For any $\sigma \in$ Syn, if $x \in X_\sigma$ then $\nu(x) \in D_\sigma$.

The set of all such functions ν is denoted by N. Given assignments V and ν to the constants and variables of $\mathscr{L}^\lambda$, an interpretation of $\mathscr{L}^\lambda$ is a function V_ν from $F^+ \cup X^+$ into D^+ such that

> 4.10 If $\alpha \in F^+$ then $V_\nu(\alpha) = V(\alpha)$; and if $\alpha \in X^+$ then $V_\nu(\alpha) = \nu(\alpha)$.

When we are considering value-assignments for particular formulae, the assignments to the variables in one of its component expressions will often be constrained by the rest of the formula. For this reason, we will need to speak about a particular assignment which yields some specific value, a, for some variable x. For convenience we will refer to such an assignment as $(\nu, a/x)$: thus,

> 4.11 For any $x \in X_\sigma$, $a \in D_\sigma$, and $\nu \in$ N, let $(\nu, a/x)$ be that function such that $(\nu, a/x)(x) = a$; while for any $y \in X^+$ distinct from x, $(\nu, a/x)(y) = \nu(y)$.

The joint assignments, V and ν, of values to the symbols of $\mathscr{L}^\lambda$ then induce an assignment, I_V^ν, of a value, or *intension*, for every well-formed expression of $\mathscr{L}^\lambda$. The function I_V^ν is defined to be such that,

4.12　If $\alpha \in F^+ \cup X^+$ then $I_V^\nu(\alpha) = V_\nu(\alpha)$

4.13　If α is $\langle \delta, \alpha_1, \ldots, \alpha_n \rangle$ where $\alpha_1, \ldots, \alpha_n \in E_{\sigma_1}, \ldots, E_{\sigma_n}$ and $\delta \in E_{\langle \tau, \sigma_1, \ldots, \sigma_n \rangle}$, then $I_V^\nu(\alpha) = (I_V^\nu(\delta))(I_V^\nu(\alpha_1), \ldots, I_V^\nu(\alpha_n))$

4.14　If α is $\langle \lambda, x, \beta \rangle$, where $x \in X_\sigma$ and $\beta \in E_\tau$, then $I_V^\nu(\alpha) = \omega$ where ω is that function from D_σ into D_τ such that if $a \in D_\sigma$ then $\omega(a) = I_V^{(V, a/x)}(\beta)$.

Condition 4.14 ensures that $\langle \lambda, x, \beta \rangle$ will be what is called an *abstract*. The intension of $\langle \lambda, x, \beta \rangle$ is a function which maps something in the category of x into something in the category of β. When $\langle \lambda, x, \beta \rangle$ is concatenated with an expression, α, of the same category as x, the value of $\langle \alpha, \langle \lambda, x, \beta \rangle \rangle$ is the same as the value β takes when α is substituted for x. We may read $\langle \alpha, \langle \lambda, x, \beta \rangle \rangle$ as roughly equivalent to: 'α is a thing such that β is true of that thing'; and the abstract $\langle \lambda, x, \beta \rangle$ can be read as: 'is a thing such that β is true of that thing'.

It should be noted that the intension of $\langle \lambda, x, \beta \rangle$ under an interpretation V_ν is independent of the value assigned by ν to the variable x. The intension of $\langle \lambda, x, \beta \rangle$ is a function which maps an object of the *same category* as x, into the value β takes when x is *replaced* by a name of that object. This function will be unchanged whatever value ν may assign to x. Thus, the intension of an expression in which *all* variables are bound will be independent of any assignment ν of values to variables. The assignments to its variables will be fully constrained by their linguistic context: by their being syntactically linked with expressions which are not variables. For instance, in $\langle \alpha, \langle \lambda, x, \beta \rangle \rangle$ the variable x serves only to link α with certain expressions buried in β. And so the function of variables is seen to be solely that of syntactic place-markers, as I recommended earlier.

5. Meanings and variables

In assigning intensions to the symbols and expressions of $\mathscr{L}^\lambda$ I have just been redeploying Cresswell's presentation of λ-categorial languages. Now I wish to suggest a way in which an interpretation, V_ν, of $\mathscr{L}^\lambda$ may induce not only an intension, but also a Lewis-type *meaning* for every well-formed expression of $\mathscr{L}^\lambda$.

As I suggested earlier, I will take λ and the variables as their own meanings. In order for this to be acceptable, we must ensure that λ and the variables are not included in D^+; otherwise their meanings may coincide with the meanings of other expressions in $\mathscr{L}^\lambda$.

The requirement that λ and the variables should not occur in D^+ may seem hard to meet. Within D^+ is included the set D_1 of 'things': and whatever things we choose to take as λ and the variables, it might seem that these things ∈ will have to be members of D_1.

However, the set of all 'things' whatsoever can never be exhaustively specified in any language. In particular, no language can specify its own truth-definition; the function which assigns a truth-value to every sentence in a language must always be specified in some other language. Thus, the set T of all the truth-definitions for all λ-categorial languages is an entity which cannot be described in any λ-categorial language. Consequently T need not be a member of any relevant domain D_1 for any λ-categorial language. So we could meet the requirements set on λ by taking it to be the set T. And we could take each set of variables, X_σ, to be the set of ordered triples (n, σ, T), for each natural number n.

Given that λ and the variables are defined in some such manner, we will be free to stipulate that they are to be taken as their own meanings. Following Lewis, we will stipulate that the meanings of the other basic symbols of $\mathscr{L}^\lambda$ should be identified with their intensions. The meaning of a well-formed expression of $\mathscr{L}^\lambda$ will then be identified with the ordered sequence of the meanings of its component symbols.

Since variables are to be taken as their own meanings, the assignment of meanings to expressions of $\mathscr{L}^\lambda$ will not depend on any assignment, ν, of values to the variables. In this respect the assignment of meanings is unlike the assignment of intensions. The intension of an expression with free variables may depend on the context in which it is embedded, since different contexts will dictate different assignments to its variables. The meaning of such an expression, however, is what determines *how* we are to calculate its intension in any given context. And so its meaning must be determined prior to its being assigned to any particular context.

Hence an assignment M_V of meanings to all the well-formed expressions of $\mathscr{L}^\lambda$ is induced solely by an assignment V of values to the constants of $\mathscr{L}^\lambda$. The definition of M_V proceeds as follows: For any interpretation, V,

5.1 If $\alpha \in F^+$ then $M_V(\alpha) = V(\alpha)$

5.2 If $x \in X^+$ then $M_V(x) = x$

5.3 If α is $\langle \delta, \alpha_1, \ldots, \alpha_n \rangle$, where $\alpha_1, \ldots, \alpha_n \in E_{\sigma_1}, \ldots, E_{\sigma_n}$, and $\delta \in E_{\langle \tau, \sigma_1, \ldots, \sigma_n \rangle}$, then $M_V(\alpha) = \langle M_V(\delta), M_V(\alpha_1), \ldots, M_V(\alpha_n) \rangle$

5.4   If α is $\langle \lambda, x, \beta \rangle$ where $x \in X^+$ and $\beta \in E^+$, then $M_V(\alpha) = \langle \lambda, x, M_V(\beta) \rangle$.

It may be wondered whether this definition of M_V might cut meanings too fine. In particular, variable-binding introduces spurious distinctions of meaning between what are called *bound alphabetic variants*. For instance, the meaning of

$$\langle \textit{Cynthia}, \langle \lambda, x, \langle \textit{spies}, x \rangle \rangle \rangle$$

will be different from the meaning of

$$\langle \text{Cynthia}, \langle \lambda, y, \langle \text{spies}, y \rangle \rangle \rangle,$$

if x and y are distinct.

This seems counter-intuitive. However, it never really matters too much if we cut meanings too fine. Spurious distinctions in meaning may simply be ignored. We may just define all operators in the language in such a way that their values are always the same for all bound alphabetic variants within their scope, even when the operator is a hyperintensional one which is sensitive to the meanings of its arguments. Or alternatively, if we wish we may always introduce a coarser definition of meanings on the basis of the above definition of too-fine-meanings. For instance, we might define the meaning-proper of an expression as the set of all the too-fine-meanings of all its bound alphabetic variants.

There is no pressing need, therefore, to worry about whether the above definition of M_V cuts meanings too fine. We should be happy provided only it cuts them fine enough.

6. *Hyperintensional operators*

We are now in a position to introduce hyperintensional operators—verbs of psychological attitudes and speech acts—into a λ-categorial language.

First of all, having defined meanings for expressions of $\mathscr{L}^\lambda$, we need to introduce a device which enables us to make use of these meanings in calculating the intensions of expressions involving hyperintensional operators. Such a device, call it θ^+, should be introduced in a similar manner to λ and the variables, ensuring that it is distinct from the other symbols of $\mathscr{L}^\lambda$ and that it is not identical with the meaning or intension of any expression in $\mathscr{L}^\lambda$. We can then permit θ^+ to be taken as its own meaning.

The formation rule for the introduction of θ^+ is simply:

6.1   If α is an expression of $\mathscr{L}^\lambda$, then $\langle \theta^+, \alpha \rangle \in E_1$.

We assign $\langle \theta^+, \alpha \rangle$ to the syntactic category 1, since we are going to treat it as a name—as the name of the expression α and its meaning. Note that θ^+ makes a name out of an expression of any syntactic category at all. Thus θ^+, like λ, is not in any syntactic category: that is, $\theta^+ \notin \mathrm{Syn}$. So it cannot have an intension or meaning in D^+. That is why θ^+ should be taken as its own meaning.

An intension and meaning for expressions containing θ^+ are then induced by an interpretation, V_v, in the following way:

6.2   If α is $\langle \theta^+, \delta \rangle$ where $\delta \in E^+$, then for any interpretation V_v,
$$I^v_V(\alpha) = \langle \delta, M_V(\delta) \rangle$$
$$M_V(\alpha) = \langle \theta^+, \delta, M_V(\delta) \rangle.$$

I will now introduce hyperintensional operators into $\mathscr{L}^\lambda$ in a way which enables us to represent concepts like the concept of belief. As I explained earlier, I will take belief to be an $(n + 2)$-place relation between an individual, an n-tuple of objects of various categories, and the meaning of an n-place predicate. Consequently, if the concept of belief were to be represented by a single operator, say *believes*, then this would have to be an $(n + 2)$-place operator—an operator which takes a varying number of arguments. This, however, is not possible in a categorial language.

Thus we will have to represent the concept of belief, in a λ-categorial language, by a range of different operators. Belief-relations may hold between an individual, a meaning, and an n-tuple of objects in various categories—that is, an n-tuple of members of $D_{\sigma_1}, \ldots, D_{\sigma_n}$, for any $\sigma_1, \ldots, \sigma_n \in \mathrm{Syn}$. Each such subclass of belief-relations will have to be represented by a different operator—by an operator which takes as its arguments a name of an individual, a θ^+-expression, and an n-tuple of members of $(E_{\sigma_1} \cup X_{\sigma_1}), \ldots, (E_{\sigma_n} \cup X_{\sigma_n})$. Such an operator will be in the syntactic category $\langle 0, 1, \sigma_1, \ldots, \sigma_n, 1 \rangle$; and each different n-tuple $\langle \sigma_1, \ldots, \sigma_n \rangle$ will determine a different operator, say *believes* $_{\langle \sigma_1, \ldots, \sigma_n \rangle}$. However, since no confusion will arise from ignoring the subscripts for these different operators, we may in general just drop the subscripts and treat all the different belief-operators as if they were one.

The formation-rule for *believes* $_{\langle \sigma_1, \ldots, \sigma_n \rangle}$ is as follows:

6.3 *If:*

    (i) a is a name or variable of category 1 (that is, $a \in (E_1 \cup X_1)$);

    (ii) $\alpha_1 \in (E_{\sigma_1} \cup X_{\sigma_1}), \ldots, \alpha_n \in (E_{\sigma_n} \cup X_{\sigma_n})$;

    (iii) α is a closed expression[4] of the form $\langle \lambda, x_1, \langle \lambda, x_2, \ldots, \langle \lambda, x_n, \langle \beta \rangle \rangle \ldots \rangle \rangle$ where $\beta \in E_0$ and $x_1, \ldots, x_n \in X_{\sigma_1}, \ldots, X_{\sigma_n}$;

then

$$\langle \textbf{\textit{believes}} \, _{\langle \sigma_1, \ldots, \sigma_n \rangle}, a, \langle \alpha_1, \ldots, \alpha_n \rangle, \langle \theta^+, \alpha \rangle \rangle \in E_0.$$

The intension of *believes* is then a function *into* the set of propositions, *from* the set of $(n + 2)$-tuples of the intensions of the arguments of *believes*. The intensions of the arguments of *believes* are, respectively, members of $D_1, D_{\sigma_1}, \ldots, D_{\sigma_n}$, and an ordered pair containing an expression of $\mathscr{L}^{\lambda}$ and a meaning. And the meaning of *believes* is identified with its intension.

The intensions of expressions containing *believes* are then determined straightforwardly, by letting the intension of *believes* under any given interpretation apply to the intensions of its arguments under that interpretation (as in 4.13). The meaning of an expression containing *believes* is also determined straightforwardly, by taking the ordered sequence containing the meaning of *believes* together with the meanings of its arguments (as in 5.3).

Hyperintensional operators like *believes* can then be classified, as I outlined earlier, into purely quotational, partially quotational, and purely Fregean operators. A hyperintensional operator takes as part of its domain the intension of a θ^+-expression, $\langle \theta^+, \alpha \rangle$: and the intension of such an expression is an ordered pair of an expression and a meaning. An operator which is applied to such an ordered pair may be more sensitive to one half of the pair than to the other. A purely quotational operator, for instance, will yield exactly the same result whatever is taken as the second element of the pair, provided only that the first element remains fixed. Of course, the expression, α say, and the meaning, $M_V(\alpha)$, are linked: given α and an interpretation V, $M_V(\alpha)$ is uniquely determined. So we cannot keep α fixed while varying the meaning $M_V(\alpha)$ unless we also vary the interpretation V. The distinction between purely quotational and other hyperintensional

4. In requiring that the sentence α have no free variables, we exclude the possibility of quantification *into* a context governed by θ^+. This is desirable, since quantification into such a context is not always acceptable. When 'quantification in' *is* desired, we must always move from an $(n + 2)$-place operator to an operator which takes one more argument: thus adding a variable outside the scope of θ^+, and adding one more argument-place to the predicate within the scope of θ^+.

operators can only be brought to the surface, therefore, by considering a class of interpretations which vary in their assignments to α, but which all agree in their assignments to the hyperintensional operator in question and its other arguments.

Thus, for instance, the value of

'Cicero' has six letters

remains unchanged however the interpretation of 'Cicero' is varied—provided that the interpretation of quotation marks and of '. . . has six letters' is held constant.

Conversely, a purely Fregean operator should yield the same result when applied to a pair of an expression and a meaning, $\langle \alpha, M_V(\alpha) \rangle$, no matter how the expression α is varied—provided that the meaning $M_V(\alpha)$ is held constant.

And so, we may set down the following definitions: If ψ is a hyperintensional operator, and if K is a set of interpretations V_ν for $\mathcal{L}^\lambda$ in which the values of ψ, a, $\alpha_1, \ldots, \alpha_n \in E^+$ remain fixed, then

6.4 ψ is a *purely quotational* operator in K iff for any V_ν, $V_\nu^* \in K$, and α, $\beta \in E^+$, if $\alpha = \beta$ then $I_V^\nu(\langle \psi, a, \langle \alpha_1, \ldots, \alpha_n \rangle, \langle \theta^+, \alpha \rangle \rangle) = I_{V*}^\nu(\langle \psi, a, \langle \alpha_1, \ldots, \alpha_n \rangle, \langle \theta^+, \beta \rangle \rangle)$.

6.5 ψ is a *purely Fregean* operator in K iff, for any V_ν, $V_\nu^* \in K$, and $\alpha, \beta \in E^+$, if $M_V(\alpha) = M_V*(\beta)$ then $I_V^\nu(\langle \psi, a, \langle \alpha_1, \ldots, \alpha_n \rangle, \langle \theta^+, \alpha \rangle \rangle) = I_{V*}^\nu(\langle \psi, a, \langle \alpha_1, \ldots, \alpha_n \rangle, \langle \theta^+, \beta \rangle \rangle)$.

6.6 ψ is a *partially quotational*, or *partially Fregean* operator in K iff it is neither a purely quotational nor a purely Fregean operator in K.

Other classifications of hyperintensional operators will also be possible, some cutting across the quotational/Fregean distinction. One sort of classification deserves special mention.

Purely and partially quotational operators are sensitive to a meaning which falls within their scope; but different operators may be sensitive to different aspects of the meanings within their scope. Now, one very important feature of meanings is that the meaning of a sentence generally determines that sentence's intension: it determines the set of possible worlds in which that sentence is true. The intension of a sentence may then be of interest in its own right. A hyperintensional operator may therefore discriminate between meanings on the basis of the intensions which those meanings determine.

Thus for instance we might define an operator, say *knows* $_{\langle 0, 1, 1 \rangle}$, which maps its arguments into a proposition which contains any given world w *only if* the meaning which the operator acts on is one which determines an intension which contains w. Thus

$$\langle knows\ _{\langle 0,1,1\rangle},\ a,\ \langle \theta^+,\ \alpha\rangle\rangle$$

will be true in a world w under an interpretation V_v only if α is true in w under V_v.

Conversely, we could define an operator, say *imagines* $_{\langle 0,1,1\rangle}$, in such a way that

$$\langle imagines\ _{\langle 0,1,1\rangle},\ a,\ \langle \theta^+,\ \alpha\rangle\rangle$$

will be true in a world w only if α is false in w.

Such definitions could be extended from two-place operators to many-place operators: so that

$$\langle knows\ _{\langle \sigma_1,...,\sigma_n\rangle},\ a,\ \langle b_1,\ ...,\ b_n\rangle,\ \langle \theta^+,\ \alpha\rangle\rangle$$

will be true in a world w only if the n-tuple of objects assigned to $b_1,\ ...,\ b_n$ in w is in the set of n-tuples assigned to the predicate α in w. Conversely,

$$\langle imagines\ _{\langle \sigma_1,...,\sigma_n\rangle},\ a,\ \langle b_1,\ ...,\ b_n\rangle,\ \langle \theta^+,\ \alpha\rangle\rangle$$

will be true in w only if the n-tuple assigned to $b_1,\ ...,\ b_n$ is *not* in the set of n-tuples assigned to α in w.

Intension-sensitive operators raise too many questions to tackle here; but the possibility of defining such operators should be worth investigating.

7. *Nested hyperintensional operators*

Suppose we wish to formalise a sentence which contains nested hyper-intensional operators, like

7.1 Cynthia believes that Ralph believes that α.

If both occurrences of 'believes' here were represented by the same belief-operator, then in the hyperintensional logic developed above, 7.1 would be given the form:

7.2 ⟨*believes, Cynthia,* ⟨θ⁺, ⟨*believes, Ralph,* ⟨θ⁺, α⟩⟩⟩⟩.

But as Cresswell pointed out in 'Hyperintensional Logic', a formula like 7.2 will lack an intension. The intension of 7.2 would have to be the value which the intension of the first *believes* yields when applied to the intensions of its arguments. But the intension of one of its arguments includes the meaning of

⟨*believes, Ralph,* ⟨θ⁺, α⟩⟩;

and the meaning of this includes the intension of *believes*. And so the intension of *believes* will occur as part of its own argument. Most set theories will require that the value of an operator must be undefined for such an argument. Consequently 7.2 will not have an intension: it will not be true in any possible worlds. It cannot therefore be an adequate formalisation of 7.1. We may call this the paradox of self-embedded hyperintensional operators.

Cresswell suggested that we modify our formalisation of 7.1 in the following manner. We introduce a new operator, θ⁻, which alters the meanings of sentences containing hyperintensional operators in such a way as to ensure that they can always be embedded within other hyperintensional operators without risking paradoxes of self-reference. θ⁻ is defined to be such that the *meaning* of an expression ⟨θ⁻, α⟩ is always just the *intension* of α. We then add to our formation rules for hyperintensional operators (i.e. to 6.3) the requirement that any hyperintensional operator should always be preceded by θ⁻. Thus we should represent

Ralph believes that α

as

7.3 ⟨θ⁻, ⟨*believes, Ralph,* ⟨θ⁺, α⟩⟩⟩.

The meaning of this formula will be just the intension of ⟨*believes, Ralph,* ⟨θ⁺, α⟩⟩—that is to say, a proposition, or set of possible worlds. So the meaning of 7.3 does not contain the intension of *believes*. Hence it can be embedded within the scope of another occurrence of *believes* without threat of paradox.

This solution is formally adequate. It does, however, have one worrying feature. Suppose we have two sentences of the form:

7.4 Ralph ψ's that α
7.5 Ralph ψ's that β

where ψ is a hyperintensional operator. Now, since ψ is a hyperintensional operator, this means that it must be sensitive to differences in meaning even between sentences which are logically equivalent. That is, if ψ is a truly hyperintensional operator, there will be *some* logically equivalent sentences α and β for which 7.4 and 7.5 will differ in intension. Yet this does not rule out the possibility that for *other* sentences α and β, 7.4 and 7.5 might have exactly the same intensions *even though* α and β differ in meaning.

Suppose then that 7.4 and 7.5 do have the same intensions, even though α and β differ in meaning. If we represent these sentences on the model Cresswell suggests, the hyperintensional operator ψ will have to be preceded by θ⁻; so that the meanings of 7.4 and 7.5 will reduce to their intensions. But then, since their intensions are the same, their meanings too will be the same.

Consider therefore what happens when 7.4 and 7.5 are embedded within a further hyperintensional operator: as in

7.6 Cynthia believes that Ralph ψ's that α
7.7 Cynthia believes that Ralph ψ's that β.

Since the embedded sentences (7.4 and 7.5) have the same meanings as well as the same intensions, 7.6 and 7.7 will have to have the same meanings and intensions too. This means that Cynthia cannot possibly believe that Ralph ψ's that α without also believing that Ralph ψ's that β.

But this is curious. The main reason for introducing hyperintensional operators was to explain how a person can believe one but not the other of two logically equivalent sentences. Yet now we find that a person *cannot* believe one but not the other of two logically equivalent *hyperintensional* sentences. Why should this be? It may indeed be true that if Ralph ψ's that α then necessarily he also ψ's that β: but surely Cynthia might not be aware of this. So surely she might *believe* Ralph ψ's α but not β?

If we abandon Cresswell's use of θ⁻, we will lose a neat solution to the paradox of double embeddings. But we will gain in the flexibility of the system. We will then be able to define hyperintensional operators like ψ, in such a way that 7.6 and 7.7 need not be logically equivalent even when the embedded 7.4 and 7.5 do happen to be logically equivalent. It may turn out to be useful to be able to define such operators. There may even be such operators in natural languages.

Consider for instance the following case. Suppose Ralph has proved a certain theorem T. A fairly obvious corollary of T is the sentence α. So we might say

7.8   Ralph has enabled mathematicians to prove that α.

It is plausible to suggest that 7.8 contains a genuinely hyperintensional operator. Ralph has not enabled mathematicians to prove everything which is logically equivalent to α.

But now, suppose that for some sentence β, the logical equivalence of α and β is even more obvious than the proof of α from T. Then, in any possible world in which 7.8 is true it will also be true that

7.9   Ralph has enabled mathematicians to prove that β.

Yet although Cynthia has heard it reported that 7.8, she does not recognise that β is easily proved from α: so she does not believe 7.9.
   Hence

7.10   Cynthia believes that Ralph has enabled mathematicians to prove that α
7.11   Cynthia believes that Ralph has enabled mathematicians to prove that β

should differ in intension, even though the embedded hyperintensional sentences 7.8 and 7.9 are logically equivalent. So 7.8 and 7.9 must differ in meaning after all, despite their containing a hyperintensional operator. This is compatible with the hyperintensional logic I defined above, without θ⁻; but it is not compatible with Cresswell's suggestion that every hyper-intensional operator should be preceded by θ⁻.

   However, if we abandon Cresswell's solution to the paradox of double embeddings, we are left with no explanation of how we are to formalise sentences like

7.1   Cynthia believes that Ralph believes that α.

One thing we might do is to make more sparing use of Cresswell's θ⁻, reserving it for just those cases where it is really needed—that is, for just those cases where one and the same operator occurs within its own scope. This might seem a fairly promising option. The above objections to θ⁻ will be less likely to apply in the case of double embeddings of the same operator.

The times when θ^- gets in the way appear to be primarily cases where a relatively insensitive hyperintensional operator occurs within the scope of a more sensitive operator: so that the meanings of the most deeply embedded elements leapfrog over the insensitive operator and influence the more sensitive operator outside. When one and the same operator occurs within its own scope, such leapfrogging is less likely to be a threat.

However, even in cases of self-embeddings some sort of leapfrogging might occur. Consider for instance the two sentences:

7.12 Cynthia has enabled mathematicians to prove in one line that Ralph has enabled mathematicians to prove in one line that α.

7.13 Cynthia has enabled mathematicians to prove in one line that Ralph has enabled mathematicians to prove in one line that β.

Suppose that a one-line proof of α can easily be converted into a one-line proof of β. Then the embedded sentences in 7.12 and 7.13 are logically equivalent. Yet 7.12 and 7.13 may not be logically equivalent. Suppose Cynthia's one-line proof in 7.12 was simply the citing of a one-line proof of α occurring in Ralph's latest publication. Then 7.12 is true: but 7.13 is false. Cynthia has given us a one-line proof that Ralph gave us a one-line proof that α. From this we can deduce that Ralph enabled mathematicians to prove in one line that β. But we can deduce this only given the further assumption that a one-line proof of α can be converted into a one-line proof of β. So we have a two-line, but not a one-line proof that Ralph enabled mathematicians to give a one-line proof of β.

Hence 7.12 and 7.13 differ in intension. And so, it seems, it will not be safe to use θ^- even in cases of double embeddings of the same operator.

We are led to the conclusion that we should do our best to dispense with θ^- altogether. This has the consequence that a hyperintensional operator can never occur within its own scope. In order to formalise a sentence like

7.1 Cynthia believes that Ralph believes that α,

we will have to represent the two different occurrences of 'believes' by two distinct operators: call them *believes*[2] and *believes*[1].

The operator *believes*[1] can be defined as an operator which takes as its domain the intensions of only those expressions of $\mathscr{L}^\lambda$ which contain no hyperintensional operators. Along with *believes*[1] we may define a whole class of first-level hyperintensional operators whose domains include no hyperintensional operators.

Given a set of first-level hyperintensional operators, we may then define a set of second-level operators like *believes*^{2}, whose domains include the domains of the first-level operators together with the intensions of those first-level operators themselves. In this manner we can construct an infinite hierarchy of hyperintensional operators. Each operator, *believes*^{n}, will yield the same values as *believes*$^{(n-1)}$ for all arguments with a 'hyperintensionality' of less than $(n-1)$. But *believes*^{n} will differ from *believes*$^{(n-1)}$ in being defined for arguments which include sentences with a 'hyperintensionality' of $(n-1)$. Similar remarks will apply to other such hierarchies of hyperintensional operators. We can then embed any hyperintensional operator any number of times, provided we always embed it in progressively higher-level operators.

This version of hyperintensional logic enables us to take account of the meanings of symbols in a sentence, no matter how far they have been embedded; and these differences in meaning may contribute to differences in the intensions of yet further embeddings. Thus this version of hyperintensional logic is more flexible than Cresswell's. It is not strikingly more intuitive, however. But perhaps it does derive some plausibility from its resemblance to other familiar and well-entrenched solutions to analogous problems. The problem of multiple embeddings of hyperintensional operators is reminiscent of a wide range of semantic paradoxes involving self-reference: the Liar paradox for instance. Such semantic paradoxes are not uncommonly resolved by retreating into infinite hierarchies of languages, each one generated in a regular way out of the ones before in very much the manner in which my suggested hierarchy of hyperintensional operators is to be generated. So in this respect, while my system lacks some of the tightly-knit elegance of Cresswell's, it does at least borrow some dignity from tradition.

8. *Translation*

Hyperintensional operators have long been troublemakers in philosophy. Sentences describing propositional attitudes, speech acts and language have persistently raised legions of deep and bewildering philosophical problems. Thus, progress even in a small corner of a topic as central as this will kindle hopes for new light on a wide range of subsidiary topics. I will mention briefly just one such topic which is likely to benefit from the recent progress in hyperintensional logic: namely, the theory of translation.

Suppose Charles does not understand German, and he hears Ludwig say, 'Du musst wissen: ich fürchte mich'. Suppose that Charles wants to know what Ludwig has said, and he is told

8.1 Ludwig said, 'Du musst wissen: ich fürchte mich'.

This is probably not the sort of answer Charles would like; it tells him nothing he did not know already. In 8.1 the operator

___ said, '. . .'

is being used as an instance of what I have called a purely quotational operator.

But suppose Charles is informed

8.2 Ludwig said that he was frightened.

Here the operator

___ said that . . .

is being used as a purely Fregean operator. In this case Charles will learn something he did not know before.

Now clearly, in some sense 8.2 may be said to provide a rough *translation* of what Ludwig said. As a translation, however, it leaves something to be desired. Charles may be grateful for the information 8.2 does give him: but he may want more information as well.

One point we may note, is that the words '. . . he was frightened' in 8.2 do not perfectly match the meanings of Ludwig's original words. It is possible that Charles might want to know more accurately the literal meanings of Ludwig's words: so he might be interested if he were told, for instance,

8.3 Ludwig said that you must know that he is frightened,

or

8.4 Ludwig said, 'You must know: I am frightened'.

8.3 and 8.4 might perhaps be said to offer a 'literal' or 'word for word' translation of Ludwig's remark.

It is unlikely, however, that Charles would be so interested in the precise meaning of Ludwig's remark. He is more likely to be interested in learning something of the *manner* in which Ludwig said that he was frightened. The words which Ludwig used may have many important features which would not be revealed simply by reporting their meanings. They may have agreeable or disagreeable auditory qualities, independently of their meanings.

5*

They may be words which are frequently used, or words which are seldom used, or words which were often used in the past but are seldom used nowadays. They may be words which are most frequently heard within certain sorts of socio-psychological contexts—in the fish markets, perhaps, or amongst thieves, or in fashion magazines, or amongst people who are on intimate terms, or between people who are fuming with anger, and so on. Or, they may be words which are well known to have been used by some famous person on a particularly historic occasion; or they may be words which occurred in some obscure piece of literature known to both speaker and hearer. And so on. Such properties as these might be more interesting to Charles than absolute precision about the literal meanings of Ludwig's words.

Thus, Charles may be willing to sacrifice some accuracy in the reporting of the meanings of Ludwig's words, provided he is compensated with other extra-semantical similarities between Ludwig's original words and the words used in the translation. And so, for instance, Charles would probably not be much misled if he were told

8.5   Ludwig said, 'I must tell you: I am frightened'.

Here the operator

_____ said, '. . .'

is not being used as a purely quotational operator. It does not provide a *direct* quotation of Ludwig's words; rather, it reports his words in a fashion closely resembling that of *indirect speech*. The words in the quote-marks must have meanings which are not too far removed from the meanings of Ludwig's words. If the meanings of Ludwig's words had been different, the truth-value of 8.5 might have been different too. So the hyperintensional operator in 8.5 is partially Fregean. But in addition, the words in the quote-marks must share certain non-semantic features with Ludwig's words—in particular, they must be as plain and colloquial in English as Ludwig's words were in German. If Ludwig had used different words with roughly the same meanings, 8.5 might not then have been an accurate report of what he said. So the hyperintensional operator in 8.5 is partially quotational. On this reading, 8.5 might well be described as a translation of Ludwig's words.[5]

Consider another example. Suppose Ludwig says,

5. It is in fact the translation G. E. M. Anscombe gives for a sentence on page 174 of Wittgenstein (1967).

8.6 'Du musst wissen: mir graut davor.'[6]

In the case of this sentence, a literal, or word-for-word translation is hard to come by, since the German 'mir graut davor' is an idiom without any exact counterpart in English. The closest thing to a literal translation I can find is,

8.7 'You must know: it gives me the creeps.'

Here, the English 'gives me' reflects the German dative 'mir'; the term 'the creeps' is, like the German 'graut', reserved for a kind of shivering which is associated with fear of the supernatural; and the English 'it' corresponds fairly closely to the German 'davor' in this context.

So 8.7 reflects the meaning of 8.6 fairly closely—more closely than any other English sentence I can think of. Yet nevertheless, 8.7 is I think a poor translation of 8.6. In particular, the German 'mir graut davor' has, I believe, an antique, dignified air about it; whereas 'it gives me the creeps' has contemporary, comic-strip sorts of associations in English. For this reason, a translator is justified in sacrificing a degree of fidelity to the meanings of Ludwig's actual words, and offering instead some such translation as

8.8 'I must tell you: it makes me shiver.'

Thus, if Ludwig utters 8.6, we may accurately report what he has said by the assertion,

8.9 Ludwig said, 'I must tell you: it makes me shiver'.

Alternatively, we might say,

8.10 Ludwig's words translate as, 'I must tell you: it makes me shiver'.

This sentence differs in one notable respect from the other hyperintensional sentences I have been considering. The subject-term in 8.10 refers, not to a person (as in most sentences describing propositional attitudes or speech acts), but to a linguistic entity (Ludwig's words). However, this departure from the general format for other hyperintensional sentences is of minor significance, and introduces no new problems of principle. The operator

_____ translates as, '...'

6. This sentence, too, is found (facing Anscombe's translation) on page 174 of Wittgenstein (1967).

will be represented in hyperintensional logic by a partially Fregean, partially quotational operator, of the same type formally as the operator *believes* introduced earlier.

It appears, then, that within hyperintensional logic it should be possible to define an operator which comes very close indeed to capturing our intuitive notion of translation. Suppose we are speaking within a categorial language $\mathscr{L}^\lambda$, and we wish to translate an expression, α, into $\mathscr{L}^\lambda$. (α may or may not itself be an expression within $\mathscr{L}^\lambda$—if α does occur within $\mathscr{L}^\lambda$ we will not, perhaps, be 'translating' it, but we will be 'paraphrasing' it.) We may then define an operator, *translates as*, in the following manner. If a is a name ($a \in E_1$) and β is an expression of $\mathscr{L}^\lambda (\beta \in E^+)$ then

$$\langle a,\ \textit{translates as},\ \langle \theta^+, \beta \rangle \rangle$$

is true under a given interpretation if and only if a names an expression, α, which stands in a particular relationship to the ordered pair of the expression β and the meaning of β under the interpretation in question. The operator, *translates as*, will map entities inside and outside the language $\mathscr{L}^\lambda$ on to sets of expressions, β, within $\mathscr{L}^\lambda$, on the basis of both the meanings, and the extra-semantical features of the expressions, β.

And so, it appears, if the language into which we are translating is one which contains hyperintensional operators, translation will be a process which can be described within that language itself. Thus, hyperintensional logics, particularly ones containing a unified treatment of opaque contexts, should provide a very promising framework for the theory of translation.

Hyperintensional logics enable us to explain how translation into a language can be described in that language itself. However, hyperintensional logics are also relevant to the theory of translation for other, more general reasons. Translation may fairly be described, I think, as a procedure of pairing a sentence in one language with those sentences in another language which share *as many as possible* of their properties with the sentence being translated. The properties we try to preserve through translation will be many and varied; but clearly the most important property we want to preserve is the sentence's *meaning*. Not only is this the most important property we want to preserve: it is also the most difficult to characterise. This is one difficulty on which hyperintensional logics may be able to assist us.

The hyperintensional logic I have outlined rests on an identification of the meanings of sentences with certain abstract, set-theoretical entities, of a kind notably associated with David Lewis. The success of hyperintensional logics in accounting for the semantics of opaque contexts can be taken as confirmation of the Lewis-type characterisation of meanings. If this characterisation of meanings is essentially correct, it will be of considerable assistance in explaining the process of translation. One sentence should be translated by another only if the set-theoretical entity which represents its meaning is an entity which stands in specifiable relationships to the representation of the other sentence's meaning.

There are other plausible approaches to the semantics of opaque contexts. I cannot pretend to have shown that the one I adopt here is the best. It has the questionable feature of resting on talk about possible worlds. But it does have an advantage over many other approaches, in that it gives a formally explicit characterisation of the structures and interrelationships of the meanings of sentences. Without such a characterisation of meanings it is difficult to see how any theoretical basis for translation could be established. Those who avoid speaking of meanings as entities with specifiable structures are likely to be led into radical scepticism about translation.

For instance, Donald Davidson, in a famous article 'On Saying That' (1968), offers an analysis of opaque contexts which does not rest on any characterisation of the meanings of sentences. His analysis does not, I think, give any clear indication of how to handle sentences of the complexity which hyperintensional logics are equipped to deal with. But the point I more especially wish to note here, is that his approach rests on taking as basic and undefined a certain sort of relation which can hold between sentences, and which he calls the 'samesaying' relation. This is, I think, precisely the relation which holds between a sentence and its translation. Thus, Davidson's analysis of opaque contexts rests on the theory of translation; and the theory of translation is, in turn, left without foundations. This blends well with Quine's famous doctrine of the indeterminacy of translation (1960, especially Ch. II). Translations may be performed with Quine's consent, but they cannot be considered objectively right or wrong; and likewise, the idioms of propositional attitudes and speech acts are suitable for use on the street, but are not to be countenanced within science itself.

In order to make translation and opaque contexts scientifically respectable, it appears that we must first of all explain how meanings can be formally characterised and represented: and I think hyperintensional logic does a good deal towards achieving this. Then, after constructing formal representations of meanings, we must show that the things we have constructed are themselves scientifically respectable, and represent something which actually exists. I believe this can be done; but I cannot do it here.

T. Burge

Self-Reference and Translation*

An obvious if little-recognised principle of translation is that translation preserves self-reference if and only if it does not preserve reference.[1] Put more precisely, if e_1 is a singular expression contained in sentence s_1 and e_1 refers to s_1 (or refers to itself), then a truth-value-preserving translation of s_1 into a sentence s_2, and e_1 into a singular expression e_2 contained in s_2 (where $s_1 \neq s_2$ and $e_1 \neq e_2$), will make e_2 refer to s_2 (or itself) if and only if e_2 does not refer to what e_1 refers to.[2] My aim is first to show that the principle is non-vacuous in translation practice—that self-reference is sometimes preserved at the expense of reference. I shall then use the principle to explain certain translations that have been regarded as anomalous. I conclude by suggesting the principle as a key to understanding certain intensional contexts in natural languages.

Let us begin with some simple sentences assertion of which (here and now) involves self-reference:

* A version of this paper was read at Stanford and at Irvine in the winter and spring of 1975. It has benefited from the remarks of various participants. I am also indebted for critical comments to Tony Anderson and Alonzo Church.

1. The principle seems to have been first stated in a fine paper by W. D. Hart (1970).
2. In this paper I shall use 'refers' in a complex sense. A singular term containing no indexical element refers to an object on any occasion if it *denotes* the object. A singular term containing an indexical element refers to an object on a given occasion if it *designates* that object on that occasion. A singular term containing indexical elements and a (possibly complex) predicative condition designates an object on an occasion if given the assignments (if any) on that occasion to the indexical elements (free variables) in the term, the object uniquely satisfies the predicative condition. In the case where the singular term contains indexical elements but no predicative condition, the term will be a single free variable (like 'this') and the term designates an object on an occasion if the term is assigned that object on that occasion. To illustrate the typical case, if I use 'the only table in the room' in an act of reference, the term designates an object under the circumstances if a given room is assigned as a result of my act of reference to the second 'the' (which is plausibly indexical), and a table uniquely satisfies the condition of being a table in that room. (I leave out of consideration the tense implicit in the description.) For a discussion of 'denotes', see Church (1956, Sect. .01). For a fuller and more precise account of indexicals see Burge (1974, 205–23). For discussion of 'designates' as applied to proper names, see Burge (1973, Sect. 2). It should be emphasised that in these articles I use 'refers' differently—to apply to an action by a person, not to a relation between term and object.

(1)   This very sentence begins with a four-letter demonstrative.

(2)   This is to serve warning not to plagiarise.

(3)   (3) makes reference to itself.

I want you, my reader, to understand these sentences as written assertively on the present occasion, and as involving self-reference. For example, you should realise that I have used 'This' in (1) to refer to (1), not to some other sentence that I am coyly concealing.

Although my points about self-reference do not depend on demonstratives (indexical expressions), demonstratives always intrude into the simplest examples. So a word about their comportment under translation is in order. Translation of demonstrative expressions normally differs from indirect discourse reporting of such expressions in that the point of view of the demonstrator is assumed in the translation. For example, in translating an utterance of 'I am hungry' into German, we would use the expression 'Ich bin hungrig', where it is understood from the context (or perhaps made clear informally by the translator) that the referent of the German first-person demonstrative 'ich' is the English-speaker, not the translator. The translator presents the speaker's point of view, rather than reports on it. On the other hand, in reporting the same utterance in indirect discourse we would say, '(He said that) he was hungry', or in German, '(Er sagte dass) er hungrig war'. The first-person demonstrative 'I' is replaced by a third-person demonstrative in order to maintain the point of view of the reporter rather than that of the original speaker.

One can easily imagine cases in which (1)–(3) would be appropriately translated in the reference-preserving way. Indeed, such a translation is probably to be preferred, other things being equal. A literal reference-preserving translation of (1) would be

(4)   Dieser Satz fängt mit einem hinweisenden Artikel mit vier Buchstaben an

where the translator makes it clear that the referent of 'dieser' ('this') is the English sentence uttered by the English speaker. If an interlocutor were to translate a teacher's utterance of (1) for a somewhat dull German student of English, he would perhaps use (4).

But sometimes the intent of the sentence's user is better captured by preserving not reference, but self-reference. If the present paper were translated into German, the reference-preserving translation of (1)—and of (2)–(3)—would be a bad one. This is because the point of using and displaying the sentences on the present occasion is to illustrate self-reference. The appropriate translation of (1) would be

(5) Dieser Satz fängt mit einem hinweisenden Artikel mit sechs Buchstaben an.

This translation preserves self-reference at the expense of reference, for the translation is to be taken to refer to itself, rather than to its English counterpart (1). It should be noted that to preserve self-reference and truth-value, we must sometimes translate expressions other than the singular term that effects the self-reference in such a way as to fail to preserve *their* referents, or extensions if they are predicates. In (5) we had to make a compensatory translation of the term 'four' into 'sechs' ('six') in order to preserve the truth-value of the self-referential sentence.

Self-referential translation is demanded in informal expositions of meta-mathematics. Gödel's proof that not all arithmetically valid sentences are provable is based on the strategy of constructing a sentence within arithmetic to the effect:

(6) (6) is not a theorem.

In translating an informal exposition of Gödel's theorem that contained (6) into German, one would preserve self-reference, not reference, in order to convey the point and coherence of the accompanying exposition. That is, the translation (even if numbered '(6)') would refer to itself not to our (6).

(6), of course, refers to itself by way of the demonstrative device '(6)'. But indexical expressions are not crucial to our point about translation. Let 'w' be a variable ranging over expressions and let 'S_1' be a name of 'w'. Then the effect of (6) can be caught without demonstratives by

(7) The result of putting the quotation of 'The result of putting the quotation of w for S_1 in w is not a theorem' for S_1 in 'The result of putting the quotation of w for S_1 in w is not a theorem' is not a theorem.

(7) says of itself that it is not a theorem. (For (7) *is* the result of the construction it describes. (7) results from starting with the expression:

The result of putting the quotation of w for S_1 in w is not a theorem and then putting the quotation of that expression for S_1 (i.e. for 'w').) A foreign translation of (7), insofar as (7) occurs in a discussion of Gödel's result, would not only have to alter the reference of the subject singular term in (7); it would also have to change the referents of the quotations, so that the appropriate foreign expression would be quoted.[3] Otherwise, the translation would not convey the point of the illustration of Gödel's method. A referential translation would indeed *describe* for foreign readers the example, but it would not translate it so as to be intelligible for someone who did not understand English. And surely the primary purpose of translation is to make foreign discourse intelligible to someone who does not understand that discourse.

I have focused on *informal* counterparts of the Gödel sentence for two reasons. First, in Gödel's original article the expressions of the language P in which the argument is carried out are introduced by being quoted. Translations of the article give the quotations the identity translation (as they should), then carry out the argument in precisely the same notation that Gödel used. Since the English translation of Gödel's article is (in the relevant passages) the identity translation, no schism between reference and self-reference occurs. Second, Gödel's argument does not strictly involve self-reference, but something analogous, self-representation via a system of Gödel numbering.[4]

The Gödel argument, however, is suggestive of an important point. Preservation of non-demonstrative self-reference is sometimes the only way to preserve the soundness of an argument under translation without adding additional premises. We may illustrate this point by a thought experiment. Suppose that a language like Quine's proto-syntax—a language containing at least the grammar of quantification theory together with resources for describing its own syntax—were widely used in English-speaking countries for formulating certain metamathematical arguments. And suppose the language were used so routinely that English-speaking logicians did not bother to take up journal space by introducing the expressions of the language explicitly: they assume the syntax and intended reading of the notation to be understood. Suppose that in Poland Polish notation (with syntactical primitives) were routinely used under analogous conditions. Now suppose that Quine's proto-syntax were employed to show its own incompleteness by

---

3. (7) is lifted verbatim from Quine (1962, 307). The only translations of this work, those into Spanish and Polish, bear out my point: cf. the Spanish translation by Jose Hierro S.-Pescador (p. 299), and the Polish translation by Leon Koj (pp. 298–9); cf. also Kleene (1950, 205); and the Spanish translation by Manuel Garrido (p. 191).

4. Kurt Gödel (1931, cf. p. 176).

means of a Gödel-like argument involving self-reference.[5] Since, under our imagined conditions, there would be no explicit introduction of the formal language, the argument would begin by setting out the axioms of quantification theory and syntax, and would go on to give definitions of notions like theoremhood. A translation of the article into Polish (and the argument into Polish notation) would have to preserve self-reference at the expense of reference. Otherwise the soundness of the argument could not be preserved unless certain metalinguistic premises (connecting Quinish and Polish) were added.

The notion of translation that I have appealed to is a notion based on actual translation practice (cf. note 3). Translations which are commonly recognised as good ones sometimes do not preserve the reference of the expressions being translated, and sometimes this results from a concern with preserving self-reference. This perspective on translation conflicts with a standard philosophical notion, to wit, that a good translation expresses the same proposition expressed by the sentence it translates. For it is widely assumed among philosophers that sentences whose terms have different references cannot express the same proposition. I do not wish to quarrel with this assumption here, or even to dispute the heuristic or normative value of the standard philosophical notion of good translation. I simply want to emphasise that (so interpreted) the notion does not accord with actual translation practice.

In one sense, the departure of actual practice from reference-preserving translation should come as no surprise to the traditional philosophical view. Good translation of literature often preserves rhyme, rhythm, alliteration, tone, or idiom, at the expense of 'literal meaning' and even reference. And poetic licence might be thought to extend beyond the domain of literature, so that preservation of self-reference might be assimilated to 'licentious', albeit common, translation practice. (What is wrong with the common translations, it might be said, is that they are so common.)

This assimiliation, patronising though it might seem, is suggestive: a unified theory of translation should treat all cases of translation under a single set of context-keyed rules. But the assimilation is also over-facile. The occurrence of self-referential translation in technical scientific work can hardly be dismissed as a literary indulgence (cf. note 3).

Liberty and licence are not virtues in translations of metamathematical treatises. What counts is preservation of 'information value' or 'cognitive content'—not tone or style. This distinction between content and style is a vague heuristic one, of course—less clearcut even than we commonly allow

5. Quine (1962, Sects. 53–60).

ourselves to assume. But intuitively our examples of self-reference do not yield to the objection that they are merely cases in which style is preserved to the detriment of content. Self-referential translations sometimes appear to be better at preserving 'information value' or 'cognitive content' than their referential counterparts. A reference-preserving translation of (7) into Polish would be less informative to a provincial Pole than its self-referential alternative. Moreover, self-referential translation of a passage containing (7), or a Gödel-like argument of the sort we imagined earlier, better preserves the coherence of the passage or the soundness of the argument as a whole. Preservation of these values (cognitive values, note) sometimes requires relinquishing the attempt to preserve the reference of some component expressions.

The moral is that good translation is responsible for preserving certain global characteristics of discourse, as well as more local features. One cannot always read off the best translation of a sentence (at an occurrence) simply by understanding the sentence itself. It is necessary to understand the wider context in which the sentence is used—the presuppositions and intentions of the user, and the character of the passage or argument in which the sentence is embedded.

Context will bear not only on the question of whether to choose the usual referential translation or to opt for a self-referential one. It will also bear sometimes on the choice of self-referential translation. For example, given that we have decided to translate:

The seventh word of this sentence has three letters

self-referentially, it still remains open whether to translate it as:

Das siebte Wort dieses Satzes hat vier Buchstaben

or as

Das sechste Wort dieses Satzes hat drei Buchstaben.

If one translation is better than the other, this will be determinable only by taking into account the English user's intentions and the character of the discussion in which the English sentence appears. In some cases, the choice may simply be a matter of indifference.

Nothing in what follows depends on precisely what role one gives self-reference in one's theory of translation. It will not matter whether or not one is attracted to the comparison between translation of poetry and self-reference-preserving translation. It is enough for my purposes that one recognises the phenomenon of self-referential translation as occurring in respectable practice. In the light of this phenomenon, an important form of argument in the philosophy of language requires reformulation. The Langford translation test runs, in Langford's words, as follows:

> There is a simple test which helps us to determine whether a word is being used or talked about, namely, that of translation. A word that is being used is to be translated, while a word that is being talked about must not be (subject matter must remain unchanged under translation).[6]

As Langford makes clear, the test assumes that reference *must* remain unchanged under translation. As we have seen, this assumption is false. The test must therefore be revised to read: An expression that is being used is to be translated, while an expression that is being mentioned must not be translated—unless an element of self-reference associated with the sentence that contains the expression requires such translation.

The Langford translation test has been deployed chiefly to argue against certain analyses of intensional contexts that treat expressions in such contexts as functioning autonomously (as referring to themselves). The best-known argument of this kind is Church's criticism of Carnap's analysis of statements of assertion and belief. Church pointed out that a sentence like:

(8)   Seneca said that man is a rational animal

translates into German as:

(9)   Seneca hat gesagt, dass der Mensch ein vernünftiges Tier sei

—not into a German sentence that mentions the English expression 'man is a rational animal'. In view of this, Church argued that (8) itself does not mention the expression 'man is a rational animal', as Carnap's analysis required, and that propositions, not sentences, are the 'objects' of indirect discourse.[7] The argument explicitly assumes the validity of the Langford translation test and thus stands in need of reformulation in the same way

6. Langford (1937, 53–4).
7. Church (1950; 1951b); Carnap (1947). Although Church cites Langford's test, he couches his argument in terms of preservation of meaning rather than preservation of reference. Most criticisms of the argument have focused on Church's assumptions about meaning. It is important to see therefore that the argument at bottom depends on the less controversial notion of reference.

that the test did. Reformulated, the argument concludes: (8) does not mention the English expression 'man is a rational animal'—unless there is some element of self-reference associated with (8), preservation of which is required for good translation.

Is there some such element of self-reference associated with (8)? According to the type of analysis Church criticises, the expressions in intensional contexts do refer to themselves. But this point does not, in and of itself, refute Church. For there is no apparent reason why this element should be preserved in good translation.[8] In order to suggest a source of self-reference in (8), I want to turn to some closely related sentences.

Ever since the Langford test became well known among philosophers and logicians, certain exceptions to the test have been recognised. In translating a piece of foreign literature or a historical report that contains dialogue or other quoted matter, it is usual and proper to translate the quoted material. Such quoted matter differs from the direct discourse cited by Church in his argument against Carnap. For whereas in the latter, reference to the quoted expressions is normally preserved under translation, in the former the quoted expressions themselves undergo translation. Yet there is little reason to doubt that the expressions that are quoted in such dialogue are being mentioned or talked about. The translatability of the expressions does not itself provide such a reason, since in mathematical expositions of the sort discussed above, it is clear from the nature and intent of the discourse that *expressions* are mentioned by the quotations (cf. (7))—yet the quoted expressions are translated. (Indeed, the quotations in (7) may be plausibly regarded as the 'purest', most uninterpreted type; for they occur in proof-theoretic discourse.) Moreover, there appears to be no independent ground for claiming that the logical form of ordinary dialogue makes no reference at all to the quoted expressions.

The cited exceptions to the Langford test have been regarded as mere literary convention or as somehow anomalous to ordinary translation practice. There has been no attempt, to my knowledge, to explain the 'anomalies'.[9]

---

8. Carnap's analysis does not make any real use of self-reference. Although we may assume that he retained his view from *The Logical Syntax of Language* that expressions in natural-language 'that-clauses' function autonomously, his formal analysis of belief contexts in *Meaning and Necessity* does not involve or cite self-reference at all. It should be emphasised that merely attributing an indexical element to the discourse (which Carnap does not emphasise, but which others have suggested on his behalf) does not explain the translation shifts. For the reference of demonstratives is typically preserved under translation.

9. A worthwhile discussion of them, however, may be found in Goodman (1974). Although the practice of translating quoted material has been demeaned as 'anomalous' and 'literary', it is sometimes invoked in translations of the most rigorous writing about

Of course, translation of foreign quoted material aims at conveying the 'point' of the passage that contains it. Our problem is to express that 'point' and explain why reference is not preserved under translation.

Our previous discussion suggests that there is some element of self-reference in these passages whose preservation forces the shifts of reference.[10] A tempting hypothesis is that the sentences containing the relevant dialogue involve implicit reference to the language in which they themselves are to be construed as occurring. On this hypothesis, the sentence:

(10)   Ivan said, 'There is a strength to endure everything'

as translated from Russian dialogue in *The Brothers Karamazov* could be paraphrased:

(11)   Ivan said, 'There is a strength to endure everything', taken as a sentence of the language of this very sentence.

where 'this very sentence' applies self-referentially to the containing sentence, (11).

In employing the term 'the language of this very sentence', a user of (11) takes advantage of a certain context-dependence that affects the use and interpretation of all symbols. Any symbol, being merely a certain shape or sound, may be used in indefinitely many ways; it could in principle be included in indefinitely many dialects or languages. So there is a sense in which any asserted sentence is inter-linguistically ambiguous—or possibly so. This inter-linguistic ambiguity (or the possibility of it) cannot be dispelled by a context-independent specification of the language in which the sentence is intended to occur. For, of course, any such specification would be subject to the same sort of ambiguity. There is thus an ineliminable element of context-dependence in the employment and understanding of symbols. We cannot specify the intended interpretation of symbols we do use (or might use—imagine a recursive specification of the interpretations of

---

language. Cf. for example, Tarski (1956b, 159, 169). The instance of the truth schema cited in the translation ('"Snow is white" is true if and only if snow is white') itself illustrates the point! It is a translation of a German instance that nowhere mentions an English expression. The phenomenon also occurs in Frege (1966, 50).

10. One might find self-reference in giving semantical analysis to quotation marks. But this would not provide us with an explanation of the reference shifts—any more than ascribing an autonomous function to expressions in indirect discourse explains such shifts. The element of self-reference must be such that its preservation is crucial to conveying the 'point' of the passage.

infinitely many expressions) without presupposing an intended interpretation for symbols we use to make the specification. Employing symbols involves intending them in a certain way on occasions of their employment. Understanding symbols involves utilising convention and context to construe them as intended. Although the sentence (11) may occur in multiple languages, we understand it as intended in understanding actual uses of it.

A paraphrase like (11) not only suggests an implicit element of self-reference in sentences like (10), it provides the basis for an explanation of why self-reference, not reference, should be preserved in translations of those sentences. The point of these sentences is to mention words in the intended language of the sentences themselves that best convey the utterance of the speaker.

This characterisation of the sentences that have been recognised as exceptions to the Langford test seems very nearly right. But there are two reasons for being dissatisfied with it. In the first place, a sentence like (11) is less plausible as a paraphrase of a sentence like (10) than as an explication. Ordinary speakers would not recognise an implicit grammatical construction in (10) that effects reference to a language, or to any other entity. The self-reference that is crucial to the point of sentences like (11) is not a part of the grammar or semantics of the sentences themselves. It is better seen as involved in a convention presupposed in the use and understanding of such sentences. In the second place, there is little reason to believe that the relevant self-reference involves reference to anything as global as a language. What is involved in rightly construing the expressions that are mentioned in problem sentences like (10) is merely the ability to understand those expressions as they would be intended if they were used by the person who uses the relevant token of the sentence in which they are mentioned. For example, rightly construing the expression 'There is a strength to endure everything' in (10) requires the ability to understand uses of that expression by the person—say, the translator—who uses (10). Of course, in the normal case we need not be acquainted with the translator to understand her would-be intentions. Familiarity with communal conventions is usually sufficient to put us in touch with the intentions of a stranger.

We may thus take the relevant uses of (10) as presupposing a convention that associates an element of self-reference with (10) and which accounts for the shifts of reference under translation. Specifically, the convention is as follows:

(C₁) Uses of a verb under its translatable direct discourse reading presuppose that the expressions mentioned in the direct object of the verb are to be understood as they would be understood if they were used as an embedded sentence (rather than merely mentioned), at the time of the use of the verb, by the person who uses the relevant token of the containing sentence.[11]

For example, if I were now to use the sentence 'Tarski said, "Snow is white" ' in the relevant sense, convention (C_1) would bid you to interpret the mentioned expression 'Snow is white' as you would if I had used it.

Convention (C_1) creates the effect of self-reference in that it relates the interpretation of the mentioned expressions to that of the very sentence in which they occur. The convention applies to the terms of other languages that translate the 'said' of translatable direct discourse. So to properly formulate the sentences in which these terms occur, it is necessary to preserve the element of self-reference that the convention provides. Thus in translating sentences like (10) into foreign expressions and back, the quoted material must be translated. Actually, if one prefers, one may formulate the relevant convention so as to apply only to 'said' (appropriately read), and then think of counterpart conventions as governing the terms of other languages that translate the 'said' of translatable direct discourse. Either way, mentioned expressions will undergo translation in order to preserve an element of self-reference associated with the relevant sentence.

Of course, in cases where the quoted expressions following 'said' contain demonstrative or indexical expressions, the user of the containing sentence (the reporter) must maintain the point of view of the speaker. Take for example, the sentence

Ivan said, 'The purpose of your visit is to convince me of your existence'.

The convention says to interpret the quoted expressions as they would be interpreted if they were used by the person who uses the relevant token of the containing sentence. In this case the person is either I or Constance Garnett, the relevant translator of Dostoevski's book. The hypothetical use is a use by the person in the role of translator (as opposed to independent

---

11. We indicate the appropriate interpretation by reference to embedded use for the following reason. The person who uses the sentence containing translatable direct discourse may himself be multilingual in such a way that the quoted expression occurs in more than one of his languages. By relating the quoted expression to the interpretation of the containing asserted sentence, we relate the interpretation of that expression to the context-dependent resolution of inter-linguistic ambiguity that we mentioned earlier. An example of the sort of embedded use I have in mind is: Ivan said, 'There is a strength to endure everything' and there is a strength to endure everything. Of course, this device does not touch intra-linguistic ambiguity. But in a formal theory this can be handled in one of the standard ways.

asserter) presenting Ivan's viewpoint. Thus the expression 'me' is to be understood as I would use it as surrogate-speaker for Ivan, so that the referent of 'me', as I would use it in this role, is Ivan. A convention analogous to (C_1) that backed indirect discourse uses of 'said' would take indexical expressions in the 'content' clause to be used from the viewpoint of the reporter rather than the speaker.

The central feature of our interpretation of sentences like (10) is the *construal* of the expressions mentioned in those sentences. In and of themselves linguistic expressions are nothing more than certain shapes or sounds that may be used or interpreted in indefinitely many ways. The interpretation of a symbol is conventional or contextual and thus depends on the customs and expectations of its local employers. In certain contexts, however, an expression may be mentioned in a way that does not prescind from its meaning or potential use in those contexts, but rather presupposes a certain meaning or potential use.

As noted earlier, this practice roughly distinguishes translatable direct discourse from the sort of direct discourse usually cited by logicians and philosophers. We may call this latter sort 'uninterpreted direct discourse' because no interpretation of the quoted material is presupposed by the reporter, so the quotation is left intact under translation. What is more, uninterpreted direct discourse implies that the quoted material was actually uttered by the speaker, whereas translatable direct discourse does not. Uninterpreted direct discourse is clearly important in disciplines, such as phonetics or proof theory, which quite self-consciously 'abstract' from the meaning of the expressions under study. In most cases, however, it is unimportant to distinguish between the two sorts of discourse (although as a matter of fact ordinary speakers do tend to presuppose an interpretation of familiar expressions when they are quoted in direct discourse). As long as we are reporting the words of a compatriot, the two will be practically equivalent.[12]

---

12. It is perhaps worth noting that whether or not the direct discourse in a sentence is translated is not an infallible criterion for determining whether the discourse is translatable or uninterpreted. Suppose William writes out the following silly and misleading, but probably valid, argument: (a) Tarski said, 'Snow is white'; (b) 'Snow is white' is Quine's favourite English sentence; so (c) Tarski said Quine's favourite English sentence. Let us suppose that (a) contains translatable direct discourse, on three grounds: suppose that although (a) is true, Tarski never uttered the words 'Snow is white'; suppose that William takes (a) from an English translation of the proceedings of a Warsaw conference on semantics in which Tarski participated (speaking Polish); and suppose that William presupposes the familiar interpretation of 'Snow is white'. (The first and third of these grounds would be sufficient to count (a) as containing translatable direct discourse.) Now suppose that we are asked to translate (a)–(b)–(c) into German. A sentence-by-sentence

Both sorts of direct discourse differ from indirect discourse. Indirect discourse differs from uninterpreted direct discourse in all the ways translatable direct discourse does. The expressions ascribed to the speaker in indirect discourse are not, of course, quoted. But they may be regarded as mentioned by the that-clause and otherwise construed in a way analogous to the way they are construed in translatable direct discourse. It should be clear how this viewpoint can be mobilised to meet the Church–Langford translation objection to taking expressions as 'objects' of indirect discourse. Indirect discourse, however, is not merely translatable direct discourse in disguise. The most important difference is illustrated by the behaviour of indexical expressions. In the that-clauses of indirect discourse, the context of the reporter is assumed, so that indexicals are used from his point of view. Indexicals occurring in translatable direct discourse, as we have noted earlier, maintain the viewpoint of the speaker. These points bear refinement in an adequate treatment of transparent (as opposed to oblique or intensional) indirect-discourse contexts. But for the present, we may allow them to stand.

The importance of translatable direct discourse as an analogue to indirect discourse has been obscured, I think, primarily by the role of uninterpreted direct discourse as a paradigm for a certain practice in metamathematics. The development of a rigorous axiomatic method in studies of geometry and proof theory depended on 'abstracting' from the intuitive meaning of symbols occurring in the axioms. It has become a convention among theorists in these fields that to mention a symbol is so far to presuppose nothing about its use. The heuristic success of this practice in metamathematics is adequate justification for it in that domain. But the practice has served to entrench a certain view of meaning which is easily associated with it. The idea is that since meaning is 'extrinsic' to linguistic expressions (which, after all, are merely certain shapes or sounds), any attempt to take the meaning of an

---

translation that ignored the context of the argument would yield: (a′) Tarski sagte 'Schnee ist weiss'; (b′) 'Snow is white' ist Quines liebster englisher Satz; (c′) Tarski sagte Quines liebsten englischen Satz. Such a translation fails to preserve validity. We might try translating the quoted matter in (b), and translate 'English' as 'Deutsch'. But such a translation, though validity-preserving (assuming (a′) and (c′) unchanged), might not preserve truth. The most likely escape would be to translate (a) as (a″): Tarski sagte, 'Snow is white'—retaining (b′) and (c′), and adding a footnote that gave the German counterpart of 'Snow is white'. Here is a case in which the normal self-referential translation of translatable direct discourse in (a) is overridden by considerations regarding global features of the surrounding passage. We end up preserving reference instead of self-reference. The footnote in effect tells the German reader how the mentioned expression is to be construed. It is construed as it would be if it were used by the English speaker, William.

expression (in a certain context) into account must explicitly relate that expression to the relevant meaning.[13]

This point of view has guided work in formal semantics since the inception of the subject. But the idea that meaning is extrinsic to an expression tends to run together two views. One is that how a symbol is to be construed depends on context and is not to be determined by analysing the symbol *per se*. This obvious point issues in the demand that a semantical theory make the 'context' explicit by relating expressions to other entities. The least controversial meeting of this demand has been the systems of extensional semantics which assign denotations or referents to expressions and explain truth conditions in terms of these assignments. But referents are not all there is to meaning.

The need to account for the elements of meaning 'over and above' referents suggests the second view implicit in the idea that meaning is extrinsic to an expression. This is the view that an account of meaning should relate an expression to some non-linguistic 'intensional' entity, which *is* its meaning. This view has come in for a lot of criticism, but the criticism has only occasionally been supplemented by an account of intensional contexts that fills the needs of a semantical theory. Most work within the formal semantical tradition has adopted the view. (I am thinking of the work of Frege and Church, of Russell, of Carnap and of the various possible-world approaches.) Here is not the place to discuss this complex issue, or various alternative ways of dealing with it. But in the space that remains I want to set out how my approach stands with respect to the two views implicit in the idea that meaning is extrinsic to an expression.

Adequate semantical accounts of translatable direct discourse and indirect discourse cannot be content with merely assigning an expression as referent of the quotation or that-clause. For it is clear from the facts of translation that in some sense the relevant speaker is related to the relevant expression only 'taken together with its meaning'. And whereas it is perfectly natural for ordinary language-users to rely on context to indicate the intended interpretation of the mentioned expression, a semantical theory should not

---

13. This point is the crux of one of Church's criticisms of Carnap (cf. note 7). To account for the contextual relativity of the interpretation of an expression, Carnap relativised expressions (which were his 'objects' of indirect discourse and belief) to a language. This move is similar to (11), except that Carnap made no provision for self-reference (cf. note 8) and thus was vulnerable to a version of the Church–Langford objection. As has been often noted, the appeal to a language really amounts to an appeal to intensional entities like meanings or propositions. And in view of the intuitive implausibility of the relativisation (noted against (11)), I would prefer Church's analysis of indirect discourse and belief to Carnap's—if appeal to intensional entities were unavoidable.

do so. For the reliance on context should itself receive analysis insofar as possible (cf. note 13).

Since sentences like (10) do not plausibly contain as part of their syntactical or semantical structures devices for referring to a language (or to a person, time, and token, as specified by convention (C_1)), the contextual relativity is not plausibly analysed in the usual way—by assigning entities to expressions in the formal representation of the sentence by some rule governing variations in context.[14] An account of the contextual relativity should be based on specifying the convention presupposed in uses of the 'said' of translatable direct discourse or indirect discourse. Of course, the convention does not spell out in advance how to interpret what the speaker 'said', any more than a theory of demonstrative constructions specifies the referents of those constructions in advance of a person's uses of them. The convention does, however, give directions for interpreting the quoted expressions or the expression mentioned by the that-clause. Note what these directions assume. They assume that to interpret uses of 'said' as it is relevantly intended in sentences like (8) or (10), we must be able to understand potential uses, by the user of 'said', of the expressions mentioned in the subsequent that-clause or quotation. The mentioned expressions' implicit relativity to an interpretation is fixed by the ineliminably context-dependent understanding of the expressions used in the containing sentence. The context-dependence treated by the convention we have cited is thus a special case of the pervasive, earlier-mentioned context-dependence—the context-dependence that is intrinsic to the use and interpretation of all symbols, natural or formal.

To illustrate more concretely this approach to expressions' relativity to an interpretation, let us focus on the form of the semantical theory. A semantical theory, as I conceive it, takes the form (partly) of a Tarskian theory of truth. Translations of sentences like (10) into the metalanguage in which the theory is given will themselves presuppose a convention like (C_1). In using such translations on the right sides of instances of Tarski's truth schema, the theorist will be mentioning certain expressions in his metalanguage. For example, in the instance for (10) he will be mentioning expressions that translate 'There is a strength to endure everything'. The convention says to interpret these mentioned expressions as one would interpret them if they were used by the theorist. Since the mentioned symbols occur in the theory and translate object-language sentences, they themselves will appear (as used) on the right side of an instance of the Tarski truth schema. Thus we can always effectively produce a case in which the mentioned expression is used, for the expression always occurs in a theorem of the

14. For an example of how this is done, see Burge (1974).

theory. Once the convention is explicitly stated, the theorist need not make explicit how the relevant mentioned expressions are used (or interpreted) any more than he need make explicit how the symbols he uses in his theory are used—assuming that those symbols are antecedently understood, or have been antecedently explained. The appropriate use of the mentioned expressions is presupposed in the very understanding of the sentence in which they are mentioned.

The idea that meaning is extrinsic to a symbol suggests not only that interpreting a symbol depends on the symbol's context, but also that a semantical theory should somehow relate symbols to intensional *entities*. The reason I gave for not treating sentences like (10) (or (8)) as implicitly relative to a contextually determined language was that understanding the mentioned sentence does not require determining anything as global as a language (cf. also note 13). This reason does not rule out relativising the sentence to an extra-linguistic proposition. We might have rephrased the convention to read: understand the mentioned sentence as expressing the proposition it would express if it were used by the relevant person at the relevant time.

My reason for not taking this course is that stating the presupposed convention does not appear to require commitment to propositions. I rely on the notion of understanding a sentence as used by a certain person at a certain time. For the present, at least, I take this notion as primitive. To formulate the convention in terms of propositions, as suggested above, would be to suggest that the notion of understanding a sentence on an occasion of use amounts to the notion of 'grasping' a proposition expressed by the sentence on that occasion. I find this implausible. Regardless of the usefulness of postulating propositions for other purposes, the notion of proposition as something to be grasped seems to be of no help in understanding understanding. Indeed, the question of the nature of the psychological relation between person and proposition has always been a soft spot in proposition theory.

Of course, explicating the counterfactual element in convention (C_1) and explicating the idea of understanding a sentence on an occasion of use are notoriously difficult projects. To embark on these projects here would be to stray. Let it suffice to say that the chief arguments for postulating propositions have never focused either on the analysis of counterfactuals *per se* or on the idea of understanding an assertive utterance. There are, to be sure, analyses of counterfactuals and of understanding that rely on propositions. But the chief arguments for such reliance derive from considerations regarding indirect-discourse and propositional-attitude contexts, and contexts involving talk about different sentences meaning the same thing. Insofar as our approach to sentences like (8) and (10) applies to these contexts, it removes the primary motivations for postulating propositions in explicating the notions in convention (C_1). These remarks are, of course, merely programmatic. In this paper, I have done no more than show how the Church–Langford argument for postulating propositions in analyses of indirect discourse may be circumvented.

It should be evident though that much more is at stake than sentences like (8) and (10). The approach I have outlined may be applied to propositional-attitude contexts—sentences that ascribe belief, desire, intention and so on—and to a wide range of other intensional idioms. But the applications are decidedly non-trivial since they demand discussion of numerous important issues in semantics, ontology and the philosophy of mind. Development of these matters will be matter for other occasions.

IV

TRANSLATABILITY, EXPRESSIBILITY, EFFABILITY

Edward L. Keenan

Some Logical Problems in Translation

... translation is just like chewing food that is to be fed to others. If one cannot chew the food oneself, one has to be given food that has been already chewed. Such food however is bound to be poorer in taste and flavour than the original.

Kumarajiva (trans. of Buddhist texts into Chinese, cited in Fung Yi-Lan, 1948)

THE PURPOSE OF this paper is to evaluate what we shall call the Exact Translation Hypothesis, given below.

The Exact Translation Hypothesis (ETH)
Anything that can be said in one natural language can be translated exactly into any other language.

We shall argue that the ETH is incorrect by exhibiting, in section 3, sentences from certain languages whose meaning is not *exactly* expressed by any sentence in certain other languages we consider. To substantiate the argument we will show that either the given sentence has certain semantic properties which the purported translations do not, or else that the purported translations have certain properties which the original fails to have. Thus it will appear that any attempted translation either overshoots or undershoots the mark.

It is obvious that for such an argument to be valid even in principle we must specify which properties of sentences are the relevant semantic ones. That is, we must be able to agree antecedent to our argument, that if one sentence has a certain property and another does not then that is sufficient to say that neither is an exact translation of the other. In section 2 we present a few such criteria which, while not exhaustive, are sufficient for our purposes.

First, however, we would like to consider several arguments that have been advanced in favour of the ETH which do not depend on the choice of translation criteria. We shall argue that these arguments do not justify the ETH, and further, that other facts we know about natural language justify the expectation that the ETH fails. That is, we shall argue that the nature of natural language is such that we do not expect perfect translatibility between languages to hold, and that the burden of proof in this matter falls on those who advocate the ETH, not on those who deny it.

1. *The primae facie case*

1.1 The first argument in support of the ETH, advanced e.g. by Steklis and Harnad (1975), is an essentially negative one. It runs as follows. In order to justify the claim that a sentence S in some language L cannot be adequately translated into e.g. English we must be able to explain (in English) what properties S has which fail to be captured in English. This explanation itself provides the basic translation of the original sentence!

This argument fails because the sentences we might naturally use to explain the meaning of the original will, in many cases, be 'metalinguistic'. That is, they may talk about the words or phrases in the original, or at least talk about their meanings. But the original sentence does not talk about words, or their meanings, so the explanatory sentences cannot themselves constitute the English sentence whose semantic properties are exactly the same as those of the original. For example, in section 3 we will argue that Hopi presents sentences whose meaning is basically the same as e.g. *John thinks that he will win*, except that the Hopi verb *win* carries a marker which forces the meaning that the person John is thinking about is necessarily different from John himself. The English sentence of course is unmarked or vague in this respect.

The above explanation of the meaning of the Hopi sentence actually talks about the meanings of parts of that sentence, so the English sentence which constitute the explanation of the meaning of the sentence are very different semantically from the Hopi sentence itself, and so cannot themselves constitute a translation of it which satisfies the ETH. For that, we must find a single (perhaps complex) English sentence which has all and only the semantic properties of the Hopi original. Note that we are not claiming that we could not find other, perhaps less metalinguistic explanations, but only that in many cases the natural explanations are metalinguistic. The claim that we could always find non-metalinguistic explanations would have to be justified. And in the absence of such justification this argument in support of the ETH fails.

1.2 A second, stronger argument in favour of the ETH comes from Katz (this volume, and 1972, 18–24) who argues that translatability of languages follows from the Effability Hypothesis which all languages are held to satisfy.

Effability Hypothesis[1] (EH)

Anything that can be thought can be said.

So if there is a sentence in some language, which expresses a thought (i.e. it is not semantically anomalous), then speakers of other languages can, by the EH, also express that thought. This informal argument, that the ETH follows from the EH, can be attacked[2] but we feel that the basic intuition is right enough that a more explicit formulation would still preserve the essentials of the argument. Where we differ from Katz however is in accepting the EH, as stated.

Note first that, by and large,[3] Katz does not argue for the EH by claiming that it follows from other independently known facts about the nature of human language. Rather, the EH hypothesis itself is taken as one of the defining parameters of a possible human language. It is what differentiates human languages from e.g. bee language on the one hand (where only a very

1. Katz's (this volume) exact formulation of the Effability Hypothesis is: 'Each proposition can be expressed by some sentence in any natural language'. For purposes of introducing the essential idea of the EH we have chosen not to introduce the technical term 'proposition'.

2. For example, perhaps the only way a speaker of one language could express a given thought expressed in a sentence of some other language would be to learn the other language. This would appear to satisfy the EH as stated but in such a case the ETH would fail.

3. Katz (1972, 19) does claim some empirical support for the EH. Namely, 'I take it as some empirical evidence for the claim that natural languages are effable that speakers almost always find appropriate sentences to express their thoughts, that difficulties in thinking of a sentence are invariably regarded as a failing on the part of the speaker rather than of the language, . . .' But the status of this 'empirical' support is equivocal. We have all experienced difficulties in attempting to express our thoughts or feelings to someone. And often our thoughts remain very imperfectly expressed. (Recall all the papers we started to write but never finished.) Who is to say that the difficulty lies in our poor ingenuity in using the language rather than in the inherent limitations of the language itself (Katz offers no empirical support for this latter claim)? Why is the case not like our inability to express the validity of the sentence *if all men are mortal and Socrates is a man then Socrates is mortal* in the language of sentential logic (in which the only logical operators are negation, disjunction, conjunction, if-then, and if and only if, and in which quantifiers and one-place predicate symbols are not grammatical categories)? It seems possible at least that Katz's opinion that the difficulty above lies in ourselves and not in our language stems from a highly Rationalist view of the universe in which everything is held to be ultimately knowable. But this is an attitude prevalent, at best, only in Western science. We note, from Lao Tzu (the 'founder' of Taoism), 'One who knows does not talk. One who talks does not know.' Or again, from the Chinese poet T'ao Ch'ien (372-427):

> The mountain air is fresh at the dusk of day;
> The flying birds two by two return.
> In these things there lies a deep meaning;
> Yet when we would express it, words suddenly fail us.

> (Arthur Waley, trans. cited in Fung Yu-Lan, 1948)

restricted class of things can be talked about, e.g. direction and distance of the honey source) and the formal languages of mathematics on the other (where, e.g. in the language of Euclidean geometry all we can talk about are points and lines, and the relations like 'is parallel to', 'intersects', etc. which obtain among them). The claim is then that it is simply the basic nature of natural language to enable people to talk about whatever they can experience and think about.

We are basically in sympathy with this point of view, but feel it represents only a partial truth about human language. We will argue here that human language must meet another requirement, the Efficiency Requirement, which entails that the EH as stated by Katz be weakened, or perhaps just stated more precisely. And the revised version of the EH *is* compatible with the failure of the ETH.

Efficiency Requirement (ER)

A human language must permit the communication of thoughts in a way that is reasonably efficient relative to the lifespan and cognitive capabilities of human beings.

The ER seems innocuous enough. It eliminates as candidates for human languagehood 'languages' in which every sentence has more than a trillion words. Such a language could not be learned within the lifespan of human beings and could not be used to communicate everyday thoughts in a way that is compatible with normal human behaviour. It would take years for example just to say 'You're standing on my foot'. This is simply too long a time span to make the utterance useful in getting the person to remove his foot from yours.

But notice, that although my example is facetious, it is trivial to construct a language which has the expressive power of English but in which all the sentences are over a trillion words long. Namely, consider simply the set of English sentences having more than a trillion words. Let us call it Kooky-English. Now any simple sentence S in ordinary English is logically equivalent to one of the form 'Either S or K, and furthermore it is not the case that K', where K is some sentence from Kooky-English. So Kooky-English meets the EH but not the ER and so is not a possible human language, and the ER is independently motivated as a constraint on the form of possible human languages.

Now we want to claim that the efficiency requirement justifies the claim that human languages are, by nature, *imprecise*. That is, we claim that human language must be imprecise in order to permit efficient communication. The reason is that not only is it the case that we must be able to talk about an unlimited range of phenomena, but we must be able to do so in an even more diverse range of communication situations. Probably each particular act of communication takes place in a situation that is unique in terms of what relevant knowledge the speaker and addressee share (and know to be shared) concerning the topic under discussion. The norm in understanding an utterance of a sentence is that the addressee infers the thought of the hearer partly on the basis of what was literally encoded in the syntax of the sentence, and partly on the basis of independent knowledge of the topic under discussion. Consequently, as a norm, a speaker does not express his thought *exactly*. He adapts the expression of his thought to (what he takes to be) the addressee's knowledge of the subject matter at hand.

We shall consider here two types of examples which justify the claim that language imprecision facilitates communication efficiency.

1.2.1   First, consider an utterance of (1).

(1)   John told Bill that he was sick.

The syntax of (1) allows that the person claimed to be sick be either John, Bill, some third party visibly present to speaker and addressee, or some fourth party previously identified in the prior discourse. But this ambiguity or vagueness is most usually not a communication hindrance, since the speaker can usually count on the independent knowledge of the addressee to grasp his thought exactly. Suppose on the other hand that the syntax of a human language forced us to always be precise concerning the vague or ambiguous reference in cases like (1) above. That would be inefficient since in most situations we would not need to code that information explicitly in order to communicate the thought.

As we are using the term then, 'efficiency' quantifies over the ordinary, everyday, types of communication situations. It is required of natural language that everyday communication be relatively easy to produce and comprehend ('easy' relative to the cognitive and perception capabilities of human beings, of course).

Further, the modifications to human language that would be necessary to accommodate the complete absence of cross-reference imprecision would weigh heavily against the ER and possibly even the EH. For example, we might try simply eliminating pronouns from the repertoires of human languages (yet all such languages have them) in favour of using full NPs instead of their pronominal 'replacements'. But this would greatly and unnecessarily increase the length and hence decrease the efficiency of many otherwise simple communications. And it is doubtful that this alternative would work in any event. What full NPs would we substitute for the pronoun *he* in *Everyone told someone that he was sick* that would unequivocally disambiguate the different readings of the sentence? (So this alternative then might violate the EH.)

Alternatively we might endow human languages with enough distinct pronouns to allow them to discriminate among any number of NPs previously mentioned in the discourse. But since a preceding discourse may be arbitrarily long this would mean we would need an unbounded, that is infinite, number of pronouns. And we would further need some additional syntax to assure that each use of a pronoun always picked out the intended antecedent. The most obvious proposal, the one used in mathematical languages, is for the 'antecedent' to carry a copy of the pronoun. So in our modified human language we might express one of the senses of (1) by something like *John$_x$ told Bill$_y$ that y was sick*. But this proposal is obviously inefficient since it requires the addressee to remember which pronouns are assigned to which NPs over arbitrarily long stretches of discourse.

1.2.2 Second, consider the communication advantage of lexical ambiguity. It appears e.g. that the English word *bachelor* has four distinct meanings, corresponding roughly to *unmarried man, male seal, knight's helper*, and *recent college graduate*. Now on most occasions of the use of sentences containing the word *bachelor* the context will make clear which sense is appropriate. So it is not necessary for successful communication that English have four distinct, unambiguous, words expressing the various senses of *bachelor*. The ambiguity permits learners of English to have a smaller basic vocabulary than would be needed otherwise. Of course enriching the vocabulary of English by a few words is insignificant, but if all words were required to be semantically unambiguous the size of the basic vocabulary would increase by several orders of magnitude.

Note finally that *all* human languages present both the lexical imprecision of the type illustrated for *bachelor* and cross-reference imprecision of the type illustrated in (1). This is solid support for the ER on human language. Consequently we feel that a more exact statement of the EH is:

Weak Effability Hypothesis (WEH)
Anything that can be thought can be expressed with enough precision for efficient communication.

The WEH preserves the basic intuition that it is the nature of human language to be a tool for expressing our thoughts but does not require that it be a perfect tool. It allows in particular that human language can make do with an approximation to the exact thought a speaker has in mind.

In situations where we want to speak with more precision than natural language normally affords we make up specialised languages which have the requisite precision properties. Thus in the languages of mathematics, for instance, the imprecision in an English sentence like *Every number is greater than some number* is intolerable (since the truth of the sentence is equivocal). Such languages do not allow semantically ambiguous predicates like *bachelor* or *is even* as does English, nor do they permit the type of cross-referential ambiguity considered earlier. To avoid this latter imprecision in particular the syntax of mathematical languages is extended in a very significant way beyond that of natural language. Infinite numbers of pronouns (= variables) are used, the surface forms of sentences contain parentheses which un-equivocally delimit constituent boundaries, and unequivocal cross-reference is effected by matching variables across arbitrarily long spans.

It is perhaps natural to query here whether mathematical languages do not suffer from the cumbersomeness or inefficiency of communication which we felt natural languages could not have and still function as natural languages. The answer I think is twofold. On the one hand the formal languages do in fact often present even short sentences which are not easy to comprehend. They must be studied and reasoned to see exactly what the meaning is (and so they are not suitable objects for the expression of everyday thoughts). In practice then mathematicians often use a mixture of natural language and formal language, availing themselves of the latter only to the extent neces-sary to assure precise communication. The advantage of the formal language is that in a case of say a novel, important, proof the entire discourse can be given with complete precision. And second, the inefficiency problem is minimised since the range of topics that can be discussed in a formal lan-guage is, as we have seen, severely restricted. Consequently, basic mathe-matical languages, like those for elementary arithmetic and Euclidean geometry, often have only a few primitive predicates, say five to twenty, and only a very few distinct sentence types—half a dozen is a usual number here. So the absolute quantity of syntax needed to use these languages is quite limited. But what syntax there is is very precise. We have in effect traded effability for precision—a trade that natural language cannot afford and still be useful in communicating in novel situations.

1.3 So far we have largely criticised arguments in support of the ETH. Here we would like to offer an argument that what we know about the general relation between form and meaning in natural language supports the expec-tation that natural languages are not perfectly translatable, and that conse-quently, the burden of proof for the ETH rests with those who support it, not those who deny it.

6*

The meanings that can be expressed in a human language can be represented by the set of sentences of the language. The set is infinite, but can be (very roughly speaking) represented in a finite way as a two-part structure: one, a finite set of *basic* sentence types, and two, a finite set of *operations* which recursively generate complex structures from simpler ones. This two-part structure also represents the set of meanings expressible in the language. The meanings of basic sentences are in general lexically specific, but the meanings of complex sentences are normally understandable as a function of the meanings of the structures the complex ones are formed from. That is, if we know the meaning of the underlying structure, and we know what meaning change is introduced by the operation which forms the complex one from the simpler one, then in general we know the meaning of the complex sentence. For example, to understand the meaning of a novel negative sentence it is sufficient that we know the meaning of the underlying affirmative from which it is generated, and that we know what meaning change is represented by negation (that is, we must know what it means to deny something). Given this knowledge we can figure out the meaning of the negative sentence, rather than e.g. having to learn it as another 'special case', analogous to the way we must understand novel basic sentences formed from e.g. predicates not in our current vocabulary.

Now it seems to us that the set of syntactically unanalysable predicates in any given language will not have a complete set of semantic equivalents in most other languages, and hence the basic sentences in one language cannot be fully translated by basic sentences of most other languages. The reason is that among the primitive predicates of most languages will be ones that reference properties peculiar to the culture in which the language is spoken; e.g. the Malagasy predicate *mikabary* has no syntactically unanalysable equivalent in English. (It means, roughly, to perform a *kabary*, which is a particular type of formal speech only given on certain types of ceremonial occasions, such as the bone turning ceremonies—see Keenan (1974) for discussion—which are particular to Madagascar.)

Furthermore, we claim that the operations which form complex structures from simpler ones in different languages are also not exactly the same. Semantically significant operations (i.e. non-paraphrastic ones) which apply very productively in some languages only apply in very restricted syntactic environments in others, and not at all in still others. This claim has been substantiated in some detail in Keenan (1975b), so here we only summarise some of the conclusions, referring the reader to that paper for the substantiating data.

As a first case, consider the distribution of passive-like rules across languages. In English direct objects and a few indirect objects can be presented as the surface subject of a passive sentence (*the book was given to Mary by John*, and *Mary was given the book by John*, respectively). Now passive is a semantically significant operation. Thus, other things being equal (and there are very many such other things), subject phrases have wider scope logically speaking than non-subjects, so an operation which makes a non-subject into a subject, as passive does, endows that NP with wider scope properties than it originally had. Thus the preferred readings (and for some speakers the only readings) of *every boy kissed a girl* and *a girl was kissed by every boy* are logically distinct in that they have different truth conditions.

But languages vary considerably with regard to the domain of application of passive-like operations. Many languages, like Hausa and other Chadic languages, or Arosi and other Melanesian languages, have no syntactic operation which corresponds to English passive. On the other hand, many Malayo-Polynesian languages like Malagasy and Tagalog (and Philippine languages generally), as well as many Bantu languages like Kinyarwanda and Chicewa can systematically promote all major NPs in basic sentences to subject status. So given a Kinyarwanda sentence like '*John saw a lion in the forest*', we can form '*the forest was seen-in a lion by John*'. Clearly then languages can vary with regard to the distribution of semantically significant operations.

As a second, and final case, consider the distribution of relative clause-forming operations. In some languages, like Malagasy and Tagalog, we can only directly relativise subject NPs. Thus we can say directly *the man who saw John* but not *the man whom John saw*, where the position relativised is the direct object position of *saw*. Clearly languages like English permit the formation of a much greater range of relative clauses than the Malagasy/Tagalog type languages. On the other hand, languages like Hebrew, Welsh, and Persian (see Keenan, 1973, for examples) which normally present a personal pronoun in the position relativised (i.e. they say *the girl that John saw her* rather than, as in English, *the girl that John saw*) generally allow relativisation to apply in a much larger range of syntactic environments than does English. For example we cannot in English relativise into other relative clauses, although this is possible in e.g. Hebrew. Thus in English we cannot relativise on *man* in *the dog that bit the man belongs to Harry*, which would yield **the man that the dog that bit belongs to Harry* (*is my cousin*). But in Hebrew we can form (in rough translation), *the man that the dog that bit him belongs to Harry* (*is my cousin*).

Now clearly, since the meaning of a relative clause (by which we mean the entire structure *the man who saw John*, not just the restricting clause *who saw John*) is different from the sentence it is formed from (e.g. *John saw a man*, or perhaps even simply, *John saw him*) it again follows that languages differ significantly with regard to the applicability of semantically significant operations.

It appears then that in considering the set of 'meanings' expressible in two languages we are faced with the following fact, in the general case: first, the *basic* meanings (i.e. those expressed by the basic sentences of the language) are not exactly the same in the two cases, and second, the ways of forming (expressions of) complex meanings from (those of) simpler ones are not exactly the same. It is surely plausible then that one of the languages would allow us to express some meanings that were not exactly expressible in the other. And it would surely be surprising, and a very strong empirical claim, that different languages using different means to express 'meanings' always arrived at *exactly* the same end. This claim is, *prima facie*, most implausible.

1.4   The argument in 1.3 also provides a slightly different answer to the query raised in 1.1. Namely, how could we have a thought without being able to express it? How would we know what thought it was? In 1.1 we argued that this could be done by describing, metalinguistically, how the content of the thought differs from one which can be expressed in the language. 1.3 however provides a different answer. Namely, we can understand, in certain cases, the thought expressed by an ungrammatical structure, without having to know whether there is in the language some grammatical means for expressing that thought. A means for doing this is as follows: native speakers (perhaps oneself) are presented with pairs of grammatical sentences in which the second differs in form and meaning from the first in a regular way. For example, we might consider pairs of simple sentences containing the NP *a bear* and the corresponding sentences in which that NP has been clefted, as in (2a) and (2b) below.

(2)   a. John saw a bear.
      b. It was a bear that John saw.

Once the speaker is conscious of how the b-sentences differ in meaning from the a-sentences we can then present him with more complex sentences containing *a bear* and see if the corresponding cleft can be formed, as in (3a) and (3b).

(3)   a. John's dancing with a bear surprised me.
      b. *It was a bear that John's dancing with surprised me.

Even if the complex cleft is ungrammatical we can, with only a little effort, understand what thought it expresses by noting that it is the thought which differs in content from the one expressed by its non-cleft version in exactly the same way as the thoughts expressed by simple clefts differ from the ones expressed by their corresponding non-clefts.

Thus we can easily entertain thoughts for which we have, at hand, no grammatical expression. And we can do this without having to know whether there is, elsewhere in the language, some grammatical expression for that thought. This fact then should debunk what some may regard as a kind of mysticism in claiming that it is in principle possible to conceive of a thought without having a grammatical expression for it.

2. *Adequacy criteria for exact translation*

For two sentences in different languages to be exact translations they must of course have the same meaning. Hence the criteria we use to determine exact translationhood are basically the same as the ones needed to determine whether two sentences in a given language are paraphrases. To present these criteria then, we may, without loss of generality, draw all our examples from English.

Our knowledge of natural language semantics is not yet sufficient to enable us to list all the properties which sentences must share in order to be full paraphrases. We can however agree on several necessary properties. Then if two sentences fail to share one of these properties we may conclude that they are not exactly the same in meaning. Further, we shall restrict our attention to semantic properties which are overtly represented in the syntactic structure of the sentences in question. That is, we are only concerned here with what semantic properties are explicitly represented in a language, not e.g. with properties which we may 'indirectly' infer, a point we make more explicit in 2.1.

2.1 *Sameness of speech act*

If two sentences are paraphrases they should be naturally usable in the same range of speech acts. Thus *has John left?* is not an adequate translation of *John has left* since its syntactic form tells us that it is used to request information (one type of speech act) rather than to make a claim (another type of speech act). If in some language declaratives and interrogatives were not syntactically distinct (Vietnamese and Luiseño are possible candidates here) we would have a *prima facie* case that the ETH would fail since a purported translation of an English question could also be used to make a statement, so the translation function would not preserve the property of being used to make only certain types of speech act.

We might contrast the above case with a hypothetical language in which (the literal translation of) *God is thirsty* can only be uttered on the occasion of the ritual decapitation of the king during the last day of the 13th lunar month of the year. That sentence could not be adequately translated in English preserving sameness of speech act since English-speaking cultures, presumably, lack such a speech act altogether. However, by hypothesis, there is nothing in the syntactic form of *God is thirsty* which restricts its usage to ritual killings, so we do not want to say that that type of speech act is overtly coded in the syntax of that language. Hence this failure of exact translation will not count against the ETH.

2.2 *Sameness of truth conditions*

Clearly if two declarative sentences have the same meaning they must say the same thing about the world—that is, they must be true under the same conditions. Clearly *John is whistling off-key* is not a paraphrase of *John is whistling* since an utterance of the former sentence is only true in a proper subset of the cases in which an utterance of the latter is true.

While this criterion is easily agreed upon in principle, its application in practice is sometimes problematic. For one thing we often do not know exactly what the world must be like for (utterances of) simple sentences to be true (e.g. *John loves Mary*). But we do have indirect access to the truth conditions of utterances in terms of the inferences they justify. Thus while we are no clearer about the truth conditions of *John does not love Mary* than we are about those of *John loves Mary* we can unequivocally assert that their truth conditions are different since only the latter justifies the inference *someone loves Mary*. (That is, if *John loves Mary* is true, then *someone loves Mary* must also be true.)

An historically, more problematic case here concerns the truth conditions of sentences containing elements (deictics) whose meaning requires that their context of utterance meet certain conditions. It is clear nonetheless that *I am a linguist* and *Chomsky is a linguist* differ in meaning since a true utterance of the former justifies the inference that its speaker is a linguist, while the truth of the latter justifies no such inference. So the utterances of the sentences are true in somewhat different conditions and hence they are not paraphrases. Note that deictic boundness is not limited to first or second person pronouns. *Some people are linguists* and *they are linguists* also fail to be paraphrases since the latter requires that both speaker and addressee have a mutually identifiable set of people about whom they are talking, whereas the former sentence placed no such requirement on the contexts in which it can be truly asserted.

Note further that deictic boundness is not a minor feature of natural languages. It is rather a design feature. All natural languages can be used in face-to-face interaction, and all natural languages present sentences whose truth places requirements of various sorts on the contexts in which they are asserted. In English for example most sentences are deictically bounded since tense marking is obligatory (in distinction e.g. to Indonesian where it is optional and perhaps most often omitted) and tense marking stipulates a relation between the time of utterance and some other time. Thus the truth of *John was a student* requires that at some time prior to the utterance time *John is a student* be true.

2.3 *Sameness of derived truth conditions*

If two sentences have the same meaning then complex structures formed from them in the same way must also have the same meaning. That is, if we change the meaning of one in a fixed way the resultant meaning should be the same as the one obtained by changing the meaning of the other in the same way. For example, if two sentences S and S′ have the same meaning then the yes-no questions formed from them must request the same information, their negations must deny the same information, and their nominalisations must refer to the same fact or event.

This criterion is often useful in distinguishing the meanings of sentences whose meaning difference is not great enough to justify a difference in truth conditions when considered in isolation. Operations which form complex structures from simpler ones however may be sensitive to the small difference in meaning between them with the result that the derived structures have different truth conditions. For example, (4a) and (4b) below have the same truth conditions.

(4) a. John sold a house to Mary.
b. Mary bought a house from John.

Yet we feel that there is some non-trivial meaning difference between (4a) and (4b). The one primarily talks about something John did, whereas the other primarily talks about something Mary did. But the truth conditions are the same since, if John did what he is claimed to have done in (4a) then Mary must have done what she is claimed to have done in (4b), and conversely. But now compare:

(5)   a. The fact that John sold a house to Mary surprised us.
        b. The fact that Mary bought a house from John surprised us.

(5a) and (5b) differ in truth conditions since in a situation in which we know John to be a disreputable salesman and Mary to be a scrupulous shopper (5a) might be false and (5b) true. Clearly the difference in truth conditions of (5a) and (5b) is attributable to the meaning difference between their subject phrases, namely the factive nominalisations of (4a) and (4b). So (4a) and (4b) must differ in meaning since their factive nominalisations do; hence (4a) and (4b) are not exact paraphrases.

Another application of this criterion concerns sentences, like (6a) and (6b) below which have the same truth conditions but whose negations clearly do not.

(6)   a. The one student who stayed until the end was asleep.
        b. The claim that exactly one student stayed until the end and that
           he was asleep is true.
(7)   a. The one student who stayed until the end was not asleep.
        b. The claim that exactly one student stayed until the end and that
           he was asleep is not true.

Clearly the truth of (7a) still justifies the inference that one student stayed until the end, whereas (7b) does not. We may infer then that (6a) and (6b) are not exact paraphrases since, even though they have the same truth conditions, their negations do not. Negation then, like yes-no question formation, is sensitive to the subtle meaning difference between (6a) and (6b). In general we will say that information which is preserved under negation (or yes-no questioning) is *presupposed* rather than merely *asserted*. (6a) and (6b) then differ in meaning in that (6a) presupposes some of the information which is merely asserted in (6b). And in general if a putative translation of some sentence into another language presents some of the presuppositions of the original as assertions we may agree that the translation is not exact (although it may well be good enough for many ordinary purposes and so would not violate the Weak Effability Hypothesis, even though it would violate the Exact Translation Hypothesis).

2.4   *Ambiguity vs. vagueness*

If one sentence is naturally used to express two distinct meanings while another expresses only one of those then neither is an exact paraphrase of the other, since the one could be true in situations in which the other would not be true. Probably no language other than English however has a sentence with exactly the fourfold ambiguity previously discussed in *John is a bachelor*. It is clear then, as Katz (this volume) would agree, that the ETH fails if preservation of ambiguity is taken as a necessary criterion on exact translation. Katz then proposes a weaker version of the Translatability Hypothesis in which translation up to ambiguity is to count as exact enough. That is, a sentence S, considered on one of its meanings *m*, is to be adequately translated by some sentence T as long as T has *m* among its meanings.

But why should we accept this weaker version? We have already argued that natural languages are inherently ambiguous. It is part of our linguistic competence that the relation between form and meaning is one in which different meanings are expressed by the same form. The fact that *flying planes can be dangerous* is judged to have two somewhat different meanings represents a basic cognitive, or logical, property of that sentence. If a purported translation of that sentence fails to have that property then it differs in meaning from it in a basic way. We shall for purposes of argument in the rest of this paper accept some version of the weaker Translatability Hypothesis in which translation up to ambiguity is allowed, although in so doing it seems to us that we have actually abandoned the Exact Translatability Hypothesis and are now only arguing about how badly it fails.

Further, it seems to us that Katz's weaker version is clearly too weak. In particular it allows the following reduction *ad absurdum* argument: imagine a hypothetical language in which the only sentence is *ôm*, and in which *ôm* is held to be multiply ambiguous, having as one of its meanings each distinct meaning expressible by some English sentence. On Katz's version of the ETH the Ôm language (for that is of necessity its name) has the same logical expressive power as English. But this is absurd. Ôm cannot make even the most primitive logical distinctions that English can. Its syntax does not force us to distinguish between the situations expressed by *John is a linguist* and *John is not a linguist*. So this weakening of the ETH seems to us too weak.

Admittedly, Ôm is not a possible human language (although the reason pertains to the Efficiency Requirement not the Effability Hypothesis) but the principle it illustrates is sound. Suppose e.g. we find a language which is systematically ambiguous in a way in which another is not. We have a *prima facie* case then that the ambiguous language fails to make logical distinctions which the other does make and so cannot provide exact translations from the other. Let us then informally define a sentence in a language to be *essentially ambiguous* as between two meanings *m* and *m'* if the language has no other sentences whose meanings are exactly *m* and *m'* respectively—that is, if the sentence cannot be unequivocally disambiguated in that language. We now require of the weakened ETH that each meaning of a sentence in one language be translated by an unambiguous sentence in each other language. If the only translations which one language provides for certain sentences of another are ambiguous then the ETH will still be held to fail. This version of the ETH has the advantage that it correctly rules out Ôm as a translation candidate for English since, in fact, every translation of any English sentence into Ôm will be ambiguous. And further, this version of the ETH still recognises that ambiguity is a basic semantic property of natural language sentences.

Finally, we must mention a theoretical obstacle to the application of the ambiguity criterion. To our knowledge no pre-theoretical intuition of ambiguity has been articulated in the literature which enables us to distinguish cases of ambiguity from mere vagueness or non-specificity. The importance of the distinction for us is illustrated by the following example: Suppose that *bachelor* is not four ways ambiguous but only vague or non-specific as between 'unmarried male', 'knight's helper', etc. Then *John is a bachelor* has only one meaning, not four, and is true in a fairly wide range of situations. Then the French sentence *Jean est célibataire* is not in any way an exact translation of it since it is true in only a proper subset of the cases (the unmarried man ones) in which the English sentence is true. But if the English sentence is ambiguous then the French sentence is an adequate translation of one of its meanings.

We can of course, within the framework of e.g. transformational grammar represent at least certain types of ambiguity. But what pre-formal criteria do we have for deciding whether a particular formulation of transformational grammar which labels a sentence ambiguous is correct or not? Note, by way of comparison, that in the case of *logical entailment* we do have such a pre-formal intuition. Namely, a sentence S *logically entails* a sentence T (both S and T assumed for simplicity of argument to be unambiguous) just in case T is true in all the situations in which S is true. A theory of logical relations must formalise the notion 'true-in-a-situation', and if a specific version of such a theory claims e.g. that *John is a linguist* entails *John is a philosopher* we may reject the theory on the grounds that someone can be a linguist without in fact being a philosopher. But no analogous intuition exists for ambiguity.

Explicating the intuition of ambiguity as distinct from vagueness would go well beyond the bounds of this paper, although initially the problem seems tractable. There are many easily-agreed-upon instances of ambiguous sentences, such as the *flying planes can be dangerous* ones. There are equally many clear cases of vagueness. Thus *the man on the table is hurt* is vague, not ambiguous, according as the man is Albanian or not. Note of course that the situations in which the man is, or is not, Albanian are quite distinct. But we feel that neither of these situations is talked about in the original sentence.

We shall propose then the following sufficient condition for a sentence to be judged vague, rather than ambiguous, in certain respects: A sentence S is *vague* according as it describes distinct situations *a* and *b* if, on a natural occasion of its use, the speaker of the sentence does not have to know (or believe he knows, a distinction we will not continue to make) whether in fact *a* or *b* is the case. Thus we may naturally assert that the man on the table is hurt without having to know whether the man is Albanian or not, so the sentence is correctly judged to be vague in this respect.

On the other hand, in a normal assertion of *the chickens are ready to eat* the speaker is expected to know whether the chickens are ready to be eaten or rather are ready to dine. So this sentence does not satisfy our criterion of vagueness, and is most plausibly judged ambiguous. Note however that our criterion of vagueness is not intended as a necessary condition on vagueness. It is possible, for independent reasons, that a speaker might have to know certain information, such as (following Descartes) whether he exists or not, but that a sentence not be judged ambiguous with respect to that information. All we are saying then is that if a speaker can remain indifferent between alternatives *a* and *b* and still meaningfully assert some sentence then the sentence is vague not ambiguous according as *a* or *b* obtains.

3. *Cases where the weakened version of the ETH fails*

We consider now several specific cases in which, I contend, the weakened version of the ETH fails. All the cases I give, however, suffer from the fact that, at the moment, it is not possible effectively to enumerate the set of meanings expressible in any given language. Consequently I can in no case prove that I have exhausted all the possible candidates for exact translations. The best I can do is discuss the natural translations that native speakers give, show that they are not exact (though good enough for most purposes), and attempt to find other ways of improving the translation. But I cannot guarantee that someone more clever than I might not come up with a better translation than any I considered.

On the other hand the examples I consider are designed to represent categories of problems for the ETH, not merely 'accidental' gaps in one or another language. In each case then we have reason to believe that the type of problem I consider will crop up again and again in slightly different guises. Hence a fully satisfactory rebuttal to my arguments should show not only that I was not clever enough to think of a translation in the particular case at hand, but that the type of case considered has a systematic solution.

3.1 *Semantic gaps*

It is sometimes argued that perfect translatability fails between languages because e.g. Eskimo (reportedly) has a word that means 'snow that has been partially melted and then refrozen', whereas English lacks such a word and English speakers lack such a concept. This is a poor argument however since English speakers can reference such snow by using a more complex structure, such as the one we used above, to reference such an object.

There is another counter argument to this claim however which seems to us to be invalid. Namely, 'we can coin a new word, say *smush* which means "snow that has partially melted . . ." and add that word to the vocabulary of English. It is the nature of human language to allow vocabulary increases without changing the identity of the language. English has not ceased to be English merely by the addition of a new vocabulary item.'

We would agree that English remains English under such conditions. But this fact is irrelevant to the ETH. For suppose that before the addition English had no way to reference such snow and no way to translate exactly the relevant Eskimo sentences. In such a case the ETH would simply fail, and the addition of *smush* to the language would increase its expressive power, even if the syntactic change in the language is judged trivial.

Now we are not arguing here against the claim that a language with limited expressive power can be augmented, perhaps in syntactically trivial ways, so as to increase its expressive power. This claim is surely true, and it trivialises the ETH, which would then have to mean 'Any language can provide exact translations of anything in any other language if we allow ourselves to increase its expressive power'. The claim we are arguing against is that any two human languages, as they stand, can be exactly translated one into the other. And this claim we shall now argue is false. The reason is that there are numerous areas of human activity which are not shared across certain language groups. We'll give just one example, but the reader can easily construct many others.

Among the indigenous languages of Australia and New Guinea it is common to find languages which have no ways of referencing numbers beyond what is inherent in the pronominal systems (which frequently distinguish singulars, duals, perhaps trials or paucals, and plurals). So the number names in those languages are limited to phrases like 'one', 'two', 'a few', and 'many'. See Hale (1971) for supporting data for this claim from Walbiri. It is safe to say then that such languages cannot, at the moment, provide translations of English sentences like *the cube root of ten is not a rational number, all subgroups of a cyclic group are cyclic*, etc. We have no doubt that Walbiri speakers could learn these mathematical concepts and enrich their language so as to be able to talk about them in Walbiri, but at the moment such discussion is impossible, which is to say that the ETH, in point of fact, fails.

3.2 Pragmatic presupposition

We have pointed out in 2 that all human languages present sentences (e.g. ones containing deictic items) whose meaning requires that the context of their utterance meet certain conditions. But these conditions vary greatly from language to language. We consider here the very simple example of the address term distinction present in many European languages. Thus (8a) and (8b) in French have quite different meanings, although both are normally translated by the same English sentence (8c).

(8)   a. Tu es malade.
     b. Vous êtes malade.
     c. You are sick.

Yet (8a) justifies the inference (9), whereas (8b) justifies a rather contrary inference, and (8c) justifies neither of these inferences.

(9)   It is probable that the speaker of (8a) is personally intimate with the addressee, or that he and the addressee are members of equal social status in some socially identified group, or that the addressee is in some socially quite inferior relation to the speaker such as being a puppy dog or a prostitute, or that the speaker is mad as hell at the addressee.

(8a) justifies this inference because it is a presupposition of the use of the familiar address term *tu* that the speaker and hearer stand in one of the sorts of relations indicated in (9). (8c) needless to say carries no such conditions on its appropriate use. Consequently (8c) can be true in situations in which (8a) is pragmatically anomalous. Stated differently, if an utterance of (8a) is a true utterance we know more about how the world is than if an utterance of (8c) is true.

Now is there a way of translating (8a) into English which covers all and only the information in (8a)? It seems to us not. We might try e.g. simply conjuncting (9) with (8c). The conjunction would then trivially justify the inference of (9), but it is not at all semantically equivalent to (8a). For one thing, (8a) does not talk about its speaker. More important, the conjunction explicitly asserts information which is only presupposed by (8a). Thus in a situation in which the addressee is sick but does not stand in the requisite social relationship to the speaker the conjunction is simply false, being a conjunction of a true sentence and a false one (if indeed we are motivated in natural language to assign a single truth value to a conjunction of sentences at all). But (8a) is anomalous in such a situation. It is only clearly false if the addressee is not sick, but does stand in the right relationship to the speaker.

Another attempt at translating (8a) would be to put the relevant information concerning the social relation between the speaker and addressee in apposition to the address term, as in *You, my dear friend, are sick*. But this alternative, at best, would justify a much stronger inference than (9), namely that the speaker and addressee were intimate, whereas it is only the grotesque disjunction (9) that is inferable from (8a). And we cannot put such a disjunction in apposition (or in any other way assert it) for this would imply that the speaker was not sure of his social relationship to the addressee, and that is not implied by (8a).

Unless I have overlooked some obvious alternative then, it appears that there is no English sentence which presents exactly the pattern of pragmatic presuppositions as does (8a). So the ETH appears to fail here on the grounds that translation between French and English does not preserve pragmatic presupposition. And perhaps we should add here that the French case was chosen only for its familiarity. A more impressive case could be made from South Asian languages like Thai, which have much more developed address term systems, or languages like Javanese or certain Australian languages in which large parts of the basic vocabulary are reserved for use between persons of certain social or kin relations (the so-called 'mother-in-law languages' in Australia—see Dixon (1972) for some references). For example, a lexicon of Javanese (see Horne, 1961) will specify for the basic content words of the language whether it is used in the high language, the low language, or both.

We may, however, anticipate a counter-argument consistent with a Katzian point of view (although I would not want to attribute exactly this argument to Katz himself). The argument would run as follows: '(8a) and (8c) do in fact express the same *proposition*, namely that the addressee (regardless of his social relation to the speaker) is sick. The sentences admittedly differ as regards their pragmatic presuppositions, but we only require of the ETH that translation preserve the propositional content of a sentence, not the requirements it places on the context of its utterance in order to be meaningful.'

This I think is a tenable line of argument, but it does further restrict, and arbitrarily so in our opinion, the significance of the claim made by the ETH.

We have already seen that all human languages require that competent speakers be able to discriminate certain aspects of the context of utterance—namely they must at least be able to distinguish speakers, addressees, and third parties, and know that the truth of their claims varies with the identities of these participants. And very many languages in addition require that competent speakers be able to discriminate among certain types of social or kin relations among the participants in a speech situation. The basic ability to make such discriminations must surely then be part of our innate linguistic competence. The ability to use *tu* and *vous* in a generally correct way in French is certainly a part of the competence of native speakers of French.

So on what basis can we rule that the ETH should only apply to certain parts of our linguistic competence but not others?

3.3 *Structure destroying operations*

It is characteristic of natural language that the operations which form complex structures from simpler ones eliminate semantically significant aspects of the structures they operate on. For example, it is very common across languages for the tense/aspect distinctions which are made in simple sentences to be lost when those sentences are nominalised. E.g. *John is speaking* and *John will speak* may both be nominalised as *John's speaking*. The resulting structures then are inherently vague or ambiguous with respect to the information lost (though the information lost may sometimes be recoverable from other aspects of the sentences in which the derived structures occur).

A particularly common type of loss (it occurs almost universally among SOV languages, probably the most widely distributed word order type across languages) concerns the formation of relative clauses on oblique case NPs. It is very usual that the pre- or post-position which indicates the exact semantic relation that the oblique case NP bears to its verb cannot be present in the relative clause. Thus while English may retain such prepositions in either of two ways as in *the knife with which John cut the meat* or *the knife that John cut the meat with*, many languages can only say *the knife that John cut the meat*. In this case one could argue that the inherent meaning of *knife* allows one to recover the instrumental relation between the head NP and the main verb of the restricting clause. But there is at least one case, locatives, where the exact semantic relation cannot be generally recovered. If a language only allows the formation of a vague relative clause like *the table where John put the basket* we cannot tell whether it is the table on top of which he put the basket, or next to which, or under which, etc. Consider the following example from Malagasy (Tagalog, and Philippine languages generally are the same as Malagasy in the relevant respects).

(10) a. nametraka ny harona teo ambon'- ny latabatra Rabe
placed   the basket there on top of-the table   Rabe
'Rabe put the basket on top of the table.'

b. nametraka ny harona teo   amban'- ny latabatra Rabe
placed   the basket there under- the table   Rabe
'Rabe put the basket under the table.'

Now the only way to relativise on 'table' from these sentences is to make 'table' a surface subject, since only subjects can be relativised in Malagasy (see Keenan (1972b) for details). And the *only* way to make 'table' a subject is to put the verb in the circumstantial voice (the voice used when any oblique NP is subjectivised, whether it be a locative, instrumental, temporal, etc.), move 'table' to the subject position (sentence final), and make it nominative, i.e. eliminate its preposition.[4] So subjectivising 'table' in either (10a) or (10b) yields, in both cases, (11), which we might roughly 'translate' as *the table was basket-put by Rabe*.

(11)   Nametrahan-dRabe ny harona ny latabatra
placed-by   Rabe the basket the table
'The table was basket-put by Rabe.'

Necessarily then the information concerning the exact locative relation which 'table' bears to the verb is lost. But it is only from (11) that we can relativise on 'table', illustrated in (12).

(12)   ny latabatra (izay) nametrahan-dRabe ny harona
the table   that placed-by   Rabe the basket
'The table where Rabe put the basket.'

Hence, while we can infer from the morphological marking of the verb voice in (12) that 'table' is an underlying oblique, and we can infer from the inherent meaning of 'table' that it must be a locative (not e.g. an instrumental or temporal), we cannot determine the exact locative relation that 'table' bears to the restricting verb.

It would appear then that English sentences containing locative specific relative clauses, like (13a) below, receive only inexact translations in

4. We might note that Malagasy has no equivalent of the 'dummy' verb *have* in English 'sentences' like *the table has a basket under it*. And precisely it does not need such dummies, since the main function they perform in English, allowing us to topicalise non-subjects, is handled by the well-developed voicing system in Malagasy.

Malagasy, like (13b). Certainly (13b) is the only naturally elicited translation of (13a).

(13) a. The table under which John put the basket was damaged.
      b. simba   ny latabatra (izay) nametrahan-dRajaona ny harona
         damaged the table   that placed-by   John   the basket
         'The table where John put the basket was damaged.'

But what other options does Malagasy afford for providing a more exact, if cumbersome, translation of (13a)? There is certainly no way of fiddling the relative clause to allow the preposition to remain. We cannot e.g. as many languages can, retain the preposition with a pronominal trace, as in *the table that John put the basket under it*. Nor could we front the preposition as in English *under which*, since *izay* in Malagasy is morphologically invariant and cannot carry prepositions, like the English relativiser *that*. Nor can we insert the relevant information parenthetically, as in *the table where John put the basket—he put it under it—was damaged*, for Malagasy allows no such parentheticals. There is in fact no formal or intonational distinction in Malagasy between restrictive and non-restrictive relative clauses, and there is a strong constraint in Malagasy against interrupting the stream of speech. Malagasy discourses contain no parentheticals in the above sense.

If we force a Malagasy to try to give a translation of (13a) which preserves the locative relation he simply factors the original sentence into two parts, like *John put the basket under some table. That table was damaged.* But this translation, even if construed with an overt conjunction, is not exact because it explicitly asserts that John put the basket under a table, whereas that information is presupposed in (13a).

Pragmatically as well the Malagasy conjunction is different from (13a) since it represents two speech acts (both assertions) whereas (13a) represents only one. This difference is more striking when we attempt to paraphrase the English question *was the table under which John put the bread damaged?* in an analogous way. The Malagasy sentence then would be (in translation, for simplicity of exposition) *John put the bread under some table. Was that table damaged?* Clearly here the Malagasy 'text' both makes an assertion and asks a question, whereas the English sentence merely asks a question but makes no assertions. So clearly the Malagasy text is not an exact translation of the English question, and the ETH once again appears violated.

Notice here that the attempted paraphrase of (13a) by a conjunction of sentences or a short text illustrates our claims concerning the Weak Effability Hypothesis. Faced with a situation in which it is important to make explicit the exact locative relation, the Malagasy can do it, but not in a way that has exactly the properties of (13a) in English. That is, he can give a rough translation, good enough for the purposes at hand, but not an exact translation.

An apparent counter-argument to our claim here would be to say that the Malagasy relative clause (12), translated by us as *the table where John put the bread* is in fact ambiguous according as it means the table on which, or under which, etc. he put the bread. Then one could claim that the natural Malagasy translation of (13a) namely (13b) had the exact meaning of (13a) as one of its senses.

However, this argument fails because, by the criterion of vagueness discussed in 2, (13b) is judged vague and not ambiguous in Malagasy. That is, a Malagasy may assert (13b) without knowing exactly where the basket was put. He may simply have seen John moving towards the table with the obvious intent of disposing of his overladen basket. It would be sensible for a Malagasy, concerned with whether the table might break if the basket were put on it, to respond to (13b) by the question 'Did he put the basket on it, or merely next to or under it?'. And the speaker of (13b) could reasonably respond 'I don't know'.

3.4 *Positive and negative co-reference*

Languages vary considerably with regard to the syntactic means they provide for stipulating that two referential positions in a sentence necessarily refer to the same object (positive co-reference) or necessarily refer to different objects (negative co-reference). English e.g. stipulates the positive co-reference between subjects and objects of a given verb by using a particular pronominal form (the reflexive one), as in (14a) below in which it is necessarily the case that the person criticised and the one doing the criticising are the same.

> (14)   a. John criticised himself.
>   b. John criticised him.

In (14b) however, on most occasions of its use, we can infer that the person criticised and the criticiser are different. But I do not want to say here that English stipulates negative co-reference. That is, the syntactic form of (14b) does not force the interpretation that the criticiser and the criticised are different. It only forces the interpretation that the speaker does not know that the criticiser and the person criticised are the same. The usual inference that they are different is a pragmatically-based one, as follows: It is a presupposition of the use of definite pronouns like *him* and of proper names like *John* that the speaker can identify their referents in some way. That is, he knows, in some way or another, who he is referring to. Most usually then he will know whether the proper noun and the definite pronoun reference the same individual or not. If they do, then he is obliged to use the reflexive pronoun. So we may usually infer from the fact that he did not use the reflexive form that the two individuals are different.

However, it is not difficult to imagine plausible cases where the speaker could identify in some reasonable way who he was talking about without knowing whether the two individuals were the same or not. And in such a case he would use the non-reflexive pronoun (regardless of whether the individuals are in fact the same). We will illustrate this case since it is important for our later argument.

Imagine that the newly appointed manager of the bank, call him Mr Schumann, is obliged, against his personal inclinations, to follow the pre-scribed bank policy of not giving loans to students. He follows the policy but writes an article in the local paper criticising the policy and advocating its change, without however identifying himself as the bank manager. Someone reading the article might report 'The bank manager is behaving unreasonably, but *Mr Schumann has recently criticised him*, so perhaps the bank will change its policy'. Here clearly the person criticised and the one doing the criticising are the same, but the speaker does not know that, and so is justified in using the non-reflexive pronoun. The speaker can of course identify, in a socially acceptable sense, the referents of 'Mr Schumann' (He is the man who wrote the article) and of 'him' (He is the bank manager).

So we shall say then that English stipulates the positive co-reference of subjects and objects (of a given verb) but does not stipulate their negative co-reference.

3.4.1 *Positive co-reference*

Many languages however, such as Gilbertese and Fijian (see Keenan, 1975d, for further examples), do not have regular syntactic means for stipulating positive co-reference in the cases cited above. Thus in Fijian the c-sentences below are the natural translations of either of the corresponding a- and b-sentences.

(15) a. John criticised him.
      b. John criticised himself.
      c. a vakalewai koya (ga)   o   jone
         criticised   him (emph) art John

(16)　a. Everyone criticised him.
　　　　b. Everyone criticised himself.
　　　　c. a vakalewai koya (ga)　　o　ira kece
　　　　　　criticised　him (emph) art pl all
(17)　a. Who criticised him?
　　　　b. Who criticised himself?
　　　　c. o　cei　a vakalewai koya (ga)?
　　　　　art who criticised　him (emph)

In analysing these cases we shall use (15a–c) as representative of the other two cases as well since all the difficulties it presents arise, *mutatis mutandis*, in the other cases. We shall point out, however, a few additional problems with (16) and (17).

In (15c) the pronominal form *koya* may refer to John or it may refer to some third party mutually identifiable to speaker and addressee. Its exact reference depends on context, much as the referent of *him* in *John thinks that Mary loves him* might be John or might be some third party, depending on the context in which the sentence is asserted.

It would appear then that (15c), the natural translation of (15a) in Fijian, is not an exact translation since it might be true in cases where the subject and object phrases refer to different persons, whereas (15a) forces their identity. To secure this argument we must, however, as in the previous case, show first that (15c) is not merely ambiguous as between a reading on which it paraphrases (15a) exactly, and another on which it paraphrases (15b) exactly. And secondly we must show that there is no other way in Fijian of exactly translating (15a).

(15c) is not ambiguous between the meanings of (15a) and (15b) because the speaker of (15c) does not have to believe that the person criticised and the one doing the criticising are the same or different. In the bank manager case cited earlier he may simply have different ways of identifying the criticiser and the criticised without knowing whether these two means actually identify one person or two. (15c) then appears closer in meaning to (15a), but even here there is a difference. For a speaker of (15c) will still assert (15c) even if he knows that the subject and object phrases are positively co-referential, whereas this is not the case in (15a). So the pragmatic implication that the speaker is unaware of the identity, which holds in (15a), fails in (15c).

Furthermore, even if (15c) were judged ambiguous rather than vague in the relevant respects we would still not have an exact translation of either (15a) or (15b). For that we need unambiguous sentences in Fijian, and we find no fully convincing way in Fijian of unequivocally disambiguating (15c). So the ambiguity, if it is one, appears to be an essential ambiguity in the sense of 2.

Several possibilities for more exactly translating (15b) do however suggest themselves. We might try for example simply replacing the object pronoun by a copy of the full NP subject as in *John criticised John (a vakalewai jone o jone)*. But such sentences are judged somewhat anomalous, and if an interpretation is forced on them it is easily possible that the two occurrences of *jone* are understood to refer to different individuals, as is the case in English. And the reason this interpretation is natural in Fijian is the same as in English: if the speaker had intended to indicate that the criticiser and the person criticised were the same he would have used a pronominal form in the object slot. Since he did not, some other meaning must be intended, and a natural one would be that the individuals referred to were different since that is the usual interpretation when both subject and object phrases are proper names.

Furthermore, repetition of the subject phrase in object position is not a generally applicable alternative since, as in English, it fails badly when the subject phrase is a quantified or interrogative NP. Thus *everyone criticised everyone* in Fijian can never mean *everyone criticised himself*, nor can *who criticised whom?* mean *who criticised himself?* Nor could we use anything like *everyone criticised that person*, (18), since the only natural interpretation of *that person (na tamata oya)* is where it refers to a third party, not where it is bound by *everyone*.

> (18) a vakalewa na tamata oya o ira kece
>   criticised art person that everyone
>   'Everyone criticised that person.'

Another alternative, which does appear to force the required co-reference, is to factor (15b) into two sentences which translate roughly as *John criticised someone, and that person was John himself* (where *himself* 'ga' here is a kind of emphatic marker, not a reflexive pronoun).

> (19) a vakalewa e due   o jone. na tamata oya a o   jone ga
>   criticised   someone art John. art person that art John emph
>   'John criticised someone. That person was John himself.'

But the same objections we levied earlier in the Malagasy 'translation by factorisation' apply here. In particular the second conjunct of (19) presupposes that John criticised someone, since *that person* means *the person who John criticised*. Thus in a situation in which John criticised no one (15b) is simply false, but the second conjunct of (19) is anomalous, since its subject phrase fails to have a referent, so it does not make any sense to ask whether the predicate *was John himself* holds or fails to hold of that person. Further (19) presents two speech acts, not one as in (15b), a fact which is made more obvious when the same type of translation is required of a question like *did John criticise himself?* which would have to be rendered as *John criticised someone. Was that person John himself?* which clearly both makes an assertion and asks a question, whereas the sentence its supposed to translate only asks a question.

Further, the conjunction alternative is a much less plausible alternative when the subject of *criticise* is a quantified or interrogative NP, since universally such NPs are less good at controlling pronominal co-reference across coordinate conjunctions (since, presumably, they are less effective in establishing a definite referent). Compare:

(20) a. John$_i$
     b. *Everyone$_i$ } worked hard but nobody thanked him$_i$
     c. **Who$_i$

Attempts to paraphrase even (20a) by a conjunction were initially met with total incomprehension by the informant. When an interpretation was finally forced it was only successful if the anaphoric phrases (i.e. the personal pronoun or phrases like *that person*) were understood to refer to third parties, not if they were bound by the quantifier phrases).

(21) *a vakalewa e dua$_i$ o ira kece$_j$ kei na tamata oya$_j$ a okoya$_i$ (ga)
     criticised someone everyone and art person that him (emph)
     'Everyone criticised someone and that person was him (himself).'

A final alternative we might try would be *John criticised someone who was John himself*, (22). (Note the more natural SVO main clause order here.)

(22) o jone a vakalewa e dua   o koya ka a o jone ga
     art John criticised someone who   rel art John emph
     'John criticised someone who was John himself.'

But as with the *John criticised John* cases, this is such an unnatural way to say *John criticised himself* that the more plausible interpretation is one in which the two occurrences of *jone* refer to different individuals. And further this alternative completely fails when the subject of *criticise* is a quantified or interrogative NP. Thus the Fijian equivalent of *everyone criticised someone who was everyone himself* is simply uninterpretable, and (23), *everyone criticised someone who was that person himself* can only be interpreted where *that person* refers to a third party.

(23) *o ira kece$_i$ a vakalewa e dua   o koya ka a na tamata oya$_i$
      everyone criticised someone who   rel art person that
      'Everyone$_i$ criticised someone who was that person$_i$.'

In the absence of other plausible translations of (15a)–(17a) then we may conclude that Fijian has no exact translations of these sentences and hence the ETH fails. But note again that the Weak Effability Hypothesis remains intact. For given that it is a presupposition of the use of definite pronouns like *koya* that the referent is known to both speaker and hearer, on normal occasions of their use, sentences like (15c)–(17c) will be interpreted correctly. Thus Fijian does provide translations which are good enough for ordinary purposes.

3.4.2 *Negative co-reference*

Languages also vary considerably in the syntactic means they provide for stipulating negative co-reference. English in particular is very limited in this respect. While it does appear that we can stipulate negative co-reference for indefinite NPs in certain environments, as in *some students were collecting the tickets while others were showing people to their seats* in which the students who were showing people to their seats must be different from those who are collecting the tickets, it is in general not natural to stipulate negative co-reference between definite NPs. Thus it is most natural for a speaker to assert *John thinks that Mary loves him* regardless of whether he intends *him* to co-refer to *John* positively or negatively.

It is however a typological trait of many American Indian languages as well as of the Eastern Highlands New Guinea languages (see Keenan, 1975b, for examples) that various types of subordinate verbs carry either one of two markers: one if the subject of the subordinate verb is the same in reference to the subject of some other verb (usually the main clause one), and the other if its subject is different in reference.

Consider e.g. the following sentences from Hopi, provided by Pamela Munro. (We use 'ss' to mark 'same subject as' and 'ds' to indicate 'different subject'.)

(24) a. John navoti:ta (pam) mo:tita-ni- qay
 John knows   he   win-   inc-ss
 b. John navoti:ta pam mo:tita-ni-q
 John knows   he   win-   inc-ds
 c. 'John knows that he will win.'

(25) a. so:soyam navoti?iyɨ wa (pɨma) mo:titota-ni-qay
 everyone knows-pl   they win-   inc-ss
 b. so:soyam navoti?yɨnwa pɨma mo:titota-ni- qat
 everyone knows   they win-   inc-ds
 c. 'Everyone knows that he will win.'

Analogous examples could be constructed where the subject of *knows* is the interrogative pronoun *who?*

Now (24a) unequivocally means that John is thinking about himself, whereas (24b) means that he is thinking about some third party known to both speaker and hearer. Analogous claims hold for (25a) and (25b). It is worth noting perhaps that similar judgments of positive or negative co-reference obtain in Japanese, a more accessible language to readers of this paper, for the (25) case above.

(26) a. daremo ga zibun ga katu to   omotte iru
 everyone subj self subj win COMP think be
 'Everyone thinks that he is winning.'
 b. daremo ga kare ga katu to   omotte ira
 everyone subj he subj win COMP think be
 'Everyone thinks that he is winning.'

Clearly the natural translations of the a- and b-sentences above are the same in English, and hence are not exact translations since they have a broader range of truth conditions than either of the ones they purport to translate.

Let us consider first how we might attempt to give more adequate translations, in particular to the b-sentences in which negative co-reference is stipulated. We might try e.g.

(27) There is someone different from John who John knows will win.

But this translation is inexact for two reasons: first, it explicitly asserts the non-identity of John and the winner, whereas this information is presupposed in (24b). That is, if (24b) is false in Hopi, we have still claimed that there is a fact which John does not know, namely the one expressed roughly in English by *he will win*, where *he* is understood to be a third party identifiable to speaker and hearer and different from John. But if (27) above is false we are merely claiming that there is no one different from John about whom John knows that he will win. Thus we are not committed by this denial to the claim that there even is anyone different from John, whereas the denial of (24b) does force this commitment. And second, (27) fails to identify a winner for the addressee. It claims that there is a winner (since it claims that there is someone who John knows will win) but it does not identify (or re-identify) that individual for the addressee. In other words, in order for the b-sentences in Hopi and Japanese to be true on an occasion of their use, both the speaker and the hearer must know who the winner is. But (27) places no such requirement on its truth conditions. A similar objection can be raised against a purported translation of (24b) by (28).

(28) John knows that someone different from himself will win.

Clearly (28) means only that what John knows is that someone different from himself will win, but it does not identify that person. So what we are claiming in a sentence like *John knows that he will win* (regardless of what reference conditions we place on *he*) is quite different since *he will win* and *someone (other than John) will win* express different facts. To avoid this problem Katz (this volume) has suggested sentences like (28) as translations of (24b).

(29) John knows that some particular person different from himself will win.

Here the use of words like *particular, specific*, or *definite*, are supposed in some way to identify the winner and so make a stronger claim than the mere existence (of a winner) claim in (28). But again this attempt is not, in my opinion, fully successful. To see this, compare first the meanings of (30a)–(30c) below.

(30) a. He will win.
      b. Someone will win.
      c. Some particular person will win.

The difference in meaning between (30a) and (30b) is obvious. (30a) requires that in the context of its utterance a third party be identified to speaker and

7

it makes a claim about him—namely that he will win. The claim is false if that individual will not win. But in (30b) no winner is identified, merely the existence of a winner is asserted, and the claim is only false if there will be no winner.

The meaning difference between (30b) and (30c) is much less clear however. For (30c) in fact gives no more information about whoever it is who will win than does (30b). The term *particular* it seems to me, functions as an indicator that the speaker of (30c) possesses further identifying information about the winner, which he can provide if necessary, but the word *particular* does not itself provide that information. This difference shows up more strikingly when (30b) and (30c) are embedded under higher predicates like *say* and *know*.

    (31)   a. John said that someone would win.

            b. John said that some particular person would win.

(31b) differs in meaning from (31a) in the following way: (31b) contains all the information in (31a), but in addition indicates that either John or the speaker of (31b) possesses further identifying information concerning the winner. Thus, suppose that what John had actually said was *Fred will win* but the speaker of (31b) knows that the addressee of (31b) does not know who Fred is. So it would be pointless for the speaker to report John's statement using the name *Fred* since that use would presuppose that the addressee would know who the referent of that name was. So the speaker may naturally report John's speech using a phrase like *some particular person* indicating that further identifying information concerning the winner can be provided.

In other words, phrases like *particular* are used precisely when the speaker judges that further identification of the person in question is not appropriate, but where he wants to indicate that he can provide further identification if needed. Hence (29) fails to be an exact paraphrase of (24b) for the same reason as does (25), namely it does not presuppose that a winner is already identified to the speaker and addressee. Hence an assertion of (29) is true in a somewhat broader range of cases than is an assertion of (24b)—for it can hold in cases where the addressee has no way to identify the purported winner.

We might add here that (29) fails to translate (24b) exactly for another reason: namely (29) has a contradictory reading in which it implies that there is someone who is different from himself. Pragmatically speaking we can ignore this reading since we can usually assume that a speaker does not intend to assert that an obviously impossible state of affairs obtains. But logically this reading is naturally determined as a function of the structure of the parts of the sentence. That is, heads of relative clauses (e.g. *someone (who is) is different from himself*) can universally control reflexive pronouns when the head functions as the subject of the restricting predicate. So (29) possesses an ambiguity not present in (24b) and for this reason again fails to be an exact translation.

Consider finally whether (24c) for example is ambiguous or merely vague as between the readings expressed by (24a) and (24b) in Hopi. Note first that even if (24c) is ambiguous, it would appear to be an essential ambiguity if the two meanings cannot otherwise be unequivocally disambiguated, as we have argued above. So the ambiguity is an essential ambiguity in the sense of 2 and for that reason (24c) still is not an exact translation of (24b).

Further it seems to us that in fact (24c) is vague not ambiguous between the meanings of (24a) and (24b). For an assertion of (24a) forces the speaker to assume the identity of the knower and the winner; and an assertion of (24b) commits the speaker to the claim that they are possibly not the same. But (24c) forces neither commitment on the part of the speaker. If the speaker has no opinion concerning the relative identities of the knower and the winner he may, as in e.g. a discussion of 'New Zealand's top track star' still report John's knowledge that he (New Zealand's top track star) will win without having to have an opinion as to whether John is, or is not, a track star. So (24c) then simply fails to code any information concerning the relative identity of the knower and the winner, whereas (24a) and (24b) each code such information.

It appears once again then that the Exact Translation Hypothesis is falsified. The question of concern now should be not whether we can say anything exactly in one language that we can say in any other, but how much languages differ with regard to the exact types of information they encode.

Jerrold J. Katz

Effability and Translation[1]

1. *Exploiting scepticism*

THIS PAPER DEALS with the foundations of a theory of natural language, specifically what such a theory ought to say about the logical structure of sentences in natural language. The general questions the paper deals with are: *What are the basic principles of a semantic theory of natural language? How should such principles be systematised?* and *What overall conception of the relation between logic and language do they provide?*

The standard approach to the fundamental principles of a theory involves familiar steps of successive abstraction from empirical generalisations.[2] An equally good way of seeing what principles are basic to a theory, which moreover has the advantage of constituting a considerable short-cut, is to exploit scepticism. We can look at the principles the sceptic challenges when denying that there can be any knowledge of the kind afforded by a theory or (what amounts to almost the same thing) we can look at the principles called into question when the sceptic tells us we can know none of the things we ordinarily believe we know about a subject. Such principles are the fundamental principles of a theory of the subject.

To appreciate the value of taking scepticism seriously, we have only to think of outstanding philosophical sceptics such as Hume and Descartes. This serves as a reminder, if one is needed, not to be deterred by what is at first sight so extreme a challenge to our entrenched beliefs of ordinary life as to incline us to dismiss scepticism immediately as *ipso facto* beyond the bounds of serious argumentation. In Descartes' case, there was an important method in the madness. Sceptics do not always really intend to prove to us that we cannot know any of the things we naïvely think we know; sometimes they merely wish to demonstrate to us that we are too naïve about how we know them.

1. The author wishes to thank the editors of this volume for the request that led, eventually, to the writing of this paper, and to thank Ms. Joan Levinson for her editorial assistance.
2. This approach is taken in Katz (1972) and in the earlier papers on semantic theory beginning with Katz and Fodor (1963).

Furthermore, the example of Hume will remind us that it can even be a mistake to dismiss the pyrrhonistic sceptic, who does indeed intend to show us that we do not know what we think we do. Too many philosophers are ready to take the view that anyone prepared to sacrifice so large a portion of our knowledge cannot be 'epistemologically responsible'. But if we do not allow ourselves to rest secure in our beliefs of ordinary life, knowing them to be too well-entrenched to be overturned by pyrrhonism, we stand to gain a great deal. For one thing, sceptics have an uncanny eye for fundamental principles: consider Hume on any of the major questions he addressed. For another, what appears at first blush as epistemological irresponsibility can turn out to be a difference in metaphysical outlook. Hume's pyrrhonistic criticism of the concept of causality stemmed not from an irresponsible libertinism but, as Kant observed (1951), from a responsible empiricism.

Thus, an appropriately pyrrhonistic sceptic in the domain of semantics ought to be useful to us in our attempt to uncover the basic principles of a semantic theory of natural language. We ought to be able to obtain very good approximations to such principles simply by negating each of the sceptic's main theses. Moreover, in pursuing this approach, we will be following to some degree Kant's strategy in his reply to Hume. Kant denied Hume's thesis that the part of the concept of causality that (as Hume himself had proven) is irreducible to co-occurrence is metaphysical nonsense, since the thesis rested not only on Hume's proof of irreducibility but also on Hume's empiricism. Kant formulated this denial positively, as the rationalist principle that the irreducible part of this concept is an innate idea. And he framed a theory of knowledge based on the systematic elaboration of this rationalist principle.

An appropriately pyrrhonistic sceptic about the possibility of a theory of meaning is readily at hand. For most of his career, Quine has been as staunch a sceptic about the concept of meaning as Hume was about the concept of causal necessitation. The underlying metaphysic in Quine's case, too, is empiricism.[3] Thus, determining against what Quinian scepticism is directed will enable us to determine the basic principles of a semantic theory.

What Quine is sceptical of is, in a word, propositions. From his earliest discussions of the status of semantic concepts in linguistics and philosophy (1953b), through his attack on the analytic-synthetic distinction (1953a; 1966b), and finally culminating in his thesis of the indeterminacy of translation (1960; 1969), Quine has consistently and continuously denied the possibility of any theory of propositions based on the traditional, intensionalist concept of meaning. Like Hume, his claim was that the part of the concept

3. For particularly clear statements, see Quine (1953a, 1966a).

of meaning that cannot be reduced to empirical co-occurrence is metaphysical nonsense. Accordingly, stimulus-meaning is, for Quine, the only legitimate kind of meaning (1960, 80–2). The thesis of the indeterminacy of translation, undoubtedly Quine's major contribution to the philosophy of language, was developed and has its primary application as an argument against propositions. Quine makes it abundantly clear that his crucial argument 'not only against our specific plan of structural-synonymy concept as a standard of propositional identity, but against the whole idea of positing propositions' (1960, 205) is the indeterminacy of translation.

Now that we have our sceptic, we may apply our strategy for arriving directly at the basic principles of semantic theory. First, we select the following passage from Quine's writings because it expresses his major sceptical theses about the theory of meaning (1960, 205–6):

> For, insofar as we take such a posit seriously, we thereby concede meaning, however inscrutable, to a synonymy relation that can be defined in general for eternal sentences of distinct languages as follows: sentences are synonymous that mean the same proposition. We would then have to suppose that among all the alternative systems of analytical hypotheses of translation which are compatible with the totality of dispositions to verbal behaviour on the part of the speakers of two languages, some are 'really' right and others wrong on behaviourally inscrutable grounds of propositional identity. Thus the conclusions reached in [the argument for indeterminacy] may of themselves be said implicitly to scout the whole notion of propositions, granted a generally scientific outlook. The difficulties cited earlier in the present section are merely by the way. The very question of conditions for identity of propositions presents not so much an unsolved problem as a mistaken ideal.

Next, we extract the main claims and form their negations. Then, we reformulate to avoid negative statements, arriving at the positive statements (1)–(4).

(1) Propositions exist and are the object of study in semantics.

(2) The question of what are the identity conditions for propositions is sound, and its answer constitutes the ideal of theory construction in semantics.

(3) Synonymy relations can be defined generally for sentences of distinct (and the same) natural languages.

(4) Alternative hypotheses of translation (or synonymy) are never compatible with the totality of dispositions to verbal behaviour on the part of speakers of two languages (or the same language). Genuinely *alternative* hypotheses, not merely different notations

expressing the same claim about sentences, are ultimately distinguishable either on grounds of evidence or methodology (i.e. simplicity, etc.); some hypothesis is 'really' right and others wrong on grounds of propositional identity.

Finally, (1)–(4) should be systematically elaborated. Perhaps some more extensive reformulation will provide a deeper account of the foundations of semantic theory.

2. *More exploitation*

Scepticism may serve different metaphysical masters. For Descartes, it was rationalism; for Hume, empiricism. As the example of Hume and Kant suggests, we ought to be able to determine the metaphysical character of a theory on the basis of the metaphysics underlying the scepticism that denies its existence: the metaphysical position of the theory ought to be the opposite of that underlying the scepticism that denies the possibility of such a theory. Hence, we may hope that an examination of the empiricism underlying Quinian scepticism will shed light on the rationalist character of a semantic theory.

I will not undertake here a full-scale examination of the empiricism on which Quine's scepticism rests. I have done this elsewhere (Katz, 1974; 1975) in the course of defending (1)–(4) against Quine's sceptical arguments. That defence had the following form. First, we exhibited the particular empiricist assumptions on which Quine's anti-intensionalist arguments rest. We showed that the premises of these arguments depend on the Bloomfieldian theory of taxonomic grammar, both its empiricist view of the structure of natural languages and its empiricist methodology for linguistic investigation. Second, we showed that none of Quine's sceptical arguments go through without these assumptions and the theory of taxonomic grammar on which they depend. Finally, we drew the obvious conclusion from recent developments in linguistics in which the taxonomic theory has been shown false and replaced by the transformational theory of grammar, namely, that as a consequence of these developments the premises of Quine's sceptical arguments too are refuted.

Assuming that this line of defence is right, let us look more closely at the kind of theory on which Quine rested his sceptical arguments. First and most significantly, that theory was fashioned on the early logical empiricist conception of scientific theories. It was thus built not only on an extremely crude picture of science but on a view highly biased in favour of the empiricist theory of scientific knowledge.[4] The logical empiricist tenet that the concepts of a scientific theory should be statable exclusively in an observation vocabulary, whose terms could be introduced on the basis of suitable operational tests, was understood to imply that a grammar of a language is a theory of nothing more than the physical structure of utterances, whose terms stand for classes into which utterances and their parts can be placed on the basis of distributional regularities. A taxonomic grammar represents the observationally distinguishable segments of utterances as members of phonological morphological, and syntactic classes, forming a hierarchy from the significant speech sounds in an utterance up to the highest constituent structure categories to which it belongs. These classes are inductive projections from phonological, morphological, and syntactic regularities, and they are defined in terms of distributional tests in which some observational property is found to remain invariant when any member is substituted for another member in an utterance. The methodology that governs the use of such tests in forming the higher levels of the classification guarantees that the concepts at any level will always be statable in an observation vocabulary of acoustic elements by demanding a strict bottom to top flow (Chomsky, 1964). At the initial stage, each class is based on segmentation and classification of physical characteristics of the speech signal, and at each subsequent stage, this methodology allows only classes definable in terms of co-occurrences among the classified segments (or strings of classified segments) from the immediately preceding stage. Hence, the members of any class at any level are always reducible to physical parts of an acoustic signal. It is no wonder, then, that transformationalist critics of this conception of grammars compared taxonomic grammars to catalogued books in a library and taxonomic theory to classificational schemes like the Dewey Decimal System.[5]

This aspect of taxonomic theory was a matter of explicit design on the part of Bloomfield and his followers for whom such a conception of grammar was the only sure safeguard against mentalism and animism. Bloomfield once said:

4. To call the early positivist views 'highly biased' may be too extreme a form of understatement, but this is exactly what is true of the theories of scientific knowledge— the explications or rational reconstructions—which emerged from these views when logical empiricists became respectable as professional philosophers of science. I have in mind the notion of translation into an empiricist language as a criterion of cognitive significance (see Hempel, 1965, 101ff). Without a strong antecedent bias against *a priori* concepts, the fact that some concept is not translatable into an empiricist language is no basis for claiming it is not cognitively significant. It might, if rationalists are right about the existence of innate ideas, not be learned from experience and not definable in terms of observation vocabularies. See, for example, Bloomfield (1955, 230-1).

5. See Chomsky's discussion of the view he calls 'taxonomic phonemics' in Chomsky (1964, 91-112).

7*

> Non-linguists . . . constantly forget that a speaker is making noise, and credit him, instead, with the possession of impalpable 'ideas'. It remains for the linguist to show, in detail, that the speaker has no 'ideas', and that the noise is sufficient . . . (1936, 93)

> Within the next generations mankind will learn that only such terms as are translatable into the language of physical and biological science, are usable in any science. The terminology in which at present we try to speak of human affairs—the terminology of 'consciousness', 'mind', 'perception', 'ideas', and so on—in sum, the terminology of mentalism and animism—will be discarded. (1933, 89)

Quine endorsed this attitude of taxonomic linguists:

> Now there is considerable agreement among modern linguists that the idea of an idea, the idea of a mental counterpart of a linguistic form, is worse than worthless for linguistic science. I think the behaviourists are right in holding that talk of ideas is bad business even for psychology. (1953b, 48)

The anti-mentalism and physicalism espoused by Bloomfield and Quine constitute essential elements in their empiricism. Since grammars are theories of what we come to know about the structure of a language in the process of acquiring fluency in it, the properties ascribed to a language by a particular grammar determines, for those who accept the grammar as a true theory, what can be said about the linguistic knowledge of its speakers. Since this knowledge is the end-product of the acquisition process, physicalism and behaviourism (at the level of theories about the grammatical structure of a natural language) support empiricism (at the level of theories about the acquisition of knowledge of a language) by allowing nothing into the characterisation of the product of the acquisition process that would prevent empiricist theories of acquisition from emerging as the best hypotheses. The physicalistic and behaviouristic character of taxonomic theory allows descriptions of natural languages to use only concepts whose content refers to observable features of the speech signal and whose conditions of application are given in terms of overt behaviour. This means that there ought to be nothing about the structure of a language that could not be acquired as an inductive extrapolation from observable regularities in speech behaviour. Since empiricism is the doctrine that our knowledge (except, of course, our knowledge of the principles of inductive extrapolation themselves) reflect nothing more than the regularities of our experience, if descriptively adequate grammars of natural languages conform to physicalist and behaviourist constraints (that is, are taxonomic grammars), there will be no linguistic facts to count against the empiricist claim that nothing more complex than an empiricist theory of acquisition is necessary. On the other hand, if the simplest and most revealing grammars of natural languages cannot be written within the constraints of a physicalist and behaviourist methodology, optimal grammars will contain concepts that refer to internal states of the organism that cannot be defined in terms of behaviour and properties of the accoustic signal. The fact that these concepts will be unexplainable on the basis of principles of inductive extrapolation and observational evidence about co-occurrence relations will lend strong support to the rationalist claim that the speaker is innately programmed with a set of highly abstract grammatical concepts reflecting the structure of the language.

The relation between the level of theories about grammatical structure and the level of theories about the acquisition of grammatical competence bears in another important way upon the empiricist-rationalist controversy in philosophy. On the taxonomic theory of grammars, the only aspects of sentence structure that have the appropriate physical reality to count as part of its grammar are its sounds and their syntactic organisation in utterances. The levels of sentential analysis in taxonomic grammars begin with the linguistically significant sounds of a language and end with the syntactic concatenations that pattern these sounds into words, phrases, clauses, and sentences. The methodology of taxonomic grammar thus guarantees that the elements at any level in such classificational hierarchies will be reducible to the significant sounds at the lowest level, and as a consequence, *it guarantees that there will be no semantic level in taxonomic grammars.* Hence, taxonomic theory claims that meaning is not part of grammatical structure.

Since meaning is external to the grammar of sentences, it is natural to treat semantic relations, as Bloomfield and Quine both did, in terms of stimulus-response associations between the organism and its environment (Bloomfield, 1933, 139-57; Quine, 1960, 8off; see Chomsky's criticisms in Chomsky, 1968b). The advantage of excluding semantics from grammar for empiricism is substantial. If knowledge of a language is what taxonomic grammarians say it is—in particular, if semantics is what they say it is, then, the sentences of a natural language can, in principle, express nothing stronger than associative connections. That is to say, a sentence like

(5)   Bachelors are male

cannot be taken to express a necessary connection but only a contingent one, since, on S-R theory, the connection they express is the kind that results from frequently repeated, contiguous pairings of things in our experience. As speakers of the language, we learn that 'bachelor' is associated with a sample of bachelors on the basis of an exposure to uses of the language. In the same way, we learn that 'male' is associated with a sample of males. We also observe that each of the things associated with the use of 'bachelor' are things associated with the use of 'male'. (5) expresses the inductive extrapolation from these observations to the generalisation that future uses of 'bachelor', too, will be associated with things that 'male' is associated with. Falsification may be unlikely, but we can never rule out the possibility that some future use of 'bachelor' will not be associated with something that 'male' will be associated with. No inductive confirmation can provide the 'super strength' of a connection between events that holds in every possible world (Katz, 1974, 285–6).

On taxonomic theory, then, what we come to know is a network of contingent associations, and there is no need for empiricists to worry that sentences like (5) will be construed as expressing necessary truths. If they were so construed, empiricism would be put in the disastrous position of having to account for knowledge of connections that hold in every possible world on the basis of a theory of the acquisition of knowledge that denies its existence. Thus, getting semantics safely outside grammar constitutes taxonomic theory's strongest appeal for empiricists like Quine. The chief advantage was that this theory interprets sentences in a way that precludes them from expressing the kind of proposition that constitutes a counter-example to an uncompromising empiricism.

Another advantage of the exclusion of semantics from the theory of the structure of sentences is that semantic concepts like meaningfulness, synonymy, analyticity, etc. play no explanatory role in the study of the structure of sentences. This was the basis for all of Quine's criticisms of semantic concepts as explanatorily empty (like Molière's *virtus dormitiva*).[6]

The relation between theories of grammatical structure and theories of how we acquire our knowledge of such structure, which, as exploited by Quine, served empiricism (as a consequence of the influence of taxonomic theory), might as well serve rationalism. It is just a question of how the theory of a language specifies the character of the knowledge speakers have about the language. Hence, it is critical to understand the nature of the generative, transformational theory which overthrew the Bloomfieldian taxonomic theory in the sixties (Chomsky, 1957; Postal, 1964; Lees, 1957).

Chomsky's theory is in every significant respect the opposite of Bloom

---

6. Quine says that the appeal to meanings is like the appeal to a *virtus dormitiva* because it 'engenders an illusion of having explained something' (Quine, 1953a, 48). See Katz (1974, 295–303) for an explanation of how the *in*clusion of semantics in the theory of the structure of sentences, on a Chomskyan conception of such a theory, defeats this criticism.

field's. It is hypothetico-deductive where taxonomic grammar is observationalist; it is mentalistic where taxonomic grammar is behaviourist and physicalist; and it is rationalist where taxonomic grammar is empiricist. Chomsky's revolution consisted in showing that a descriptively adequated grammar for a natural language could not be written without violating the methodological constraints and the form of taxonomic grammar. He showed that the grammatical structure required to explain a range of facts about grammatical relations, syntactic ambiguity, sentence-type relations, well-formedness, etc. is not reflected in the 'surface structure' of sentences, but only in levels of structure underlying it.[7] Such 'deep structure' was shown to be determinable on the basis of hypothetical postulations of unobservable syntactic relations. These took the form of a model of a new level of syntactic structure from which it was possible to handle the facts that could not be handled within the taxonomic framework. Since the most plausible construal of the reality of deep syntactic structure was psychological, Chomsky was led to change the conception of formal grammars from data-cataloguing devices to models of the mental principles that constitute the native speaker's fluency in the language.

This change led directly to a rationalist theory of acquisition. Chomsky argued that if the best account of grammatical structure commits us to hypothetical postulations of highly complex syntactic structures underlying sentences that are in no way reflected in the physical form of their utterances, then, given the degenerateness of samples of the language in regard to such underlying syntactic structures, the speed with which language acquisition takes place, the existence of a critical period and so on, only a nativist model of the preconditions for language acquisition is reasonable. He thus formulated an account of how we acquire our knowledge of a language in which what cannot be acquired by inductive extrapolation from observable features of utterances is supplied by the operation of innate mechanisms for language acquisition—that is, species-specific, genetic programming that store the universals of language.[8]

This change in the conception of the nature of grammars opens the way

7. All the now famous examples, such as 'John is easy to please' and 'John is eager to please', 'Flying planes can be dangerous', and so on, were put forth as illustrations of how grammars whose syntactic apparatus is restricted to the representation of surface structure will fail to explain grammatical facts. For instance, the first pair of sentences was cited as an illustration of how such grammars could not account for the fact that in the former sentence 'John' is the object of 'to please' but in the latter it is the subject.

8. Chomsky (1962). Also, Chomsky (1967) and Katz (1966, 240–82). These works have sparked an empiricist rejoinder, as might be expected; see the recent anthology, Stich (1975), Goodman (1967), and Chomsky's reply (Chomsky, 1968a, 70–3).

for construing meaning as part of grammatical structure. Once the Chomskyan conception of grammars as theories of the internalised linguistic knowledge of speakers replaced Bloomfield's view of grammars as compact catalogues of corpus data, there can no longer be an objection to including semantic rules together with phonological and syntactic rules in grammars. Such semantic rules could be conceived of as hypotheses about the representations of the meanings of sentences and could be verified in the same way that hypotheses about underlying phonological and syntactic structure are verified, by deducing predictions about appropriate grammatical properties and relations of sentences and checking these predictions against the judgments of fluent speakers of the language.[9] The appropriate grammatical properties and relations in the case of semantic rules are semantic properties and relations such as meaningfulness, ambiguity, synonymy, analyticity, etc. If such prediction proves successful, the entire set of Quinian arguments that semantic concepts play no explanatory role in the grammatical account of sentence structure collapses. In helping to predict the semantic properties and relations of sentences, semantic concepts help explain the ability of speakers of the language to recognise that sentences have these semantic properties and relations (Katz, 1974, 295–303).

We may take stock now and ask what light has been shed on the rationalist character of semantic theory by virtue of its forming a component of the Chomskyan theory of language. First, semantic rules will be part of a theory that takes the form of a hypothetico-deductive postulation. They must dovetail with the syntactic rules of the grammar, but because some of these rules are quite far from surface syntax, semantic rules, too, may be highly abstract. Second, semantic rules will be part of a mentalistic theory of language. They are postulations about an internal representation whose content is not exhausted by its behavioural consequences in speech. Third, both by virtue of its abstractness and its psychological reality, semantic representations can be taken to represent a language-universal conceptual structure, a body of language-invariant propositions expressed with different sound and syntax from language to language. Finally, since Chomskyan theory is rationalist in taking the speaker's knowledge of the language to be a product not only of their experience with its sentences but also of innate

9. It is sometimes mistakenly supposed that such verification presupposes that a speaker must understand semantic properties and relations. But, although it is presupposed that a speaker's judgments result from an internal representation of the structures underlying such properties and relations, there is no need to suppose that a speaker has any intellectual grasp of them, that is, that speakers have to understand words like 'synonymy', 'ambiguity', etc. in their ordinary sense since the judgments can be similarity judgments with respect to preselected stimulus material. See Katz (1967).

universals of language, semantic theory (the theory of semantic rules) will be an important component in a theory about the organisation of our linguistic experience in the form of a grammar of a language.

3. *Toward a systematisation of the basic principles*

Scepticism has now outlived its usefulness to us, and we now turn to the question of what theoretical basis for semantics emerges when we try to systematise the principles (1)–(4). What will a full-fledged rationalist and mentalist theory of semantic structure look like and how will the problems of the philosophy of language and logic look from outside an empiricist position?

(1) makes propositions, entities to which the laws of logic apply, the objects of study in semantics. What does this mean? Semantics, as traditionally conceived, is the study of linguistic meaning, concerning itself with questions about the senses of expressions and sentences in a language. How, then, can the objects of study in semantics be the things to which laws like *modus ponens* apply? The simplest and most direct answer takes propositions to be senses of sentences. On this answer, a proposition is identified with the sense of a sentence in exactly the manner that physical science identifies water with H_2O.

The justification of (1), on this construal, must proceed in the same way that arguments for theoretical identification in other sciences proceed. The thrust of our justification would be that, given such an identification of propositions with senses of sentences, we simplify the overall ontology of linguistic semantics and deductive logic and we eliminate answerless questions about the basis of the alleged correlations between the behaviour of objects in one realm and the behaviour of corresponding objects in the other. Such an argument is not hard to formulate. The realm of deductive logic concerns the structure of valid arguments. Propositions are the idealised objects that make up arguments. The realm of language concerns the structure of sentences. The notion of sense is the basis for the distinction between the information content of a sentence and its sound pattern and syntactic organisation. But regardless of the differences in the way these realms conceive of their objects, there is as close a correspondence between facts about propositions and facts about senses of sentences as there is between facts about water and facts about H_2O. For example, logicians distinguish between sentences that express a proposition (enter into logical relations in arguments) and sentences that do not express a proposition (fail to enter into such relations).

(6) Charity drinks procrastination

is an example of the latter and

(7) Charles drinks prune juice

is an example of the former. Also, logicians distinguish between sentences that express a single proposition and those that express more than one proposition. The latter are traditionally taken to pose a danger for inference. Logicians often say that an argument like

(8) He insulted an old man and woman
(9) So, he insulted two old people

commits a fallacy of ambiguity because the premise (8) expresses more than one proposition. Further, logicians take some sentences to express the same proposition. Such sentences are taken to be interchangeable in arguments. Thus,

(10) Prune juice is drunk by Charles

is freely interchangeable with (7) in arguments because exchanging one for the other leaves the structure of the argument intact. Now consider the corresponding linguistic facts. Linguists describe a sentence like (6) as meaningless, that is, as having no sense, and they contrast it with sentences like (7). They say that a sentence like (8) is polysemous, that is, has more than one sense. Again, linguists say that sentences like (7) and (10) are synonymous, that is, have the same sense.

What are we to say about this correspondence? It seems wrong to say that there is a correlation. Aside from the fact that this position forces us to countenance both propositions and senses of sentences, thus twice as many things as we might have to countenance, how are we to explain this correlation? If we say that the logicians are talking about one kind of object and the linguists about another, what explanations are we to give of the fact that whenever a sentence expresses no proposition it has no sense and whenever it has no sense it expresses no proposition, or the fact that whenever a sentence expresses more than one proposition it is polysemous and whenever a sentence is polysemous it expresses more than one proposition, or the fact that whenever two sentences express the same proposition they are synonymous and whenever two sentences are synonymous they express the same proposition. It thus seems far better to say that there is not a correlation but an identity. This answer halves the number of objects to which we have to ascribe independent existence, and it eliminates embarrassing questions about the peculiar, unfathomable connections between propositions and senses of sentences. The identification increases in plausibility as a function of the effort made to answer the questions that arise on the correlation position.

(1) can be interpreted as saying that propositions and senses of sentences are the same things under different descriptions. On the description familiar to the logician, the object is represented independently of its embodiment in the linguistic forms that express it. On the description familiar to the linguist, it is represented as an inherent aspect of the grammatical structure of such forms. Questions naturally arise about whether it makes sense to speak about propositions in the way we speak about senses of sentences or to speak about senses of sentences in the way we speak about propositions, but these do not undermine the theoretical identification (Katz, 1972, 123–4). The reason it doesn't seem odd to say 'He refuted the proposition' but does seem odd to say 'He refuted the sense of the sentence' is explained by reference to the speech habits that result from superficial differences in usage reflecting the way that the two systems of description are customarily employed. We wouldn't translate God's command in *Genesis* as 'Let there be electro-magnetic radiation', but this is not because light is not electromagnetic radiation.[10]

What, then, about the further claim of (1), that propositions exist? Since what it means to say that something exists depends on what kind of thing it is, we have to first consider what kind of things propositions are. Within a framework that does not require its theoretical entities to be reducible to actual utterances or its theoretical terms to be definable exclusively in terms of overt behaviour, two views are possible. One is a realist view like Frege's (1956) on which propositions are abstract entities, and the other is a conceptualist view on which they are psychological objects of some sort, perhaps mentalistic constructions, perhaps certain kinds of brain states. On the former view, one would be obliged to say about propositions whatever

---

10. Other doubts about the identification of propositions with senses of sentences arise in connection with the senses of performative sentences. One might ask here whether it makes sense to identify the sense of a sentence like 'I hereby promise to go' with a pro-position in logic when the latter have truth values and the former do not. The question turns out to have a false presupposition about propositions. An examination of the issue shows not that the identification is mistaken but that logic requires more general notions of 'proposition' and 'validity' on which the concept of truth does not enter into either notion. See Katz (1977a).

platonist philosophers of mathematics say about numbers and sets.[11] On the latter one would say that propositions exist in whatever sense psychologists or neurophysiologists say that mental objects or brain states exist. The question of existence, insofar as it involves more than whether propositions are legitimate objects of theoretical speculation is not specifically about semantics but more generally about the foundations of semantics and related disciplines. We shall postpone trying to say something concrete about the nature of the existence claims in (1), partly for this reason, and partly because questions of existence are less important at the outset of theory construction, due to the fact that often a theory has to be obtained first and then, as a consequence of the existence of the theory, we discover in what sense the objects referred to in the theory can be said to exist (e.g. the case of the theory of the planetary motions).

On the basis of the theoretical identification, we can clarify the relation of (2) and (3) to each other and the relation of both to (1). (2) says, first, that the task of finding the identity conditions for propositions is reasonable. One hears it said that Quine is wrong in demanding a statement of the identity conditions for propositions as a condition for accepting as clear the notion of proposition. One hears the argument that we are not tempted to dispense with sentences even though we are in no position to provide a statement of their identity conditions. This, I think, misses Quine's point. Quine is saying that before we can accept a notion as clear in philosophy we have to have an explication or rational reconstruction of it. Antecedent to such an explication or reconstruction we might have one or another intuition, but to pass from opinion to knowledge requires such a philosophical theory that is impossible without explicit conditions of identity for the objects of the theory. We are not tempted to dispense with sentences, so Quine would argue, precisely because we think that we can construct a theory in which their identity conditions are explicitly stated.

(2) also says that an explicit statement of the identity conditions for propositions is the ideal of theory construction in semantics. Given our identification of propositions with senses of sentences, we can construe this ideal as that of defining the relation 'x is the same sense as y'. This permits us to individuate propositions in terms of their connections with sentences in natural languages, thereby enabling us to bring the full theory of grammatical structure to bear on the question of stating conditions of identity for propositions. Thus, the claim (3) makes is the central presupposition of

11. It is often not easy to figure out what such philosophers of mathematics want to say about them, particularly, the foremost platonist today, Gödel. See Chateaubriant (forthcoming) for a highly informative discussion of Gödel's position and criticisms of it.

theory construction in semantics. If synonymy could not be defined generally for sentences, there would be no possibility of giving the identity conditions for propositions in a semantic theory of natural language.

To so give these conditions, we require that semantic theory specify a set of properties and relations K such that 'x is the same sense as y' can be defined in terms of x and y having K-properties and K-relations in common. That is, K is the set of properties and relations such that the sense of a sentence S_i is the same as that of another S_j just in case, for any property in K, S_i has it if, and only if, S_j has it, and for any relation in K, S_i bears it to $S_1, \ldots, S_n$ if, and only if, S_j bears it to $S_1, \ldots, S_n$. Not every property and relation of linguistic expressions is in K. Since K defines an identity relation only for senses, the property of length, the relation of rhyme, the relation of sameness co-occurrence pattern,[12] etc. are outside K. K is the set of *semantic* properties and relations.

We can now say, abstractly, what a semantic theory is. It is a specification of the membership of K, a set of definitions, one for each member of K, which explicate the semantic properties and relations, and finally, a representation system for the semantic level of grammars in terms of which we can formally specify, relative to the definitions, the conditions under which a linguistic expression has a particular property in K or bears a particular relation in K to some n-tuple of linguistic expressions.[13]

How do we determine the membership of K? As I proposed elsewhere (Katz, 1972, Ch. 1), the most natural way is to take some property or relation to belong to K if, and only if, it is the subject of one of the subquestions to which the basic question of semantics, namely, 'What is meaning?', breaks down. That is to say, if a question about the nature of some grammatical property or relation has to be answered in order to answer the general question of what meaning is, then that grammatical property or relation is semantic. Since the questions 'What is sameness of meaning?' 'What is meaningfulness?' 'What is redundancy of meaning?' 'What is truth by virtue of meaning?' 'What is implication by virtue of meaning?' and so on, are such questions, the properties and relations of synonymy, semantic anomaly, redundancy, analyticity, entailment, and so on are members of K. The 'and so on' clause refers to other properties and relations that will turn out to belong to K because the principles on which semantic theory defines the

12. To show that some relation like 'same co-occurrence pattern as' is outside K, we have to exhibit a case in which a pair of expressions in its extension is not in the extension of the identity relation determined by properties and relations we know to be in K, or the other way around. See Katz (1974, 296).

13. This latter specification is the model of a semantic component for grammars.

clear cases of semantic properties and relations serve to define them, too (Fodor, 1968, 10–11).

From these considerations, we can see that (2) and (3) imply that the definitions of semantic properties and relations are universals, that is, synonymy, ambiguity, semantic anomaly, analyticity, and the other semantic properties and relations are the same in every natural language. This, however, is no stronger a sense of universality than applies to the phonological properties and relations of rhyme, alliteration, metre, etc.; though the particular structures that have such properties and relations may vary, the homomorphism among structures that defines a property or relation are invariant from language to language. Rhymes, for example, may be different in English and Mohawk, but rhyme is the same thing in both languages and in every other; likewise, synonyms and antonyms will differ in different languages but synonymy and antonymy are always the same thing.

Where semantics differs from phonology (and from syntax) is in the universality of its representations of linguistic expressions. That is, in contrast to the other areas of grammar, in semantics not only are the properties and relations universal but so are the structures that exhibit them in natural language. This is part of what (3) asserts. It can be made somewhat more precise as the 'determinacy thesis':

(11)　For any pair of natural languages L_i and L_j, and for any sentence S in L_i, and for any sense σ of S, there is at least one sentence S' in L_j such that σ is a sense of S',

which is so termed to contrast it with Quine's 'indeterminacy thesis'. Two comments on (11). First, sentences in natural languages are, in general, ambiguous. Hence, notions like synonymy have to be taken as equivocal, covering both a notion of 'full synonymy' (two expressions are synonymous just in case every sense of one is a sense of the other) and a notion of 'partial synonymy' (two expressions are synonymous just in case there is a sense of one that is also a sense of the other). We choose (11) as our determinacy thesis because there is no philosophical reason for wanting a stronger thesis framed in terms of the notion of full synonymy and such a stronger thesis is certainly empirically false. The alternative determinacy thesis would claim that S and S' (rather than a sense of S and a sense of S') have their semantic properties and relations in common. But it is a foregone conclusion that natural languages are not as closely related in morphological and syntactic structure as this stronger thesis requires.

Second, the notion of translation that we use in understanding the occurrences of this term in (4) depends on whether we adopt (11) or the stronger thesis. Since we have adopted (11), translation is a special case of partial synonymy (it is the special case of the relation of partial synonymy that holds between sentences from different languages). As a consequence, our notion of translation allows

(12) The children were asked to stop shouting in the house
(13) Someone asked the children to see to it that no shouting took place in the house

to be translations, whereas a notion based on full synonymy would not. It also precludes semantically anomalous sentences in different languages from counting as translations, whereas a stronger thesis which said that S and S' have their semantic properties and relations in common would imply that all semantically anomalous sentences are translations of one another.[14]

Both our notion of translation and the stronger one based on full synonymy should be distinguished from various non-logical notions. The difference is simply a matter of whether the properties and relations that need to be considered in determining if one sentence is a translation of another are only those belonging to K. Two sentences are translations in the logical sense just in case a proposition expressed by one has exactly the same semantic properties and relations as a proposition expressed by the other. In areas of scholarly activity where questions of literature rather than logic are central, the notion of translation is somewhat different. There the term 'translation' is used for a relation or set of relations that have to be defined not only in terms of the properties and relations in K but also in terms of some outside K, e.g. syntactic and phonological properties, properties of the discourse context, etc. Consequently, all sorts of sentences that count as translations in the logical sense would fail to count as (adequate) translations in a non-logical sense. For the time being, however, we shall concern ourselves with just the logical notion of translation based on (11).

(4) introduces the notion of hypotheses of translation and claims that they are fully on a par with hypotheses of other kinds in other sciences. Given what has been said so far, such hypotheses are statements that one sentence has a sense in common with another. The question in connection with (4)

14. The distinction between these two theses reflects the distinction between semantic properties and relations of expressions and semantic properties and relations of senses (ambiguity being an example of the former and analyticity being an example of the latter). See Katz (1977a, Ch. 3). We should point out here that accepting the weaker thesis does not prevent us from making use of the stronger one in areas where it applies, as we shall see when we discuss the hierarchy of translation relations.

is what form such statements must take in order for them to be on a par with hypotheses in other sciences with respect to scientific methodology.

The answer follows from our abstract characterisation of a semantic theory as a list of definitions of semantic properties and relations and a representation system for the semantic level of grammars. Since the meaning of a sentence (i.e. its set of senses) determines its semantic properties and relations, the representation system and the definitions must be framed in the same notation, so that formal properties of semantic representations in the grammar define semantic properties and relations in semantic theory. Since the formal statement of a particular semantic property or relation is an explication of it relative to the explication that semantic representations provide of senses of sentences, the definitions (14)–(17) are determined.[15]

(14)   A sentence S is semantically anomalous (lacks a sense) just in case the optimal grammar of the language assigns no semantic representation to S.

(15)   A sentence S is meaningful (has a sense) just in case the optimal grammar of the language assigns S at least one semantic representation.

(16)   A sentence S is ambiguous (has more than one sense) just in case the optimal grammar of the language assigns S two or more semantic representations.

(17)   The sentences S_1 and S_2 are (partially) synonymous just in case the optimal grammar of the language assigns them the same semantic representation.

Since translation is the special case of the synonymy relation where the sentences come from different languages, we have the definition:

(18)   The sentences S_1 and S_2 are translations just in case S_1 is a sentence of L_i and S_2 is a sentence of L_j, $L_i \neq L_j$, and the optimal grammar of L_i assigns S_1 the same semantic representation that is assigned to S_2 by the optimal grammar of L_j.

Hence, whether or not we predict that one sentence is a translation of another depends on whether or not the grammars we have constructed for the two languages assign them the same semantic representation. Accordingly, a hypothesis of translation is an assignment of the same semantic representation to sentences from different languages, and such hypotheses are special cases of 'hypotheses of synonymy'.

15. Others, of course, are not determined on so general a basis.

The form of such hypotheses depends, therefore, on what empirical investigations of grammars reveal about an optimal grammar, in particular about the representation of sentences and senses in the grammars of natural languages. The empirical question is simply what formal structure must semantic representations of sentences have in order for us to predict their semantic properties and relations. Empirical investigation proceeds by trying out various formalisms and revising them when they prove to be false or offer no predictions about a significant range of semantic properties and relations.

The claim in (4) that the choice between alternative hypotheses of translation is always decidable on the basis of evidence (given the usual methodological canons) is simply an aspect of this empirical investigation into the formal structure of semantic representations. If definitions of semantic properties and relations are given in the formalism of semantic representations, then, presented with a set of alternative hypotheses, we can deduce which make what predictions about the semantic properties and relations of each sentence that comes along. Given such predictions, we can then obtain judgments from speakers of the language about the semantic properties and relations of the sentence and thereby confirm or disconfirm some of the hypotheses. The claim that 'some hypothesis is "really" right and others wrong on grounds of propositional identity' is the claim that, in this manner, a false hypothesis can always be refuted by some extension of the present sample of judgments about semantic properties and relations on the part of speakers and only the true hypothesis will remain unrefuted by the totality of such judgments. This is to say no more than that semantics, and grammar generally, are no different from other branches of science. (4) is the form that the general scientific faith in the existence of laws and in the adequacy of reason to discover them takes in the special science of linguistics.[16]

4. *The role of effability in semantics*

The principle I have called 'effability' (Katz, 1972, 18–24) was propounded in somewhat different form by Frege (1963), Tarski (1956a, 19–21) and Searle (1969, 19–21). It might be stated, succinctly, as:

(19)   Each proposition can be expressed by some sentence in any natural language.

16. We return to this in section 8 where we argue that Quine's behavioristic methodology is all that supports his claim that non-equivalent hypotheses of translation can be consistent with all possible evidence.

In my earlier discussion of this principle, I argued that it comes much closer to expressing the essence of natural language than any other proposal made so far. In particular, I argued that even Chomsky's principles of creativity, appropriateness and stimulus freedom, significant as they are to our conception of natural language, fail to put their finger on just what it is that makes a natural language unique (Chomsky, 1966, 3–30). I argued that only the ability of natural languages to provide a sentence for any thought that differentiates them from artificial languages (which gain their expressive power parasitically from natural languages),[17] and from animal communication systems (which, although they can bear amazing resemblance to natural languages,[18] are patently non-effable).

Let us briefly examine this question before turning to the role of effability in the foundations of semantics. Recently, empiricist psychologists like the Gardners, Premack and others, have taken issue with Descartes' claim that language is a uniquely human attribute by arguing that, with the proper training and with the proper physical realisation of linguistic units, chimps can be taught a language or something differing only inessentially from a language. Their empirical results, however, do not refute Descartes' claim. Nothing in the chimp studies to date suggests that they can do anything more significant than we already had reason to think they could do (in the realm of cognitive processes) or that a cat or dog does when it rings a bell to communicate its desire to go outside. A chimp does, of course, acquire a far more complex set of discriminations in learning to arrange chips as a signal for food, but such a difference in degree does not amount to *the* difference in kind required to refute Descartes' claim. Unfortunately, this conclusion has not emerged as clearly as it might, in part because the criticisms that rationalist linguists and psychologists make of the work of these empiricist psychologists assume that what makes human language essentially different from other communication systems is wholly a matter of its syntax. Fodor, Bever and Garrett argue as follows (1975, 449):

> ... *all* of what Premack calls productivity in Sarah's use of language consists in her 'generalizing' from the trained content ... there is no indication that Sarah has ever done the most characteristic thing that a productive syntax permits human speakers to do: namely, use a sentence of a syntactically novel form

17. Artificial languages are parasitic in the sense of containing definitions of terms and predicates that are stipulative definitions, abbreviatory conventions, whose condition is expressed in a natural language. Hence, the primitive basis of the artificial language contains vast portions of the natural language used in such definitions.

18. The main example is the communication systems of social bees (see Lindauer, 1961, for general background).

without being specifically trained on sentences of that form. Productivity in human languages exploits iterative syntactic mechanisms which generate *novel constituent sequences.*

In short, chimps fail to produce the novel constituent structures from which we can infer internalised syntactic rules. Fodor, Bever and Garrett are right, but, as we shall see, having generative syntactic rules is only a necessary condition for speaking a natural language.

Descartes had empirical support for his claim that language is uniquely human. He pointed out that

> . . . men who, being born deaf and dumb, are in the same degree, or even more than the brutes, destitute of the organs which serve the others for talking, are in the habit of themselves inventing certain signs by which they make themselves understood. (Quoted in Chomsky, 1966, 4)

Recent work on American Sign strengthens this argument by producing evidence that the 'gesture language' of the deaf is not essentially different from spoken natural languages (Bellugi–Klima and Klima, 1975). Since a gesture system can qualify as a natural language, and since chimps can produce as wide a range of gestural configurations as can humans, it would seem that the best hypothesis to explain why chimps never develop a gesture natural language is simply that they lack the capacity to acquire any natural language.

The question to which Descartes addressed himself is Aristotle's question of what makes human beings unique. The question here is what makes natural language unique. Even if natural language is not uniquely human, it can still differ from other communication systems. For example, if it were to turn out that porpoises have the capacity for natural language, we would still be in the dark about the nature of the communication systems we share with porpoises. This can be seen from the following Gedanken experiment. You have just seen the TV broadcast of the first English–Porpoise bilingual performing feats of English-translation comparable to any other feats of translation. Do you now know any more about the *nature* of natural language?

Although the two questions are conceptually distinct, they are by no means unrelated. One way to see their relation is to note that those with the same philosophical outlook will answer the two questions in the same way. Rationalists like Chomsky follow Descartes in claiming both that natural language is uniquely human and that natural language is qualitatively different from even the most elaborate and highly ramified associative systems.

Empiricists like Skinner are disposed to think that natural language may well not be uniquely human and that what is special about them, if anything, is merely the great complexity of the associative connections making them up. The reason for these preferences is not hard to see.

Rationalists hold that the acquisition of linguistic competence is to be explained as a process in which innate schema expressing the form of a grammar are realised as particular hypotheses about the grammatical structure of a language. Empiricists, on the other hand, take the language learner's hypotheses to be determined by the form of the distributional regularities in the available speech sample. Empiricists emphasise the environment by taking the rules of a language to be inductive extrapolations from observed regularities. Thus, the empiricist's case for an environmental basis for natural language would be confirmed if it were the case that the more intelligent the species, the more language it can learn (assuming that conditions are constructed to compensate for such irrelevant things as vocalisation limitations). On the other hand, the rationalist's case for a genetic basis for natural language would be confirmed if the presence and absence of language were to coincide with the dramatic species difference between humans and non-humans.

The uniqueness of language is also relevant to the rationalist-empiricist controversy. If what is unique about natural language is simply its greater degree of associative connections, then empiricist models of learning offer plausible accounts of how languages are learned. If, instead, what is unique about natural languages is something entirely different from a network of associative connections, then some rationalist account postulating innate schema rich enough to explain the special structure of natural languages will be necessary.

Recent work in transformational grammar shows that a rationalist account of some sort is necessary. This work reveals levels of underlying syntactic and semantic structure that make it unreasonable to suppose that the rules of a language are acquired inductively from distributional relations in the superficial form of actual utterances.[19] But, beyond saying this, it is not clear

19. The argument, made by Chomsky and others, is, in a nutshell, that the underlying syntactic and semantic structure to a great extent has no reflection in the observable form of sentences, so that the language learner who is trying to induce the rules of the grammar from a sample of utterances would have to somehow form a hypothesis about such underlying, unobservable structure from a sample that is too degenerate with respect to this structure to permit such hypotheses as *inductive* extrapolations. The claim is that the only way that we can explain the fact that appropriate hypotheses obviously are considered is to suppose that their form is specified innately, thereby making up for the degenerateness of the evidence.

what can be said about the relative contributions of nature and nurture. Research in psycholinguistics based on transformational grammar has had little to say about the properties of a model of language acquisition. There is, to be frank, no nativistic acquisition model to which one might turn after rejecting empiricist models.

Rationalist linguistics has had equally little to say about the uniqueness of natural language. There are only scattered suggestions, principally by Chomsky himself. These, however, turn out to be too weak to work as an explanation of the uniqueness of natural language. Effability can thus be recommended as a preferable explanation, since, at least, it is not too weak to work as such an explanation.[20]

Chomsky reports that the Cartesians suggested 'the creative aspect of language use' as 'the essential and defining characteristic of human language' (Chomsky, 1966, 19):

> ... man has a species specific capacity ... which manifests itself in what we may refer to as the 'creative aspect' of ordinary language use—its property of being both unbounded in scope and stimulus-free. Thus Descartes maintains that language is available for the free expression of thought or for appropriate responses in any new context and is undetermined by any fixed association of utterances to external stimuli or physiological states. (ibid., 4–5)

There are, then, three components to the creative aspect of language use. First, there is *unboundedness*: this is understood as depending on the infinitude of the set of sentences. In principle a fluent speaker can produce or understand any of infinitely many sentences (thus ones that may never have occurred before). Second, there is *stimulus-freedom*: this is understood as the absence of control over verbal behaviour by external stimuli or internal, non-volitional states. Third, there is *appropriateness*: this is understood as something like 'fitting the situation', meaning how suitable or natural the verbalisation is in the situation. (The honey bee's waggle-tail dance is appropriate and unbounded but, presumably, under some strong degree of stimulus-control, while the shorthand of a drunken stenographer might be an instance of inappropriateness coupled with unboundedness and no stimulus control.)

All three of these features are significant aspects of language use, but it doesn't seem likely that any or all of them constitute the uniqueness of natural language. Unboundedness is a consequence of a system having

---

20. The other deficiency is a problem of far larger proportions. I have nothing to say about it except insofar as the remarks I will make about the uniqueness of natural language bears on the question of how a model of acquisition should be built.

recursive structure, and since such structure can be exceedingly simple, exceedingly simple systems, too simple to be a natural language, are unbounded. An automaton that just enumerates strings of a's of any length qualifies as unbounded. Stimulus-freedom and appropriateness, moreover, do not even seem particularly matters of language. They seem matters of performance rather than competence and matters of general behaviour rather than linguistic behaviour. Surely, a schizophrenic who makes inappropriate remarks under rather rigid control of external stimuli need not be taken to have any deficiency in linguistic competence. There is the same reason for saying that there is no deficiency in linguistic competence in such a case as there is for drawing the competence/performance distinction in the first place.

Premack reports that Sarah is capable of the productive use of conjunction (1969; 1971). Suppose she can produce strings of the form 'Sarah take apple, and candy, and banana, and . . .' with no upper limit on the number of conjuncts. Suppose also that she does this after having been trained on cases with only two conjuncts. This example, as it is, does not show that Cartesians are wrong in taking creativity to be the uniqueness of natural language, since with just this rule and a finite vocabulary of names Sarah's output is restricted, in principle, to a finite number of sentences. But, now, suppose Sarah's ability were to develop so that she learns a productive rule for names. Say she learns to iterate a chip n times to refer to n of the things to which the chip can refer. The 'chip-sentence' 'Sarah wants apple apple apple' translates as the English sentence 'Sarah wants three apples'. With this easily imaginable extension, Sarah's output is, in principle, infinite. Moreover, since her behaviour is stimulus-free in the proper sense and appropriate, it would appear that her communication system is creative. The fact that it is clearly not a natural language shows that we must look further for the distinctive characteristic of natural language.

The failure of the Cartesian hypothesis might be due to the fact that we can have infinite output even though there is no abstract structure. We may thus try a related hypothesis, based on the Fodor, Bever and Garrett's claim that Sarah failed to exhibit constituent structure and thus failed to be using language. Again, we can do a Gedanken experiment. Suppose the same rule for unbounded conjunctions as above, but, instead of the previous rule for producing infinitely many words, suppose Sarah's rule is the $[\Sigma, F]$ grammar G.

(G) $\Sigma : Z$
$\quad\quad$ F : Z $\rightarrow$ apple banana
$\quad\quad\quad$ Z $\rightarrow$ apple Z banana

Sarah's 'sentences' now include 'Sarah wants apple apple banana banana', and so on, but they no longer include strings such as 'Sarah wants apple'. In describing a grammar such as (G), Chomsky points out (1957, 30–1) that

> ... we have introduced a symbol Z which is not contained in the sentences ... This is the essential fact about phrase structure which gives it its 'abstract' character.

Thus, Sarah's strings now exhibit constituent structure. But the introduction of structure here has, if anything, made the case even less likely to qualify as a natural language, since Sarah no longer has the ability to ask for a single fruit or for fruits of the same kind. This criterion for the presence of language thus fails to offer us any better hypothesis.

The unifying theme of all these failures is the attempt to find the uniqueness of natural languages at the syntactic level. This suggests that the uniqueness of natural language has to do with its *semantic* as well as its syntactic and phonological levels. Thus, effability, the thesis of the completeness of the semantic level of language and the power of the syntactic and phonological levels to express the objects at the semantic level, has considerable initial plausibility.

Let us spell out some further aspects of its initial plausibility. First, it has something to say about semantic structure. It would be hard to believe that the unique feature of natural language has as little to do with semantic structure as the syntactic hypotheses suggest. Second, we immediately explain why we feel that in each of our Gedanken experiments Sarah fails to satisfy the real criterion for having a natural language. Third, this hypothesis squares with our notion that competence in a foreign language is being able, in principle, to say or understand anything in the foreign language. Indeed, the only way to know that our English–Porpoise bilingual is genuinely bilingual would be by some test to determine whether any thought we might ask to be translated is properly translated. Fourth, the hypothesis succeeds in making a distinction between natural languages, on the one hand and systems of animal communication and artificial languages on the other. The unbounded systems of animal communication with which we are familiar, like that of the honey bee, can now be dismissed as not a natural language since we know that its 'sentences' fail to say anything about anything except the location of food sources and nesting areas (and even fail to express information about elevation). Artificial languages like those in logic and computer sciences are the clearest case of the desirability of characterising natural languages in terms of expressive power.

The systematisation of the basic principles of semantics that was sketched in section 3 can be based on the principle of effability since the identification of propositions with senses of sentences is not restricted to any natural language or proper subset of natural languages. Since, in developing this basis, we want to compare effability with theses like the determinacy thesis (11), it is convenient to formulate effability as (20). Since we conceive of propositions, antecedently, as the objects for which the laws of logic hold, we may also state effability as the principle (21). This formulation suggests the complementary principle (22) for consideration.

(20) Every proposition is a sense of some sentence in each natural language.

(21) For every logical implication $P_1 \rightarrow P_2$ and for any pair of languages L_i and L_j, there is a sentence of S of L_i and a sentence S' of L_j such that P_1 is a sense of S and P_2 is a sense of S'.

(22) For any language L, and any meaningful sentence S of L, where σ is a sense of S, there is at least one logically valid implication of the form $P_1 \rightarrow P_2$ such that $\sigma = P_1$ or $\sigma = P_2$.

Now, although (22) is not directly relevant to whether we can understand the structure of the objects of which laws of logic hold within the theory of the grammatical structure of natural languages, (22) is of deep concern to the relation between logic and language. For (22) raises the question of whether the logical structure of natural language is restricted to the sentences that express assertive propositions. If there are logical implications between non-assertive propositions like those expressed by performative sentences that ask questions, issue requests, make promises, give warnings, etc., then (22) could be true; it is otherwise false. Elsewhere (Katz, 1977b) we argue extensively that there are such implications and that the conception of logic that denies this is, not surprisingly, the Quinian conception on which only the so-called logical particles determine implications (see also Katz, 1974; 1975; 1977a). We may, therefore, take (22) as a further basic principle of semantics, noting that it, too, could have been obtained by the strategy of extracting the central sceptical claims Quine makes and taking their negations as our basic principles.

Let us look at the general philosophical significance of the principle of effability and then at some of its theoretical implications. We understand the notion of a law of logic in terms of the following conception of logic. This conception is quite standard in denying that logic is the study of the laws of thought. Rather than trying to arrive at scientific generalisations about how actual thoughts follow one another and explanatory principles about their underlying dynamics, on our conception, logic is an account of the laws of validity to which inferential steps ought to conform. Our conception construes propositions as the abstract objects whose tokens are the various thoughts that occur in the process of thinking, just as sentences are construed as the abstract objects whose tokens are the various utterances that occur in the process of speech. Thus, the principle of effability (19) has to be distinguished from the psychological principle (23) which we may call 'expressability'.

(23) Each thought can be expressed by some utterance of a natural language.

This principle is implied by this conception of thoughts as the exemplifications of propositions in mental activity, the assumption of full grammatical competence, and the principle of effability. (23) thus represents the idealised functional relation of language to mind, on which language, as an instrument for communicating thoughts, is optimally adapted to its function (as such an instrument). If anything weaker than (23) were true, language would not, in principle, be perfectly adapted to serve as our essential means for communicating our thoughts to other minds.

In practice, of course, nothing like the strongest form of expressibility exists, because of 'performance limitations'. Expressive capacity is less than optimal when the apparatus for manipulating thoughts is for one reason or another unable to cope with exemplifications of certain propositions because the thoughts would be too complex or too extensive. Such cases are counterparts to the cases in speech production and recognition where the mechanism is unable to process exemplifications of certain sentences, e.g. those with many centre embeddings or composed of trillions and trillions of words.[21] These cases then do not constitute an objection to the claim that language is optimally adapted to thought. They reflect features of the mechanisms with which humans are equipped to use language and think. Creatures from outer space with astoundingly different performance capacities might fully share our natural languages and logic (i.e. speak English or French and reason in conformity with the same standard of validity) even though

21. Chomsky (1965, 10–18). In syntactic performance theories, the goal is to find the particular cognitive mechanism responsible for the failure in processing, e.g. Chomsky suggests that the very limited size of the storage facilities in immediate memory is responsible for the breakdown in the processing of sentences with multiple centre-embeddings. The same sort of goal ought to be adopted in semantic performance theories, with semantic representation playing the same role there that syntactic representation plays in standard syntactic performance theories.

propositions and sentences of a complexity that confound us are mere child's play to them.

Effability provides a theoretical basis for conceiving of the functionality of language that is optimal with respect to the class of propositions. This qualification is important. What makes Frege's claim that the syntactic and phonological rules of a natural language make available a 'form of words' for each thought significant is that the range of thoughts is, in principle, the full range of propositions. That a set of syntactic and phonological rules matches up with a set of thoughts can be uninteresting if the set of thoughts in question are highly restricted. The amazing thing about natural languages is that their grammatical correlation of sound and meaning involves no restriction on semantic structure. This sets them apart from any animal communication system and from any artificial language that is not simply a recoding of some natural language.

As rationalists, we explain the fact that effability is characteristic of natural language as a species specific biological trait, originating in a genetic disposition to programme language learning in accord with a very narrow set of linguistic universals. On the semantic side, these universals determine a conceptual space in which every proposition can be represented by some set of semantic primitives and some principles of semantic combination.[22] On the syntactic and phonological side, these universals determine a grammatical space in which every system of deep-to-surface structure mappings can be represented by an appropriate set of primitives and principles of combination. At present, we have nothing more than a sketch of an explanation. An actual explanation would show us why the semantic primitives and rules of combination determine a complete conceptual space and why the primitives and principles of combination in syntax and phonology determine systems of deep-to-surface structure mappings that match up properly with a complete conceptual space. At present, we cannot even say what either set of primitives and either set of combinatorial principles are. Nonetheless, we can't wait until after we have such explanations to ask what the kind of explanation it is that we want.

Such an explanation of effability automatically explains why natural languages are (as we assume) intertranslatable in the sense of (11). Assume (20). Then arbitrarily choose a pair of natural languages L_i and L_j and select any sentence S from L_i. If the proposition A is a sense of S, then, by (20), A is also the sense of some sentence S' in L_j. Since a sense of S is identical to a sense of S', these sentences are translations. Since the argument is

22. The primitives are the primitive semantic markers and the principles of combination are the projection apparatus.

general for any languages and sentences, effability implies intertranslatability. Thus the rationalist explanation of effability is also an explanation of inter-translatability. If it is a biological fact about the human species that under-lying its rational capacities is a conceptual framework with the potential to generate the set of propositions (all the thoughts that it is in principle possible to think), then each human language community has the same stock of possible thoughts. If, furthermore, it is a biological fact about the human species that underlying its linguistic capacities is a mechanism for acquiring syntactic and phonological rules that are functionally optimal with respect to the semantic structure of any language they can learn, then each human language community will speak a language that is in principle fully translatable into any other.

This rationalist viewpoint is, of course, in stark contrast with the empiricist account of the relation of language to thought and of language acquisition. Effability sharply focuses the rationalist-empiricist controversy on the con-crete questions of the relation of language to thought and the character of language acquisition. Quine and other linguistic relativists, such as Whorf and Sapir, make the empiricist assumption that the objects manipulated in thought are or correspond directly to the particular sentences learned in acquiring a language. Quine is particularly clear (1960, 76):

> Thus who would undertake to translate 'Neutrinos lack mass' into the jungle language? If anyone does, we may expect him to coin words or distort the usage of old ones. We may expect him to plead in extenuation that the natives lack the requisite concepts; also that they know too little physics. And he is right except for the hint of there being some free-floating, linguistically neutral meaning which we capture, in 'Neutrinos lack mass', and the native cannot.

To make it perfectly clear, Quine adds that it is an illusion to think that less theoretical, so more readily translatable sentences,

> ... are diverse verbal embodiments of some intercultural proposition or meaning, when they are better seen as the merest variants of one and the same intercultural verbalism. The discontinuity of radical translation tries our meanings: really sets them over against their verbal embodiments, or, more typically, finds nothing there.[23]

This is the very opposite of a rationalist view. For rationalists, cases of failure to translate theoretical sentences represent only a temporary inability of

---

23. In this connection, see Katz (1972, 20–21) where we discuss the reasons for thinking that the absence of an appropriate technical vocabulary does not preclude inter-translatability.

8

speakers, based on their lack of knowledge of the relevant sciences, to make the proper combination of primitive semantic concepts to form the appropriate proposition. That is, the failure represents a temporary vocabulary gap (rather than a deficiency of the language) which makes it necessary to resort to paraphrase, creation of technical vocabulary, metaphorical extension, etc. in order to make translations actual in practice, as well as possible in principle.

The empiricist assumption that our concepts come from experience is responsible for the empiricist's view that natural languages are not intertranslatable; similarly, the rationalist assumption that our concepts come from our genes is responsible for the rationalist's view that natural languages are intertranslatable. The well-known doctrine of linguistic relativity, which states that cultural differences produce incommensurate conceptual frameworks, derives neither from the discovery of exceptional facts about exotic languages by linguists like Whorf nor from important breakthroughs in the study of methodology by philosophers like Quine. Rather, the doctrine derives from the empiricism common to these linguists and philosophers.[24]

5. *The epistemological status of effability*

Because effability is a highly abstract principle,[25] it has seemed vulnerable to the charge that it is not empirical because it is not verifiable. Rationalists do not wish their hypotheses about language to be empiricist, but they do wish them to be empirical. Hence, we shall consider how effability might be verified.

Effability is a testable hypothesis: if there is any proposition that can be expressed in one language but not in another, effability is false. Thus, it can be refuted by showing that some meaningful sentence in some natural language cannot, in principle, be translated by any sentence of another natural language.[26] Effability implies intertranslatability in the sense of (11). Thus, the facts about intertranslatability in natural language bear on the

24. Whorf (1956) and Sapir (1921). Quine is not a linguistic relativist in exactly the same sense as Sapir and Whorf, as he himself points out (Quine, 1960, 77-8). His basic point is that it is mistaken to even suppose that the choice between conflicting translations of a sentence is like ordinary choices in science, where there is a right and wrong choice (see Quine, 1960, 75-6 and 205-6). My point stands, nonetheless, insofar as his doctrine also depends on his empiricism (see Katz, 1974, 1975).

25. That is, it is very far removed from empirical facts about what semantic properties and relations this, that, and the other sentence exhibits.

26. Katz (1972, 20-21). I would no longer want to say that 'the basic issue' is that of whether translation is always possible between any pair of natural languages, but simply that this is *a* basic issue.

truth of effability, precluding the easy criticism that effability is untestable.

Indeed, there are empirical arguments in the literature designed to deny that every natural language has the same expressive power. It will be worthwhile to consider an example of an argument which tries to show that some sentences in one language that cannot be translated properly by any sentence of some other language. Presentation of such an argument will establish that effability is empirical and examination of its structure will reveal the conceptual mistakes linguists are prone to make in attempting to test abstract principles about the relation of logic and language.

One example I have chosen is the argument in Keenan's recent paper 'Logic and Language'. He states his notion of translation as follows (Keenan, 1974, 193):

> ... for any two sentences of different languages to be exact translations of each other they must be semantically related to other sentences of their respective languages in exactly the same way.

This, construed straightforwardly, is a consequence of our conception of translation. If two sentences are translations, they have the same semantic properties and relations (with respect to a particular sense of each). Hence, they have to be semantically related to every other sentence of their respective languages in exactly the same way (again, with respect to a particular sense of each, since the claim fails for translation in the sense of full synonymy).[27] Keenan goes on to particularise his notion as follows: '... if, in some language, a sentence S presupposes a sentence T then any exact translation of S into another language must presuppose the exact translation of T' (1974, 193). He points out that restrictive relative clauses contribute to the presuppositions of a sentence: the presupposition of (24) includes the presupposition that there is a man who took the addressee's watch.

(24) The man who took your watch is over at the door.

From the fact that Hebrew allows relative clauses in sentential contexts where English does not, Keenan argues that 'sentences containing these relative clauses are not naturally translatable into English in a way that preserves the presuppositions of the original' (ibid., 194). The example on which he bases this argument is the Hebrew sentence:

(25) Zot ha-isha she-ami makir et ha-ish she-natan la et ha-sefer.

27. See the previous section.

(25), according to Keenan, has no translation into English with 'the same pattern of assertions and presuppositions', and thus Hebrew and English are not identical in expressive power.

If what Keenan claims about (25) were true, effability would have been refuted, and this illustrates a relevant empirical test for effability and shows it to have empirical content. But Keenan's claim is wrong. There are English sentences, of which (26)–(28) are examples, with the same pattern of assertions and presuppositions.

> (26) (a) This is the woman such that she was given a book by the
> man I know
> (b) This is the woman who received a book from the man I know
> (c) This is the woman who was given a book by the man I know

Each presupposition of (25) is a presupposition of (26) (a), (b) and (c), and each assertion of (25) is an assertion of (26) (a), (b) and (c); conversely, each presupposition of (26) (a), (b) and (c) is a presupposition of (25), and each assertion of (26) (a), (b) and (c) is an assertion of (25).

Consider another example from a more recent paper of Keenan's (1975, 18), the Hopi sentences (27) (a) and (b). These sentences reflect a feature of some but not all languages.

> (27) (a) pam navoti:ta (pam) mo:titani-q
> [he   thinks   (he)   win   -≠]
> (b) pam navoti:ta (pam) mo:titani-qate
> [he   thinks   (he)   win   -=]

The subordinate verb can carry one of two affixes depending on whether its subject is or is not co-referential with some noun phrase in another clause. (27) (b) expresses strict co-reference: the referent of the subject of 'win' is the same as the referent of the subject of 'think'. English will translate this sentence using a masculine singular first-person pronoun followed by its reflexive form as the subject of 'win'. (27) (a), like (25), is supposed to exhibit the limitation of English, since English has no form corresponding to the reflexive for marking referential difference. But, again, if we depart from the non-logical constraint to have translations parallel the syntactic form of the foreign sentence, we can translate (27) (b) by either (28) (a) or (b).

> (28) (a) He thinks that some specific male other than himself will win
> (b) He thinks that someone else, some particular male, will win

It should be noted that (28) (a) uses the grammatical device of, as it were, subtracting from the meaning of an expression to obtain one with a meaning that is neither too broad nor too narrow to be an exact translation of a certain foreign expression. With such grammatical devices in every natural language, arguments for differences in the expressive power between natural language face the extremely difficult task of attempting to show that no such device in combination with additive devices can produce the exact translation that such arguments deny. It is not even clear how to argue for the existence of expressions that such devices cannot zero in on.

The fact that our translations of Keenan's sentences are not syntax preserving does not make them any the less exact translations. Translation, as Keenan's own notion makes clear, has to do exclusively with semantic relations. Moreover, expressive power is always understood in terms of the propositional content of sentences rather than their syntactic or morphological form. If we take features of form to count in determining expressive power, we can get Keenan's conclusion that natural languages are unequal in expressive power quite trivially (namely, by considering phonological features, which there is no reason to exclude if one is going to include the syntactic and morphological features to which Keenan appeals). Keenan's mistake, as I see it, is a confusion of the logical notion of translation with other, non-logical notions that are prominent in the study of language use, which, unlike the logical notion, employ syntactic, morphological, and phonological relations in addition to semantic ones. We distinguish these notions below.

Intertranslatability doesn't, on the other hand, imply effability. It could be the case that every natural language is translatable into every other in the sense of (11), but at the same time none is effable in the sense of (20). That is to say, it might be that every natural language is limited in expressive power in exactly the same way. Although each natural language can express the propositions as any other, none of them is able to express every proposition. Given that the implication goes only one way, we might wonder why we should count as empirically verifiable the part of the principle that is not equivalent to determinacy. One might argue from analogy that having shown that a logical consequence of a principle is verifiable is not enough, since (29)

(29) Grass is green

is a logical consequence of the conjunction (30)

(30) The absolute is perfect and grass is green,

and is verifiable, yet it is not at all clear that this confers the slightest credit on the other conjunct of (30).

It is unnecessary to reply that the analogy fails because determinacy is not related to effability in the way that (29) is related to (30). We can imagine conditions under which effability would be false that are independent of whether or not determinacy is true.[28] The study of the laws of logic may proceed apart from the study of the grammar of natural languages. It may proceed as a study of valid inference and be carried out within a suitable artificial language. If the best theory of inference countenances as valid the implication $P_1 \to P_2$ and it turns out that the optimal grammar of some natural language does not employ a semantic representation for P_1 or P_2 as its account of the sense of a sentence of the language, then, as the formulation (21) shows, effability is false. The point is that a theory of validity might require the propositions P_1 and P_2 to state some valid implication, but the simplest theory of the semantic properties and relations of the sentences of some natural language might not require P_1 or P_2 as a sense of any of its sentences.

Effability is the strongest of the expressability principles upon which a semantic theory might be founded, and in the absence of evidence against it, it is, therefore, the most desirable of these principles to adopt. Anything weaker would be an arbitrary restriction on the expressive power of natural languages. Principles weaker than effability would say either that the semantic structure of natural languages is incomplete, some logical structures between which implications hold are not senses, i.e. not constructable from the semantic primitives and projection apparatus, or that the syntactic and phonological structure of natural languages is incomplete, some constructable senses are not correlated with sentences in the grammar's sound-meaning correlation. Choosing a weaker principle seems arbitrary because it claims that one, the other, or both of these incompletenesses obtain, without specifying what propositions are not senses or what senses are not expressed by sentences, or explaining why.[29]

One consequence of effability is that the class of propositions has the cardinality of the natural numbers. The set of sentences of a natural language has the cardinality of the natural numbers, and since propositions are senses of sentences and the number of senses of a sentence is finite, the propositions must be of the same cardinality as the sentences, that is, the cardinality of the

28. I am indebted to Fred Katz for the suggestion on which this point is based.
29. There is also the possibility, which cannot be pursued here, of motivating effability in terms of its advantages in theoretical systematization internal to the theory of logic and language. Such advantages are exhibited in Katz (in preparation).

natural numbers. Accordingly, one might claim that a deep ineffability still remains. The cardinality of the realm of facts would seem to be higher than that of the propositions, since presumably for each real number it is a *fact* that that real number is a number (less than some other number).[30] There thus seems to remain an 'ineffability' in the relation of facts to propositions, namely, not every such fact is described in some proposition which states just that fact; some elude conceptual representation. This seems relatively harmless when we note that it is not inconsistent with our continuing to theorise in mathematics in exactly the same manner as we presently do. Yet the possibility of exchanging this 'fact-to-proposition' ineffability for 'proposition-to-sentence' ineffability exists. One might wish to claim that every fact is described by a proposition but deny that every proposition is expressed by a sentence. This option, however, denies the identification of propositions with senses of sentences and thereby reopens the question of how we are to conceive of the connection between propositions and senses of sentences in those cases where the former are expressed by sentences. Taking this option is, therefore, tantamount to rejecting the theory of the relation of logic and language set out above. Conversely, to the degree that this theory offers an attractive account of the relation of logic and language, it offers a basis for rejecting this option.

6. *Non-logical translation*

Our discussion of Keenan's argument against the claim that every natural language has the same expressive power showed that further conceptual analysis is required to obtain a sufficiently clear picture of what facts are relevant to decide about effability and determinacy. It also showed that, for such analysis to provide a clear picture of what facts would be decisive against these principles, it will have to distinguish logical translation from non-logical translations and further distinguish among the latter. Confusions such as Keenan's were shown to be due to formulations of translation claims that are so vague that more than one distinct kind of translation is covered in a formulation, thereby allowing evidence that is logically independent of one kind to appear relevant to deciding the truth of claims about that kind of translation. Thus, once a conceptual analysis of non-logical translation is completed, it ought to be easy to sort out the features of sentences that count as confirming or disconfirming various claims about translation relations in natural language.

A semantic theory based on (1)–(4) determines the logical notion of trans-

30. I am indebted to Henry Newell for discussion of this point.

lation in terms of the class K of semantic properties and relations. Accordingly, non-logical notions must be determined on the basis of linguistic considerations beyond meaning. These must enter into the identity conditions for such notions over and above the membership of K. The logical notion thus forms a 'base line' for a hierarchy of translation relations, in which the higher the translation relation the narrower its extension in the set of sentences. The levels of such a hierarchy may be given by the classes of properties and relations that determine the identity conditions for these relations. K is the lowest level and each higher one, $K_1, \ldots, K_n$, is obtained from the preceding level by the addition of some set of non-semantic properties and relations. Since each set $K_1, \ldots, K_n$ determines the identity conditions for a higher translation relation in exactly the manner that K determines the identity conditions for logical translation, a particular translation relation R_i holds between the sentences S and S′ just in case S and S′ have the same properties and relations at K_i.

A proposal for such a hierarchy of translation relations depends on a theory of language for hypotheses about the kinds of non-semantic properties and relations sentences can have. Without attempting to make a concrete proposal, we may present an example based on current transformational theory:

(31) K = the semantic properties and relations of senses
  K_1 = K + the deep syntactic properties and relations
  $K_2 = K_1$ + the surface syntactic properties and relations
  $K_3 = K_2$ + the phonological properties and relations.

K_1 consists of the semantic properties and relations plus those syntactic properties and relations that are definable over the phrase markers representing the deep structure of natural languages. Thus, (26)–(28), although logical or, as we might say relative to (31), K translations of (25), are not K_1 translations of (25), nor are

(32) I need someone who has earned the degree of doctor of medicine or the equivalent

and

(33) Necesito un doctor

K_1 translations of each other. K_2 consists of the semantic properties and relations, the deep syntactic properties and relations, plus those syntactic properties and relations definable over the structures from which a natural language chooses the surface form of its sentences. Thus,

(34) The boy drinks whisky and the girl wine

and

(35) Le garçon boit le whisky et la jeune fille boit le vin

would not be K_2 translations of each other, and

(36) Whisky is drunk by the boy

would not be a K_2 translation of the first clause of (35). K_3 consists of all the properties and relations definable in terms of the entire representational apparatus that the theory of grammars makes available for the construction of grammars. Since it surpasses K_2 by having phonological properties and relations like rhyme, alliteration and metre, sentences like

(37) The rain in Spain falls mainly in the plain

and

(38) Deszcz v Hispanii pada przeważnie na dolinie,

which are K_2 translations, fail to be K_3 translations.

A hierarchy such as (31) is naturally construed as a part of a theory of multilingualism. The object of this theory can be specified, like Chomsky's specification of the object of a grammar, as a description of grammatical competence. We introduce the theoretical fiction of an *ideal multilingual* corresponding to the ideal speaker-hearer, who is an ideal speaker-hearer of every natural language,[31] and say that a theory of multilingualism is a theory about such a speaker's knowledge. As a special case, consider an *ideal bilingual*, that is, an ideal speaker-hearer of some pair of languages, whose competence is sufficient to determine, for any sentence in either language and any grammatical property or relation, whether or not the sentence has that property or relation. In both the general case and the special one, the theory has to contain the definitions of the theory of grammar plus the grammars of the relevant languages.

31. We have departed from Chomsky (1965, 3–9).
8*

Does it need to contain more? Is the theory of grammar plus optimal grammars of natural languages enough for a theory of multilingualism, or do there have to be further levels $K_4, \ldots, K_n$ whose properties and relations are non-grammatical?

The ideal bilingual is an abstraction from actual bilinguals engaged in imperfectly performing tasks of translation. Imagine our ideal bilingual engaged in the same tasks, but operating under none of the performance limitations that underlie the imperfections of actual translation. Accordingly, the range of these tasks is a matter to be determined by examining different kinds of translation activities and seeing what sorts of distinctions they depend on. The hierarchy, as part of a theory of multilingualism, will have to exhibit the properties and relations reflected in the various distinctions found in the activities of translators. For instance, because it would be reasonable to criticise (32) as a translation of (33) on the grounds of its excessive length, the K_1 properties and relations underlying prolixity should appear in an adequate hierarchy. Also, because it would be reasonable to criticise (38) as a translation of (37) on the grounds that it fails to capture the rhymes in the original, such K_3 properties and relations should appear in an adequate hierarchy. To decide whether or not the hierarchy should contain another level, we can look to see whether there are distinctions made between better and worse translations that rest on properties and relations not found in the levels K, K_1, K_2 and K_3.

I think (31) is incomplete. At least one further level is required, shown by a criticism standardly made of translations that they fail to carry the appropriate connotation. The criticism is that the expression or sentence in question fails to suggest the same constellation of stereotypic beliefs about the referent as the item undergoing translation. For example, neutral words like 'Negro' or 'Black' and 'Hebrew' or 'Jew' are not adequate translational renderings of pejorative terms like 'nigger' and 'kike'. The reason is that some aspect of the text may depend on the offensiveness of these terms, which is then lost in translation. The pejorativeness of terms associated with racial and religious stereotypes is not the only property that stereotypic beliefs contribute to the connotations of words. There is the regal connotation of 'lion' (but not 'felis leo') or the cute connotation of 'doggie' (but not 'canine animal').

Thus, the theory of translation and language use has a place for the kind of account of stereotypic concepts recently proposed by Putnam (1970; 1975). If such an account provides a systematisation of the attitudinal and belief structures underlying stereotypes, we will be able to define the properties and relations for a new level K_4, thereby making the theory of multilingual competence a far better idealisation of real translation as we know it, particularly in literature. But three things need to be taken into consideration if such a systematisation is to be obtained. First, in the form Putnam presents his account of stereotypic concepts, they are not distinguished from concepts that form part of the sense of a word in the language, especially natural-kind concepts.[32] In part, this is because Putnam mistakenly thinks that he has succeeded in disproving the existence of semantic representation of the kind on which the properties and relations in K are defined; he thus thinks it necessary to make stereotypic concepts carry the full burden of serving as the conceptual determinate of reference.[33] If, however, we make the distinction drawn in *Semantic Theory* (Katz, 1972, 450–1; see also Katz, forthcoming, section 1.1) between *narrow concepts* and *broad concepts*, the former being the senses of words, expressions, or phrases in the language (what determines its properties and relations at the level K) and the latter being the stereotype that emerges from the beliefs we have about the referent of a word, expression, or phrase (what determines its connotation indirectly through our beliefs about the typical member of its extension), then stereotypic concepts can be distinguished from semantic ones in a way that accords each their proper role in a hierarchy of translation relations. Semantic concepts set the base line at synonymy and figure in every translation relation, whereas stereotypic concepts determine the tightest translation relation in the hierarchy in terms of identity of the broad concepts of corresponding constituents.

Second, the attempt at a systematisation will also have to take account of the growing research in both psychology and linguistics related to the nature and use of stereotypic concepts in language, as well as the vast range of material in literary criticism bearing on connotation in the present sense. Third, there are puzzling cases resembling connotation of the kind already discussed in some respects but not others. An example is the contrast between obscene words and their technical equivalents, which seems quite similar to the contrast above between pejorative words and their neutral equivalents, but which seems dissimilar in lacking the underlying belief structures. This

32. I say this even though Putnam says explicitly 'What the essential nature [of something] is is not a matter of language analysis but of scientific theory construction' (Putnam, 1970, 188), because he criticises my semantic theory, which is solely a matter of 'language analysis', on the grounds that it does not offer insights into natural kinds, that is, the essential nature of things (ibid., 194). My point in the text is that Putnam fails to distinguish claims about the meanings of words *in the language* from claims about our knowledge of their extensions as presented in scientific theories about the world.

33. The 'disproof' is based on Putnam's robot cat case and others like it being counter-examples to analytic sentences like 'cats are animals'. See my rejoinder in Katz (1975) and Katz (1977b).

raises the question whether we have in K_4 the final level of the hierarchy or whether there are still other levels reflecting as yet unexamined aspects of language use, but this is a question, as they say, 'for further research'.

7. *The irrelevance of modal theories*

We can, however, show that so-called modal theories of meaning, or possible world semantics, provide no relevant properties and relations for a translation hierarchy (cf. Lewis, 1969; and more recently Hintikka, 1969; Montague, 1974a). In fact, the realities of translation provide what is perhaps the most revealing insight into the failure of possible world semantics.[34]

Modal theories represent the meaning of an expression or sentence in terms of its extension in all possible worlds. These theories sometimes take meanings to be functions that relate expressions and sentences to possible worlds, but such functions determine semantic properties and relations in the same way as they are determined by their extensions in the possible worlds.[35] Thus, instead of definitions like (14)–(18), we will have definitions like these (see Lewis, 1969, 174):

(39) Two expressions or sentences are the same in meaning just in case they have the same extension in every possible world.

(40) A sentence is true by virtue of meaning just in case it is true in every possible world.

(41) A sentence is false by virtue of meaning just in case it is false in every possible world.

(42) A sentence is contingent just in case it is true in some possible worlds and false in others.

Now, if we were to change K so that it contains properties and relations definable in modal semantics instead of in semantic theory, the translation relation would be a case of (39). Any sentences that are true and false in exactly the same sets of possible worlds are translations of one another. Measured against real translation, even of the loosest sort, the absurdity of this is truly staggering. It means that all logical and mathematical theorems are translations of each other, all contradictions are translations of each other, expressions like 'the even prime' are translations of ones like 'the number

---

34. Other revealing insights are found in Katz (1972, 182–4) and in more detail in Katz (1975, section 6) and Katz (1977).

35. That is, if two expressions have the same extension in every possible world, then, however the functions representing the intensions of these expressions are set up, they will have to provide a basis for asserting that the expressions are the same in meaning.

two' and expressions like 'the round square' are translations of ones like 'a right-handed southpaw'. Imagine trying to learn mathematics from a translation that is the work of a doctrinaire possible world semanticist!

8. *Indeterminacy revisited*

Quine's indeterminacy thesis concerns only K translation. Given a hierarchy of translation in which a number of different translations relations are distinguished, we are faced immediately with a number of different indeterminacy theses. Thus, besides Quine's, the K-indeterminacy thesis, we have at least a K_1-indeterminacy thesis, a K_2-indeterminacy thesis, a K_3-indeterminacy thesis, and a K_4-indeterminacy thesis. Having adopted (11), we are of course still free to reject them all and then agree or disagree with any of the counterparts of (11) based on other relations in the hierarchy, since rejecting an indeterminacy thesis is simply allowing the theoretical ideal of identity conditions of the kind in question, while rejecting a determinacy thesis can amount to nothing more than the factual claim that full intertranslatability at the level in question does not happen to exist. But, clearly, we want to hold that none of these indeterminacy theses is correct while taking no position *a priori* on the question of the empirical truth of any of the determinacy theses beyond (11).

The multiplicity of indeterminacy theses suggests that Quine's argument against propositions might suffer from a failure to distinguish among such theses just as Keenan's argument against the empirical truth of the determinacy thesis suffers from a failure to distinguish among translation relations. Let us look again at how Quine structures the case that raises the question of indeterminacy of translation. He imagines a situation in which the field linguist is working with a native informant who provides judgments of assent or dissent concerning the proper application of words in the informant's language (Quine, 1960, 26–80). Dispositions to such assent and dissent constitute 'the totality of dispositions to verbal behaviour on the part of speakers', the sole source of data available to the linguist. Structuring the situation in this way makes the linguistic data on which we decide between alternative hypotheses of translation the product of all sorts of factors beyond semantic competence. Moreover, factors reflected at every level of the hierarchy of translation relations enter into the make-up of such dispositions without a trace of the degree or kind of influence they have had on these dispositions or will have on the judgments. For example, the informant judgments on which the linguist will have to decide whether to 'equate a native expression with any of the disparate English terms "rabbit"',

"rabbit stage", "undetached rabbit part", etc.' will reflect the beliefs, customs, and attitudes that enter into K_4-translation.

But such decisions will not have to face the stronger test of conformity to native intuitions of semantic structure. Such equations are not, on Quine's structuring of the situation, required to predict whether bilingual speakers have the intuition that 'gavagai' is similar in meaning to 'branch', 'arm', 'heal', etc. or to 'tree', 'body', 'foot', etc. (see Katz, 1974, 290–1). Quine would, of course, be sceptical about the existence of such pure semantic intuitions, but this scepticism is part and parcel of his overall sceptical position and as such not to be *assumed* without begging the question.

From Quine's viewpoint, then, it seems foolish indeed to think that 'some hypothesis [is] "really" right and others wrong on grounds of propositional identity'. On the other hand, from the non-sceptical viewpoint developed here, it seems quite reasonable to think that. The difference lies in the differences between the viewpoints, first, the distinction between semantic properties and relations and others, inside and outside grammar; second, the construction of identity conditions for propositions in terms of semantic properties and relations; third, the creation of a theoretical framework in which semantic properties and relations can be defined and these definitions used to predict when particular sentences have particular properties and relations; fourth, a conception of the evidential basis for grammars that accords a role to the speaker's intuitions of semantic structure in testing such predictions; and finally, a methodology that characterises the notion 'simplest hypothesis of translation' in a way that gives definite meaning to the claim that one hypothesis is 'really' right.

To say that one hypothesis H is 'really' right is to say that the semantic representation it assigns to a sentence and its translation, S and S', is the simplest representation from which to predict each and every property and relation of S and S' in K. A representation is counted as maximally simple just in case no representation with fewer symbols predicts each and every property and relation of S and S' in K.[36] The fact that there can be more than one maximally simple semantic representation can be discounted just as we discount the fact that tree notation and parenthesisation provide equally simple syntactic representations. The methodological principle to which we appeal here is that, since maximally simple representations predict the required range of facts with no unnecessary assumption about structure, they count as notational variants. If two representations are equally simple,

36. I am making the standard assumption in generative grammar that we can devise notations for each level of representation in a grammar such that the simplicity of representations can be computed by a symbol count. See Chomsky (1965, 37–47).

predict the same facts, and make no unnecessary assumption, but are not notational variants because they offer different accounts of the structure in question, then there must be facts that they have as yet not been asked to predict and about which they will give different predictions. This principle is a special case of the classical rationalist principle that the real is rational.

Quine once suggested that the fact that 'different neural hookups can account for identical verbal behaviour' is an analogy of semantic indeterminacy (Quine, 1960, 79). If we take the set of properties and relations that determine the equivalence of functional theories in speculative neurology to consist of just relations between stimuli and verbal behaviour produced in response, then the fact that we can imagine different neural hookups in cases where the same input-output relations obtain is irrelevant. Functional neural theories are not concerned with anatomical hardware. On the other hand, if it is insisted that anatomical structure and input-output relations must form parts of the same neurological theory, that they cannot be separated, then properties of anatomical structure (how things are hooked up in the brain) should be in the set of facts that determine the choice between neurological theories. But, then, the hookups in the brain turn out to be a proper basis for confirming and disconfirming theories. One cannot have it both ways. Either some aspect of structure is in the set that determines empirical verification or it is out. If in, it can confirm or disconfirm; if out, then there can be no objection to ignoring it by counting otherwise equal theories as notational variants.

Quine's indeterminacy thesis wants to have it both ways. On the one hand, the thesis requires that *different* analytical hypotheses remain even after we consider not only all the available evidence but after we consider all the possible evidence (Quine, 1968). It must be the case both that hypotheses

(43) 'gavagai' translates into English as 'rabbit'

and

(44) 'gavagai' translates into English as 'undetached rabbit part'

assert incompatible accounts of structure and that no possible evidence confirms one over the other. If the former fails, the hypotheses are merely notational variants, different formalisms for expressing the same translation relation, and if the latter fails, indeterminacy degenerates into ordinary inductive risk. If, as we suggested above, there could be evidence from bilinguals bearing on the choice, indeterminacy would reduce to ordinary inductive underdetermination. What makes this dilemma fatal to Quine's indeterminacy thesis is that, outside of a methodological framework rigged to exclude intuitions of semantic structure from counting as genuine linguistic data, judgments from the relevant informants about which of the hypotheses match their intuitions, no matter what the practical problems of elicitation, would count as an empirical basis for choice. The point can be made 'crystal clear' by transposing Quine's indeterminacy thesis from semantics to phonology. Thus, corresponding to the question of whether (43) or (44) expresses an identity of senses, we have the question of whether (45) or (46) expresses an identity in pronunciation. Quine's

(45)   The German 'Herr' is pronounced the same as the English 'hair'.

(46)   The German 'Herr' is pronounced the same as the English 'teeth'.

indeterminacy thesis here amounts to the claim that such hypotheses are incompatible but remain even on all possible evidence, where the notion of evidence excludes the intuitions of bilinguals about rhyme, alliteration, and any other phonological properties or relations.

How hypotheses about synonymy can be incompatible and consistent with all possible evidence, how, that is, two hypotheses can make inconsistent predictions when there is nothing for them to differ about, is not easy to see.

Talmy Givón

Universal Grammar, Lexical Structure and Translatability

1. *Preamble: on slicing the pie*

IN THE PAST decade linguistics has been gravitating slowly towards a more traditional universalist view of language in general and its semantic base in particular. Unlike the classical Rationalists and subsequent Port Royal grammarians, this new-found universalism is more firmly grounded in the study of linguistic diversity and in particular of languages whose typological characteristics range far and wide of the standard Eurocentric fare. This expanded data base, while leaving the linguist in great awe of the typological diversity of human language, has nevertheless succeeded in firming up his old intuition concerning the universality of the human semantic base. This universality, in turn, may be attributed to a number of factors whose relative weight and potential interdependencies remain to be assessed: neuro-genetic constraints on the organism, physical universals concerning the biotop and its pragmatic properties, universal of socio-cultural structure and function. Still, even granting the ultimate correctness of the current return to universality, the problem of inter-linguistic translation persists. This problem springs from the fact that the great bulk of typological differences between languages involve the way in which they map their semantic structures onto surface expression. This mapping involves two interdependent components that together mediate between meaning and signal: syntactic structure and lexical organisation. One may find it useful to talk about each of the two in isolation, as indeed I will attempt to do here. Still, it must be conceded that in terms of typological characterisation of a language, syntax and lexicon constitute a single complex whose two components define each other.[1]

Lexical differences between natural languages may be of several kinds. Some may appear rather trivial to the linguist, involving accidental gaps[2]

1. I am disregarding here the 'shallowest' component of the overall mapping from semantic to surface structure, i.e. the ponological rules.

2. Given the socio-cultural context of a speech community, vocabulary gaps are seldom accidental. They most commonly reflect lack of pragmatic need or lack of dynamism within a certain sub-portion of the socio-cultural universe of the speech community.

in the membership of large lexical classes such as nouns, verbs, adjectives or adverbs. Though traditionally well publicised (cf. the Sapir–Whorf Hypothesis), gaps of this type are theoretically of interest only when the sociocultural specificity of languages is under consideration. And while this is a rather absorbing subject, it falls outside the scope of this paper.

Of more interest to a theory of translation are systematic vocabulary gaps, i.e. the presence, absence or skewed distribution of classes of morphemes, in particular so-called grammatical morphemes. One may conceive of three types of cases falling under this general category:

(i) Where the very same propositional contents or semantic structure is mapped differentially into surface morphemes or 'words', as in:

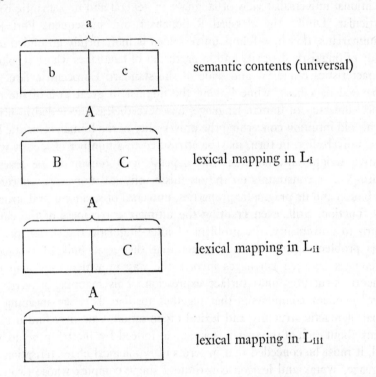

In situations of this type, both L_i and L_{ii} have adequate means of mapping the same propositional contents into their respective surface expressions, but they bunch up the semantic primitives in slightly different ways, as dictated by their syntactic-lexical typology. Neither is said to have an advantage over the other in terms of expressive power, they merely slice the same pie in two different ways.

(ii) Another type, more vexing from the point of view of the translator, involves inter-linguistic differences in the degree of expressive *specification*. Suppose a universal semantic element a may have two more specific sub-categories b and c, both equally universal at the semantic level. Suppose now three languages map this complex, hierarchic semantic structure as follows:

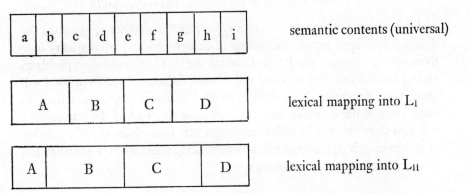

| a | b | c | d | e | f | g | h | i | semantic contents (universal) |

| A | B | C | D | lexical mapping into L_i |

| A | B | C | D | lexical mapping into L_{ii} |

With respect to the semantic sub-universe a, one may now say that L_i is the most specified in its lexical mapping, having lexical items expressing the generic a as well as the two specific sub-categories b and c. L_{ii} is less specified, lacking a lexical item to express the more specific sub-category b. While L_{iii} is the least specified of the three, having only a single lexical item to express both the generic and the specific categories. Now, the linguist may choose to dismiss this type as 'ambiguity' or 'vagueness', but the fact remains that as compared to L_i, both L_{ii} and L_{iii} are lacking in expressive specificity.[3]

(iii) Finally, at least in theory there ought to exist cases where due to some peculiarity of its syntactic-lexical organisation a language is incapable of mapping a certain portion of the universal semantic base onto surface expression. There are reasons to believe that instances of this type are not common and that they are limited to certain areas of semantic structure which are to some extent less central to the main tasks of human communication. Nevertheless, they do exist and to the inter-linguistic translator they represent, at least in principle, a peculiarly insurmountable obstacle.

In this paper I will illustrate mostly translation problems arising from the first two types discussed above, using the grammar of definiteness, referen-

---

3. Ultimately, lack of expressive specificity may easily be construed as lack of expressive power. Thus, as suggested to me by Ed Keenan, consider a language which maps all possible combinations of semantic contents onto a single lexical item, say GROCK. Now, while the linguist may still claim that this is a multiply-ambiguous surface structure, it is clear that in terms of communicative value such a language is useless, since it exhibits zero correlation between meaning and signal.

tiality, pronominal reference and topicalisation in various languages. More briefly I will illustrate the existence of the third type, drawing mostly upon data of verb-phrase operators in a number of languages.

2. *Lexical mapping of definiteness and referentiality*

In this section I will contrast the way in which a number of typologically different languages handle the coding of definiteness and referentiality onto their surface expressions. I will illustrate the types of translation problems arising from differential mapping and areas of differential specification. I will show how, progressively, considerations of syntactic structure related to other areas of the grammar may impinge upon the work of the translator. I will also show the way in which languages may take advantage of a number of universal principles concerning definiteness, referentiality, negation and more generally discourse structure.

2.1. *Some universal considerations*

Whether a common noun used in a sentence may be *definite, indefinite* or *non-referential* depends to a lesser or greater extent on its case-position within that sentence, as well as on the type of verb employed. If one disregards generic expressions as well as finer details of discourse structure, the following constraints may be observed to hold for most human languages, based on a summary of two recent works on referentiality.[4]

(3) Referentiality

(i) The three basic sentence-scope modalities in language are FACT and POSSIBLE, with NEG patterning itself as a stronger case of POSSIBLE;

(ii) Some of the operators responsible for the POSSIBLE modality are sentential in their scope, such as QUESTION, FUTURE, CONDITIONAL, PROBABILITY modals and at least some type of NEGATION. The scope of other operators responsible for this modality is verb phrase scope, excluding the sentence's subject (though including subjects of sentential verb complements), such as internal NEGATION, non-implicative (intentional) verbs such as WANT, SEEK, ORDER, REQUEST, inherently negative verbs such as

---

4. See details in Jackendoff (1972) and Givón (1973). The referential opacity discussed in these two works may be labelled 'existential' opacity, and is not to be confused with the 'degree of definiteness' type of opacity discussed in Keenan (1972a).

REFUSE, FORBID, PREVENT, DENY, or non-factive
verbs such as THINK, BELIEVE;

(iii) Nouns falling under the scope of the POSSIBLE modality
may be interpreted either referentially or non-referentially.
Otherwise all nouns are always interpreted referentially.[5]

In addition to the principles governing referentiality, other principles which
relate to discourse structure govern definiteness. They may be summarised
as follows:

(4) Definiteness

(i) Referential object nouns under the scope of NEG can only
be definite, but not indefinite;[6]

(ii) The subject nouns in most languages, especially in the main
clause, will tend to be *definite*. In some languages this is an
absolute constraint on 'competence', in other languages a
frequency constraint on text frequency;[7]

(iii) In languages with an absolute constraint against indefinite
subjects, indefinite nouns may appear as subjects of existential
or presentative constructions, which are 'marked' in several
senses;[8]

(v) The object position in sentences, on the other hand, is most
commonly used for introducing indefinite nouns into the
discourse;[9]

(v) In languages in which the notion of subject is viable[10] there is
a strong tendency for the subject to appear first in the sentence. This reflects a more general tendency for the topic or
old information to appear first. Thus, one of the most striking
characteristics of existential-presentative constructions, in
which indefinite (i.e. 'new information') nouns are introduced

5. There are convincing arguments, presented in both Jackendoff (1972) and Givón
(1973), for assuming that in natural languages the existential quantifier is the unmarked
case.

6. This may be probably extended to subject nouns as well. For detailed discussion of
this as a discourse-motivated constraint, see Givón (1975a).

7. For details see Keenan (1975a), Givón (1974, 1975b), Kirsner (1973) and Hetzron
(1974).

8. See discussion in Hetzron (1974), Givón (1974, 1975b).

9. I will restrict the discussion here only to direct or accusative objects. For further
details see Givón (1974, 1975b).

10. For a number of works concerning the typological validity of the notion 'subject',
consult Li and Thompson (1975a).

into the discourse as sentential subjects, is a tendency to defer them from sentence-initial positions;

(vi) The notions of definite and indefinite, referring only to referential nouns, are used here strictly in the pragmatic/discourse sense of 'assumed by the speaker to be uniquely identifiable to the hearer' and 'not assumed by the speaker to so be', respectively.

In the following pages I will contrast the treatment of definiteness and referentiality in a number of languages, using English as the constant point of reference. The two modal environments POSSIBLE and NEG will be used, in addition to the modally-unmarked FACT.

2.2. *Definiteness and referentiality: Bemba (Bantu)*

In Bemba the lexicon makes no provision for a definite/indefinite distinction *per se*, though the language does have a full complement of space-deictic demonstratives. In contrast, the morphology makes full provision for marking the referential/non-referential distinction, by contrasting the VCV-form of the noun prefix (referential) with the CV-form (non-referential). In a non-modal environment one finds only VCV-prefixes, on either subjects or objects:

(5) a. *umu*ana aasomene *ici*tabo
'*The* child read *a/the* book'
b. **mu*ana aasomene *ici*tabo
'**Any* child read *the/a* book'
c. **umu*ana aasomene *ci*tabo
'**The* child read *any* book'.

Further, in this language the subject, especially of the main clause, can only be interpreted as definite. But a referential object may be either definite or indefinite, as is evident from (5a) above. One may thus say that at the object position Bemba is *under*specified with respect to the marking of definiteness as compared to English. At the subject position, however, since Bemba abides absolutely by the universal convention (4ii), this underspecification has no undesirable consequence to the translator. However, to translate an English sentence with an indefinite subject into Bemba one must resort to an existential construction in which the indefinite noun does appear with a VCV-prefix, as in:

(6) pa-ali *umu*ana a-á-soma *ici*tabo
THERE-was child he-CONS-read book
'(Once) there was a child and he read a book'.

One may thus summarise the mapping between English and Bemba under the FACT scope as:

(7) *English*   *Bemba*

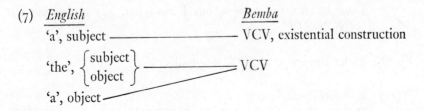

'a', subject ——————————— VCV, existential construction

'the', { subject / object } ⟩ VCV

'a', object

While this is not an overwhelming translation task, neither is it an automatic morpheme for morpheme mapping. The translator must be conscious of the case-function of the noun and the viability of constraint (4ii) in Bemba. Further, the translation problem is not the same in both directions, and while the translator from English to Bemba must be aware of the existential syntactic construction, the translator from Bemba to English must be sensitive to the case-function of the noun as well as to the discourse context— from which alone could one determine the definiteness of the object noun.
    Under the scope of POSSIBLE, one finds:

(8) a. umuana aafwaaya *ici*tabo
{ 'The child wanted *the* book' (DEF)
  'The child wanted *a* specific book' (REF, INDEF) }
b. umuana aafwaaya *ci*tabo
'The child wanted *a* book (be it any)' (NON-REF)

Here English is underspecified with respect to referentiality, while Bemba remains underspecified with respect to definiteness. For the translator the mapping may be represented as:

(9) *English*   *Bemba*

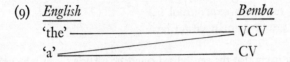

'the' ——————————— VCV
'a' ——————————— CV

And again, the translator from Bemba to English must consider the discourse context in order to decide how to translate VCV-prefixed nouns, while the translator from English to Bemba must consider, somehow, the intent of the subject as seen via the eyes of the writer in order to translate the indefinite article. Here the pragmatics of the discourse could furnish considerable help, thus consider:

(10) I am looking for *a* book *that* was written by Goethe (REF?)
      I am looking for *a* book, *it* was written by Goethe (REF)
      I am looking for *a* book, but I can't find *any* interesting *one* (NON-REF).

Finally, under the scope of NEG one finds:

(11) a. umuana taasomene *ici*tabo
         'The child did not read *the* book' (DEF)
      b. umuana taasomene *ci*tabo
         'The child did not read a/any book' (NON-REF).

Here, due to the universal constraint (4i), there is no translation problem of great magnitude, since the referential VCV prefix of Bemba maps onto 'the' in English, while the non-referential CV maps onto either the non-emphatic 'a' or the emphatic 'any'.[11] In summary, the translator must be conscious of the modal scope, grammatical function, discourse-topic considerations and discourse-intentional considerations.

2.3. *Case and gender agreement: Israeli Hebrew (Semitic)*

In modern Israeli Hebrew indefinite nouns are alleged to be unmarked, the definite is marked by a noun prefix and a definite-accusative preposition also exists. In fact, in non-modal environments both indefinite subjects and objects are marked, if singular, by the unstressed numeral *one* which requires gender agreement with the head noun, and in the plural by the invariant, quantifier 'some'. Thus:

(12) a. ish *exad* ba hena etmol . . .
         '*A* man came here yesterday . . .'
      b. raiti isha *axat* etmol . . .
         'I saw *a* woman yesterday . . .'

---

11. It is most likely that the generalised emphatic particle *fye* may be used in Bemba to augment the CV noun prefix in mapping the English 'any'. The translation problem is further complicated, though not too much, by the fact that 'any' is emphatic only under stress, a cue that is not available in written texts.

c. kaniti *kama* sfarim/maxbarot etmol . . .
'I bought *some* books/notebooks yesterday . . .'
d. *ha*-ish ohev *et-ha*-isha
the-man love ACC-the-woman
'*The* man loves *the* woman'.

The mapping between English and Hebrew in this environment may be summarised as:

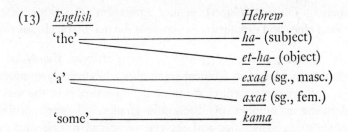

(13) *English*   *Hebrew*
'the' ————————————— *ha-* (subject)
                    ————————— *et-ha-* (object)
'a' ————————————————— *exad* (sg., masc.)
                    ————————— *axat* (sg., fem.)
'some'————————————————— *kama*

The translator, particularly from English to Hebrew, must be conscious of case-function, as well of the lexical gender of indefinite nouns (which is not always morphologically obvious).[12]

Under the scope of POSSIBLE a number of added complications emerge. The unmarked noun is interpreted non-referentially. The unstressed, gender-inflected numeral 'one' marks the referential-indefinite, but the stressed 'one' reverses that into a non-referential interpretation:

(14) a. ani mexapes *et-ha*-sefer
'I am looking for *the* book' (DEF)
b. ani mexapes sefer/sfarim
'I am looking for *a* book/books(any)' (NON-REF)
c. ani mexapes séfer *exàd*
'I am looking for *a* (specific) book' (REF-INDEF)
d. ani mexapes sèfer *exád*
'I am looking for *óne* book' (NON-REF).

Finally, under the scope of NEG the coding situation simplifies, due in large part to the universal constraint (4i):

12. A gender agreement problem of sorts already exists in Bemba, where the noun prefixes vary according to gender and singularity/plurality. However, the citation form of the noun always includes the prefix, so that the translator needs to be concerned only with translating the VCV/CV forms of the prefix. Though for translating into a Bantu language in general he must master the grammar of gender/number agreement.

(15) a. lo karati *et–ha*-sefer
'I did not read *the* book' (DEF)
b. lo karati *af/shum* sefer
'I did not read *any* book' (NON-REF)
c. lo karati sefer
'It's not true that I read *a* book' (external, NON-REF?).

To summarise the translation problems between Hebrew and English, one needs to worry about the modal environments (FACT, POSSIBLE, NEG), case-functions (subject, object), gender agreement (masculine, feminine), intonational clues and discourse environment for pragmatic clue as to intent.

2.4. *Word order, verb typology and diachronic change: Mandarin*
Definitisation in Mandarin Chinese represents an extremely complex array of devices, where the system of mapping definitisation is in the very midst of undergoing a number of diachronic changes in word order, verb morphology/syntax/semantics and the rise of special morphemes to mark definite and indefinite nouns. In addition, word-order devices to mark definitisation shade into marked-topicalisation, another universal process closely related to definitisation.[13]

Chinese is one of the languages which abides absolutely by constraint (4ii) above. That is, subjects in the normal subject-first word order may only be definite (or generic):

(16) kèrén zhùo-gōng

$$\left\{ \begin{array}{l} \text{'Guests always work'} \\ \text{'A guest always works'} \end{array} \right\} \text{(GENERIC)} \\ \text{'The guest(s) always work(s)' (DEF)} \right\}$$

If the singular/plural distinction as well as the generic/definite are to be disambiguated, the distal demonstrative 'that' may be used. But this requires the use of noun classifiers (for both the singular and plural), and thus the introduction of noun gender which is not marked on the noun itself. Further, the demonstrative 'that' loses its deictic value only in the singular, but retains it in the plural:

(17) nèi-ge kèrén zhùo-gōng
that-cl. guest work
'The guest works'

13. For the data on Mandarin Chinese I am much indebted to Charles Li (private communication), but see also Li and Thompson (1974; 1975a, b).

nèi-xié kèrén zhùo-gōng
that-cl. guest work
'Those guests work'.

For morphologically complex, historically transitive verbs such as 'work'
(do-work), the only way to indefinitise the subject is via the existential construction using the verb 'be/exist':

(18) yǒu kèrén zhùo-gōng
      be   guest   work

$\left\{ \begin{array}{l} \text{'There is a guest who works'} \\ \text{'There are some guests who work'} \end{array} \right\}$ (REF-INDEF).

And to disambiguate the singular from the plural, the numeral 'one' plus
the singular/plural noun classifier may be used:

(19) yǒu yī-ge kèrén zhùo-gōng
      be one-cl. guest work
      'There is a guest who works' (REF-INDEF)
      yǒu yī-xié kèrén zhùo-gōng
      'There are some guests who work' (REF-INDEF).

When the verb is intransitive and morphologically simplex, existential constructions may be also used for indefinitising the subject, as in (18) and (19)
above. But in addition, one may simply reverse the subject-verb order to
verb-subject to achieve the same end, as in:

(20) a. kèrén lái   le
         guest come asp.
         'The guest(s) arrived' (DEF)

      b. lái   kèrén le
         come guest asp.
         'A guest/some guests arrived' (REF-INDEF).

Let us now turn to the mapping of definiteness and indefiniteness in
accusative objects. The first device involves the use of the erstwhile serial
verb *bǎ* in an SOV word order. This device is preferred for morphologically
complex verbs and obligatory when those verbs also take certain manner
adverbs. However, it cannot be used when the verb is morphologically
simplex. Consider first:

(21) a. wǒ bǎ zhuāngzi dǎ-pò le
I   BA window hit-broken asp.
'I broke *the* window(s)' (DEF)

b. wǒ dǎ-pò le   zhuāngzi
I   hit-broken asp. window
'I broke *a* window/*some* windows' (REF-INDEF).

To disambiguate the singular/plural indefinite, the numeral 'one' together with a classifier may be used in the same SVO order, as in:

(22) wǒ dǎ-pò le yī-ge zhuāngzi
'I broke *a* window'

wǒ dǎ-pò le yī-xié zhuāngzi
'I broke *some* windows'.

Finally, using the same SVO order one may also disambiguate the singular/plural definite accusative by using the demonstrative 'that', but the deictic meaning is retained in the plural, as in:

(23) wǒ dǎ-pò le nèi-ge zhuāngzi
'I broke *the* window'

wǒ dǎ-pò le nèi-xié zhuāngzi
'I broke *those* windows'.

There are many verbs which cannot use the BA construction for definitising their objects, and in general those are verbs for which the surface direct object is semantically not a patient/accusative, such as 'see', 'hear', 'read', 'feel', 'write' and others. Their objects may be definitised via the use of the demonstrative with SVO word order, as in (23) above. Their unmarked object in the SVO order is interpreted as indefinite as in (21b), and the singular/plural may be disambiguated as in (22) above. In addition, one may definitise the object via two word order devices, SOV and OSV orders, as in:

(24) a. wǒ tīng le   yīnyuè le
I   hear asp. music prt.
'I listened to (some) music' (REF-INDEF)

b. wǒ yīnyuè tīng le
I   music hear asp.
'I listened to the music' (DEF)

c. yīnyuè wǒ tīng le
music I hear asp.
'I listened to the music' (DEF).

Under the scope of POSSIBLE, with verbs that use the BA construction, one obtains definitisation with the SOV word order, as in:

(25) wǒ yào tā bǎ zhuāngzi dǎ-pò le
I want he BA window hit-broken asp.
'I wanted him to break the window(s)'.

The unmarked noun in the SVO order is opaque, yielding either the non-referential or referential-indefinite interpretation, as in:

(26) wǒ yào tā da-pò zhuāngzi
I want he hit-broken window
$\left\{\begin{array}{l}\text{'I want him to break } a/some \text{ (specific) window(s)' (REF-INDEF)}\\ \text{'I want him to break } a/some \text{ (any) window(s)' (NON-REF)}\end{array}\right\}$

The same ambiguity is obtained if the numeral 'one' is used, together with the classifier, to disambiguate the singular from the plural in the SVO order. Except that in the non-referential reading, the quantifier value of 'one' is more apparent, that is, it hasn't been completely de-marked onto a bona-fide indefinite marker.

For verbs which cannot use the BA construction, one faces another problem: the SOV and OSV orders cannot be used in an embedded clause. That is, they have the same restrictions one normally finds on marked topicalisation devices.[14] Thus, in the context used here, the object may be definitised only with the use of the demonstrative in an SVO order, as in:

(27) a. wǒ yào tā kàn bàozhi
I want he read paper
$\left\{\begin{array}{l}\text{'I want him to read } a/some \text{ paper(s)' (NON-REF)}\\ \text{'I want him to read } a/some \text{ specific paper(s)' (REF-INDEF)}\end{array}\right\}$

b. wǒ yào tā kàn yī-fèn bàozhi
I want he read one-cl. paper

14. See some discussion further below, as well as Givón (1974). This is not a restriction due to the scope of the modality POSSIBLE *per se*, but rather a general restriction pertaining to embedded clauses.

$$\left\{ \begin{array}{l} \text{'I want him to read } a \text{ (specific) paper' (REF-INDEF)} \\ \text{'I want him to read } a \text{ (any) paper' (NON-REF)} \end{array} \right\}$$

c. wǒ yào tā kàn yī-xié bàozhi
I want he read one-cl. paper

$$\left\{ \begin{array}{l} \text{'I want him to read } some \text{ specific papers' (REF-INDEF)} \\ \text{'I want him to read } some \text{ (any) papers' (NON-REF)} \end{array} \right\}$$

d. wǒ yào tā kàn nèi-fèn bàozhi
'I want him to read the paper' (DEF)

wǒ yào tā kàn nèi-xié bàozhi
'I want him to read the papers' (DEF)

(28) a. *wǒ yào tā bàozhi kàn (*SOV)

b. *wǒ yào bàozhi tā kàn (*OSV).

Under the scope of NEG, with verbs using the BA construction, one obtains:

(29) wǒ méi bǎ zhuāngzi dǎ-pò
I neg BA window hit-broken
'I did not break *the* window(s)' (DEF).

And the singular/plural may be again disambiguated by the use of 'that' with the classifiers in an SVO word order. The unmarked object in an SVO order yields only a non-referential reading, as in:

(30) wǒ méi dǎ-pò zhuāngzi
I neg hit-broken window
'I did not break any window(s)' (NON-REF).

However, contrary to constraint (4i) above, when the numeral 'one' is used to disambiguate for singular/plural, it precipitates a referential-indefinite reading, as in:

(31) wǒ méi dǎ-pò yī-ge zhuāngzi
I neg hit-broken one-cl. window
'There is a specific window that I did not break' (REF-INDEF)

wǒ méi dǎ-pò yī-xié zhuāngzi
I neg hit-broken one-cl. window
'There are some windows that I did not break' (REF-INDEF).

Construction (31), while considered 'grammatical', is nevertheless unpreferred, and the native speaker prefers to render it as the existential construction, where the referential-indefinite noun is first introduced as the subject of 'be/exist' in a VS word order.[15]

(32) yǒu yī-ge zhuāngzi wǒ méi dǎ-pò
be one-cl. window I neg hit-broken
'There is a window that I did not break' (REF-INDEF).

Finally, the objects of verbs which cannot use the BA construction may definitise under negation via using the demonstrative plus classifier in an SVO word order, as in:

(33) wǒ méi kàn nèi-fèn bàozhi
I neg read that-cl. book
'I did not read *the* paper' (DEF).

And again the plural demonstrative retains its deictic force, as in:

(34) wǒ méi kàn nèi-xié bàozhi
'I did not read *those* papers' (DEF).

In addition, the SOV and OSV orders may be used for definitisation if the negation is in the main clause, as in:

(35) wǒ bàozhi méi kàn
'I did not read *the* paper(s)' (DEF, SOV)
bàozhi wǒ méi kàn
'I did not read *the* paper(s)' (DEF, OSV).

The unmarked object yields again only a non-referential reading, as in:

(36) wǒ méi kàn bàozhi
'I did not read any paper(s)' (NON-REF).

The marked indefinite with 'one' yields a referential-indefinite reading, as in:

15. As I have noted in Givón (1975a), in English too an apparent violation of constraint (4i) is possible, as in e.g. 'Mary did not read *a* book that was assigned, and as a result she flunked the exam'. While this is definitely 'grammatical', text counts reveal that the frequency of this usage is *zero*, so that the universality of constraint (4i) is in fact demonstrated to hold in *discourse* ('performance'), though not in 'competence'.

(37)	wǒ méi kàn yī-fèn bàozhi
		'There is a paper that I did not read'.

But again an existential construction as in (38) is preferred over (37):

(38)	yǒu yī-fèn bàozhi wǒ méi kàn
		be one-cl. paper I neg read
		'There is a paper that I did not read'.

As one can see, the complexity for the translator between English and Mandarin is rather staggering. In addition, the BA construction itself as a device for definitisation is restricted in its distribution almost to the same extent as the SOV and OSV word orders, and may appear only in a number of that-S type complements of assertive verbs ('say', 'think', but not of 'know').[16] This raises the general question of whether the BA, SOV and OSV devices for definitisation are really that, or rather whether they are devices for marked-topicalisation. Their distributional restrictions strongly suggest the latter rather than the former. A topic-shifting devices universally allow either generic or referential-definite nouns, which is precisely what the SOV and OSV orders in Mandarin allow (as well as what the subject in the SVO order allows). This problem will be discussed in greater detail in section 3.

2.5. *Degree-of-definiteness opacity: Frisian and Malagasy*
The referential opacity discussed so far, which appears only under the scope of non-FACT modalities, involves roughly the existential quantifier, i.e. the lack of commitment of the speaker himself/herself to believing in the actual existence of an individual about which they make a certain proposition. There exists another type of referential opacity, one which I shall label here 'degree-of-definiteness' opacity, which may appear under the scope of FACT modalities. It involves situations where the speaker believes in the existence of a unique individual about which a proposition is made, but may not be able to actually identify that individual, i.e. he may not know which one it actually is.[17] Let us consider the following example:

16. Both Hooper and Thompson (1973) and Hooper (1974) have observed that the sentential complements of assertive (as against 'presuppositional') predicates allow more syntactic freedom, in particular with respect to various stylistic transformations labelled as 'Root Transformations' by Emonds (1970). For a more general discussion of this, see Givón (1974).
17. For extensive discussion of this type, see Keenan (1972a).

(39)   The man who killed Smith is blind.

A speaker, say Sherlock Holmes, may utter (39) under the condition that he actually knows who Smith's murderer is, or alternatively under the condition where he only knows that whoever it was who killed Smith must have been blind. Under the first reading, the restrictive relative clause functions as a definite identity operator and the whole subject NP may be replaced by a proper name, say 'John'. Under the second reading, the restrictive relative clause has an *attributive* function and the entire NP may not be replaced by a proper name. Now, in most languages there is no lexical mapping to resolve this type of ambiguity between the transparent (definite identity) and opaque (attributive) interpretation. However, Keenan and Ebert (1973) have shown two cases in which such lexical mapping actually exists. The first is Frisian, where two articles exist, one of which is used ambiguously as in (39) above:

(40)   John wonert ham dat *di* maan wat woon bisööben wiar
       John wonder him that *the* man who won drunk   was
       'John was surprised that the man who won was drunk'.

Sentence (40) may either mean that John knew who the man was, say 'Bill', and that Bill's being drunk surprised him. Or alternatively, that John was surprised that *a winner*, whoever it be, was drunk. The other article in Frisian has only the opaque reading:

(41)   John wonert ham dat *a* maan wat woon bisööbert wiar
       John wonder him that *the* man who won drunk   was
       'John was surprised that the man who won was drunk'.

In Malagasy, there is a definite article which allows either the opaque or the transparent reading, as in:

(42)   Gaga Rakoto fa mamo *ny* mpandresy
       surprised Rakoto that drunk *the* winner
       'Rakoto was surprised that *the* winner was drunk'.

But there also exists another article which allows only the transparent reading:

9

(43) Gaga   Rakoto fa   mamo *ilay*   mpandresy
      surprised Rakoto that drunk *the* winner
      'Rakoto was surprised that the winner was drunk'.

While this degree of expressive specificity is not very common, it is clear that languages such as English, which are probably the large majority, are expressively under-specified in this area of the grammar, as compared to Malagasy or Frisian.[18]

3. *Definiteness, topicality and pronominal agreement*

The Mandarin examples cited in section 2.4 above already suggested that it is not always possible to keep definiteness apart from other discourse-related devices used to map various situations in which an argument is mentioned not for the first time in discourse. In this section I will cite a number of examples in which the grammar or mapping of definiteness in language shades into other discourse devices, such as topicalisation, pronominalisation or grammatical agreement, and in particular how different languages may choose to draw the lines which divide these discourse-mapping devices from each other at different point. I will begin by a short outline of some universal discourse situations pertaining to the manner in which a previously-mentioned *topic* may be *recalled* into discourse.

3.1. *Complexity and recall of discourse topic*

Probably the most simple and least problematic environment for recalling a discourse topic is that in which the topic argument is mentioned directly prior to its recall, is mentioned there alone with no other argument which may possibly confuse the hearer, and in an otherwise unambiguous fashion. Most languages will recall it in this environment by the use of *anaphora* (simple deletion) if they have no pronominal system, or by the use of anaphoric pronouns, if available. This should be considered the least complex, least marked topic-recall environment, since the position (directly prior) and nature (unambiguous) of the prior mention of the topic makes the hearer's task of assigning co-reference almost automatic. Let us label this device *simple pronominalisation*, as in:

(44) *John* worked, and then *he* rested.

18. It is also of some interest that neither Frisian nor Malagasy has resolved the ambiguity completely, so that each one has only *one* unambiguous article, while leaving one reading to be covered by an ambiguous expression.

Almost as simple a device, in terms of the hearer's task of assigning co-reference relations (or recalling the topic), is that of simple definitisation, which up to this point we have taken for granted. This device is used in a number of non-contrastive situations where the use of pronouns will not suffice to identify the individual. This may be because a large gap exists between the prior and subsequent mention of the topic, during which other arguments have been discussed whose pronominal gender is not distinct. Or when one is confident that the hearer could identify the topic from his own context, i.e. even when it has not been overtly mentioned in previous discourse. Some of the situations here involve pragmatic considerations of dependency, quite often resulting in the use of possessive pronouns as the definitising markers, as well as reliance on various cultural conventions. Why it is clear that this is a more-marked discourse environment than anaphoric pronominalisation, is because it seems that the speaker assumes the hearer will have more difficulty in identifying the co-referent, and is thus supplying more specific information—i.e. the entire noun, rather than relying only on the most generic features which characterise the pronominal system.[19] Let us label this device *definitisation*, as in:

(46) Once upon a time there lived *a gracious king*. He reigned over a lovely country, was married to a beautiful queen and had three lovely children, a parakeet and a court jester. Now one day *the king* . . . (large gap)

(47) *The sun* is so bright today. (uniqueness)

(48) *My wife* arrived yesterday. (uniqueness via cultural and pragmatic conventions)

(47) *The rascal* is at it again. (uniqueness via personal experience)

The next type of an environment shares a number of the constraints on anaphoric pronominalisation, except that it is contrastive. Two (or more) topics are mentioned in directly prior discourse, but they are of different pronominal genders, so that the pronominal system of the language can handle this situation and establish unique reference for both. This device may not be used by languages with zero pronouns or languages with only one gender, unless further conventions of primacy hold. Since primacy conventions usually involve, in this case, subject and object relation, a situation which would unambiguously require contrastive pronouns is one where both topics have the same case-function. Further, this device usually requires stressed pronouns. Let us label it *contrastive pronominalisation*, as in:

19. For a detailed discussion of this, see Givón (1975b).

(48) I saw *the queen* and *the king*. *She* wore black, while *he* wore red.

Quite often the use of this device also involves certain parallelism in the grammatical structures of the sentences involved, as well as contrastive conjunctions such as 'but', 'while', 'though', etc.

The next situation, again non-contrastive, is in some sense a further complication over simple definitisation. It involves topic-shifting to the left, most commonly with an intonational break and quite commonly with a pronominal reflex in the main proposition. It is quite hard to differentiate the environment for this device from that which precipitates the use of simple definitisation, short of to say that it involves two extra, possibly interdependent considerations. One may involve such a large gap between the prior and subsequent mention of the topic so that the speaker suspects that the hearer may have trouble recalling the topic if only simple definitisation is used. However, it seems to me that this may be coupled with another condition. Topics are normally not simply mentioned in discourse once and then dropped. They linger on, entire stories or paragraphs deal with them. Now, when more than one potential topic is mentioned in prior discourse, then the speaker proceeds to deal with one of them in great length, and then he shifts back to another one, i.e. he changes topic—at that point, it seems to me, the use of topic-shifting becomes felicitous. The actual topic-introducing devices may vary enormously. Thus consider:

(49) Once upon a time in a faraway land there lived a king, who was married to a beautiful queen. The king ruled over a vast country, he had many slaves and servants, not to mention mere vassals, and frequently went to wars in order to increase the size of his treasury.
  (a) *Now the country* over which he ruled was rather flat . . .
  (b) *Now, as to his country, it* was rather flat . . .
  (c) *As to his kingdom, it* was rather flat . . .
  (d) *Let us now speak of his kingdom. It* was rather flat . . .

Thus, topic-shifting devices do not merely indicate that a different topic is being mentioned, but further that a new topic has now been picked up as the subject matter of the discourse.

Let us now turn to *contrastive topic-shifting*. It stands in the same relation to topic-shifting as contrastive pronominalisation to simple pronominalisation, and on occasion uses the same devices, plus additional ones. The discourse context roughly involves topic-shifting to an argument that stands in contrast, in terms of what the speaker says about it, to the preceding topic argument. Thus typically this involves pairs, parallel constructions and quite often contrastive conmunctions such as 'but', etc. Considering (49) above, 'country' is not a very good contrastive topic-shift *vis-à-vis* 'king', since it is semantically so different so that there are relatively few properties of the two which are likely to be contrasted. Suppose however that the following discourse environment occurred, where both 'king' and 'queen' are mentioned as prior topics, then recalled contrastively:

(50)   Once upon a time there lived a gracious *king* together with his lovely *queen* in a faraway land. They had one son, the young prince, who caused them no end of grief. He would destroy his toys, torture his pets and chop up the livingroom furniture. *Now the king*, he took it all in his stride, muttering into his beard about the sorrows of child rearing. *But the queen*, *she* got sadder and sadder every day . . .

It is not very clear whether in all cases one ought to consider the first member of the pair a contrastive shifted-topic, though clearly the second one qualifies and further, in many languages both the first and second require the use of devices that are only characteristic of contrastive topic-shifting. Further, in many languages there are certain topic-shifting devices which can be used only contrastively, and more often than not involve neither intonation break nor recalled pronouns. Thus consider:

(51)   a. I went to buy presents *to all the members of my family. To my older boy* I bought a bicycle, and *to my little girl* (I bought) a plastic paratrooper.
       b. I hate almost all *vegetables*, especially *spinach. Now potatoes* I like.

There are grounds to believe that this contrastive device does not involve changing the subject of the discussion, so that in fact it is less marked in terms of discourse environment than contrastive topic-shifting as seen in (50) above. In other words, the discourse device in (51) is used to contrast topics when the continuity of the subject of discourse is not broken.

There are two universal constraints which seem to apply to topic-shifting devices cross linguistically. The first limits these constructions only to main clauses, with some allowances made for that S-type complements of assertive predicates.[20] Though the evidence is not unambiguous, I suspect

20. See discussion in section 2.4 above as well as footnote 16.

the restriction is not as absolute on non-shifting contrastive topicalisation as in (51).

The second universal restriction, shared by all topic-shifting constructions, by definites, contrastive topics and the *subject* nouns of languages such as Mandarin or Bemba, is that of definiteness: the nouns participating in these constructions may be either definite or generic, but never *referential-indefinite*. This is an obvious restriction tagging these constructions as once in which a new argument *cannot* be introduced into discourse. With all this in mind, let us now consider a number of examples to contrast them with the English data presented above.

3.2. *Mandarin: topic and definitisation*

Without repeating the data presented in section 2.4 above, one should recall that it was left unclear whether the SOV and OSV word-order devices for definitisation were indeed 'mere definitisation' or topic-shifting devices. The nouns occurring in them could be either definite or generic, which is a general restriction holding to definite NPs as well as topic-shifting. The distributional restrictions in these word-order devices in Mandarin, including the BA construction, strongly hint that they are topic-shifting rather than definitisation devices. Now, since the use of demonstratives for definitisation, particularly in the plural, does not rid them of their deictic force, one may argue that it is not a proper equivalent for mere definitisation. And if this is true, then Mandarin shows certain gaps in expressive specificity in the area of mere definitisation, particularly in embedded clauses. These gaps are, in all probability, largely illusory, since the greatest need for differentiation and elaboration, particularly with respect to discourse phenomena, lies in the main clause.[21]

3.3. *Japanese: topic pronoun and definitisation*[22]

Japanese has a definite marker, *sono*, as well as a topic case suffix *-wa* that is used with unstressed nouns for topic-shifting and in combination with stress for contrastive topics. The restrictions on the distribution of this device parallel those mentioned above, i.e. it may be used only in in main clauses and bars referential-indefinite readings.[23] Finally, Japanese uses mostly

21. See discussion in Givón (1974).

22. For the Japanese data used here I am indebted to Katsue Akiba (personal communication), but see also Kuroda (1972) and Kuno (1974).

23. The contrastive use of *-wa* phrases may appear in embedded clauses, but it is not absolutely clear that it is still functioning as a topic device as distinct from contrastive *focus*, i.e. where the entire preposition is presupposed and the noun in focus is identified in contrast to other(s).

zero pronouns in anaphoric situations. This presents the first problem for the translator, since in situations where English can use contrastive pronouns, Japanese must use the full noun with -*wa*:

(52) *Simple pronominalisation:*
I saw *John*, but I did not greet *him*
watashi-*wa* John-*ni* at-ta ga Ø aisatsu-*o* shi-nak-atta
I-TOP   John-DAT see-past but (Ø) greeting-ACC
                                                                    do-neg-past

(53) *Contrastive pronominalisation:*
I saw *John* and *Mary*. I greeted *him* but I did not greet *her*.
watashi-*wa* John-to-Maria-*ni* at-ta. John-*ni-wa* aisatu-*o* shi-ta
                          ga Maria-*ni-wa* aisatsu-*o* shi-nak-atta
I-TOP   John-and-Mary-DAT see-past. John-DAT-TOP
greeting-ACC do-past but Mary-DAT-TOP greeting-ACC do-
                                                                    neg-past.

Further, one could show that the use of -*wa* phrases in Japanese shades into the use of non-contrastive pronouns, as in situations such as:

(54) I saw the man and the dog (and) I greeted *the man*
watashi-*wa* otoko-to-inu -*ni* at-ta. otoko   -*wa* aisatsu-*o* shi-ta
I-TOP   man-and-dog-DAT see-past. man-TOP greeting-
                                                                    ACC do-past.

Thus, although the definite article *sono* exists in the language, it does not cover exactly the same discourse function as its equivalent in English, since part of that function seems to be covered by the non-contrastive use of -*wa*. But that use of -*wa* can only be available in main clauses, so that for the *same* function of definitisation in non-main clauses one must resort to the use of the definitiser *sono*, as in:

(55) a. otoko-*ga* tegami-*o* kai-ta
man-SUBJ letter-ACC write-past
'The man wrote a letter'
   b. watashi-*ga* otoko-*ni*   tegami-*o* kaku-yoo-*ni*-it-ta
I-SUBJ   man-DAT letter-ACC write-inf-DAT-say-past
'I told the man to write *a* letter'
   c. *watashi-*ga* tegami-*wa* otoko-*ni*   kaku-yoo-*ni*-it-ta
I-SUBJ   letter-TOP man-DAT write-inf-DAT-say-past

   d. watashi-*ga* otoko-*ni*   *sono*-tegami-*o* kaku-yoo-*ni*-it-ta
      I SUBJ   man-DAT *the*-letter-ACC write-inf-DAT-say-past
      'I told the man to write *the* letter'.

One could argue that 'letter' could be topic-shifted with -*wa* over the subject of the main clause, as in:

   (56) (*sono*)-tegami-*wa* watashi-*ga* otoko-*ni* kaku-yoo-*ni*-it-ta
         (the)-letter-TOP I-SUBJ   man-DAT write-inf-DAT-say-past
         'As to the letter, I told the man to write it'.

However, it is not entirely clear that in this case the value of the -*wa* phrase remains equivalent to mere definitisation, rather than becoming topic-shifting.

   There are various other complications arising from the use of -*wa* as a mere definitiser. One of those involves the problem of surprising shift in the discourse from the 'unmarked' or 'conventionally expected' pattern of continuation. For example, consider the following, in the context of 'Once upon a time there was a beautiful princess':

   (57) Ohimesama-*wa* shiawase-deshita.
         Princess-TOP happy-was
         'The princess was happy'
      a. Ohimesama-*wa* takusan-*no* tomodachi-*ga* arimeshita.
         princess-TOP   many-GEN friend-SUBJ was
         'The princess had many friends'
      b. *Sono* ohimesama-*ga* ookami-*ni* osow-are-ta
         the-princess-SUBJ wolf-BY   attack-PASS-past
         'The princess was attacked by a wolf'.

The sentence (57a) continues predictably from its antecedent, i.e. 'happy' → 'have friends'. Sentence (57b), however, if substituted for (57a), breaks that continuity rather rudely and unpredictably, i.e. 'happy' → 'attacked by wolf'. And in that context -*wa* as a topic marker or definitiser cannot be used, but rather the subject case-marker -*ga* is used, together with the definitiser *sono*.

   Finally, to illustrate one more consideration that is clearly pragmatic, consider the following case, where (58a) is the discourse context and either (58b) or (58c) may be the continuation:

(58) a. A new quarter has started
      b. *The students* were given new books
         Seito-tachi-*wa*   atarashii han-*o* kubar-are-ta
                  **ga*
         student-pl.-TOP new   book-ACC distribute-PASS-past
                  *SUBJ
      c. *New books* were distributed to the students
         atarashii hon -*ga*   seito-tachi-*ni* kubar-are-ta
                  **wa*

         new   book SUBJ student-pl.-DAT distribute-PASS-past.
                  *TOP

The pragmatics of 'a new quarter', within the university context, establishes both 'books' and 'students' as potentially legitimate topics, as may be
seen by the legitimacy of (58b) and (58c) in the equivalent English discourse.
But in some sense in Japanese, and I suspect also in English, 'students' are
considered more *topical* than 'books' in this context. That this is the case in
English may be shown by the peculiar oddity, in the very same context (58a),
of (58c') below:

(58c') The new quarter has started.
        ?*The books* were distributed to the students.
        ?*The new books* were distributed to the students.
        ?The students were given *the new books*.

Though notice how the anchoring of 'books' to 'students' rescues the sentence:

(59) The students were given *their new books*.

This seems, then, to be a problem related to definitisation or topic recall,
rather than topic-shifting *per se*.

3.4. *Bikol: topic, subject, dative and passivisation*
In spite of the various complications seen in Mandarin and Japanese, above,
both are typologically languages in which the notion of 'subject' is reasonably viable, if that notion is defined by a number of semantic, discourse and
syntactic distributional properties.[24] In this section I will illustrate the

24. For a detailed discussion of 'subject properties', see Keenan (1975a). For a dis-
senting view concerning the status of 'subject' in Mandarin and Japanese, see Li and
Thompson (1975b).
9*

definitisation problems in a Philippine language, Bikol, whose typological characteristics with respect to the notion 'subject'—as distinct from 'topic'—are of a rather different sort.[25]

In this language one argument in the simple sentence ('main clause') is assigned a topic status marked by a prefix (*ʔang*), and in many ways this argument functions as the subject. It may be either *definite* or *generic*, a restriction shared by the subjects of some languages (Mandarin, Bemba) and by marked-topicalised constructions of all languages. The accusative ('patient') is marked, when indefinite, by another prefix (*ning*). It may be definitised in three different ways, one of which involves switching the *ning* prefix into the normal dative/locative prefix *sa*. The other two involve promotion of the accusative to the 'topic' status, i.e. the use of the marker *ʔang*. Promotions of this type also involve changing the verb-marking prefix ('focus marker'), which indicates which of the arguments of the verb is in the *ʔang* case:

(60) *nag*-pákul ʔang-babáye ning-kandíng
      AGT-hit TOP-woman ACC/INDEF-goat
      'The woman hit *a* goat'

(61) p-*in*-ákul kang-babáye   ʔang-kandíng
      ACC-hit AGT/DEF-woman TOP-goat
      'The woman hit *the* goat'

(62) *na*-pákul kang-babáye ʔang-kandíng
      ACC-hit AGT-woman TOP-goat
      'The goat was hit by the woman'

(63) nag-pákul ʔang-babáye sa-kandíng
      AGT-hit TOP-woman DAT/DEF-goat
      'The woman hit the goat'.

Thus, while both (61) and (62) assign the topic marker to the patient, (62) is judged to be 'more like a passive', while (61) is 'more like definite accusative'. And further, it is not quite clear how exactly to represent the difference between definitising the accusative/patient by promotion, as in (61), as against definitising it by the dative marker, as in (63). The most intelligent guess is that (62) > (61) > (63) > (60) hierarchise as to degree of topicality, with the indefinite in (60) being clearly non-topic, and the topic-marked patient in (62) being clearly the highest. Further, while the argument

25. For a discussion of the typology of 'subject' and 'topic' in these languages, see Schachter (1975). For the Bikol data I am indebted to Manuel Factora.

in the *ʔang* case can only be definite (or generic),[26] once an agent is 'demoted', it could either take the agentive *kang* prefix (as in (61) and (62) above) and be definite, or take the *ning* case as indefinite, as in:

(64) p-*in*-ákul ning-babáye   ʔang-kandíng
     ACC-hit INDEF-woman TOP-goat

$$\left.\begin{cases} \text{'A woman hit the goat'} \\ \text{'The goat was hit by a woman'} \end{cases}\right\}$$

(65) *na*-pákul ning-babáye   ʔang-kandíng
     ACC-hit INDEF-woman TOP-goat
     'The goat was hit by a woman'.

So far then, one may say that any constituent in the *ʔang* case is definite, and out of the *ʔang* case for agents the contrast DEF/INDEF is marked by *kang/ning*, while for patient by *sa/ning*, respectively.

An added complication involves the dative/locative case. It is normally marked by *sa*, but for some verbs that *sa* is only to be interpreted as definite, and for indefinites one must substitute *ning*, as in:

(66) a. *nag*-laʔúg   ʔang-kandíng sa-harúng
     AGT-enter TOP-goat   DAT/DEF-house
     'The goat entered *the* house'

   b. *nag*-laʔúg   ʔang-kandíng ning-harúnh
     AGT-enter TOP-goat   INDEF-house
     'The goat entered *a* house'.

On the other hand, with other verbs the *sa* marker is ambiguous and can mean either DEF/INDEF, and *ning* cannot be used, as in:[27]

(67) a. nag-dumán ʔang-laláke sa-tindáhan
     AGT-go   TOP-man DAT-store
     'The man went to *the*/(*a*?) store'

   b. *nag-dumán ʔang-laláke *ning* tindahán.

26. It may easily be argued that generic topics are 'definite within the universe of *types*' just like non-generic ones are definite with respect to the universe of *tokens*. It is less clear whether the same contextual constraints make a *type* topic as those which make a *token* topic.

27. It is not altogether clear that this is a question of the semantic properties of the verb as distinct from the pragmatics of the setting in which those verbs are most frequently used. For example, if the verb '*put* (x) *on* (y)' is normally used within the sub-universe 'house', where 'table', 'chair', 'bed', 'shelf', etc. may be unique dependent variables of the house or rooms in it, chances are the locative goal of 'put' is likely to always appear as definite.

There are reasons to believe that even a complete lack of *indefinite*-marking for either locatives or datives would, at the discourse level, be a relatively *small* loss. Datives are mostly *human* and much more likely to be topic/definite in discourse.[28] And locatives are either conventionally/pragmatically unique, or else they usually belong to the *setting* for an action, which is normally mentioned in discourse *before* the action, and is thus likely to be *definite* when the actions/events concerning agents, patients and datives are described.

Now, when dative/locative arguments are 'promoted' to the topic case (*?ang*), they may only be definite (or generic), as is the general constraint:

(68) d-*in*-uman-*án* kang-laláke ?ang-tindáha
　　　LOC-go　　　AGT-man TOP-store
　　　'The man went to the store'

(69) *na*-duman-*án* kang-laláke ?ang-tindáha
　　　LOC-go　　　AGT-man TOP-store
　　　'*The store was gone-to by the man'.

Since locative, benefactive and instrumental arguments can be all 'promoted' to topicality (*?ang*) as in (69), these 'passivisation' devices in Bikol are not altogether analogous to the English passive, which is restricted mostly to accusative objects and some datives.

Since the 'promotion to *?ang*' process is not fully equivalent to passivisation, is it then more equivalent to marked-topicalisation? There is a strong piece of evidence which suggests that this could not be the case. Marked-topicalisation devices, as I have shown above, are confined mostly to the main clause. However, the *?ang* NPs in Bikol have a complete distribution in all embedded clauses. In fact, in relative clauses the equi-NP within the embedded sentence must in most Philippine languages[29] be in the TOPIC case, otherwise relativisation cannot proceed:

(70) a. nag-pákul áko　　sa-laláke　*na na*-gadán ning-kandíng
　　　　　AGT-hit TOP-I DEF-man *that* AGT-kill INDEF-goat
　　　　　'I hit the man who killed a goat'

　　　b. *nag-pákul áko sa-laláke *na* g-*in*-adán ?ang-kandíng
　　　　　　　　　　　　　　　　　　　　　ACC-kill TOP-goat

28. See discussion in Givón (1975b).

29. In Bikol there are a number of exceptions to this rule, mostly involving datives/locatives, which under certain circumstances may be relativised even though they are not the *?ang* phrase in the embedded sentence.

c. nag-pákul áko   sa-kandíng *na* g-in-andán kang-laláke
   AGT-hit TOP-I DEF-goat *that* ACC-kill AGT-man
   { 'I hit the goat that was killed by the man' }
   { 'I hit the goat that the man killed' }

d. *nag-pákul áko sa-kandíng *na* nag-dumán ʔang-laláke
                            AGT-kill TOP-man

Finally, it is not very clear whether Bikol has the same mapping of marked-topicalisation as in English, Mandarin, Japanese or Bantu. The 'neutral' topic marker ʔ*ang* most likely covers at least part of this function. And a deictic particle *si*, which can appear only as a substitute of ʔ*ang*, may cover part or most of this function, without any 'movement to the left' which is so universally characteristic of marked topicalisation.

3.5. *Bantu: topic, pronoun and grammatical agreement*

In a number of languages topicalisation and its associate pronominalisation shade into definitisation and often into grammatical agreement. In principle this is a highly universal process[30] which is motivated by the convergence of several synchronic and diachronic driving forces. In this section I will briefly illustrate this phenomenon by examples from two Bantu languages.

In Rwanda one may observe the following mapping of definiteness and referentiality in objects of negated verbs:

(71) a. ya-boonye *umu*gabo
    he-saw   man
    'He saw *a* man' (REF-INDEF)

b. nhi-ya-boonye *umu*gabo
    neg-he-saw   man
    'He did not see *any* man' (NON-REF)

c. *umu*gabo, nhi-ya-*mu*-boonye
    { 'The man, he did not see *him*' }
    { 'He did not see *the* man' }   } (DEF, TOP).

Thus, the only way to definitise the object of a negated verb is by topic-shifting plus an obligatory anaphoric object *pronoun*. The pronoun thus becomes an integral part of the lexical marking of definiteness (in objects), and this has been further extended in the affirmative to the point where the

30. For detailed discussion see Givón (1975b).

topicalisation movement is not obligatory here, and in fact there is a contrast between 'definite'—with only the pronoun, and 'topicalised' with both left-movement and pronoun:

(72) a. *umu*gabo, ya-*mu*-boonye
          'As to the man, he saw *him*' (DEF, TOP)

      b. ya-mu-boonye *umu*gabo
          'He saw *the* man' (DEF).

The difference between (72a) and (72b) is critical, because which topic-shifted constructions such as (72a) can appear *only* in main clauses, (72b) may already begin to appear in embedded clauses.

A further extension of this process is found in Swahili, where for inanimate (or non-human) nouns the normal definitisation process of objects is via the anaphoric pronoun, in both the negative and affirmative:

(73) a. ni-li-*ki*-soma kitabu
          'I read *the* book'

      b. si-ku-*ki*-soma kitabu
          'I did not read the book'

      c. ni-li-soma-kitabu
          'I read a book'

      d. si-ku-soma kitabu *chochote*
          'I did not read *any* book'.

For human objects, however, pronominalisation—or object agreement—has become obligatory, and definitisation must be marked by other devices:

(74) a. ni-li-*mw*-ona mtu mmoja
          'I saw one person'

      b. si-ku-*mw*-ona mtu *yeyote*
          'I did not see *any* one'

      c. ni-li-*mw*-ona mtu *yule*
          'I saw *that* man'

      d. ni-li-mw-ona *yule* mtu
          'I saw *the* man'.

As I have shown elsewhere, the progression topic/pronoun > definite >

grammatical agreement represents a diachronic cline, along which a language may progress by gradual de-marking of constructions. Thus the interaction of grammatical agreement with topicalisation and definitisation in language is a rather natural phenomenon.[31]

4. *Lexical structure and expressive power*

In the preceding sections I have treated cases which raise translation problems of the first two types, (a) differential mapping, and (b) differences in expressive specificity. Although these two types are theoretically not of the highest order of interest, they nevertheless cover the majority of problems to be encountered in inter-linguistic translation. In this section I would like to show that type (c) also exists, i.e. cases where there is a real difference between the expressive power of two languages, so that some meanings (or 'propositional structures') defined as possible by the universal semantic base may not find any surface realisation in a specific language. By demonstrating that cases of this type exist one should not necessarily imply that they pose a great problem for translation. Most of the cases I've found so far involve rather delicate areas of focus and emphasis which, one suspects, can be got around by using longer, more cumbersome, complex structures to achieve roughly the same effects. They all involve the verbal structure of languages, and in particular the morphemic status of various operators, such as tense-aspect, negation, modal and adverbial markers. As I will show, when a language has these operators bound to the verbal word (rather than free and movable morphemes), a number of expressive power problems may arise in the area of focus, emphasis and negation.

4.1. *Adverbs and the scope of assertions: Bemba*
It is a universal of language that a certain disparity holds between affirmative and their corresponding negative sentences with regard to the scope of the assertion. Affirmative sentences containing objects or adverbs may be read differentially, where in one reading the scope of the assertion ('new information') encompasses the entire VP, including the verb and objects/adverbs, while in another reading the scope is narrower, excluding the verb and including only the complement. Thus, (75a) below may be given as an answer to the wider (VP) focus question (75b), or to the narrow (COMP) question (75c):[32]

---

31. For further details on Amharic, Spanish, Ge'ez, Aramaic and others, see Givón (1975b).
32. For further discussion see Givón (1975a).

(75)   a. He worked for two hours
       b. What did he then do?
       c. For how long did he then work?

Further, in the affirmative the narrower (COMP) scope implies the truth of the wider (VP) scope:

(76)   John worked for 2 hrs. ⊃ John worked.

Finally, a language could disambiguate the narrower (COMP) scope by stress-focus, as in:

(77)   He worked *for two hóurs*.

Under the scope of NEG, however, the ambiguity of (75a) is lost, and only the narrower scope (COMP) is negated. That is:

(78)   John *did not* work for two hours ≯ John did not work.

Now, this universal phenomenon has overt morphological expression in some Bantu languages. In Bemba, for example, there are seven tense-aspect minimal pairs with respect to the distinction VP vs. COMP focus, si of them in past time and one in the habitual tense. When a VP contains an object or adverb complement, either focus may appear, as in (79a, b). But when it doesn't contain a complement, only the VP-focus aspect may appear, viz. (79c).

(79)   a. a-*àlí*-boombele saana
          'He *worked hard*' (VP focus)

       b. a-*à*-boombele saana
          'He worked *hárd*' (COMP focus)

       c. *a-*à*-boombele (*COMP focus)

       d. a-*àlí*-boombele
          'He *worked*' (VP focus)

Under the scope of NEG, however, only the COMP focus aspect may be used:

(80) a. ta-*à*-boombele saana
        'He did not work *hárd*' (COMP focus)
      b. *ta-*àlí*-boombele saana
        (*VP focus)

Now, in this language, 24 independent tense-aspect markers exist and they are all bound to the verbal word. In both the past and future the language makes four time divisions, all marked by these bound morphemes without the use of time adverbials. For example:

(81) a. a-*àlí*-boombele
        'He worked' (before yesterday) (VP focus)
      b. a-*àlíí*-boomba
        'He worked' (yesterday) (VP focus)
      c. a-*àcí*-boomba
        'He worked' (earlier today) (VP focus)

Now, since these time divisions are expressed by a morpheme which is bound to the verbal *word*, on the surface of (81a, b, c) there is no complement, and therefore the corresponding COMP-focus aspects cannot be used—and the narrower focusing such as in English (cf. (77) above) *cannot* be achieved:

(82) a. *a-*à*-boombele
        (before yesterday) (COMP focus)
      b. *a-*á*-boombele
        (yesterday) (COMP focus)
      c. *a-boombele
        (earlier today) (COMP focus)

One may argue that the language may still resort to the use of separate adverbial words, which it has, in order to allow the narrower (COMP) focusing, so that this restriction is, in this case, more a seeming than real constraint on expressive power. Thus:

(83) a. a-*à*-boombele *bulya bushiku*
        'He worked *the day before yesterday*'
      b. a-*á*-boombele *maailo*
        'He worked *yesterday*'
      c. a-boombele *leelo*
        'He worked *today*'.

However, the use of these overt expressions, at least in (83b) and (83c), is odd, because it is hard to contrast 'yesterday' with any other time when one uses a tense marker which could only mean yesterday. And similarly, it is hard to contrast 'earlier today' when one uses a tense marker that could not mean any other time. So only (83a) above is really felicitous.

A similar problem arises in Bemba with respect to a number of manner-adverb meanings, which are expressed as verb suffixes and thus may not be independently focused. They include notions such as 'repeatedly', 'continuously', 'now-and-then', 'here-and-there', 'intensively' and perhaps others. As compared with the separate adverbial 'much', 'hard' (*saana*, cf. (79), (80)), one obtains here:

(84) a. a-*àlí*-boomb-eeshye
          'He *worked intensively*' (VP focus)
      b. *a-*à*-boomb-eeshye
          'He worked *intensively*' (*COMP focus)
      c. a-*àlí*-boomba-boomba
          'He *worked on and on*' (VP focus)
      d. *a-*à*-boomba-boomba
          '*He worked *on and on*' (*COMP focus)
      e. a-*àléé*-boomba
          'He *was working*', 'He *worked continuously*' (VP focus)
      f.
          '*He worked *continuously*'[33]

It is not very clear that one could indeed find an exact equivalent to the verb-bound aspectual morpheme which could be an independent word (or clause) and thus be focused on via a narrower (COMP scope) focus. And in at least one language (Yaqui, see below) a similar situation exist where *no* independent morpheme exists in the language.

The next case, again from Bemba, represents in a sense the reverse situation: a language in which some lexical distinctions are bound to the verb turns out here to have more expressive power than a language in which the very same distinctions are marked by free morphemes. Consider the case of English, where the adverb 'yesterday' is a free morpheme, and where its use precludes the use of the perfective aspectual 'have', as in:

(85) a. He *did not* eat *yesterday*
      b. *He *has not* eaten *yesterday*
      c. He *has not* eaten (*since yesterday*)
      d. He *has not* eaten *today*

33. In progressive tense-aspects no COMP-focus morphology even exists.

The restriction barring (85b) is relatively universal, though in the affirmative variants including 'already' (but not its negative counterpart 'yet') may change the situation, as in:

(86) a. *He *has not yet eaten yesterday*
      b. *He *has* eaten *yesterday*
      c. He *has already* eaten *yesterday*

Now in Bemba, where the terminated/lingering distinction can be made in three of the four past-time divisions, sentences equivalent to (85b), which is starred in English, are quite natural:

(87) a. ta-*à*-liile
         'He did not eat' (before yesterday) (no relevance to present)
      b. ta-*à*-lya
         'He has not eaten (at some time before yesterday)' (relevant to the present)
      c. a-*àlí*-lya
         'He has eaten (at some time before yesterday)' (and this is relevant to the present)

Now, while one could justifiably say that the use of 'already' in (86c) makes it equivalent to the Bemba construction (87c) in the affirmative, English remains deficient in expressive power in the negative, since (86a) is not grammatical, while its Bemba equivalent (87b) is. And further, in Bemba one could go on and specify (87b) with an *overt* time adverbial, as in:

(88) ta-*à*-lya bulya *bushiku*
      'He did not eat the day before yesterday' (and this is relevant to the present)

In this limited area of the grammar, the simple facts of lexical organisation give Bemba greater expressive power than English.

4.2. *Modal verbs: Yaqui*[34]
In Yaqui, a Uto-Aztecan language, modality verbs such as 'want', 'begin', 'end', 'succeed', 'fail', 'intend', 'refuse', 'plan', etc. are bound suffixes on the 'main' verb, as in e.g.:

34. The data are taken from Lindenfeld (1973).

(89) a. batoi-mak-ne nok-*pea*
  people-with-I talk-*like*
  'I *feel-like* talking with people'
 b. itom asoa tekipanoa-*bae*
  our son work-*want*
  'Our son *wants* to work'
 c. aapo yi?i-*taite*
  he dance-*start*
  'He is *starting* to dance'
 d. bempo bwik-*su*-k
  they sing-*finish*-past
  'They *have* already sung', 'They have *finished* singing'
 e. inepo usi-ta-mak eteho-*n*
  I child-DEP-with chat-*continue*
  $\left\{ \begin{array}{l} \text{'I was chatting with a child'} \\ \text{'I } \textit{continued} \text{ chatting with a child'} \end{array} \right\}$
 f. inepo enc-a mak-*ne*
  I you-it give-*will*
  'I will give it to you'.

Some of these verbs have already been re-analysed as tense-aspect markers, as in (89d, e, f) above. Now, in English and other languages in which modality verbs (as well as tense-aspect markers) are separate words, one may use sentences such as (90a) below as an answer to both the *wider* (VP) and *narrower* (COMP) focus questions (90b) and (90c) below, respectively:

(90) a. He started to work.
 b. What did he do then?
 c. What did he start to do then?

In a language like Yaqui, however, where the modality verb is bound to the verbal word, only the wider scope (entire VP) interpretation is possible. Further, in English one could stress-focus or cleft-focus the modality and 'main' verb independently, as in:

(91) a. He started *to wórk* (rather than started something else)
 b. He *stárted* to work (rather than finished)
 c. What he started to do then was *work*.

In Yaqui focus operations like this cannot be done. Further, the negative morpheme in Yaqui (*kaa*) appears at the beginning of the verb phrase, as in:

(92) nee *kaa* maria-ta   bica-k
      I   *neg* Maria-DEP see-past
      'I did not see Maria'.

Now, in English, where modality verbs are independent words, one may negate either the modality verb or its complement, and with verbs such as 'start' this makes a semantic difference, as in:

(93) a. He *did not start* doing his homework.
      b. He started *not doing* his homework.

In Yaqui, due to the bound status of modality verbs, the variants involving a *lower* scope of NEG (93b) cannot be expressed. Now, while verbs such as 'want' are universal 'neg-raising' verbs, in which the meanings of the two scopes of negation neutralise to all intent and purpose (Horn, 1975), 'start' as well as other modality verbs such as 'continue', 'succeed', 'remember', 'hope', 'be afraid', etc. do allow two distinct scopes in English, so that in a language in which only the wider scope is possible, a clear loss of expressive power is demonstrated.

5. *Summary*

I have shown that all three types of differential lexicalisation exist among natural languages, and that all three may create problems for the translator. Problems arising from type (a), i.e. differential slicing of the semantic pie, may not be *per se* too baffling, but it is very likely that in most cases they must also involve type (b), i.e. situations where one language is expressively under-specified in an area of its lexicon as compared to another. And this already represents a problem of expressive power. I have also shown that type (c), i.e. where a language is incapable—due to some peculiarities of its lexical organisation—of expressing certain meanings expressible by other languages. I expect that the translation problems arising from this type may be in some sense marginal. The most burdensome task for the translator, I believe, does not arise from the theoretically more interesting types (b) and (c). Rather, it arises from the more innocuous type (a), with its potentially enormous complexity of constraints, involving syntactic structure, verb classification, case marking, noun gender and agreement and other factors, which one must take into account when translating between two languages both of whom possess adequate lexical machinery for mapping the same semantic contents onto surface expressions. Since the constraints involved often transcend the simple sentence's boundary, the translator must eventually resolve to translate discourse equivalents, rather than lexical or even sentential structures.

V

FORMAL MODELS OF TRANSLATION

H. Kamp

The Adequacy of Translation between Formal and Natural Languages

Introduction

THIS PAPER WAS written in 1970.[1] It arose out of a project led by Mr John Olney of the System Development Corporation in Santa Monica in which I had participated during part of the period 1966–8 when I was at the University of California at Los Angeles. This project tried to throw light on the semantics of English discourse by translating parts of English texts (all chosen from the *Scientific American*) into symbolic notation. The immense difficulties accompanying such an effort should be evident to anybody who has ever stopped to think about the complexity and variety of devices which we employ in ordinary speech, whatever it is that we wish to communicate. Indeed, the participants occasionally wondered whether anything would have come of the project if there had been a sufficiently vivid perception of these difficulties from the start. It soon became clear that the problem was not so much that of translating the English texts into an already existing formal system, such as first order or higher order logic, but rather that the available symbolic languages themselves had to be reappraised and extended at every turn. Almost every simple new English sentence required the introduction of new symbolic notation or else a carefully argued defence of the use of already existing symbolism to render a locution which had not yet been dealt with before.

Although this work was by no means useless, it had carried so strong a flavour of the ad hoc that we felt it was necessary to reflect upon the general methodological question of how and in what sense 'translations' of the sort we were attempting to give could contribute to linguistic theory. The present paper is the result of my own efforts to come to grips with this problem. It tries to provide a general and formally precise account of what should be understood by a translation from one language into another. It should be

1. The work reported herein was supported by SDC and Grant 1-R01-LM-00065-01, English Discourse Structure, for the Public Health Service, U.S. Department of Health, Education and Welfare.

evident that such a formal account requires an underlying formal characterisation of what a language is. In view of the nature of the problem which led to the present investigation this characterisation had to encompass so-called 'formal' or 'symbolic', as well as natural, languages.

I presume that this identification of formal and natural languages will now meet with less resistance than it would have done in 1970. Even then, however, the view was not original. Indeed, it had at that time already been defended by the late Richard Montague. Montague's influence on the form and content of this paper is so deep and pervasive that it seems pointless and misleading to credit him separately with any specific ideas that will appear below. Yet some remarks concerning his influence seem in order. My notions of a formal syntax and an accompanying semantics differ only in details from a similar proposal of Montague's—such as that which can be found in his 1968 paper 'English as a Formal Language'—or in the article 'Universal Grammar' which was written at essentially the same time as the pages following this introduction (see Montague, 1974a). 'Universal Grammar' contains, moreover, a formal definition of the concept of translation; like everything else in that paper it is a very elegant statement, considerably more elegant than what the reader will find here. Indeed, I discovered after completion of my own paper that it paralleled 'Universal Grammar' in so many respects that its publication only seemed desirable if it were substantially expanded, preferably with some concrete applications. The great merit of Montague's work on grammar is that it provides absolutely precise accounts, along the lines of his theoretical persuasion, of actual parts of English. This has made him vulnerable to a good deal of criticism from linguists; but on the other hand, it is because of the painstaking rigour and lucidity of these concrete applications that his ideas have succeeded in capturing the imagination of so many linguists and philosophers over the past seven years.

The original purpose of this paper made the inclusion of such applications unnecessary. After all, the translations which the project produced were in principle available to anyone who requested them. However, the reader of this volume could hardly be expected to go through the trouble of obtaining them. In any case they are in a state so far removed from the ideal expounded in this paper that their effect would probably have been to destroy, rather than strengthen faith in the theory. I did consider adding to this article a concrete example of a translation from a fragment of one natural language into another; we now know more than we did five years ago about the syntax and semantics (of the sort which is explained and used in this paper) of fragments of natural languages, in particular languages other than

English, and also about the semantics of various extensions of the standard systems of symbolic logic, which might be used as intermediaries in translations between natural languages. Finally, however, I decided against such a project. It would have added another ten pages to an already lengthy paper; and, more crucially, I lacked the time to accomplish the task adequately. I realise, however, that in the absence of such an addition much of what this paper has to offer will appear schematic and divorced from the reality of translating actual languages.

Some readers will have doubts about my approach to the theory of translation which even a concrete example of the sort I envisaged would not dispel. I will try, in the remainder of this introduction, to give some indication of how those doubts might eventually be put to rest.

The problems with which the actual translator must cope often seem difficult beyond solution. Many of these difficulties are no doubt incidental. Yet some of them may well be the symptoms of a much deeper and more universal issue, much discussed in recent philosophical literature as the 'indeterminacy of translation'. It seems even now to be a matter of dispute exactly what the doctrine of indeterminacy amounts to. Since the appearance of Quine's 'Word and Object' various authors have proposed different and usually non-equivalent formulations of the doctrine; and as we try to render the arguments for and against these different versions more precise, ever finer distinctions will have to be drawn.

It would defeat the purpose of this introduction to go into these matters in detail. So let me offer just one possible statement of the indeterminacy thesis, which approximates, I believe, fairly closely what most would regard as the central claim: the meaning of many expressions of any natural language L is underdetermined by the verbal dispositions of the speakers of L; and in view of this, there may exist alternative schemes for translating L into some other language L' such that there simply is no criterion that designates one of these as the correct scheme; moreover, this situation may arise even in a case where the translations s' and s'', according to the respective schemes, of the same sentence s of L are incompatible sentences of L'.

The theory developed here ignores the indeterminacy issue completely. Superficially it may even seem to contain the implicit denial that indeterminacy occurs. Those for whom indeterminacy is the fundamental problem of translation would probably regard such denial as sufficient reason to dismiss the theory as irrelevant. This obliges me to give, even at this early stage, a brief outline of the analysis whose details are spelled out in the main body of the paper.

A *translation* from a language L into a language L′ is defined as a certain function from the syntactic analyses of expressions (in particular, sentences) of L to syntactic analyses of expressions of L′ of the same semantic type; the *adequacy* of a translation is defined relative to a certain fixed association of a model for L′ with each of the models of L. Relative to such an association a given translation T is adequate if:

(1) it transforms each L-expression ϕ in its domain into an L′-expression $T(\phi)$ such that for each model α for L, α assigns to ϕ the same semantic value as the model for L′ associated with α assigns to $T(\phi)$; and

(2) the domain of T includes all (analyses of) sentences of L.

This characterisation may seem to be without empirical content insofar as it depends on a prior association of the models of the two languages. But this appraisal would be too harsh. Consider the case of Quine's linguist who joins a completely unknown tribe to learn their language L without any help from interpreters, earlier compiled dictionaries, or the like. Among the models for the language L there must be one in particular which represents the actual world. The natives' knowledge of L includes their ability to decide of (some of) the sentences of L whether they are true (either true absolutely, or true on particular occasions of use). Within the format of the grammar used in this paper, that ability comes to this. The speaker can identify, at least in principle, one of the models which belong to the semantics for L as representing the world surrounding him (from the perspective of his particular speech situation). Similarly, the linguist's knowledge of his own language L′ amounts to a parallel ability to identify the world surrounding him as some model of the semantics for L′. It is these two abilities which form the empirical basis of the association relation relative to which the adequacy of a translation scheme must be judged: when a speaker *s* of L and a speaker *s′* of L′ are placed in the same situation, the model for L′ which *s′* selects as corresponding to the situation must be the value which the association function assigns to the L-model selected in that situation by *s*.

What is the empirical significance of the claim that it is the model α which a speaker selects on a certain occasion as representing the world from that particular perspective? This is a difficult question; and it is, among other things, in the answer to this question that our views regarding the indeterminacy thesis will manifest themselves. If the language L were very simple, say a language of first order predicate logic whose primitive predicates all represent clearly recognisable and sharply demarcated qualities, and if, moreover, it were possible to point at objects without ambiguity, then the claim could be tested by asking the native speakers, pointing at various objects in turn, whether or not they belong to the extensions of the primitive predicates. This test could be pursued as far as desired, and if the claim is correct, this could in principle be so discovered.

With actual spoken languages the situation is bound to be much more complicated. The empirical evidence that can be gathered from the language behaviour of the speakers of L is in all probability not sufficient to determine which L-models correspond to particular contexts of use. It may well be argued therefore that the association relation is only partially defined. (The same considerations will of course apply to the correspondence between contexts of use and models of the translator's language L'.)

The indeterminacy of the association relation is not the only point where indeterminacy may manifest itself. The translator who starts from scratch, without any previous knowledge of the language L he is to translate into his own language L', will, if he is to proceed along the lines of the theory of this article, first have to formulate a syntax and semantics for L. And what criteria are there to decide whether that part of his task has been properly accomplished? In the last analysis the only criterion is the success of the translation scheme the translator manages to formulate on the basis of his syntax and semantics for L; and the success of a translation scheme can only be measured in terms of the quality of the explanation that it provides of the language behaviour of the speakers of L—or rather, of the explanation of this behaviour that is provided by a theory of which this scheme is part, but of which it needs not be the only part. It is an interesting, though complicated, question whether, or to what extent, the data about language behaviour will allow the translator to assess separately the adequacy of any one of the various components into which his theory of the language L breaks down (if it is set out along the lines followed in the present paper). I am afraid however that little about this can be said unless much more specific assumptions about L (as well as about L') are considered.

The rapidly expanding literature on model theoretic semantics for natural languages has to my knowledge been silent on the relation between the formal models its theories postulate and the phenomena of actual language use (such as assent to and dissent from sentential utterances, or language learning) to which we have more or less direct access. This is a gap which must ultimately be filled if we wish to develop model theoretic semantics into a comprehensive theory of language which is securely anchored to the linguistic facts we can observe. What follows does nothing to narrow that gap. I can only hope that the reader will have some idea of how my proposal could be applied to concrete cases; for without it he will find what follows a sterile exercise.

1. *Formation rules*

We will first develop a general, purely syntactical, notion of a *language*. A language will be essentially a set of well-formed expressions; to each expression is assigned some *grammatical category* of the language. Rules referring to these grammatical categories determine how given expressions may be combined into more complicated ones. These rules are called *formation rules*. The expressions of the language will all be strings of symbols that are drawn from a certain set which is given in advance.

Our first concern will be with the characterisation of what sorts of operations on strings we will allow. One might hope that only one operation might suffice, viz. that of concatenation of strings. But this hope is vain. Restriction to this sort of formation alone would lead to syntaxes for natural languages which, if they could be given at all, would be cumbersome and implausible (e.g. the number of grammatical categories they would have to contain would be very large).

Thus we will have to allow for other types of formation as well. Among the formation operations which are especially important is the one which gives for any strings x, y and symbol a, the string that results from re-placing a in x everywhere by y. (We will henceforth refer to this operation as 'substitution'.)

On the other hand, the notion of a formation rule should not be too wide. In particular, formation rules should always be effective, in the sense that for any given rule there will be an effective procedure by means of which we can decide, for any expressions $e_1, \ldots, e_n, e_{n+1}$, whether e_{n+1} comes from applying the rule to $e_1, \ldots, e_n$ or not.

A notion of a formation rule that satisfies all these requirements can be developed in terms of the notion *formation language* defined below. This language is a system of first order predicate logic which contains only two non-logical constants, a 2-place predicate constant $\subset$ (where $\tau \subset \tau'$) is to be read as: 'τ is a substring of τ'') and a 2-place operation constant $\frown$ (where $\tau \frown \tau'$ is to be read as: 'the concatenation of τ and τ''). Formation rules will be characterised as operations which can be defined both by a purely existential, and by a purely universal formula of the system. This characterisation will on the one hand provide us with e.g. substitution, and on the other hand warrant the effectiveness of all formation rules.

Definition 1: let S be a set and F an n-place function. The *closure of* S *under* F (in symbols $cl_F(S)$) is defined as follows: Let

(i) $S_0 = S$;

(ii) for $n = 0, 1, 2, \ldots$ let
$S_{n+1} = S_n \cup \{x: \text{there are } x_1, \ldots, x_n \in S_n \text{ such that } x = F(x_1, \ldots, x_n)\}$.
$cl_F(S) = \underset{n \in \omega}{\cup} S_n$.

We say that F is *well-founded on* S iff $S = cl_F(S - \text{Range F})$.

Definition 2: by the *formation language*, F1, we understand the first order language which is defined as follows:

Symbols: (1) variables: $v_0, v_1, v_2, \ldots$;
(2) logical constants: $\sim, \wedge, \vee, =$;
(3) a 2-place predicate constant C and a 2-place operation constant $\frown$;
(4) parentheses (,).

Terms: (i) v_i is a *term*;
(ii) If τ, τ' are terms then $(\tau \frown \tau')$ is a *term*.

Formulae: (i) If τ, τ' are terms then $\tau = \tau'$ and $\tau \subset \tau'$ are *formulae*;
(ii) If ϕ, ψ are formulae, then $\sim\phi$, $(\phi \wedge \psi)$, $\vee v_i \phi$ are *formulae*.

Interpretations:

An *interpretation* for F1 is a pair $\langle D, P \rangle$ where

(i) D is a non-empty set;
(ii) P is a two-place function with domain D;
(iii) P is well-founded on D;
(iv) If $x, y, z, \in D$ then $P(x, P(y, z)) = P(P(x, y), z)$;
(v) If $x, x', y, y' \in D$ and $P(x, y) = P(x', y')$ then either $(x = x'$ and $y = y')$ or there is a $z \in D$ such that $(x = P(x', z)$ and $y' = P(z, y))$ or there is a $z \in D$ such that $(x' = P(x, z)$ and $y = P(z, y'))$.

For any interpretation $\mathcal{A} = \langle D, P \rangle$ for F1, any sequence[2] d of members of D and any expression (i.e. term or formula) ϕ of F1, the *value assigned by* d *in* $\mathcal{A}$ *to* ϕ (in symbols: $[\phi]_{\mathcal{A},d}$) is defined as follows:

(i) $[v_i]_{\mathcal{A},d} = d_i$;
(ii) $[\tau \frown \tau']_{\mathcal{A},d} = P([\tau]_{\mathcal{A},d}, [\tau']_{\mathcal{A},d})$;
(iii) $[\tau = \tau']_{\mathcal{A},d} = \begin{cases} 1 \text{ if } [\tau]_{\mathcal{A},d}, \text{ is equal to } [\tau']_{\mathcal{A},d} \\ 0 \text{ otherwise} \end{cases}$

2. By a *sequence* we understand a function the domain of which is the set of natural numbers.

$$\text{(iv) } [\tau \subset \tau']_{\alpha,a} = \begin{cases} 1 \text{ iff there are } a, b, \in D \text{ such that} \\ \quad \text{either } [\tau']_{\alpha,a} = P(a, [\tau]_{\alpha,a}) \\ \quad \text{or } [\tau']_{\alpha,a} = P(P(a, [\tau]_{\alpha,a}), b) \\ \quad \text{or } [\tau']_{\alpha,a} = P([\tau]_{\alpha,a}, b) \\ 0 \text{ otherwise} \end{cases}$$

$$\text{(v) } [\sim\phi]_{\alpha,a} = \begin{cases} 1 \text{ if } [\phi]_{\alpha,a} = 0 \\ 0 \text{ otherwise} \end{cases}$$

$$\text{(vi) } [(\phi \wedge \psi)]_{\alpha,a} = \begin{cases} 1 \text{ if } [\phi]_{\alpha,a} = 1 \text{ and } [\psi]_{\alpha,a} = 1 \\ 0 \text{ otherwise} \end{cases}$$

$$\text{(vii) } [\vee v_i \phi]_{\alpha,a} = \begin{cases} 1 \text{ if there is an } a \in D \text{ such that} \\ \quad [\phi]_{\alpha,a_{(a/i)}} = 1^3 \\ 0 \text{ otherwise} \end{cases}$$

The *elementary formulae* of F1 are characterised by:

(i) $\tau = \tau'$ is an *elementary formula*;

(ii) If ϕ, ψ are elementary formulae then $\sim\phi$, $(\phi \wedge \psi)$, $\vee v_i(v_i \subset v_j \wedge \phi)$ and $\wedge v_i(v_i \subset v_j \rightarrow \phi)^4$ are *elementary formulae*.

Definition 3: a k-*place formation rule* of F1 is a pair $\langle \phi, \psi \rangle$ of elementary formulae of F1 such that $v_0, \ldots, v_k, v_{k+1}$ are all the free variables of ϕ and all the free variables of ψ, and for any interpretation $\alpha = \langle D, P \rangle$ and sequence d of elements of D, $[\vee v_{k+1}\phi]_{\alpha,a} = [\wedge v_{k+1}\psi]_{\alpha,a}$.

Let $\langle \phi, \psi \rangle$ be a k-place formation rule of F1. Let $\alpha = \langle D, P \rangle$ be an interpretation for F1 and let $d_0, \ldots, d_{k-1}, d_k$ be members of D. We say that $d_0, \ldots, d_{k-1}, d_k$ *satisfy* $\langle \phi, \psi \rangle$ *in* α iff for any sequence d of members of D, if for $i = 0, \ldots, k, d_i = d_i$, then $[\vee v_{k+1}\phi]_{\alpha,a} = 1$.

It is obvious that concatenation itself corresponds to a formation rule. Indeed, it is characterised by the pair $\langle v_3 = v_3 \wedge v_2 = v_0 \frown v_1, v_3 = v_3 \rightarrow v_2 = v_0 \frown v_1 \rangle$. To show that substitution can also be given as a formation rule is somewhat more involved. Since the construction of the proper pair $\langle \phi, \psi \rangle$ is both cumbersome and straightforward, we omit it.

The notion of formation rule developed here has the disadvantage that it is not recursive; i.e. the set of those pairs of elementary formulae ϕ and ψ with $v_0, \ldots, v_k$ free such that $\vee v_k \phi$ and $\sim \vee v_k \sim \psi$ are materially equivalent in all interpretations, fails to be recursive (in the ordinary sense of recursive). A more satisfactory notion of formation rule—i.e. one which is also suf-

3. If d is a sequence then by $d\frac{b}{i}$ we understand the sequence which is like d except that $\left(d\frac{b}{i}\right)(i) = b$.

4. We understand expressions like $\wedge v_i \varphi$ and $(\varphi \rightarrow \psi)$ as metalinguistic abbreviations.

ficiently powerful, but is such that the set of formation rules is itself recursive—could probably be developed by means of systems of equations analogous to those used to define the set of primitive recursive functions of natural numbers.

2. Syntax

We now proceed to develop a general notion of syntax.

Convention: throughout the remainder of this paper let E be a non-empty set and let P be a 2-place operation on E such that E and P satisfy the conditions (i), (ii), (iii) in the definition of an interpretation on page 281; and let $\mathscr{E} = \langle E, P \rangle$. Clearly E – Range P is non-empty. We refer to the members of E as the *expressions* of $\mathscr{E}$ and to the members of E – Range P as the *symbols* or *basic expressions* of $\mathscr{E}$.

Definition 4: by a *formal syntax* (for $\mathscr{E}$) we understand a pair $\langle \mathscr{B}, \mathscr{R} \rangle$, such that

(i) $\mathscr{B}$ is a function, the domain of which is the union of $\{0, 1\}$ and a subset of E and the range of which consists of sets of symbols.

(ii) $\mathscr{R}$ is a set of triples such that:

(iii) For each triple $\langle r, \phi, \psi \rangle \in \mathscr{R}$ there is a number k such that r is a $k + 1$-place sequence of subsets of the domain of $\mathscr{B}$ and $\langle \phi, \psi \rangle$ is a k-place formation rule.

With any formal syntax $\mathscr{S} = \langle \mathscr{B}, \mathscr{R} \rangle$ for $\mathscr{E}$ we associate a function $\zeta_{\mathscr{S}}$, with the same domain as $\mathscr{B}$, as follows:

(i) For $\alpha \in \text{Dom } \mathscr{B}$ let $\zeta_{\mathscr{S}}^{0}(x) = \mathscr{B}(\alpha)$.

(ii) If n is a natural number and $\alpha \in \text{Dom } \mathscr{B}$, then $\zeta_{\mathscr{S}}^{n+1}(\alpha) = \zeta_{\mathscr{S}}^{n}(\alpha) \cup \{\gamma \in E$: there is a natural number k, and a member $\langle r, \phi, \psi \rangle$ of $\mathscr{R}$, where r is $k + 1$-place and there are $\gamma_0, \ldots, \gamma_{k-1} \in E$ such that for $i = 0, \ldots, k - 1, \gamma_i \in \zeta_{\mathscr{S}}^{n}(\beta)$ whenever $\beta \in r_i$, and $\langle \gamma_0, \ldots, \gamma_{k-1}, \gamma \rangle$ satisfies $\langle \phi, \psi \rangle$ in $\mathscr{E}$; and $\alpha \in r_k\}$.

(iii) For $\alpha \in \text{Dom } \mathscr{B}$, let $\zeta_{\mathscr{S}}(\alpha) = \bigcup_{n \in \omega} \zeta_{\mathscr{S}}^{n}(\alpha)$.

We think of the members of Dom $\mathscr{B}$ as names of grammatical categories. For each $\alpha \in \text{Dom } \mathscr{B}$, $\zeta_{\mathscr{S}}(\alpha)$ will be regarded as the category the name of which is α; the members of the $\mathscr{B}(\alpha)$'s will be referred to as the *basic expressions* of $\mathscr{S}$. We will call the members of $\bigcup_{\alpha \in \text{Dom } \mathscr{B}} \zeta_{\mathscr{S}}(\alpha)$ the *well-formed expressions* of $\mathscr{S}$; the members of $\zeta_{\mathscr{S}}^{(0)}$ will be the *formulae* of $\mathscr{S}$; and the members of $\zeta_{\mathscr{S}}^{(1)}$ the *variables* of $\mathscr{S}$.

As an example might serve the case where E – Range P consists of all words of English (and perhaps interpunction signs and blank space), one of the members of Dom $\mathscr{B}$ is the expression 'common noun phrase', $\mathscr{B}$ ('common noun phrase') is the set of all English common nouns (as 'tree', 'house', 'thought', 'noun'), and $\zeta_{\mathscr{S}}$ ('common noun phrase') consists of all common noun phrases, i.e. common nouns together with compound phrases like 'big tree', 'house with a garden', 'thought that is wrong', 'common noun phrase', etc.

The members of $\mathscr{R}$ are called the *rules of grammar* of the syntax $\langle \mathscr{B}, \mathscr{R} \rangle$. They tell us not only how to obtain compound expressions from expressions which belong to particular categories, but also to which categories the resulting compound expression belongs. It is perhaps often assumed (either explicitly or tacitly) that a simpler concept of syntax, in which no other types of formation play a role than concatenation, would be sufficiently general—and thus, in view of its simplicity, preferable to the notion defined above. Applying this simplification to the concept just defined we would obtain:

A *formal syntax* is a pair $\mathscr{S} = \langle \mathscr{B}, \mathscr{R} \rangle$, where $\mathscr{B}$ is as above and $\mathscr{R}$ consists of finite sequences of members of Dom $\mathscr{B}$. The categories $\zeta_{\mathscr{S}}(\alpha)$ of such a syntax would be defined by:

(i) $\zeta_{\mathscr{S}}^{0}(\alpha) = \mathscr{B}(\alpha)$;

(ii) $\zeta_{\mathscr{S}}^{n+1}(\alpha) = \zeta_{\mathscr{S}}^{n}(\alpha) \cup \{\gamma \in \mathrm{E}$: there is a number k, and $r \in \mathscr{R}$ and $\gamma_0, \ldots, \gamma_{k-1} \in \mathrm{E}$ such that:

(a) r is a $k + 1$-place sequence;

(b) for $i = 0, \ldots, k - 1$ $\gamma_i \in \zeta_{\mathscr{S}}^{n}(r_i)$;

(c) $\gamma = \mathrm{P}(\ldots(\mathrm{P}(\gamma_0, \gamma_1), \ldots), \gamma_{k-1})$;

(d) $\alpha \in r_k\}$;

(iii) $\zeta_{\mathscr{S}}(\alpha) = \cup \zeta_{\mathscr{S}}^{n}(\alpha)$.

Indeed, the syntaxes of all well-known finite languages of symbolic logic are usually given in this simpler form; and that syntaxes for natural languages, like English, can be developed in this same simpler fashion, is not impossible. It is, however, as was indicated before, unlikely that one would obtain a *natural* syntax for English in this way. Such a syntax would probably involve an unduly large number of categories and would also probably be incapable of resolving certain syntactic ambiguities (such as those related to personal pronoun anaphora) and thus push such problems back to the semantical level, where, in our opinion, they do not belong. The lack of success met by attempts to develop a formal syntax for English that employs no other formation rules than simple concatenation suggests that this approach is unsatisfactory. As Montague has pointed out—and as has since also come to be accepted by an increasing number of linguists—a particularly important formation rule is substitution. But there is no reason why formation rules other than concatenation and substitution should not be equally indispensable. A class of likely candidates is e.g. that of the various deletion rules that have been discussed by transformationalists. It may turn out that various other transformations will have to be adopted to achieve the simplest theory of language.

The reasons why we have allowed the members of r to be *sets* of category names, are similar to those which prompted us to introduce other means of formation besides concatenation. Allowing only single names of categories as members of the first components of formation rules would in practice lead to unnaturally large numbers of categories and would, moreover, make it more difficult to extend a formal syntax for a certain fragment of a natural language to one which would cover a larger part of that language.

For every well-formed expression of a given formal syntax there is a certain 'construction' which establishes its well-formedness. Such 'constructions' are essentially finite trees; and that is how we will represent them. We call such construction trees *analyses*.

The definition of the notion of an analysis is quite straightforward. It requires, however, some concepts related to the mathematical concept of a tree, the definitions of which we will give first.

Definition 5: (a) A tree is a set T of finite sequences of natural numbers, such that

    (i) the empty sequence, o, belongs to T;
    (ii) if $s \smile \langle n \rangle$[5] belongs to T then s belongs to T and for all $m < n$, $s \smile \langle m \rangle$ belongs to T.

(b) If T is a tree and $t, t' \in T$ then we will say that t' *is below* t (in symbols: $t' < t$) iff t is a proper initial segment of t'. If $t \in T$ and there is no $t' \in T$ such that t' is below t then t is called an *endpoint of* T. If $t, t' \in T$, $t' < t$ and there is no $t'' \in T$ such that $t' < t''$ and $t'' < t$, then we say that t' is a *successor* of t.

(c) Let T be a tree. T' is a *subtree of* T iff T' is a set such that for some $t \in T$ it is the case that

5. By $s \smile t$ we understand, in general, the concatenation of s and t.

(i) for all sequences t', $t' \in T'$ iff $t \smile t' \in T$.

If (i) holds for T, T', t then we call t a *top* of T' in T.

(d) A *decorated tree* is a function whose domain is a tree. We refer to the points, endpoints, etc. of a tree T also as the *points, endpoints*, etc. of any decorated tree whose domain is T.

(e) By a *subtree* of a decorated tree T we understand a function T' such that Dom T' is a subtree of Dom T and that if t is a top of Dom T' in Dom T, $T'(t') = T(t \smile t')$.

Definition 6: (a) Let T be a tree. A subset B of T is called a *bar* of T if B satisfies the following conditions:

(i) If $t \in T$ then there is a $t' \in B$ such that either $t \leqslant t'$ or $t' < t$;
(ii) if $t, t' \in T$, and $t < t'$ and $t \in B$ then $t' \notin B$.

(b) If T is a decorated tree then B is called a *bar* of T iff B is a bar of Dom T.

Definition 7: (a) Let $\mathscr{S} = \langle \mathscr{B}, \mathscr{R} \rangle$ be a formal syntax. Let γ be a well-formed expression of $\mathscr{S}$. An *analysis of γ in $\mathscr{S}$* is a finite decorated tree A such that:

(i) The range of A consists of pairs;
(ii) if t is an endpoint of A, then $[A(t)]_0$ [6] belongs to the range of $\mathscr{B}$ and $[A(t)]_1 = \langle \langle \{\alpha : [A(t)]_0 \in \mathscr{B}(\alpha)\} \rangle, 0, 0 \rangle$;
(iii) if t is not an endpoint of A and $t_0, \ldots, t_{k-1}$ are all the successors of t in A then there is a k-place rule $\langle r, \phi, \psi \rangle \in \mathscr{S}$, such that:

   (a) for $i = 0, \ldots, k - 1$, if $\alpha \in r_i$ then $[A(t_i)]_0 \in \mathscr{B}(\alpha)$;
   (b) if $\alpha \in r_k$ then $[A(t)]_0 \in \zeta_{\mathscr{S}}(\alpha)$;
   (c) $[A(t_0)]_0, \ldots, [A(t_{k-1})]_0, [A(t)]_0$ satisfy $\langle \phi, \psi \rangle$ in $\mathscr{E}$;
   (d) $[A(t)]_1 = \langle r, \phi, \psi \rangle$;

(iv) $[A(0)]_0 = \gamma$.

(b) A is an *analysis in $\mathscr{S}$* iff there is a well-formed expression γ of $\mathscr{S}$ such that A is the analysis of γ in $\mathscr{S}$.

Since the formation rules of $\mathscr{S}$ are recursive, the concept of an analysis in $\mathscr{S}$ will be recursive also provided $\mathscr{S}$ has a finite number of rules. Even then it does not follow, however, that the concept of a well-formed expression of $\mathscr{S}$ is recursive. For in the first place, definition 7 does not exclude the possibility of infinite analyses. But even where all analyses in $\mathscr{S}$ are

---

6. If s is a finite sequence then by $[s]_i$ we understand the ith component of s.

finite it may be impossible to determine in terms of some directly identifiable features of the string ϕ (such as e.g. its length) any upper bound of the analyses which ϕ would have if it were indeed well formed. In each of these cases it may well be impossible to formulate a decision procedure for well-formedness in $\mathscr{S}$. If, however, (i) we have a uniform way of computing for arbitrary expressions γ of $\mathscr{S}$, a tree size such that if γ has any analysis, then it has an analysis of at most that size; (ii) for every expression γ in E there are only finitely many pairs consisting of a k-place rule $\langle r, \phi, \psi \rangle \in \mathscr{R}$ and a sequence of k expressions $\gamma_0, \ldots, \gamma_{k-1} \in E$ such that $\gamma_0, \ldots, \zeta_{k-1}, \gamma$ satisfy $\vee v_{k+1}\phi$ in $\mathscr{E}$; and (iii) we have a recursive method for finding, for any $\gamma \in E$, all those pairs $\langle\langle r, \phi, \psi \rangle\langle\gamma_0, \ldots, \gamma_{k-1}\rangle\rangle$; then the concept of well-formedness in $\mathscr{S}$ is indeed recursive.

Condition (i) is obviously satisfied if $\mathscr{S}$ has no formation rules other than concatenation; but it is also a condition likely to be satisfied by syntaxes which also have certain other formation rules (such as e.g. substitution). That an expression could result in an infinite number of different ways from the application of a rule to a certain number of other expressions, should not be discarded automatically as absurd. For example, an expression P(1) results from substitution of 1 for any symbol x different from P, in P(x). However, here the pairs of a rule and a sequence of expressions to which the rule should be applied to yield the expression in question, though perhaps infinite in number, are very similar; if for the expression in question there exists an analysis involving one of those pairs, presumably a similar analysis will exist involving any of the other pairs. So it seems possible to modify condition (ii) in such a manner as to permit cases like the one just mentioned and still yield a recursive concept of grammaticality—provided that condition (iii) is also modified correspondingly.

Condition (iii) would probably hold in those syntaxes in which for each γ there are, as (ii) requires, only finitely many pairs. One can easily conceive of the way in which (iii) could be so adapted to more flexible alternatives of condition (ii), so that the recursiveness of the set of well-formed expressions remains guaranteed.

As a rule formal syntaxes for languages of symbolic logic are such that every well-formed expression has exactly one analysis. It is wrong however to demand this of formal syntaxes for natural languages. Indeed, syntactic ambiguity is a well-known phenomenon; and we could deprive ourselves of the means to account for this phenomenon if we insisted that each grammatical expression has a unique analysis.

In view of the possibility that a grammatical expression may have more than one analysis we will from now on talk almost exclusively about analyses even though our real interest will remain directed towards expressions. It is only the possible ambiguity of the expressions that excludes them as the immediate objects of the present technical development.

3. *Levels of analysis; translations*

The primary task of a translation (say, of one natural language into another) is to transform the principal vehicles of communication, i.e. sentences, of the first language into sentences of the second. Thus, if we were to regard only this basic function of translations we could characterise them simply as maps from sentences to sentences.

However, the way in which translations are defined and learned usually involves not only sentences, but other kinds of expressions as well. A translation from one natural language into another, for example, is normally given in the form of a dictionary (which usually pairs words with other expressions) together with certain stipulations which specify how one should render grammatical constructions of the first language within the second language. We take this to be an essential feature of translations. Therefore we will define a translation Tr (from a formal syntax $\mathscr{S}$ into a formal syntax $\mathscr{S}'$) as a pair consisting of a function Tr_0, which maps certain expressions of $\mathscr{S}$—henceforth referred to as the *elementary* expressions of Tr—onto expressions of $\mathscr{S}'$, and a function Tr_1, which maps n-place rules of grammar of $\mathscr{S}$ onto n-place rules of $\mathscr{S}'$.[7] The translation of an expression of $\mathscr{S}$ which results from applying the rule ρ of $\mathscr{S}$ to the elementary expressions $e_1, \ldots, e_n$ will then be the result of applying the rule corresponding to ρ by Tr_1 to the values of $e_1, \ldots, e_n$ under Tr_0; etc.

The elementary expressions of the translations can be of various levels of complexity: they can be words; but they also might be complex noun phrases, complex verb phrases, etc. A translation will be less 'revealing' about the relations between the respective structures of the languages which it links as its elementary expressions are more complex. Thus, from this point of view, the simpler its elementary expressions are, the better the translation is—the ideal being a translation the elementary expressions of which are the basic expressions of the syntax to which it applies. However, in practice one will often have to be content with translations, not all of the elementary expressions of which are basic.

Thus it is natural to develop a concept of translation which allows for other sets of elementary expressions than just the set of basic expressions of the

7. This is not quite correct, since it neglects the possibility that the ranges of Tr_0 and Tr_1 contain *schemata* (which will be defined later on).

syntax under consideration. But not every set of expressions is acceptable as the set of elementary expressions of a translation: if an expression *e* occurs in the analysis of *e'*, then *e* and *e'* should not be elementary expressions of the same translation. In order to single out those sets which are acceptable as sets of elementary expressions, we introduce the notion of a *level of analysis*.

Definition 8: Let $\mathscr{S} = \langle \mathscr{B}, \mathscr{R} \rangle$ be a formal syntax.

(a) A *level of analysis in* $\mathscr{S}$ is a function $\mathscr{L}$ such that:

(i) the domain of $\mathscr{L}$ consists of analyses in $\mathscr{S}$;

(ii) for any analysis A in Dom $\mathscr{L}$, $\mathscr{L}(A)$ is a bar of A;

(iii) if A is an analysis in $\mathscr{S}$, A' is a subtree of A and *t* is a top of A' in A, then if A is in the domain of $\mathscr{L}$ and there is a *t'* in $\mathscr{L}(A)$ such that $t' \leqslant t$ then A' is in the domain of $\mathscr{L}$ and $\mathscr{L}(A') = \{t': (\exists\, t'' \in \mathscr{L}(A))\, t'' = t \smile t'\}$.

(b) If $\mathscr{L}$, $\mathscr{L}'$ are levels of analysis for $\mathscr{S}$ then we say that $\mathscr{L}$ is *at least as deep as* $\mathscr{L}'$ if (i) Dom $\mathscr{L}' \subseteq$ Dom $\mathscr{L}$; and (ii) if $A \in$ Dom $\mathscr{L}'$ and $t' \in \mathscr{L}'(A)$ then there is a $t \in \mathscr{L}(A)$ such that $t \leqslant t'$.

It is often the case that an expression of one language cannot be translated into any particular expression of some other language, but that its function can be rendered by some grammatical construction in that language. This phenomenon is sufficiently common to be accounted for in our formal characterisation of a translation. The notion of a schema, defined below, will serve this purpose. A more detailed explanation of the notion follows the definition.

Definition 9: (a) Let $\mathscr{S} = \langle \mathscr{B}, \mathscr{R} \rangle$ be a formal syntax. A *k*-place *schema in* $\mathscr{S}$ is a pair $\langle S, t \rangle$ such that

(i) S is a decorated tree;

(ii) *t* is a *k*-place sequence of distinct endpoints of S;

(iii) for all $t \in$ Dom S, S(*t*) is a pair;

(iv) if *t* is an endpoint of S which is not a member of *t*, then S(*t*) is a pair $\langle \gamma, \rho \rangle$ where $\gamma \in \cup$ Range $\mathscr{B}$ and $\rho = \langle \langle \{\alpha : \gamma \in \mathscr{B}(\alpha)\} \rangle, 0, 0 \rangle$;

(v) for $i = 0, \ldots, k - 1$, $[S(t_i)]_0 = 0$ and $[S(t_i)]_1$ is a triple the 0th member of which is a set of category names of $\mathscr{S}$ and the 1st and 2nd members of which are 0;

(vi) if *t* is a point of S, but not an endpoint, then $[S(t)]_1$ is a rule $\langle r, \phi, \psi \rangle \in \mathscr{R}$. Further, if $t_0, \ldots, t_{n-1}$ are the immediate successors of t in S then $[S(t)]_1$ is an n-place rule; and if, for $i = 0, \ldots, n - 1$, r_i' is the last component of $[[S(t_i)]_1]_0$ then $r_i \subseteq r_i'$. Finally, if for no $i < k$, $t_i < t$ then $[S(t_0)]_0, \ldots, [S(t_{n-1})]_0, [S(t)]_0$ satisfy $\langle r, \phi, \psi \rangle$; and if for some $i < k$, $t_i < t$ then $[S(t)]_0 = 0$.

(b) Let $\langle S, t \rangle$ be a k-place schema in $\mathscr{S}$ and let $A_0, \ldots, A_{k-1}$ be analyses of $\mathscr{S}$ such that, for $i = 0, \ldots, k - 1$, if $\alpha \in [[S(t_i)]_1]_0$ then $[A_i(0)]_0 \in \zeta \mathscr{S}(\alpha)$. A *result of applying* $\langle S, t \rangle$ *to* $A_0, \ldots, A_{k-1}$ (in symbols: $\langle S, t \rangle (A_0, \ldots, A_{k-1})$) is an analysis A of $\mathscr{S}$, such that

(i) Dom S $\subseteq$ Dom A;

(ii) if $t \in$ Dom S and for $i = 0, \ldots, k - 1$, $t_i \neq t$ then $[A(t)]_1 = [S(t)]_1$;

(iii) for $i = 0, \ldots, k - 1$, A_i is a subtree of A and t_i is a top of A_i in A;

(iv) if $t \in$ Dom S and for no $i < k$, $t_i < t$ then $A(t) = S(t)$.

It should be clear that for every k-place rule ρ of $\mathscr{S}$ there is a k-place schema S such that whenever $A_0, \ldots, A_k$ are analyses of $\mathscr{S}$ then A_k is the result of applying S to $A_0, \ldots, A_{k-1}$ iff $[A_k(0)]_0$ comes from $[A_0(0)]_0, \ldots, [A_{k-1}(0)]_0$ in the sense of definition 4(ii).

The notion of a schema, as it is defined here, should be regarded as a generalisation of the concept of a schema as it occurs in symbolic logic. There by a k-place schema one usually understands a formula with k free variables, e.g. a formula of sentential calculus with k free sentential variables $p_0, \ldots, p_{k-1}$. The result of applying the schema S to k formulae $\phi_0, \ldots, \phi_{k-1}$ is then simply the formula which we obtain if we replace in S p_0 everywhere by $\phi_0, \ldots, p_{k-1}$ everywhere by ϕ_{k-1}.

Schemata play an important role in translations. They appear indispensable when an expression γ of the language $\mathscr{L}$ from which we translate, does not correspond to any particular expression of the language $\mathscr{L}'$ into which we translate, even though every expression ϕ of $\mathscr{L}$ which is formed from γ and other expressions $\gamma_0, \ldots, \gamma_{k-1}$ does correspond, in a uniform way, to a complex expression ϕ' of $\mathscr{L}'$ formed out of the correspondents $\gamma_0', \ldots, \gamma_{k-1}'$ in $\mathscr{L}'$ of $\gamma_0, \ldots, \gamma_{k-1}$. In such a case we can usually represent the construction which gives us ϕ' from $\phi_0', \ldots, \phi_{k-1}'$ by a schema. As an example, consider the situation where $\mathscr{L}$ is a sentential calculus which contains the sentential connective $\wedge$ (representing conjunction), and $\mathscr{L}'$ is a sentential calculus, which has the same sentential constants as $\mathscr{L}$, but contains no other connectives than $\sim$ (negation) and $\rightarrow$ (material implication). A natural translation from $\mathscr{L}$ into $\mathscr{L}'$ will transform a formula $(\phi \wedge \psi)$ into, say, $\sim(\phi \rightarrow \sim\psi)$. A possible example from translations between natural languages is provided by the respective means of expressing the possessive in, say, Dutch and German, where Dutch expresses this relation with the help of the preposition 'van', and German by using the genitive. This means that 'of' will not be explicitly translated, but the (possessive) Dutch contexts in which it occurs are nonetheless systematically translatable into German equivalents. It should not be too hard to determine what schema will do this. (I speak here of a 'possible' example, as it is not excluded that the genitive ending in German should be treated as a separate lexical item. It is just conceivable that in this case we could translate Dutch 'van' into this item, and formulate the relevant recursive clauses of the translation definition in such a way that e.g. 'het boek van mijn vader' is converted into 'das Buch meines Vaters'.)

Definition 10: let $\mathscr{S} = \langle \mathscr{B}, \mathscr{R} \rangle$ and $\mathscr{S}' = \langle \mathscr{B}', \mathscr{R}' \rangle$ be formal syntaxes and let $\mathscr{L}$ be a level of analysis in $\mathscr{S}$. A *translation from $\mathscr{S}$ into $\mathscr{S}'$ down to $\mathscr{L}$* is a pair $\text{Tr} = \langle \text{Tr}_0, \text{Tr}_1 \rangle$ of functions Tr_0 and Tr_1 such that:

(i) the domain of Tr_0 consists of all those analyses A in $\mathscr{S}$ such that $\mathscr{L}(A) = \{o\}$;

(ii) for each A in the domain of Tr_0, $\text{Tr}_0(A)$ is either an analysis in $\mathscr{S}'$, or else a schema in $\mathscr{S}'$;

(iii) the domain of Tr_1 is $\mathscr{R}$;

(iv) if ρ is a k-place rule in $\mathscr{R}$ then $\text{Tr}_1(\rho)$ is a k-place schema in $\mathscr{S}'$.

Definition 11: let $\mathscr{S}$, $\mathscr{S}'$, $\mathscr{L}$ be as above and let $\text{Tr} = \langle \text{Tr}_0, \text{Tr}_1 \rangle$ be a translation from $\mathscr{S}$ into $\mathscr{S}'$ down to $\mathscr{L}$. We define a function Tr^*, whose domain consists of some (though not necessarily all) analyses A in the domain of $\mathscr{L}$, as follows, by recursion:

(i) if $\mathscr{L}(A) = \{o\}$ then $\text{Tr}^*(A) = \text{Tr}_0(A)$;

(ii) if $A \in \text{Dom } \mathscr{L}$, $\langle o \rangle, \ldots, \langle k - 1 \rangle$ are all the one-place sequences in Dom A and for $i = o, \ldots, k - 1$, there are analyses A_i such that (i) $\langle i \rangle$ is a top of A_i in A, and (ii) $\text{Tr}^*(A_i)$ is defined, then

(a) if for all $i < k$ $\text{Tr}^*(A_i)$ is an analysis in $\mathscr{S}'$ and $[A(o)]_1 = \rho$ then $\text{Tr}^*(A) = \text{Tr}_1(\rho)(\text{Tr}^*(A_0), \ldots, \text{Tr}^*(A_{k-1}))$;

(b) if there is a $j < k$ such that $\text{Tr}^*(A_j)$ is a $k - 1$-place schema of $\mathscr{S}'$ and for $i < k$, $i \neq j$, $\text{Tr}^*(A_i)$ is an analysis in $\mathscr{S}'$ then $\text{Tr}^*(A) = \text{Tr}^*(A_j)(\text{Tr}^*(A_0), \ldots, \text{Tr}^*(A_{j-1}), \text{Tr}^*(A_{j+1}), \ldots, \text{Tr}^*(A_{k-1}))$.

It is clear that in general, Tr^* will *not* be defined for *all* analyses Dom $\mathscr{L}$. We say that Tr is *adequate* if the domain of Tr^* includes all those analyses in Dom $\mathscr{L}$ such that $[A(o)]_0 \in \zeta_{\mathscr{S}}(o)$. Thus we are willing to call the translation adequate as long as all *formulae* of $\mathscr{S}$ (which do not fall 'below' our level of analysis $\mathscr{L}$) are translated by Tr. This criterion is to a certain extent arbitrary and may well be strengthened so as to include the requirement that other categories in $\mathscr{S}$ also be fully translated. Our actual choice of the criterion above reflects our viewpoint that the basic goal of a translation is the proper transformation of sentences.

Let $\mathscr{S}$ be a formal syntax. Then for any other formal syntax $\mathscr{S}'$ we can ask the question if $\mathscr{S}'$ is adequate for translation from $\mathscr{S}$ into it. This question seems, in this absolute form, rather meaningless. But we have just seen that, relative to a level of analysis $\mathscr{L}$ for $\mathscr{S}$, the question does make sense: $\mathscr{S}'$ can be regarded as adequate for translation from $\mathscr{S}$, relative to $\mathscr{L}$, if there is a translation Tr from $\mathscr{S}$ into $\mathscr{S}'$, down to $\mathscr{L}$, such that the domain of Tr* includes every analysis $A \in \mathrm{Dom}\,\mathscr{L}$ such that $[A(o)]_0 \in \zeta\mathscr{S}(o)$. For given $\mathscr{S}$ and $\mathscr{S}'$ the answer is less likely to be positive as the level of analysis $\mathscr{L}$ is deeper. Indeed, if $\mathscr{L}$ is at least as deep as $\mathscr{L}'$ and there is an adequate translation from $\mathscr{S}$ into $\mathscr{S}'$ down to $\mathscr{L}$, then there is also an adequate translation from $\mathscr{S}$ into $\mathscr{S}'$ down to $\mathscr{L}'$.

The concept of a translation could be strengthened in various ways, even if we stay within the present, purely syntactic framework. A natural requirement would be, e.g., that the functions Tr_0 and Tr_1 be recursive. However, we will not further pursue the question whether the notion of a translation should or could be strengthened in such ways. A truly meaningful discussion of translations is possible only if the meanings of the translated expressions and of their translations are taken into account: a translation should preserve the meaning of the expressions which it translates.

4. *Types*

We will characterise the meanings of well-formed expressions of any formal syntax $\mathscr{S}$ in terms of intensional models for that syntax. Intensional models should be regarded as indexed 'collections' of possible worlds. (We hesitate to use the word 'collection', since cross-reference from one such possible world to others usually occurs in intensional models.) A well-formed expression will denote at each index of an intensional model an entity of the appropriate kind. By the *intension* which an intensional model assigns to a well-formed expression γ we understand the function which, for each index of the model, gives the entity denoted by γ at that index.

We said that a well-formed expression γ of a formal syntax $\mathscr{S}$ should denote at each index of an intensional model for $\mathscr{S}$ an object 'of the appropriate kind'. What we mean by this might be best elucidated by means of an example. Suppose that $\mathscr{S} = \langle \mathscr{B}, \mathscr{R} \rangle$ is a formal syntax for English, according to which proper nouns and common nouns are well-formed expressions. It is natural that any proper noun should denote in each intensional model for $\mathscr{S}$ at each index an individual of that intensional model; similarly a common noun should always denote a class of individuals. Thus the objects denoted by a proper and a common noun, respectively, are of different sorts: individuals as against classes of individuals. The question what *sort* of entity an expression denotes should be distinguished from the question *which* entities are denoted by the expression at particular indices in particular models.

It is somewhat problematic whether this question should be considered as belonging to semantics or to syntax. It is syntactic insofar as the type of object that an expression denotes ought to depend—it seems—only on the syntactic categories to which the expression belongs. Thus the question what sorts of objects are the denotata of well-formed expressions seems to be on a level which is intermediate between syntax and semantics. We will therefore treat it separately from, and prior to, our formal development of semantics itself.

Definition 12: for any natural number $n > 0$ the *types of n-sorted* logic are defined recursively as follows:

(i) For $i = 3, \ldots, n + 2$, $\langle i \rangle$ is a *type*;

(ii) if m is any natural number > 0 and $\tau_0, \ldots, \tau_{m-1}, \tau_m$ are types then
$\langle 1 \rangle \smile \tau_0, \smile \cdots \smile \tau_{m-1} \smile \langle 0 \rangle$ and
$\langle 2 \rangle \smile \tau_0 \smile \cdots \smile \tau_{m-1} \smile \tau_m \smile \langle 0 \rangle$ are *types.*

Definition 13: let S be a *n*-place sequence of sets.

(a) For any type τ of *n*-sorted logic the *realisation of τ in S* (in symbols: $\mathrm{Res}(\tau)$) is defined recursively by:

(i) for $i = 3, \ldots, n + 2$, $\mathrm{Res}(\langle i \rangle) = S_{i-3}$;

(ii) (a) if $\tau = \langle 1 \rangle \smile \tau_0 \smile \cdots \smile \tau_{m-1} \smile \langle 0 \rangle$, $\mathrm{Res}(\tau) = \mathscr{P}(\mathrm{Res}(\tau_0) \otimes \cdots \otimes \mathrm{Res}(\tau_{m-1}))$;[8]

(b) if $\tau = \langle 2 \rangle \smile \tau_0 \smile \cdots \smile \tau_{m-1} \smile \tau_m \smile \langle 0 \rangle$ then $\mathrm{Res}(\tau) = \mathrm{Res}(\tau_m)^{\mathrm{Res}(\tau_0) \otimes \cdots \otimes \mathrm{Res}(\tau_{m-1})}$.

(b) C is a *category connected with S* iff C is the realisation of some type of *n*-sorted logic in S.

8. If x, y are sets, then we understand by $x \otimes y$ the cartesian product of x; by x^y the set of all functions with domain y and range included in x; and by $\mathscr{P}(x)$ the power set of x.

The intensional models in terms of which we will characterise the semantics for formal syntaxes, will be *multi-valued*, i.e. we will not limit ourselves to models which are based upon two truth values, True and False, but in principle admit any non-empty set of truth values. Thus the basic constituents from which a model is built up are: (i) a set of indices (I); (ii) a set of individuals (D); and (iii) a set of truth values (V). The sorts of entities in the model are completely determined by these three constituents. Among them are—the set of individuals (D): the proper kind of denotata for proper names; the set of functions from I into D: the proper kind of intensions for proper nouns; the set of functions from I into $\mathscr{P}(D)$: the proper kind of intensions for common nouns; the set of functions from I into V: the proper kind of intensions for sentences; etc. In general we will identify these sorts of entities of the model with the realisations of types in $\langle I, V, D \rangle$. Thus the set of possible models for a given formal syntax $\mathscr{S}$ is limited by the types which are associated with the well-formed expressions of $\mathscr{S}$. Each expression ought to have as its intension, in a model built from I, V, D, an entity in the realisation in $\langle I, V, D \rangle$ of the type of the expression. Thus the set of possible models for a formal syntax $\mathscr{S}$ is relative to a function which tells us for each of the well-formed expressions of $\mathscr{S}$ the type of that expression.[9] In view of the principle that the type of an expression ought to be determined entirely by the syntactic categories to which the expression belongs, such functions can be characterised as follows:

Definition 14: let $\mathscr{S}$ be a formal syntax.

(a) A *type function for* $\mathscr{S}$ is a function $\mathscr{T}$ such that:

(i) the domain of $\mathscr{T}$ consists of all non-empty sets S of category names of $\mathscr{S}$ for which $\bigcap_{\alpha \in S} \zeta_{\mathscr{S}}(\alpha) \neq \phi$;

(ii) the range of $\mathscr{T}$ consists of types of 3-sorted logic;

(iii) if Γ is a set of category names and there is a subset Γ' of Γ and a well-formed expression γ of $\mathscr{S}$ such that for any category name α of $\mathscr{S}$, $\alpha \in \Gamma'$ iff $\gamma \in \zeta_{\mathscr{S}}(\alpha)$, then $\mathscr{T}(\Gamma) = \mathscr{T}(\Gamma')$;[10]

9. In familiar symbolic languages, such as first and higher order predicate logic, or the theory of types as formulated by Church, the syntactic categories are themselves the types, so that no further specification of this function is necessary.

10. The significance of condition (iii) is this. I want to assume that the type of an expression is completely determined by the categories to which it belongs. The precise intention of this assumption is that whenever $\alpha_1, \ldots, \alpha_n$ are all the categories to which a certain expression γ belongs, and γ has type τ, then any other expression belonging to $\alpha_1, \ldots, \alpha_n$ must also be of type τ, irrespective of whether it belongs to yet some other categories. Thus any superset of $\{\alpha_1, \ldots, \alpha_n\}$ which is in the domain of τ must get the same value that $\{\alpha_1, \ldots, \alpha_n\}$ itself receives.

(iv) if $o \in \Gamma$ then $\mathscr{T}(\Gamma) = \langle 2 \rangle \smile \langle 3 \rangle \smile \langle 4 \rangle \smile \langle o \rangle$.[11]

(b) Let $\mathscr{T}$ be a type function for $\mathscr{S}$. For any well-formed expression γ of $\mathscr{S}$ we understand by $\mathscr{T}(\gamma)$ the type τ such that if Γ is the set of α such that $\gamma \in \zeta_{\mathscr{S}}(\alpha)$ then $\tau = \mathscr{T}(\Gamma)$. If A is an analysis of $\mathscr{S}$, then by $\mathscr{T}(A)$ we understand $\mathscr{T}([A(o)]_o)$.

Type functions for formal syntaxes provide us with a further natural criterion for adequacy of translations: the type of the translation of an expression should be the same as the type of the expression itself. This seems perfectly plausible for certain types, such as the type of sentences or the type of singular terms. Whether the principle should hold for *all* types of expressions to which the translation function applies is perhaps not quite so obvious. However, the semantic criteria for adequacy discussed below will explain why it is indeed natural to demand that translations preserve type without exception.

Thus we arrive at the following definition of adequacy.

Definition 15: let $\mathscr{S}$, $\mathscr{S}'$ be formal syntaxes; let $\mathscr{T}$, $\mathscr{T}'$ be type functions for $\mathscr{S}$, $\mathscr{S}'$ respectively; and let $\mathscr{L}$ be a level of analysis for $\mathscr{S}$. A translation Tr of $\mathscr{S}$ into $\mathscr{S}'$ down to $\mathscr{L}$ is *adequate relative to* $\mathscr{T}$ *and* $\mathscr{T}'$ iff:

(i) Tr is adequate; and
(ii) for each analysis $A \in \mathrm{Dom}\,\mathscr{L}$, $\mathscr{T}'(\mathrm{Tr}^*(A)) = \mathscr{T}(A)$.

The principle that the type of an expression should be uniquely determined by the syntactic categories to which it belongs is always observed in the syntaxes and semantics of languages of formal logic. Moreover, presently existing grammars for natural languages are for the most part in agreement with it. For example, English expressions which, according to traditional English grammar, belong to the same category (categories) do as a rule denote objects of the same type. There are, however, exceptions to this rule. An example is the traditional category of adverbs. Certain adverbs (e.g. 'utterly') can be used both as modifiers of verbs and of adjectives, and as modifiers of other adverbs.

It seems to me that grammars whose categories do not always determine the type are unsatisfactory and should be replaced by more refined systems in which the type of an analysis only depends on the categories of its top.

---

11. The last condition warrants that the realisation of the type of a formula of $\mathscr{S}$ in $\langle I, V, D \rangle$ will always be a function from I into V.

5. *Interpretations*

Our last characterisation of adequacy for translations is still not satisfactory. A translation should preserve the meaning of the expressions it translates, not just the semantic *types*. In order to do justice to this stronger requirement we will now turn to the interpretations, or *models*, themselves. As we said above, our models are built from three basic sets: the set of indices, the set of truth values, and the set of individuals. In addition to these basic sets a model will include a function which assigns to each 'basic' expression an entity of the appropriate kind—the intension of the expression—and a function which assigns to each rule a function which will yield the intension of an expression formed by means of that rule when applied to the intensions of the component expressions.

We have spoken in the previous paragraph about 'basic' expressions. We do not want to restrict ourselves to the case where these 'basic' expressions are simply the members of the basic categories of the syntax $\mathscr{S}$ in question. We also want to consider cases where the 'basic' expressions—or, rather, their analyses—are those which are basic relative to some level of analysis for $\mathscr{S}$. The reason for this is the following. We want to say that a translation Tr from $\mathscr{S}$ into $\mathscr{S}'$, down to level $\mathscr{L}$, is adequate if it preserves the meaning of all the analyses translated. But only those analyses are translated which belong to the domain of $\mathscr{L}$. Thus we are interested only in *their* meanings; and it seems unnatural to demand in these circumstances that the meanings of analyses in Dom $\mathscr{L}$ be analysed further in terms of meanings of subtrees of these analyses which do not belong to Dom $\mathscr{L}$. Indeed, it may well be the case that we do not have such a semantical analysis at all, even though we do have a satisfactory semantical analysis of the meaning relations between the analyses which belong to Dom $\mathscr{L}$. On the other hand, the models for $\mathscr{L}$ which assign meaning only to those analyses which belong to Dom $\mathscr{L}$ should include those which we obtain when we 'restrict to Dom $\mathscr{L}$' any model for $\mathscr{S}$ relative to some level $\mathscr{L}'$ which is deeper than $\mathscr{L}$; i.e. for any model for $\mathscr{S}$ which assigns meanings to all analyses in Dom $\mathscr{L}'$ there should be a model which assigns meanings only to the analyses in Dom $\mathscr{L}$, and coincides with the former on all of Dom $\mathscr{L}$. This requirement causes a certain difficulty in connection with variables.

In general, some of the basic expressions of a language will function as variables. This is true not only of formal languages, but also of natural languages, where in particular the personal pronouns play such a role (in some, though not in all cases). Such expressions will not denote particular objects, but 'range' over classes of such objects. Expressions which contain variables will generally not denote particular entities either, for their denotations may vary with the denotations of the variables they contain. On the other hand, such complex expressions, unlike the variables themselves, will generally not range over the class of *all* entities of the appropriate type. For example, the phrase 'house owned by x' will generally denote different sets of individuals, according as x denotes different persons, but these sets will always be sets of houses. Thus among the models relative to a level of analysis $\mathscr{L}$ on which 'house owned by x' is a basic expression, there should be at least some in which this expression ranges over a subset of the appropriate category which is neither a singleton nor the whole category.

The question remains if we have any means to determine for any of the analyses which are basic in $\mathscr{L}$, whether it is a constant (i.e. ought to denote always a particular object), a pure variable (i.e. ought to range over the whole set of appropriate entities) or an expression which could range over other sets of entities of the appropriate sort. If we have no knowledge at all of that part of the syntactic analysis of an expression which lies 'below' $\mathscr{L}$, then we can distinguish among the expressions whose analyses are not below $\mathscr{L}$, only: (i) pure variables, (ii) basic expressions of the syntax which are not variables, and (iii) compound expressions; of the latter we would never know whether they 'contain free variables' or not, and so any subset of entities of the appropriate sort should be regarded as a possible range for such an expression. However, the natural situation in the present context seems to be one where we have, on the one hand, a complete syntactic analysis but, on the other hand, only a partial semantical theory, i.e. a semantic analysis which does not go down to the lowest level of our syntax. (This is— approximately—the present state of linguistic description of English.) In this situation we can, since we know the complete syntactic analysis of each expression, include among the constants at least those expressions the analyses of which contain no variables at all. If we could in addition recognise whether a variable occurs *free* in the analysis then we could include among the analyses which are to denote particular objects also those which, though containing variables, do not contain free occurrences of variables. Since, however, we have not discussed any syntactic characterisations of freedom and bondage, we will not go into this matter any further.

Thus far we have spoken of denotations as well as of intensions. In the technical development, however, it will be expedient to pay exclusive attention to intensions. In view of our stipulations about the connection between intensions and denotations it is clear that where denotations exist, the intension can always be retrieved from them. Thus if every expression did indeed have denotations (at all indices in each model) as well as an intension we could, in principle base the semantic account entirely on denotations, and then, if we so desired, introduce intensions by explicit definition. It is not clear however that every expression has denotation. The intension of a sentential connective, for example, seems to be a function from propositions (i.e. functions from indices to truth values) to propositions. But what is the denotation of a sentential connective at a particular index? We could stipulate that at each index the denotation of the connective is what we have just called its intension. But that procedure would seem to be rather artificial. And I do not know of any compensating advantages that might justify us in adopting it in spite of this artificiality.

Thus intensions will be our central semantic entities; and type functions for formal syntaxes should be understood as giving the type of the *intension* of an expression, and not of its denotations (clause (iv) of definition 14 should be understood in this perspective).

It will turn out that the objects that models assign to analyses are not themselves intensions, but functions from assignments to intensions. This unpleasant complication arises because, on the one hand, the intensions of expressions that 'contain free variables' will vary with the assignments and, on the other hand, the intension of a compound expression under a given assignment will depend not only on the intensions of the components under that particular assignment, but also on the intentions of the components under other assignments. (This is, in general, the case if one of the component expressions is a variable binding operator—as are, for example, the quantifiers in predicate logic.)

Definition 16: let $\mathscr{S} = \langle \mathscr{B}, \mathscr{R} \rangle$ be a formal syntax. Let $\mathscr{L}$ be a level of analysis for $\mathscr{S}$ and $\mathscr{T}$ a type function for $\mathscr{S}$. Let $\mathscr{I} = \langle I, V, D \rangle$ be a triple of non-empty sets.

(a) An *assignment range for* $\mathscr{S}$, $\mathscr{T}$ *in* $\mathscr{I}$, *down to* $\mathscr{L}$, is a function U such that:

(i) the domain of U consists of the analyses A of $\mathscr{S}$ such that $\mathscr{L}(A) = \{0\}$;

(ii) if $A \in \text{Dom } U$ and $[A(0)]_0 \in \zeta\mathscr{S}(1)$ then $U(A) = \text{Re } \mathscr{I}(\mathscr{T}(A))$;

(iii) if $A \in \text{Dom } U$ and for all $t \in \text{Dom } A$, $[A(t)]_0 \notin \zeta\mathscr{S}(1)$ then there is an $x \in \text{Re } \mathscr{I}(\mathscr{T}(A))$ such that $U(A) = \{x\}$;

(iv) if $A \in \text{Dom } U$, $[A(0)]_0 \notin \zeta\mathscr{S}(1)$, but for some $t \in \text{Dom } A$, $[A(t)]_0 \in \zeta\mathscr{S}(1)$ then $U(A) \subseteq \text{Re } \mathscr{I}(\mathscr{T}(A))$.

(b) Let U be an assignment-range for $\mathscr{S}$, $\mathscr{T}$ in $\mathscr{I}$, down to $\mathscr{L}$. The *set of assignments in* U (in symbols: As(U)) is the set of all functions F such that:

(i) Dom F = Dom U; and

(ii) for all A ∈ Dom F, F(A) ∈ U(A).

(c) A *model for $\mathscr{S}$, $\mathscr{T}$, down to $\mathscr{L}$, based upon $\mathscr{Y}$* is a quadruple $\langle I', V', U, G \rangle$, where

(i) $I' \subseteq I$ and $V' \subseteq V$;

(ii) U is an assignment range for $\mathscr{S}$, $\mathscr{T}$ in $\mathscr{Y}$, down to $\mathscr{L}$;

(iii) G is a function the domain of which is $\mathscr{R}$;

(iv) for each k-place rule $\rho = \langle r, \phi, \psi \rangle$ in $\mathscr{R}$, G(ρ) belongs to

$$(\text{Re }_{\mathscr{Y}}(\mathscr{T}(r_k))^{\text{As}(U)})\text{Re }_{\mathscr{Y}}(\mathscr{T}(r_0))^{\text{As}(U)} \otimes \ldots \otimes \text{Re }_{\mathscr{Y}}(\mathscr{T}(r_{k-1}))^{\text{As}(U)}.$$

(d) Let $\alpha = \langle I', V', U, G \rangle$ be a model for $\mathscr{S}$, $\mathscr{T}$, down to $\mathscr{L}$, based upon $\mathscr{Y}$.

(i) For any analysis A in Dom $\mathscr{L}$, the *value of* A *in* α (in symbols: $\alpha^*(A)$) is defined as follows:

(a) if A ∈ Dom U, then $\alpha^*(A) = \{\langle F, F(A) \rangle : F \in \text{As}(U)\}$;

(b) if $\alpha \in$ Dom $\mathscr{L}$ − Dom U, $[A(o)]_1 = \rho$, ρ is k-place, and for $i = o, \ldots, k − 1$, $\langle i \rangle$ is a top of A_i in A, then $\alpha^*(A) = G(\rho)(\alpha^*(A_0), \ldots, \alpha^*(A_{k-1}))$.

(ii) For any analysis A ∈ Dom $\mathscr{L}$ we understand by the *assignment range* of A *in* α (in symbols: $U^*_{\alpha}(A)$) the range of $\alpha^*(A)$.

(iii) Let A be an analysis in Dom $\mathscr{L}$ and let $[A(o)]_0$ be a formula of $\mathscr{S}$. We say that A *holds in* α iff for all $F \in U$ and for all $i \in I'$, $\alpha^*(A)(F)(i) \in V'$.

As is apparent from the previous definition V' should be regarded as the set of truth values which each correspond to some form of truth in the theory of many valued logics; the members of V' are usually referred to as the 'designated truth values'. It is important to allow for the possibility that the set I' be a *proper* subset of I. The need for this arises for example within certain accounts of necessity and possibility, where we want to say that A holds in a given model α if what (the sentence) A (represents) is true at some one particular index of α which represents the actual world. The remaining indices are nonetheless required for the recursive definition of intension.

Definition 17: (a) A *semantics for $\mathscr{S}$, $\mathscr{T}$, down to $\mathscr{L}$*, is a class of models for $\mathscr{S}$, $\mathscr{T}$, down to $\mathscr{L}$.

(b) Let $\mathscr{C}$ be a semantics for $\mathscr{S}$, $\mathscr{T}$, down to $\mathscr{L}$. Let A be an analysis in Dom $\mathscr{L}$ and suppose that $[A(o)]_0 \in \zeta \mathscr{S}(o)$. We say that A is *analytic in* $\mathscr{C}$ iff whenever $\alpha = \langle I, V, U, I', V', U, G \rangle \in \mathscr{C}$, $F \in As(U)$, and $i \in I'$, then $\alpha^*(A)(F)(i) \in V'$.

Models, as defined here, are both intensional and multi-valued. If we were only interested in the characterisation of sets of analytic formulae, a simpler definition would have been sufficient. Indeed, in that case it would have been sufficient to consider either 'two-valued' intensional models (i.e. models in which $V = \{0, 1\}$ and $V' = \{1\}$) or else multi-valued 'extensional' models (i.e. models in which I is a singleton and $I' = 1$). To be precise, if $\mathscr{C}$ is any semantics for $\mathscr{S}$, $\mathscr{T}$, down to $\mathscr{L}$, and Γ is the set of analyses in Dom $\mathscr{L}$ which are analytic in $\mathscr{C}$, then there is a semantics $\mathscr{C}'$ for $\mathscr{S}$, $\mathscr{T}$, down to $\mathscr{L}$, consisting of two-valued models only, such that Γ is the set of analyses in Dom $\mathscr{L}$ which are analytic in $\mathscr{C}'$. Similarly there is a semantics $\mathscr{C}'$ consisting of extensional models only, such that Γ is the set of analyses in Dom $\mathscr{L}$ which are analytic in $\mathscr{C}''$. I have nonetheless characterised models in the general way of Definition 16, since I believe that the construction of intuitively natural semantics for natural languages may well require both a variety of possible worlds, and a wide range of truth values. (Indeed, it appears now that vagueness—a phenomenon so pervasive in, and, it seems, so essential to, languages which serve the needs of normal communication—can best be treated in a model theory employing a large truth-value space which, however, has the structure of a Boolean algebra, rather than that of a linear ordering: see e.g. Fine, 1975; Kamp, 1975.)

Our definition of a model says hardly anything about the semantic interpretation of the various rules of the syntax $\mathscr{S}$. Indeed, our conditions only warrant that the semantic entity assigned to a compound expression will be of the right type. However, it seems natural to impose further restrictions on the semantic operations that correspond to the rules of grammar. For example, it is plausible that, like the formation rules themselves, these operations should be recursive. Another natural restriction would be given by the condition that whenever $\langle I, V, D, I', V', U, G \rangle$ and $\langle I, V, D, I', V', U, G' \rangle$ are models for $\mathscr{S}$, $\mathscr{T}$, down to $\mathscr{L}$, then $G' = G$. A stronger limitation than this last one would result if we were to characterise the interpretations of the grammar rules as formulae of some appropriate language which define operations of the appropriate sort. The intension of an expression γ in a model α, based upon $\langle I, V, D \rangle$, where γ results from applying the rule ρ to $\gamma_0, \ldots, \gamma_{k-1}$, would then be the result of applying to the intensions in α of $\gamma_0, \ldots, \gamma_{k-1}$ respectively the operation defined in $\langle I, V, D, As(U) \rangle$ by the formula which interprets ρ. Furthermore, by admitting only formulae of certain forms as interpretations of rules of grammar we could guarantee recursiveness.[12]

12. Montague's general recursion theory, would be suited to this purpose.

I realise that many questions in this area are left unanswered, but will not go into this matter any further.

Definition 18: Let $\mathscr{S}$, $\mathscr{T}$, $\mathscr{L}$ be as above and let $\mathscr{L}'$ be a level of analysis for $\mathscr{S}$ such that $\mathscr{L}$ is at least as deep as $\mathscr{L}'$.

(a) Let $\mathcal{A} = \langle$ I, V, D, I', V', U, G $\rangle$ be a model for $\mathscr{S}$, $\mathscr{T}$, down to $\mathscr{L}'$. The *restriction of $\mathcal{A}$ to $\mathscr{L}'$* is the septuple $\langle$ I, V, D, I', V', U', G $\rangle$ where U' characterised as follows:

  (i) The domain of U' consists of all those analyses A of $\mathscr{S}$ such that $\mathscr{L}(A) = \{0\}$;

 (ii) if A $\in$ Dom U' and A $\in$ Dom U then U'(A) = U(A);

(iii) if A $\in$ Dom U' and A $\notin$ Dom U then U'(A) = U$^{*}_{\mathcal{A}}$(A).

(b) Let $\mathscr{C}$ be a semantics for $\mathscr{S}$, $\mathscr{T}$, down to $\mathscr{L}$. The *restriction of $\mathscr{C}$ to $\mathscr{L}'$* is the class of restrictions to $\mathscr{L}'$ of members of $\mathscr{C}$.

It should be clear that if $\mathcal{A}'$ is the restriction to $\mathscr{L}'$ of a model $\mathcal{A}$ for $\mathscr{S}$, $\mathscr{T}$, down to $\mathscr{L}$, then $\mathcal{A}'$ is a model for $\mathscr{S}$, $\mathscr{T}$, down to $\mathscr{L}'$; that for every assignment F in the assignment range of $\mathcal{A}$ there is an assignment F' in the assignment range of $\mathcal{A}'$ such that for all A $\in$ Dom $\mathscr{L}'$, $\mathcal{A}'^{*}(A)(F') = \mathcal{A}^{*}(A)(F)$; and that the restriction to $\mathscr{L}'$ of a semantics for $\mathscr{S}$, $\mathscr{T}$, down to $\mathscr{L}$ is a semantics for $\mathscr{S}$, $\mathscr{T}$, down to $\mathscr{L}$.

The concept of a semantics for a formal syntax enables us to formulate various new adequacy criteria for translations. I find it difficult to decide, within the present general framework, which of these criteria should be preferred and will therefore present the various possibilities that have occurred to me. These semantic adequacy criteria will all be variations of the principle, from which we started, that translations should preserve the meaning of the expressions translated. This principle can be stated only if with the expressions translated as well as with their translations there is associated some kind of meaning. This will indeed be the case if, for the syntax $\mathscr{S}$ from which we translate and for the syntax $\mathscr{S}'$ into which we translate, there are models $\mathcal{A}$ and $\mathcal{A}'$, respectively, down to sufficiently deep levels of analysis for $\mathscr{S}$ and $\mathscr{S}'$. If $\mathcal{A}$ and $\mathcal{A}'$ are based on the same sets, and if their sets of 'true' truth values and relevant indices coincide, the principle that translations ought to preserve meaning can be formulated without too much difficulty. If the models do not correspond in this way, however, the meanings of a translated expression and its translation can in general no longer be easily compared. Even in such situations certain, more complicated, formulations of the principle could be given; but we will not pursue this. We will consider the principle only in connection with models which correspond in the manner just explained.

I have said already it is not the task of linguistic theory to specify the intended models uniquely. We must deal with classes of models. Let us suppose that $\mathscr{S}$, $\mathscr{S}'$ are formal syntaxes, that $\mathscr{T}$, $\mathscr{T}'$ are type functions for $\mathscr{S}$, $\mathscr{S}'$, that $\mathscr{C}$ is a semantics for $\mathscr{S}$, $\mathscr{T}$, and that $\mathscr{C}'$ is a semantics for $\mathscr{S}'$, $\mathscr{T}'$. In what sense can a translation from $\mathscr{S}$ into $\mathscr{S}'$ preserve the intensions that the expressions to which the translation applies are being given by the various members of $\mathscr{C}$? There is perhaps no unique answer to this question. But one possible answer is the following: for each model $\mathcal{A}$ in $\mathscr{C}$ there ought to be a model $\mathcal{A}'$ in $\mathscr{C}$ such that any analysis A to which the translation applies has the same intension in $\mathcal{A}$ as its translation has in $\mathcal{A}'$. Consistent with the limitations which we set ourselves above, we will require that $\mathcal{A}$ and $\mathcal{A}'$ are based upon the same sets and have the same sets of true designated truth values and relevant indices.

Thus the adequacy of a translation will be relative to a function from $\mathscr{C}$ into $\mathscr{C}'$ which gives us for each $\mathcal{A}$ in $\mathscr{C}$ a thus corresponding $\mathcal{A}'$ in $\mathscr{C}'$. (In case $\mathscr{C}'$ is a semantics for a natural language, one might perhaps require that the function be *onto* $\mathscr{C}'$, but in the case where $\mathscr{C}'$ is a semantics for a formal language, this requirement would be counter-intuitive. To see this it suffices to think of the translations from English into first-order logic which, under the name 'symbolisations', play an important part in any introductory course of formal logic. The 'schemes of abbreviations' (see e.g. Kalish and Montague, 1964) on which such translations are usually based, can be regarded at least in part as devices to determine which of the possible models for first-order logic correspond to models for English, and thus which models for first-order logic should be disregarded in this connection.

A translation, as defined in section 3, is always from a syntax $\mathscr{S}$ into a syntax $\mathscr{S}'$, *relative to a level of analysis $\mathscr{L}$ for $\mathscr{S}$*. Only analyses in Dom $\mathscr{L}$ are translated, and thus a semantics $\mathscr{C}$ for $\mathscr{S}$ *down to $\mathscr{L}$* will suffice for a proper formulation of the new adequacy criteria for such a translation. But what kinds of semantics for $\mathscr{S}'$ does such a formulation require?

We could demand that the semantics for $\mathscr{S}'$ always consist only of models which assign meanings to all analyses in $\mathscr{S}'$. Indeed, if $\mathscr{S}'$ is a syntax for a formal language, this condition normally will be satisfied. But if $\mathscr{S}'$ is a syntax for a natural language, this requirement seems unduly severe. On the other hand, it is clear that certain semantics $\mathscr{C}'$ for $\mathscr{S}'$ will not yield complete adequacy criteria for a given translation from $\mathscr{S}$ into $\mathscr{S}'$, simply because the models in $\mathscr{C}'$ may well fail to assign intensions to some of the translated analyses. We could in such cases weaken the principle and demand only that *whenever* a model in $\mathscr{C}'$ assigns an intension to the translation of an analysis A in $\mathscr{C}$, this intention must be the same as the intention assigned to A by the corresponding model(s) in $\mathscr{C}$. We will, however, not consider this possibility and discuss only the situation where the models in $\mathscr{C}'$ do indeed give intensions to all analyses in the range of the translation function.

Let us return for a moment to the case in which $\mathscr{C}$ and $\mathscr{C}'$ are singletons. Let $\mathscr{C} = \{\mathcal{A}\}$ and $\mathscr{C}' = \{\mathcal{A}'\}$, and let us assume that $\mathcal{A}$ and $\mathcal{A}'$ are based upon the same sets and that their sets of relevant indices and true truth values coincide. Let further Tr be a translation from $\mathscr{S}$ into $\mathscr{S}'$, down to $\mathscr{L}$, and let $\mathcal{A}'$ assign intensions to all members of Range Tr*. Tr is adequate, we have said, if 'the intension assigned by $\mathcal{A}$ to any analysis A in Dom Tr* is the same as the intension that $\mathcal{A}'$ assigns to Tr*(A). This statement, however, is in need of explanation, as a model assigns to an analysis not simply an intension but rather a function from assignments to intensions. As a matter of fact, for many an analysis this function is constant. This will be the case whenever the analysis in question is of an expression which does not 'contain any free variables'. One may, in many cases, be interested only in expressions of this sort, and thus prepared to regard the translation as adequate as long as it preserves *their* intensions. This condition will be satisfied in particular if the translation preserves the assignment ranges of *all* analyses it translates.

We will adopt a condition which is even stronger and demand that to each assignment F(F') in the assignment range of $\mathcal{A}(\mathcal{A}')$ should correspond to an assignment F'(F) in the assignment range of $\mathcal{A}'(\mathcal{A})$ such that for all $A \in \text{Dom Tr*}$, $\mathcal{A}'^*(A)(F') = \mathcal{A}^*(A)(F)$. Unfortunately there is no obvious way of pairing assignments in $\mathcal{A}$ with assignments in $\mathcal{A}'$, and thus the procedure of defining such a correspondence will be slightly involved.

Definition 19: let $\mathscr{S}$, $\mathscr{S}'$ be formal syntaxes; let $\mathscr{T}$ and $\mathscr{T}'$ be type functions for $\mathscr{S}$ and $\mathscr{S}'$, respectively; let $\mathscr{L}$ be a level of analysis for $\mathscr{S}$, $\mathscr{C}$ a semantics for $\mathscr{S}$, $\mathscr{T}$ down to $\mathscr{L}$, Tr a translation from $\mathscr{S}$ into $\mathscr{S}'$, down to $\mathscr{L}$, and $\mathscr{C}'$ a semantics for $\mathscr{S}'$, $\mathscr{T}'$ down to some level $\mathscr{L}'$, such that for all $A \in \text{Dom Tr*}$, $\text{Tr*}(A) \in \text{Dom } \mathscr{L}'$.

(a) A *weak interpretation of* Tr, *relative to* $\mathscr{C}$, $\mathscr{C}'$ is a function In from $\mathscr{C}$ into $\mathscr{C}'$, such that for all $\mathcal{A} \in \mathscr{C}$, $\mathcal{A}$ and $\text{In}(\mathcal{A})$ are based upon the same sets and have the same sets of relevant indices and designated truth values.

(b) Let In be a weak interpretation of Tr relative to $\mathscr{C}$, $\mathscr{C}'$. We say that In is *adequate* if for all $\mathcal{A} \in \mathscr{C}$ and $A \in \text{Dom Tr*}$ $U^*_{\mathcal{A}}(A) = U^*_{\text{In}(\mathcal{A})}(\text{Tr*}(A))$.

(c) Tr is called *weakly adequate relative* to $\mathscr{C}$, $\mathscr{C}'$ iff there is an adequate weak interpretation for Tr, relative to $\mathscr{C}$, $\mathscr{C}'$.

(d) A *strong interpretation of* Tr, *relative to* $\mathscr{C}$, $\mathscr{C}'$, is a pair $\langle \text{In, Co} \rangle$ such that:

(i) In is a weak interpretation of Tr, relative to $\mathscr{C}$, $\mathscr{C}'$;

(ii) Co is a function, with domain $\mathscr{C}$;

(iii) for $\mathcal{Cl} \in \mathscr{C}$, $\text{Co}(\mathcal{Cl})$ is a many-many correspondence[13] between the assignment ranges of $\mathcal{Cl}$ and of $\text{In}(\mathcal{Cl})$.

(e) Let $\langle \text{In, Co} \rangle$ be a strong interpretation for Tr, relative to $\mathscr{C}$, $\mathscr{C}'$. We say that $\langle \text{In, Co} \rangle$ is *adequate* if whenever $A \in \text{Dom Tr}^*$, $\mathcal{Cl} \in \mathscr{C}$ and $\langle F, F' \rangle \in \text{Co}(\mathcal{Cl})$ then $\mathcal{Cl}^*(A)(F) = (\text{In}(\mathcal{Cl}))^*((\text{Tr}^*(A))(F')$.

(f) We say that Tr is *strongly adequate relative* to $\mathscr{C}$, $\mathscr{C}'$, iff there is an adequate strong interpretation of Tr relative to $\mathscr{C}$, $\mathscr{C}'$.

Of course, various other notions of semantic adequacy could be introduced as well. In particular we could limit the requirement that a translation preserve the intensions of the expressions it translates to expressions of a certain kind: to the class of all formulae; to the class of all expressions not containing free variables; to the class of all sentences (provided that the notions of freedom and bondage have been given); or others. In each such case we may distinguish between weak and strong adequacy; however, in some cases, such as the last two of the three mentioned above, the two notions will coincide.

The notions of semantic adequacy defined above have the following properties. Let $\mathscr{S}$, $\mathscr{S}'$, $\mathscr{T}$, $\mathscr{T}'$, $\mathscr{L}$, $\mathscr{C}$, $\mathscr{C}'$, Tr, $\mathscr{L}'$, be as in definition 19.

(1) Let $\mathscr{C}''$ be a semantics for $\mathscr{S}'$, down to $\mathscr{L}'$, and let $\mathscr{C}' \subseteq \mathscr{C}''$. If Tr is weakly (strongly) adequate, relative to $\mathscr{C}$, $\mathscr{C}'$ then Tr is weakly (strongly) adequate relative to $\mathscr{C}$, $\mathscr{C}''$.

(2) Let $\mathscr{C}''$ be a semantics for $\mathscr{S}$, down to $\mathscr{L}$ and let $\mathscr{C} \subseteq \mathscr{C}''$. If Tr is weakly (strongly) adequate relative to $\mathscr{C}''$, $\mathscr{C}'$ then Tr is weakly (strongly) adequate relative to $\mathscr{C}$, $\mathscr{C}'$.

(3) Let $\mathscr{L}''$ be a level of analysis for $\mathscr{S}$ such that $\mathscr{L}$ is at least as deep as $\mathscr{L}''$ and let $\mathscr{C}''$ be the restriction of $\mathscr{C}$ to $\mathscr{L}''$. Then if Tr is weakly (strongly)

---

13. We call a binary relation R a *many-many correspondence* if whenever $x \, R \, u$, $y \, R \, u$ and $y \, R \, v$, then $x \, R \, v$. If Dom R = A and Range R = B then we say that R is a *many-many correspondence between A and B*.

adequate relative to $\mathscr{C}$, $\mathscr{C}'$, there is a translation Tr′ from $\mathscr{S}$ into $\mathscr{S}'$, down to $\mathscr{L}''$ which is weakly (strongly) adequate relative to $\mathscr{C}''$, $\mathscr{C}'$.

Thus it is no more difficult to give a semantically adequate translation when the semantics of the language *into* which one translates is *less* specific (i.e. contains more models) or the semantics for the language *from* which one translates is *more* specific (i.e. contains fewer models). And if a level of analysis $\mathscr{L}$ for a syntax $\mathscr{S}$ is at least as deep as some other level $\mathscr{L}''$, then it will be easier to give a semantically adequate translation from $\mathscr{S}$ into $\mathscr{S}'$ down to $\mathscr{L}''$ than it is to give an adequate translation from $\mathscr{S}$ into $\mathscr{S}'$ down to $\mathscr{L}$—provided that the semantics for $\mathscr{S}$ down to $\mathscr{L}''$ is indeed the restriction of the semantics down to $\mathscr{L}$.

7. *Translations as a means of formulating semantics*

So far our discussion of translations has been based on the assumption that the languages they link are characterised as formal syntaxes and semantics of the sorts defined in the previous sections. However, at the present moment no such characterisation is available for any natural language, in particular not for English, the language with which the project was concerned.[14] One may therefore wonder how this paper could have any significance for the particular translations which were produced on this project and the usefulness of which we promised to explain. For what would the claim that such a translation is adequate amount to, in the term 'adequate' is meaningful only with respect to a semantics for English of which at best fragments are available?

In answer to this question one might reply that, even though at the present time we have no complete description of English in terms of a formal syntax and semantics, such a description nevertheless 'exists', in some abstract sense of 'exist'. Thus our claim that the translations are adequate is meaningful, insofar as it refers to this unknown, but yet existing, description.

From this point of view it is difficult to see how we could ever be *justified* in claiming a particular translation to be adequate. For such a justification would undoubtedly require knowledge of the description to which this claim implicitly refers.

We can, however, interpret the claim that a translation is adequate as a claim *about* the semantical structure of English: the semantics must be such that relative to it and the semantics of the formal language the translation is

[14] Cf the introduction of this paper.

adequate. Indeed, given the semantics for the latter language and a formal syntax $\mathscr{S}$ for English, the translation uniquely specifies a semantics for English, consisting of interpretations down to the same level of analysis as that to which the translation itself goes. Each model of this semantics corresponds to a model belonging to the semantics for the language into which we translate; it is based upon the same sets as this latter model, and assigns to the elementary expressions of the translation and to the rules of $\mathscr{S}$ what the latter model assigns to the translations of these expressions and rules.

In fact, one of the most natural ways to formulate semantics for natural languages (at least in the present state of semantical theory) may be just this: to develop a formal language (in the sense of this paper) and then to give translations from the natural language into it. This is essentially what we have tried to do in the translation part of this project. The formal language developed there is by no means complete, and in particular only fragments of its semantics have as yet been developed. But the general lines along which the details of the theory should be worked out are clear enough to lend substance to the claim that the translations are correct.

R. Cooper

Montague's Theory of Translation and Transformational Syntax[1]

Introduction

THE FIRST PART of this paper presents an informal description of certain aspects of Montague's theory of translation as it is set forth in 'Universal Grammar' (UG) (in Montague, 1974a) and sketches the way in which deep structures of transformational grammars may be translated in accordance with it. A detailed exposition of this is to be found in Cooper and Parsons (1975). The second part of the paper shows how Montague's theory can have consequences for proposals that have been made in the transformational literature. Two examples are discussed. The first, that of the analysis of relative clauses, is discussed briefly since more detailed discussion is to be found in Partee (1972; 1975). The second example is discussed in more detail. This shows consequences of Montague's general theory and his particular treatment of adverbs in 'The Proper Treatment of Quantification in Ordinary English' (PTQ) (in Montague, 1974a) for the hypothesis that English sentences have the underlying order Verb Subject Object.

1. Translation and transformational syntax

Montague believed that it is possible to define a model-theoretic semantics following in the philosophical tradition of Tarski and Carnap not only on formal languages as had been done previously but also on natural languages such as English. In UG and PTQ he did this not by interpreting English directly but by first translating it into a formal language which was more perspicuously related to the semantics and then inducing an interpretation for English by interpreting the formal language. The interpretation of the formal language can be seen as fulfilling a second role as the interpretation of

1. This paper contains revised material from Cooper (1975a and b). I am extremely grateful to Emmon Bach, Frank Heny, Terry Parsons and in particular Barbara Partee for insightful suggestions on various aspects of this paper. This research was supported by NSF grant GS 39752 to the University of Massachusetts at Amherst.

English.[2] Montague's reason for translating in this fashion was clarity of presentation; the formal logic is not a necessary step in the interpretation of English, although, of course, it is not without significant interest that English can be related to a formal language in such a way that the formal language serves to induce an interpretation for English.

The translation procedure relates each expression of a language to a single expression of the formal language and, since each expression of the formal language is related to one meaning, thereby also to a single meaning. For this reason it is necessary to define the translation procedure not on a representation of English itself, since English is an ambiguous language (i.e. certain of its expressions are related to a set of meanings) but on a slightly adjusted disambiguated version of English which is then related syntactically to expressions of the ambiguous language English.[3] In order to show that the interpretation of the formal language determines an interpretation for English it is necessary for the disambiguated version of English and the formal language to stand in a specific relationship to each other. Montague restricted the relation between the logic and English approximately as follows:

(i) there is one and only one category (or type) in the logic corresponding to each category in the syntax of English. The translation of any English expression is of the logical type corresponding to the category of the English expression.

(ii) each basic expression (lexical item) has only one translation into a member of some category in the logic. This may be a complex member of a category in the logic; e.g. the basic expression *John* translates into $\widehat{P}P\{^\wedge j\}$—this represents the characteristic function of the set of properties belonging to the intension of the individual John. This logical expression is a member of a category but is not a basic expression.

2. This is a slight simplification of the general theory presented in UG where the interpretation of the formal language is not precisely the same as the interpretation of English, though the interpretation of the formal language together with the translation procedure determines a unique interpretation for English. The differences arise when complex syntactic operations of the formal language correspond to simple syntactic operations of English. The interpretation of the formal language specifies semantic operations corresponding to each of the simple syntactic operations of the formal language. The interpretation of English has semantic operations corresponding only to syntactic operations of English and not to those syntactic operations of the formal language which do not correspond to any syntactic operation of English.

3. For an adjustment to Montague's theory where expressions of English are mapped into sets of expressions of the logic, thus eliminating the disambiguated version of English, see Cooper (1975b).

(iii) for each complex expression in the disambiguated version of English there is one and only one corresponding expression in the logic, whose constituents correspond to the translation of the constituents of the English expression. In addition there is just one syntactic rule in the logic which corresponds to the syntactic rule in English which combines the constituent expressions. A complex of syntactic rules in the logic may correspond to a single syntactic rule in English. For example, there is a simple syntactic rule in English which combines a proper name such as *John* with an intransitive verb such as *run* and produces the sentence *John runs*. The translations of the constituents are $\widehat{P}P\{^\wedge j\}$ and **run'** respectively. The syntactic operation of the logic which corresponds to that of English consists of two separate operations—one which forms $^\wedge$**run'** from **run'** and another which applies the function $\widehat{P}P\{^\wedge j\}$ to $^\wedge$**run'** producing the expression $\widehat{P}P\{^\wedge j\}(^\wedge$**run'**$)$.

(iv) sentences of English correspond only to sentences in the logic.

These four principles of translation are an approximate informal prose version of the definition of a translation base given in UG Section 5: (i) corresponds to (1) of Montague's definition; (ii) to (2) and (3); (iii) corresponds approximately to (4) and (5); (iv) corresponds to (6).

What is important about these restrictions on the translation relation for the examples we shall discuss is what we have represented here as (iii). This may be called the requirement of compositionality, the origins of which have been ascribed to Frege. Essentially it requires that the translation of any constituent is the result of some particular operation applied to the translations of its immediate subconstituents. The particular logical operation chosen depends on the syntactic operation of the logic corresponding to each syntactic operation of English. The compositionality requirement makes interesting distinctions between different proposals for the syntactic treatment of certain English constructions in a transformational framework.

The requirement that the logical type of the translations of expressions of a particular category always be the same is closely related to the compositionality requirement. If there is one syntactic rule of the logic corresponding to each syntactic rule of English then, since each syntactic rule makes reference to specific categories, there must also be one logical type corresponding to each category of English. If, for instance, noun-phrases corresponded to logical expressions of two types and yet there were just one rule that combined verb-phrases with noun-phrases to form a sentence, there would still have to be a single rule of the logic corresponding to the rule of

English. The logical rule would not be able to combine expressions of both the types corresponding to noun-phrases with the translations of verb-phrases since this would no longer be one rule but two rules of the logic.

It should be emphasised that these requirements are not constraints which Montague placed on the system in order to make a general claim about the nature of natural language. Rather they are part of a technique for assigning meanings to an infinite number of English expressions using only finite means. It is a non-trivial matter to do this if the translation does not parallel the syntax as is required by Montague's theory.

In Cooper and Parsons (1975) and Cooper (1975b) it was shown how the deep structures of a transformational grammar could be viewed as a disambiguated language related to the ambiguous language of surface structure by transformations and translated into the intensional logic which Montague defines in PTQ while at the same time preserving the general definitions and theory which he puts forward in UG. The basic technique for this, which will only be sketched here (the reader is referred to the references above for a detailed account), is essentially extremely simple. The translation rules are similar to projection rules as they have been defined, for example, in Katz and Fodor (1963). They may be viewed as processing first the terminal nodes of the deep structure and then assigning logical expressions to each successively larger tree until the root of the tree is reached. The translation assigned to any given sub-tree will be the result of a specific operation applied to the translations assigned to its immediate sub-trees. The translation procedure differs from the Katz–Fodor system in as far as it assigns meaningful expressions of intensional logic to each sub-tree rather than sets of semantic features.

Thus, for instance, in both the definitions of the fragment in Cooper and Parsons (1975) a possible deep structure for the sentence *John finds a unicorn* is (1).

(1)

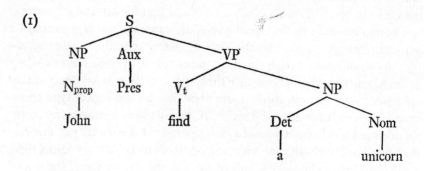

This tree is translated in the following manner. *Unicorn* corresponds to a constant of intensional logic which is represented as **unicorn'**. Any non-branching tree receives the same translation as the tree rooted by the node immediately below its topmost node. Thus Nom receives the same

$$\text{Nom} \atop | \atop \text{unicorn}$$

translation as *unicorn*. The determiner *a* receives the complex translation: $\lambda Q \hat{P} \exists x [Q\{x\} \wedge P\{x\}]$.[4] Det receives the same translation since this is a non-

$$\text{Det} \atop | \atop a$$

branching tree. The translation rule corresponding to the phrase-structure rule which expands *NP* as *Det Nom* requires that we apply the translation of the tree rooted by *Det* to the result of placing the intension operator in front of the translation of the tree rooted by *Nom*. Thus the translation of the NP is $\lambda Q \hat{P} \exists x [Q\{x\} \wedge P\{x\}](^\wedge \mathbf{unicorn'})$. *Find* corresponds to a constant of intensional logic which is represented as **find'** and thus the translation of V_t is **find'**. The rule that translates the VP requires that we apply the

$$V_t \atop | \atop \text{find}$$

function represented by **find'** to the intension of the translation of the NP. Thus the translation of the VP is $\mathbf{find'}(^\wedge \lambda Q \hat{P} \exists x [Q\{x\} \wedge P\{x\}](^\wedge \mathbf{unicorn'}))$. As there is no present tense operator in this particular logic we assign *Pres* the zero translation and thus *Aux* does not get represented in the translation of this particular example. *John* translates as $\hat{P}P\{^\wedge j\}$. The translation of NP is therefore also $\hat{P}P\{^\wedge j\}$, since this is a non-branching tree. The

$$\text{NP} \atop | \atop \text{Nprop} \atop | \atop \text{John}$$

translation rule which corresponds to the phrase structure rule expanding *S* as *NP Aux VP* requires that we apply the translation of the NP to the intension of the translation of the VP. Thus the translation of the whole sentence is $\hat{P}P\{^\wedge j\}(^\wedge \mathbf{find'}(^\wedge \lambda Q \hat{P} \exists x [Q\{x\} \wedge P\{x\}](^\wedge \mathbf{unicorn'})))$. This expression is shown by the semantics of the logic to be equivalent to $\exists x [\mathbf{unicorn'}(x) \wedge \mathbf{find'}_*(j, {^\vee}x)]$. The precise rules that yield this translation from (1) are to be found in Cooper and Parsons (1975).

4. I assume here familiarity with the notations and conventions of the intensional logic defined in PTQ. A detailed introduction to it can be found in Partee (1975). Q and P are variables over properties of individual concepts. $Q\{x\}$ may be read as 'the individual concept x has the property Q'.

Montague's theory rules out a translation procedure which does not climb up the tree in this fashion. For example, it would not be possible within Montague's theory to have a translation rule which operated just on the translations of the subject and object NPs in this structure obtaining a part of the translation which did not correspond to any particular sub-tree of the structure. Neither would it be possible to have two translation rules corresponding to any one phrase-structure rule.

2. *Some implications*

Partee (1972; 1975) has already pointed out that these requirements select between competing analyses that have been put forward for the structure of English relative clauses.[5] She shows, for example, that the phrase *the boy who lives in the park* must have a structure something like that in (2b) rather than that in (2a).

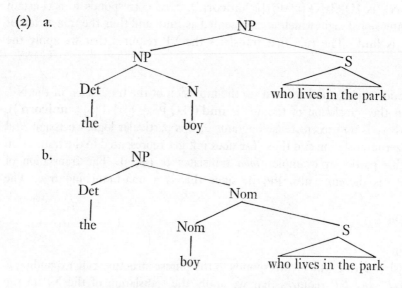

(2) a.

    b.

In translating (2a) we would obtain the normal translation of the NP *the boy*, i.e. (in reduced form) $\widehat{P}\exists y[\forall x[\text{boy}'(x)\equiv x=y]\wedge P\{y\}]$. The translation for the relative clause would have to be something like in the park$'(\hat{\ }$live$')(x_0)$ (again in reduced form). It is not possible to put these two expressions

5. Actually, Emmon Bach has convinced me that this is an argument of elegance rather than necessity when one takes into account the techniques used in an analysis of Hittite relative clauses proposed in Cooper (1975b). See also Bach and Cooper (forthcoming) for discussion. Although the NP S analysis of relative clauses proposed there is possible it is at the cost of considerable complication to the semantics and as yet it seems that Occam's razor still selects the Nom S analysis.

together to obtain the restrictive reading for the relative clause. Applying the translation of the NP to the result of abstracting over x_0 in the translation of the sentence gives us (3a) which is equivalent to (3b) and represents a non-restrictive reading of the relative clause.

(3)   a. $\widehat{P}\exists y[\forall x[\text{boy}'(x)\equiv x=y]\wedge P\{y\}](\hat{x}_0[\text{in the park}'(^\wedge\text{live}')(x_0)])$

      b. $\exists y[\forall x[\text{boy}'(x)\equiv x=y]\wedge\text{in the park}'(^\wedge\text{live}')(y)]$

(3b) might be paraphrased as 'there is one and only one boy and that boy lives in the park'. Of course, these translations do not serve to represent the meaning of an NP since they are of the type corresponding to a sentence rather than that corresponding to an NP. In order to get the restrictive reading the relative clause must modify something within the scope of the universal quantifier in the translation of *the*. In order to achieve this we must have a constituent *boy who lives in the park* to whose translation the translation of *the* applies. This is achieved by the structure (2b). We may think of the larger Nom as representing a complex property formed by a conjunction of the property corresponding to *boy* and the property corresponding to *who lives in the park*. Thus we might translate the larger Nom as (4a) which can have the translation of *the* applied to it as in (4b) which is equivalent to (4c.)

(4)   a. $\hat{x}_0[\text{boy}'(x_0)\wedge\text{in the park}'(^\wedge\text{live}')(x_0)]$

      b. $\lambda Q\,\widehat{P}\exists y[\forall x[Q\{x\}\equiv x=y]\wedge P\{y\}](\hat{x}_0[\text{boy}'(x_0)\wedge\text{in the park}'$
        $(^\wedge\text{live}')(x_0)]$

      c. $\widehat{P}\exists y[\forall x[\text{boy}'(x)\wedge\text{in the park}'(^\wedge\text{live}')(x)\equiv x=y]\wedge P\{y\}]$

(4c) may be thought of as representing the property set of the unique entity which is both a boy and lives in the park. This provides us with the correct restrictive interpretation of the relative clause and also a translation of the right type corresponding to an NP, i.e. (4c) is able to combine with the translation of a VP to form a sentence whereas (3b) could not since it is already a complete formula.

In the remainder of this paper I shall examine a similar though slightly more complex example where it seems that Montague's theory has consequences for some syntactic proposals that have been made in the linguistic literature. The argument here relies not only on Montague's theory of translation but also on his particular theory of VP-adverbs for which we provide a semantic argument. The basic point is that if we translate deep structures in accordance with Montague's theory and if we represent certain adverbs as predicate modifiers as Montague proposed then we must have

VPs in underlying structure. This excludes an analysis of English which has been widely held by linguists of the generative semantics school, where it has been argued (notably in McCawley, 1970) that the basic underlying order for English sentences is Verb Subject Object (VSO). Thus, for example, on such an analysis the underlying structure for the sentence *John finds Mary* might be approximately:

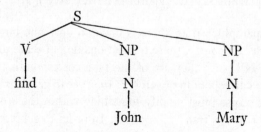

It has been claimed that such underlying structures allow us to provide both a better syntactic and a better semantic account of English.

In PTQ Montague distinguishes two categories of adverbs. The adverbs of one category correspond to logical expressions of type $\langle\langle s,t\rangle,t\rangle$, that is: expressions which represent functions from propositions to truth values. In the syntax of English these adverbs combine with a sentence to form a new sentence. The only example in the fragment of PTQ is *necessarily*. (5a) shows a deep structure for *Necessarily John finds Mary* in the fragment as defined in Cooper and Parsons (1975) and (5b) shows a reduced form of its translation.

(5)   a.

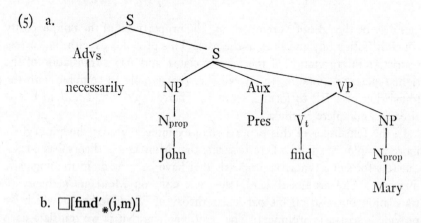

   b. $\Box[\mathbf{find'}_*(j,m)]$

The adverbs of the second category correspond to logical expressions of type $\langle\langle s,\langle\langle s,e\rangle,t\rangle\rangle, \langle\langle s,e\rangle,t\rangle\rangle$, representing a function from properties of individual concepts to a predicate which takes individual concepts as arguments. In the syntax of English these adverbs combine with a VP to form a new VP. We take as an example the adverb *rapidly*. (6a) shows a deep structure for *John finds Mary rapidly* as defined by the fragment in Cooper and Parsons (1975) and (6b) shows a reduced form of its translation.

(6) a.

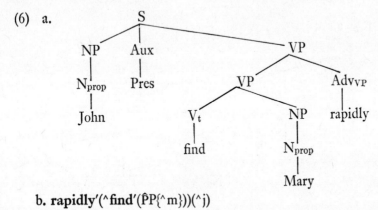

b. **rapidly′(^find′(P̂P{^m}))(^j)**

Putting *rapidly* and *necessarily* into these separate categories provides a more adequate semantic treatment than if they were in the same category. Suppose, for instance, that *rapidly* were a sentence adverb like *necessarily*. (I do not think that anybody has seriously proposed such a treatment though Thomason and Stalnaker (1973) have suggested that it is possible to reduce all adverbs to sentence adverbs by introducing appropriate meaning postulates into the system, though the result would be cumbersome.) Assuming that it is possible to define a transformation which postposes *rapidly* but not *necessarily*, we would obtain (7) as a possible deep structure if we revised the fragment in just this respect.

(7)

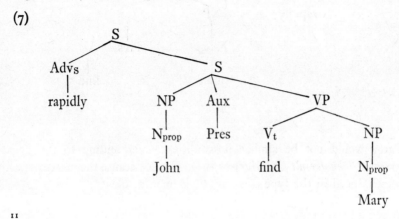

(7), of course, would replace (6a) in this revision of the fragment. Consider now what the deep structures in this revised fragment would be for *Necessarily John finds Mary rapidly*. There would be different possibilities depending whether *rapidly* or *necessarily* were higher in the tree. These possibilities are illustrated in (8).

(8)   a.

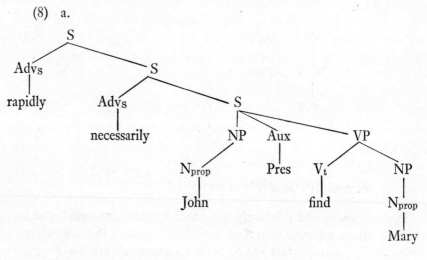

b.

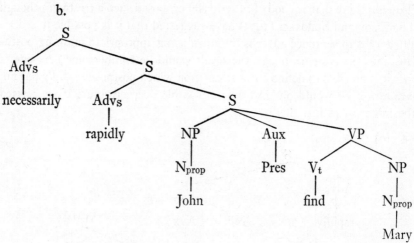

There would not be similar possibilities corresponding to the negative sentence *John doesn't find Mary rapidly*. This is because the negative particle is introduced in the type of structure shown in (9).

(9)

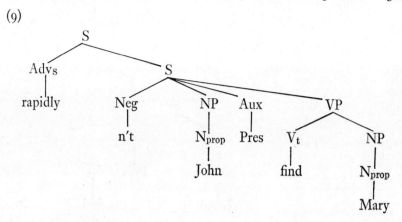

However, if we wished, we could make another small adjustment to the fragment which would allow a similar deep structure ambiguity for this sentence. This would involve changing the phrase-structure rules so that *Neg* would be introduced in the structure   S   .[6] This would now yield the deep structures shown in (10).

(10) a.

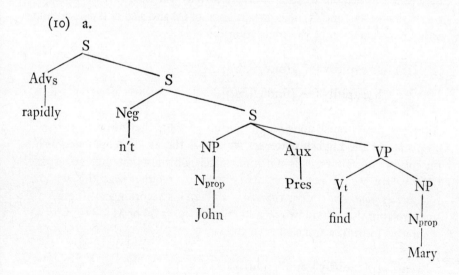

6. Since this would allow iteration of *Neg*, we would also have to adjust the *Neg-placemen* transformation in order not to generate *John doesn'tn't find Mary rapidly* if there were two occurrences of *Neg* in deep structure and also prevent similar examples where there is more than one *Neg*.

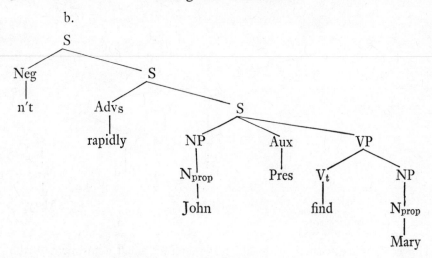

Certain of these structures look as if they might cause problems when we come to interpret them since our intuitions tell us that the translation of *rapidly* should always have narrower scope than the translation of *necessarily* or *Neg*. If we assume now that **rapidly′** symbolises a constant of the same type as the translation of *necessarily* (which is $\hat{p}[\Box\,{}^\vee p]$, where p is a variable over propositions) our existing translation rules will yield (11a) as a reduced translation of (8a) and (11b) as a translation of (9) and also of (10a) assuming a slight modification of the translation rules.

(11)   a. **rapidly′**[^□[**find′**$_*$(j,m)]]

b. **rapidly′**[^∼[**find′**$_*$(j,m)]]

Although these translations seem unintuitive since they seem to represent a reading for the English sentences which has the wrong scope relationship for the two operators, it is not immediately obvious that they are wrong. Clearly, we would not want our system to require that the sentence *Necessarily John finds Mary rapidly* is ambiguous according to whether the scope relationship of the two operators was as in (11a) or as in (12) which is a reduced form of a translation of (8b).

(12)   □[**rapidly′**[^**find′**$_*$(j,m)]]

However, it seems a simple enough matter to rectify this by requiring that (11a) and (12) are logically equivalent. We could do this by introducing the meaning postulate (13) which requires the commutativity of **rapidly′** and □.

(13) $\Box[\text{rapidly}'[^\wedge\Box[\varphi]]\equiv\Box[\text{rapidly}'[^\wedge\varphi]]]$ where: $\varphi \in ME_t$

We would probably need meaning postulates similar to (13) if we were to extend our fragment to include sentences such as (14) which were brought to my attention by Barbara Partee.

(14) a. John found Mary in the park at noon.
     b. John found Mary at noon in the park.

These sentences appear to be logically equivalent and yet their translations would presumably give different relative scopes to the translations of *at noon* and *in the park*. The introduction of the meaning postulate (13) does not seem to have any bad consequences. However, this is not the case if we introduce a similar meaning postulate requiring that **rapidly'** and $\sim$ are commutative. This meaning postulate is given in (15).

(15) $\Box[\text{rapidly}'[^\wedge\sim[\varphi]]\equiv\sim[\text{rapidly}'[^\wedge\varphi]]]$ (φ as in (13))

The problem arises when we consider the fact that *rapidly* is a subsective adverb, a fact that is treated in the Montague framework in Bennett (1974) (meaning postulate (5) on page 45) and discussed by him in section 3 of Chapter II. This means that an adequate semantics must account for the fact that (16a) entails (16b).

(16) a. John finds Mary rapidly.
     b. John finds Mary.

In order to account for the subsective property of *rapidly* in the modified version of the fragment we would have to introduce the meaning postulate (17).

(17) $\Box[\text{rapidly}'[^\wedge\varphi] \supset \varphi]$ (φ as in (13))

However, this will lead to trouble when **rapidly'** has wider scope than $\sim$. Now (11b) will entail $\sim[\text{find}'_*(j,m)]$. Thus the English sentence *John doesn't find Mary rapidly* will entail *John doesn't find Mary*. This is not in accordance with the facts of English. Although it is arguable that there is a reading of this sentence which entails that John finds Mary (perhaps he may have found her slowly) there is no reading that entails that he does not find her.[7] Given the meaning postulate (17), the meaning postulate (15) will only make matters worse since it will ensure that *John doesn't find Mary rapidly* will always entail that John does not find Mary whatever the arrangement of *Neg* and *rapidly* is in underlying structure.

It seems then that we cannot use our semantic apparatus to preserve the hypothesis that *rapidly* is a sentence adverb like *necessarily*. We might, however, consider another type of solution. As it is the structures where *rapidly* occurs outside either *necessarily* or *Neg* which cause the trouble we might consider formulating a constraint which filters out derivations containing the troublesome deep structures and then we would have no need of the meaning postulates (13) and (15). Barbara Partee has pointed out to me that a simple extension of the derivational constraint preventing the crossing of logical predicates as proposed, for example, in Lakoff (1971) would achieve this. Lakoff's constraint may be paraphrased approximately as follows:

Crossing constraint
If a logical predicate L_1 commands[8] another logical predicate L_2 in underlying structure, then in order for the derivation to be well formed either L_2 does not command L_1 in shallow structure[9] or L_1 precedes L_2 in shallow structure.

For Lakoff the set of logical predicates includes quantifiers such as *every* (and thus if we were adapting the constraint to the present system would presumably include the set of determiners), the negative particle, however it is represented, and also the connectives *and* and *or*. We might extend this notion of logical predicate now to include the sentence adverbs *necessarily* and *rapidly*. This would mean that the structures (8a), (9) and (10a) would not underly well-formed surface structures since the rule that postposes *rapidly* to the end of the sentence would violate the crossing constraint. The structures (9b) and (10b), however, would underly well-formed surface

7. It is important here not to be confused by the possibility of an external negation reading for *John doesn't find Mary rapidly* which might be paraphrased as, *It is not the case that: John finds Mary rapidly*. This reading entails neither that John finds Mary nor that he does not find her.

8. A node A *commands* another node B if and only if (i) neither A nor B dominates the other and (ii) the S-node that most immediately dominates A also dominates B. See Langacker (1969).

9. Shallow structure is a level between underlying structure and surface structure, possibly the output of the cyclical rules but preceding the operation of post-cyclic transformations. For the sake of the present discussion we might consider shallow structure and surface structure to be identical.

structures since in these structures *rapidly* is commanded either by *necessarily* or *n't* and the postposing rule would not violate the constraint. Thus this extension of Lakoff's constraint would rule out precisely those underlying structures which yield the readings we wish to avoid. This syntactic solution, then, works, but unfortunately the main thrust of Lakoff's general claim is lost. Lakoff was attempting to show that the crossing constraint is not merely a syntactic generalisation but a partially semantic generalisation defined in terms of the semantic notion of logical predicate. Unfortunately, in the present semantic system this notion of logical predicate is undefined and thus the crossing constraint, if it represents a generalisation at all, represents merely a syntactic one. This is because there is no particular semantic type which corresponds to the syntactic elements which are prevented from crossing by the constraint. For instance, quantifiers (i.e. determiners) in the present system are of the type $\langle\langle s,\langle\langle s,e\rangle,t\rangle\rangle$, $\langle\langle s,\langle\langle s,e\rangle,t\rangle\rangle,t\rangle\rangle$, that is they represent functions from properties of individual concepts to functions from properties of individual concepts to truth-values. Sentence adverbs, on the other hand, correspond to the type $\langle\langle s,t\rangle,t\rangle$, that is functions from propositions to truth-values and negation can be thought of as corresponding to the type $\langle t,t\rangle$, that is functions from truth-values to truth-values. It would be easy enough, however, to define a set of sentence operators including negation by making negation correspond to $\langle\langle s,t\rangle,t\rangle$. (This would probably be the most natural treatment if we introduced negation as in (10).) However, we would still be left with the fact that there is no semantic correlate to a syntactic class consisting of determiners and those syntactic categories which correspond to sentence operators. It might be objected in view of this that the treatment of quantifiers here is wrong and that they should be treated as functions from propositions to truth-values. However, it still cannot be the case that the crossing constraint is a generalisation about those elements which correspond to sentence operators. The future tense operator which corresponds to *will* in English is also treated as a sentence operator and yet it clearly has to be crossed by *Neg* in order to obtain the more usual reading of *John won't come*. The more usual reading may be paraphrased by *It is not the case that John will come* where *Neg* has outside scope. If the crossing constraint were defined for sentence operators, however, the only allowed reading would be the less usual one paraphrased by *It will be the case that John does not come*. This reading is almost trivially true since there is sure to be some point in time in the future at which John does not come. The reading where *Neg* crosses over *will* has more content since it claims that there is no (relevant) time in the future at which John comes. Thus in the present system the crossing constraint does not represent a semantic generalisation and we would have to define *logical predicate* in a rather ad hoc manner by referring to several categories of lexical items. Thus we might say that a logical predicate is any lexical item of the category Det, Neg or Advs.[10] This, of course, represents a purely syntactic definition and at that does not seem to represent any intuitive generalisation.

Nevertheless it seems that we have demonstrated that it is possible to define an adequate version of the fragment which does not contain VP-adverbs and which therefore might allow us to preserve the VSO-hypothesis. Assuming for the sake of argument that the two definitions could be demonstrated to be equivalent in some way, we might consider what sort of general theory of language might select between the two. The following points become relevant for this choice. The version with only sentence adverbs:

(i) makes the claim that the syntactic behaviour of adverbs like *necessarily* and *rapidly* (i.e. the fact that *necessarily* occurs at the beginning of the sentence whereas *rapidly* occurs at the end of the sentence)[11] has nothing to do with the meanings assigned to them. This is in contrast to the analysis with VP-adverbs which rests on the semantic distinction between a function from properties to predicates and a function from propositions to sentences.

(ii) requires a governed rule not necessary in the VP-adverb analysis which postposes particular adverbs. The adverbs which it moves would have to be listed since there is no semantic or syntactic generalisation which would distinguish them from those which it would not move.

(iii) requires the syntactic crossing constraint which is unnecessary in the VP-adverb analysis to account for the adverb data.[12]

It is difficult to imagine what general theory would select the analysis with only sentence adverbs which is syntactically more complex and misses a semantic generalisation over the VP-adverb analysis which is syntactically simpler and captures a semantic generalisation. It seems to be of some

10. As connectives are introduced syncategorematically in the present system we cannot include *and* or *or* here.

11. These are, of course, not the only positions in which these adverbs can occur in English but nevertheless any grammar would have to show that they occur in different positions.

12. In the I-grammar version of the fragment presented in Cooper and Parsons (1975) this constraint would not account for quantifier scope possibilities either since quantifier scope is not represented in the syntax.

significance that the more concrete syntax actually allows us to capture a semantic generalisation which is missed by the more abstract analysis since many of the arguments for abstract syntax involve semantic generalisations.

I have dwelt on this argument for VP-adverbs and against an analysis which nobody has ever seriously proposed because I believe that a strictly analogous argument can be made against an extremely ingenious proposal made in unpublished work by George Lakoff some years ago. Lakoff's insight was that the facts that Thomason and Stalnaker (1973) had used to justify the existence of VP-adverbs were equally well predicted if one considered these adverbs semantically more or less as relations between individuals and propositions and syntactically more or less like normal equi verbs. This obviated the need for a VP in underlying structure and preserved the hypothesis that English is a VSO language. (18) is what I believe to be a close imitation of Lakoff's underlying structure for *John finds Mary rapidly*.

(18)

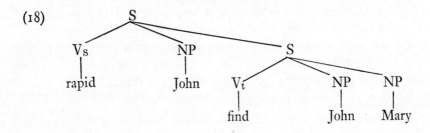

According to fairly obvious translation rules we might get (19) as a logical expression corresponding to (18).

(19) **rapidly'**(^j,^**find'**$_*$(j,m))

We assume here that **rapidly'** now represents a logical constant of the appropriate type. In order to guarantee the subsective property of **rapidly'** in this framework we would have to introduce the meaning postulate (20).

(20) $\Box$[**rapidly'**$(x,{}^\wedge\varphi) \supset \varphi$]   where $\varphi \in ME_t$

We run into trouble again when we consider the possibility of the embedded sentence in (18) being negated. According to (20) this would represent a reading for *John doesn't find Mary rapidly* which entails *John doesn't find Mary*. Again we could invoke an extended version of Lakoff's crossing constraint but again this would merely be a syntactic account which does not appear to capture much of a generalisation. Once again avoiding VP-adverbs gives us a more complex syntax and misses the semantic generalisation. In the case of this alternative the syntactic complications are considerable. This analysis requires

(i) the crossing constraint.

(ii) a governed rule of adverb lowering applying to certain equi verbs such as *rapid* but not those such as *want* or *try*. The lexical items to which this rule applies would have to be listed since there appears to be no semantic or syntactic generalisation which distinguishes them.

(iii) a rule of *ly*-addition to change *rapid* to *rapidly*. This might be considered as part of adverb lowering.

(iv) some mechanism which prevents *rapid* from receiving its own tense so that we do not obtain a reading for a sentence such as *John will have found Mary rapidly* which might be paraphrased as *John will stand in the rapid relation to the proposition that John has found Mary*.

(v) a rule of equi and its associated conditions on co-referentiality. Both of these seem unnecessary if one adopts a treatment of complementation along the lines which Thomason (1974) has proposed.

It seems then that if we want to have a semantic account of the behaviour of adverbs such as *rapidly* we need to represent them semantically as predicate modifiers.[13] Given our present theory and assuming that adverbs like *rapidly* are allowed to iterate there must be some deep structure category corresponding to predicates in order for these adverbs to be treated as predicate modifiers at the same time as preserving Montague's theory of translation. Thus the semantic analysis for which we have argued depends crucially on having a VP category in underlying structure. If there must be a VP in underlying structure then clearly English cannot be underlyingly a VSO

13. This is not strictly true. We could equally well treat them as ad-1-verbs and ad-2-verbs as Montague did in 'English as a Formal Language' (in Montague, 1974a). What is important is that the adverb not be able to take a sentence within its scope. Montague's treatment in 'English as a Formal Language' requires that each adverb correspond to two logical expressions of different types depending on whether it modifies a transitive or intransitive verb. This requires, following Montague's general theory, that each adverb of English be represented twice in the syntax of English. It seems there are no English adverbs which modify only transitive or only intransitive verbs and there seems little justification for the analysis in 'English as a Formal Language' compared with the more elegant analysis in PTQ where adverbs always modify VPs and therefore only correspond to meanings of one type.

language as has been widely suggested in the generative semantic literature.[14]

In this paper we have discussed in detail one case where it seems that Montague's theory of translation and semantics is not only compatible with a non-abstract syntax but also that the non-abstract syntax actually allows a more adequate semantic treatment.

---

14. Frank Heny has pointed out to me that this argument only holds if we assume that adverbs like *rapidly* are allowed to iterate. If we assume that there are only finitely many positions in a sentence where such adverbs can occur then it would be possible to preserve both the VSO hypothesis and the theory of adverbs as predicate modifiers by giving the sentence *John finds Mary rapidly* a deep structure something like:

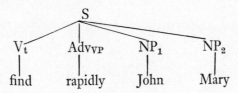

If the translation rule for this structure specified the translation to be of the form: $NP_1'(\char"005E Adv'(\char"005E V'(\char"005E NP_2')))$ as would be allowed by the theory, then we might obtain an expression equivalent to (6b) for this structure. As far as I know this structure is unlike anything that has been proposed in the generative semantic literature since it has always been assumed there that adverbs like *rapidly* iterate.

L. Åqvist and F. Guenthner

Quantification Theory for Natural Language Based on Multi-dimensional Modal Logics with Demonstratives[1]

1. *Introduction*

In the Appendix to Åqvist (1973) an axiomatic system Ä of two-dimensional propositional modal logic was proved to be semantically sound and complete relatively to a modal theory, which had a good deal in common with the cylindric algebras of Tarski and with structures studied by other so-called algebraic logicians (e.g. Halmos, 1962). An alternative, but basically similar, treatment of systems of 'bi-modal' logic was given in Segerberg (1973). As for the philosophical and/or linguistic interest of such calculi, let us point out the following facts:

(i) The need for developing systems like Ä arose in connection with the treatment of subjunctive conditionals and counterfactuals given in Åqvist (1973).

(ii) In Åqvist (1976) a reconstruction was provided of the familiar account of verb tenses due to Reichenbach (1947), based on a two-dimensional approach to Priorian tense logic.

(iii) In Åqvist and Guenthner (1975) the just mentioned development of tense logic was extended so as to enable us to give a logical treatment of various so-called verb aspects (including what linguists and grammarians label *Aktionsarten* and *Verbalperiphrasen*). A conspicuous feature of the employed system of tense logic is due to its containing modal operators enabling one to speak of what takes place uninterruptedly throughout bounded intervals of time, for instance.

Let us add that a valuable attempt is made in Segerberg (1973) to trace historically the growing need felt by 'philosophical logicians' for what we

1. The authors express gratitude to the Deutsche Forschungsgemeinschaft (DFG) for supporting the research reported here.

shall call multi-dimensional modal logics; this is particularly apparent among authors doing tense logic.

So much for previous work in the area. In the present paper we consider another application and extension of the system Ä, called DM2 (see section 3 below), whose intended interpretation is such that we can adequately translate (sections 4–7 below) a certain restricted system QT2 (section 2) of ordinary classical first-order predicate logic into it, viz. one that contains exactly (and only) two distinct variables over individuals. Instead of thus possessing individual variables, DM2 has two demonstrative (or indexical) terms, δ and ∂, to be tentatively read as '*this* individual' and '*that* individual'. Also, instead of quantifiers in the received sense of variable-binding sentence-forming operators, DM2 uses certain one-place modal operators, called *quantificational modalities*, which, by the formation rules of DM2, are 'linked' or 'tied' to those demonstratives. Again, in order for a language of DM2 to be disambiguated, DM2 will have to contain one pair consisting of a quantificational modality together with its matching demonstrative for each 'variable to be explained away', to speak Quinish for a while. (See in particular section 3 below.) For that reason, the degree of complexity of DM2 will be seen to be much higher than would perhaps be expected.

Among further developments of our present enterprise from which we have to refrain here, the most obvious one is that of generalising DM2 to DMn, for any arbitrary natural number n; by using the techniques of this paper, one would then be able to explain away n individual variables, of course, not just 2. (However, in section 8 below, we indicate how to extend DM2 (in another 'direction') with operators forming definite as well as indefinite descriptions.) Instead, we now feel more concerned about motivating the claim that systems of multi-dimensional modal logic with demonstratives, like DM2, are more adequate tools for the study of quantification in natural languages than standard predicate calculi such as QT2.

First of all, let us formulate a question with respect to natural languages like English: which are, if any, their individual variables in a reasonable sense of the word? Bearing that question in mind, consider now the following Aristotelian sentence:

(1)   Every philosopher is wicked.

A standard formalisation of (1) within some language of first-order predicate logic then gives us:

(1a) $\forall x(Fx \rightarrow Gx)$

where 'F' and 'G' are respectively read as 'is a philosopher' and 'is wicked', and where ∀ is read as 'for every' and → as 'only if'. So, if we translate (1a) *back* into ordinary English, we obtain the following somewhat clumsy, but perfectly intelligible result:

(1b) For every x, x is a philosopher only if x is wicked.

Suppose now that a linguist is confronted with (1b). If he is kind enough not to 'star' it as ungrammatical at the outset, he may at least raise the following perfectly legitimate question: how are we to read the letter 'x', which occurs thrice in (1b)? If we answer: just read it as 'x', i.e. read it by pronouncing the 24th letter of the English alphabet, our response is likely to be rejected as a (bad) joke. A more serious suggestion is to the effect that 'x' in (1b) be read as 'individual', 'thing', 'object', or what have you. Unfortunately, the proposal yields an altogether nonsensical result, viz.

(1c) For every individual, individual is a philosopher only if individual is wicked.

It is interesting to observe here, though, that the grammaticality (well-formedness, meaningfulness) of (1c) is restored when in it we prefix the second and the third occurrence of the common noun 'individual' by a demonstrative article, such as 'this' or 'that', whereby one obtains:

(1d) For every individual, that /this/ individual is a philosopher only if that /this/ individual is wicked.

Note here, then, that (1d) does *not* result from (1b), or (1a), by our uniformly substituting any expression whatsoever for the variable 'x'. At best, we have obtained (1d) from (1b) by substituting the common noun 'individual' for the first occurrence of 'x' in (1b) and the demonstrative noun-phrase 'that individual' for the remaining occurrences. Clearly, this is not to provide for a uniform reading of 'x' in (1b) at all, as was obviously required by our supposed questioner. The same awkward failure of uniform substitutability results from our trying the personal pronoun 'he' for 'x': we can only replace the second and the third occurrence of 'x' in (1b) by 'he', but not the first one, if we insist on remaining grammatical speakers of English. Generalising quickly, we think that there is no uniform reading of 'x' in sentences of the form (1a) that works for English.

Our discussion so far gives rise to an interesting new problem: what is the logical form of the admittedly grammatical sentence (1d)? In order to answer this question, let us first add the fixed monadic predicate I, 'is an individual', to the stock of logical constants of our language of first-order logic. Since that theory is concerned precisely with quantification over individuals (as opposed to other entities), I will have to be a tautological, or universally applicable, predicate, which is definable by, say, the schema: $Ix =df (x = x)$. We then suggest that (1d) be represented somewhat as follows:

$$(1e)\quad U_I(F_{\underline{\mathscr{D}}I} \to G_{\underline{\mathscr{D}}I})$$

which is to be understood in accordance with these stipulations:

(i) When occurring as a subscript or index to U and $\underline{\mathscr{D}}$, I is to be read simply as 'individual', i.e. in those positions I functions outright as a common noun and the element of predication, expressed by 'is a . . .', vanishes.

(ii) U is a one-place sentence-forming (modal) operator indexed by common nouns, like I, to be read as 'for every', so that the whole compound U_I (with index, then) is read as 'for every individual', by (i) above.

(iii) $\underline{\mathscr{D}}$ is a one-place term-forming (demonstrative) operator taking common nouns (like I) as its arguments. We read $\underline{\mathscr{D}}$ as 'that', say; thus, the compound $\underline{\mathscr{D}}I$ is read as 'that individual', appealing again to (i) above.

Using these three instructions, together with some obvious rule of word-order change, we can almost automatically translate (1e) back into (1d), provided that, in the context at hand, 'F', 'G' and $\to$ are still read as 'is a philosopher', 'is wicked' and 'only if', respectively.

Let us now return to the question raised in the beginning of the present discussion: which are, if any, the individual variables of a natural language like English? More specifically, let us ask it with respect to our sentence (1d) and its formal translation (1e). The best first answer we can then come up with is this: if you agree to call the common noun 'individual', formally I, a variable when it occurs as an index (or subscript) to U and $\underline{\mathscr{D}}$, as it does in (1e), then common nouns are the variables of English. This answer, although sensible enough as it seems, should be rather hard to swallow from a traditional logical point of view, due to the following facts:

An individual variable, like 'x' in (1a) and (1b), is usually treated by logicians as being on a par with a name or singular term purporting to denote an individual, as is clear from most versions of the model-theoretic semantics for first-order predicate logic. On the other hand, the grammarian's common noun, like 'individual' in (1d) and I in (1e), is rather like the logician's monadic predicate (with the element of predication deleted, as remarked in stipulation (i) above), which is usually interpreted semantically as denoting some set of individuals, as opposed to single ones. Therefore, even if one agrees to speak of common nouns as variables of English, there is no question about their being individual ones. A better candidate for the position of individual variable of English would then seem to be the demonstrative noun-phrase 'that individual', formally $\mathscr{D}_I$, which should at least be treated by the logician as a singular individual-denoting term, let alone of a special kind. But note then carefully that, in the formalisation (1e), the term $\mathscr{D}_I$ is not bound by the initial U_I-operator in the same way as the later occurrences of 'x' in (1a) and (1b) are bound by the initial quantifier-phrase $\forall x$ ('for every x').

Where do all these considerations leave us, then, with respect to the problem of quantification in natural language? In a complete mess? Hopefully not. But they do show, we take it, that there is room, and need, for developing and studying systems of predicate logic where sentences like (1d) have natural direct representations like (1e). DM2 is precisely such a system, having demonstrative terms or noun-phrases instead of bindable individual variables, and quantificational modal operators instead of variable-binding quantifiers in the received sense. This completes our general, linguistically-oriented, motivation for the study of DM2.

Let us round off this introduction by indicating some simplifications and further developments.

(i) Since I was thought of as a fixed and universally applicable predicate (in our first-order framework), we might as well drop it as an index to U and $\mathscr{D}$, on the basis of proper definitional schemata like these:

$$\mathscr{D} =\text{df } \mathscr{D}_I$$
$$UA =\text{df } U_I A,$$

where A is a well-formed DM2-formula of a certain appropriate kind to be indicated below (section 3).

Here, the defined, non-italicised symbol $\mathscr{D}$ can be thought of as a *zero-place term-forming operator*, or simply as a (demonstrative) term in the logical sense, which is again to be read as, say, 'that individual'. By the same token, U will be read as was U_I: 'for every individual'; by way of contrast, recall that the proper reading of ∀ is 'for every' rather than 'for every individual'.

(ii) Going back to our example:

(1)   Every philosopher is wicked

one might reasonably suggest that it is really of the form

(1f) $U_F G_{\mathcal{D}^{\mathscr{G}}F}$

where F occurs as an index to U as well as to $\mathcal{D}^{\mathscr{G}}$, and thus functions as the *common noun* 'philosopher' (with 'is a . . .' deleted). Translating (1f) back into English, we then obtain

(1g)   For every philosopher, that philosopher is wicked

which result is certainly equivalent to (1), and is also closer to (1) than (1d); (1) and (1g) resemble one another in *not explicitly* using words like 'only if' and 'individual', which are forthcoming in (1d). Our comment here is simply that it is possible in DM2-languages to introduce a syntactic construction such as (1f) and, via appropriate definitions, prove it to be equivalent to (1e), which can in turn be proved to be an adequate translation of the standard formalisation (1a) of (1)—'adequate' in the straightforward sense of our Translation Theorem for QT2 and DM2 (section 5 below), which is, from a technical point of view, the main result of this paper.

Perhaps our present argument about (1f) and its relation to other sentences considered gives some support to the hope that even so-called linguistic *surface structures* can be formalised by logical means, provided only that one operates within the right kind of framework.

(iii) We leave to the reader the task of handling examples of ordinary English that involve *existential* rather than universal quantification. Also, we postpone consideration in this paper of examples requiring the use of *more than one* variable. But, as DM2 contains two demonstratives (each with matching quantificational modalities, universal as well as existential), we should be able to handle quite a few examples, which are ordinarily taken to require the use of *two distinct* individual variables. Handle them in the spirit of (1)–(1d)–(1e)–(1f)–(1g), that is to say.

2. *Languages, semantics, and axiomatics of QT2*

We start by considering a formulation of classical first-order non-modal quantification theory with identity in exactly two distinct variables, which will be called 'QT2'.

Languages of QT2

A language L of QT2 is a structure made up of the following disjoint *basic syntactic categories*:

(i) A two element set $\text{Var}_L = \{x, y\}$ of *individual variables*. Syntactic or metalinguistic notation: x.

(ii) An at most denumerable set Cons_L of *individual constants* or *names*. Syntactic notation: $a, b, c, a_1, \ldots, a_n$.

(iii) For each $n = 0, 1, 2$: a denumerable set Pred_L^n of *n*-adic *predicate letters*. Syntactic notation: P^n ($n = 0, 1, 2$).

(iv) The *logical constants* $-$, &, $\vee$, $\rightarrow$, $\forall$, $\exists$ and $=$; for, respectively, negation, conjunction, disjunction, material implication, universal as well as existential quantification, and identity. In particular, $\exists$ is read as 'for some' and $\forall$ as 'for every'.

The set Tm_L of *terms of L* is then defined as $= \text{Cons}_L$. Note that Tm_L contains *no* individual variables in Var_L among its members.

We say that A is an atomic formula (or atomic sentence) of a QT2-language L, in symbols: $A \in \text{AtW}_L$, iff (i.e. if and only if), either (1) A is a 0-adic predicate letter (or proposition letter) $P^0 \in \text{Pred}_L^0$; or (2) A is $P^n a_1, \ldots, a_n$ for some $P^n \in \text{Pred}_L^n$ and some $a_1, \ldots, a_n \in \text{Tm}_L$, where $n = 1, 2$; *or* (3) A is $(a = b)$ for some $a, b \in \text{Tm}_L$.

Again, the set W_L of *wffs* (i.e. well-formed formulas or sentences) *of L* is defined as the smallest set S such that

(i) $\text{AtW}_L \subseteq S$ (i.e. every atomic formula of L is in S),

(ii) if A, B are in S, so are $-A$, $(A \& B)$, $(A \vee B)$, $(A \rightarrow B)$, *and*

(iii) if $x \in \text{Var}_L$, $a \in \text{Cons}_L$, if A is in S and contains a but not x, then $\forall x A^x/a$ and $\exists x A^x/a$ are in S. (Here A^x/a is the result of replacing every occurrence of a in A by one of x.)

Semantics for QT2

Let us now consider how QT2-languages L are to be interpreted 'semantically' in the precise sense of logical model theory.

By a QT2-*model* for L we understand any ordered triple $M = \langle D, d_0, V \rangle$ where

(i) $D \neq \emptyset$ (i.e. D is to be a non-empty set 'of individuals'),
(ii) $d_0 \in D$ (a 'designated' element of D), *and*
(iii) V is a *valuation* of L *on* the domain D in the sense of a one-place assignment-function satisfying the following conditions:

(a) $V(a) \in D$ for each $a \in \text{Cons}_L$;
(b) $V(P^0) \in$ the set of truth-values $\{1, 0\}$ for each $P^0 \in \text{Pred}_L^0$; and
(c) $V(P^n) \in$ the cartesian product D^n for each $P^n \in \text{Pred}_L^n$ where $n = 1, 2$.

Given any QT2-model $M = \langle D, d_0, V \rangle$, we can now define what it means for any wff $A \in W_L$ to be *true in* M, in symbols: $\models^M A$. As usual, the definition is by induction on the length, or complexity, of wffs:

(1) $\models^M P^0$ iff $V(P^0) = 1$

(2) $\models^M P^n a_1, \ldots, a_n$ iff $\langle V(a_1), \ldots, V(a_n) \rangle \in V(P^n)$, where $n = 1, 2$;

(3) $\models^M (a = b)$ iff $V(a)$ is identical to $V(b)$

(4) $\models^M {-}A$ iff not: $\models^M A$

(5) $\models^M (A \& B)$ iff both $\models^M A$ and $\models^M B$

(6) $\models^M (A \vee B)$ iff $\models^M A$ or $\models^M B$ (or both)

(7) $\models^M (A \rightarrow B)$, iff, if $\models^M A$ then $\models^M B$

(8) $\models^{M = \langle D, d_0, V \rangle} \forall x A$ iff $\models^{\langle D, d_0, V' \rangle} A^a/x$ for each valuation V on D such that $V' =_a V$ (see explanation below; we assume here that $a \in \text{Cons}_L$ does not occur in A, and that A^a/x is the result of substituting a for x everywhere in A).

(9) $\models^{M = \langle D, d_0, V \rangle} \exists x A$ iff $\models^{\langle D, d_0, V' \rangle} A^a/x$ for some V' on D with $V' =_a V$.

Explanation. Let V, V' be valuations (of L) on a domain D ($\neq \emptyset$) and let

$a \in \text{Cons}_L$. We say that V′ *differs from* V *at most with respect to a*, in symbols: $V' =_a V$, iff,

(i) $V'(P^n) = V(P^n)$ for each $P^n \in \text{Pred}_L^n$ ($n = 0, 1, 2$); and

(ii) $V'(b) = V(b)$ for each $b \in \text{Cons}_L$ that is distinct from a.

A *set* S of *L*-wffs is said to be (simultaneously) QT2-satisfiable, iff there is a QT2-model M such that for all wffs A in S: $\overset{M}{\models}$A. Any *wff* A is QT2-satisfiable iff its unit set {A} is. Also, A is said to be QT2-valid iff $-$A is not QT2-satisfiable, i.e. iff $\overset{M}{\models}$A for each QT2-model M.

Remark. The designated element d_0 in QT2-models is readily seen to play no interesting role whatsoever in the present formulation of QT2. There are, however, two reasons for already bringing it in at this stage, viz.: (i) its presence facilitates our subsequent proof of the adequacy of the translation given below of QT2 into the modal system DM2 with demonstratives, and (ii) d_0 is needed when one adds descriptions (indefinite as well as definite) to QT2 in a Fregean fashion (as we recommend) and translates the resulting extension into a matching extension of DM2.

Axiomatics for QT2

We now axiomatise QT2 by stipulating that any instance of the schemata Q0–Q4 below are to be axioms and by adopting r0–r2 below as rules of proof (or inference) for the deductive system:

Q0. All tautologies

Q1. $\forall xA \to A^a/x$ where $a \in \text{Cons}_L$

Q2. $A^a/x \to \exists xA$ where $a \in \text{Cons}_L$

Q3. $a = a$ where $a \in \text{Cons}_L$

Q4. $a = b \to (A \to A^a//b)$ where $a, b \in \text{Cons}_L$ and $A^a//b$ is any result of replacing various (not necessarily all, or even any) occurrences of b in A by occurrences of a.

r0. $$\dfrac{A, A \to B}{B}$$

r1. $$\dfrac{A \to B^a/x}{A \to \forall xB}$$ where $a \in \text{Cons}_L$ occurs neither in A nor in B.

r2. $\dfrac{B^a/x \to A}{\exists x B \to A}$ with the same proviso.

We then define the set of QT2-*provable* L-wffs as the smallest set S such that (i) every instance of Q_0–Q_4 is in S, and (ii) S is closed under r0–r2. Also, we say that $A \in W_L$ is QT2-*derivable from* a set S of L-wffs, iff, there are $B_1, \ldots, B_n$ ($n \geqslant 0$) in S such that $B_1 \& \ldots \& B_n \to A$ is QT2-provable. Again, $S(\subseteq W_L)$ is QT2-*consistent* iff there is an L-wff A such that A is *not* QT2-derivable from S; otherwise, S is said to be QT2-*inconsistent*.

Finally, we record two familiar results:

Strong semantic soundness and completeness of QT2. For all subsets S of W_L: S is QT2-consistent iff S is QT2-satisfiable.

As usual, this result yields as a corollary:

Weak semantic soundness and completeness of QT2. For all $A \in W_L$: A is QT2-valid iff A is QT2-provable.

3. *Languages, semantics and axiomatics for DM2*

In the present section we describe our system DM2 of two-dimensional modal logic with identity and exactly two demonstratives. DM2 will be seen to contain the system Ä presented in the Appendix of Åqvist (1973).

Languages of DM2

A language L of DM2 is a structure determined by the following disjoint basic syntactic categories:

(i) An at most denumerable set $Cons_L$ of individual constants or names. Metalinguistic notation: $a, b, c, \ldots, a_1, \ldots, a_n$.

(ii) Two demonstrative (or indexical) terms: δ and $\wp$, to be read tentatively as '*this* individual' and '*that* individual', respectively. δ and $\wp$ may alternatively be thought of as zero-place term-forming operators, definable as indicated above in the introduction.

(iii) For each $n = 0, 1, 2$: a denumerable set $Pred_L^n$ of n-adic predicate letters. Metalinguistic notation: P^n.

(iv) Logical constants:

(a) classical: $-$, &, $\vee$, $\to$, and $=$, as in the case of QT2-languages L;

(b) two pairs of one-place quantificational modalities (or modal operators): $\square$, U (both to be read as 'for each individual it holds that') and $\diamondsuit$, E (both to be read as 'for some individual it holds that');

(c) the one-place modal operators $\boxed{u}$, $\boxed{o}$ and $\boxed{X}$ known from the Appendix of Åqvist (1973).

Duals $\boxed{\Phi}$, $\boxed{\Diamond}$ and $\boxed{\langle x \rangle}$ of the operators in (c) are defined in the usual way as $-\boxed{u}-$, $-\boxed{o}-$ and $-\boxed{X}-$, respectively.

Furthermore, the set $\mathrm{Tm_L}$ of L-*terms* is defined as $= \mathrm{Cons_L} \cup \{\delta, \mathcal{A}\}$. The set $\mathrm{AtW_L}$ of *atomic formulas of* L is then defined as in the case of QT2. Note that in the present case of DM2-languages L we deal with larger sets of terms and atomic formulas because of the presence in L of δ and $\mathcal{A}$. We adopt the same metalinguistic notation for $\mathrm{Tm_L}$ as for $\mathrm{Cons_L}$.

Again, the set $\mathrm{W_L}$ of L-*wffs* is the smallest set S such that

(i) $\mathrm{AtW_L} \subseteq S$;

(ii) if A, B are in S, so are $-A$, $(A \& B)$, $(A \lor B)$, $(A \rightarrow B)$, $\boxed{u}A$, $\boxed{o}A$, and $\boxed{X}A$;

(iii) *if* a is in $\mathrm{Cons_L}$, *if* A is in S and satisfies the following conditions:
  (a) A contains (occurrences of) a,
  (b) A contains no occurrences of δ,
  (c) A contains no occurrences of $\boxed{u}$, $\boxed{o}$ or $\boxed{X}$,
  then $\Box A^{\delta}/a$ and $\Diamond A^{\delta}/a$ are in S; *and*

(iv) *if* a is in $\mathrm{Cons_L}$, *if* A is in S and satisfies the conditions:
  (a) A contains a;
  (b) A contains no occurrences of $\mathcal{A}$;
  (c) A contains no occurrences of $\boxed{u}$, $\boxed{o}$ or $\boxed{X}$,
  then $UA^{\mathcal{A}}/a$ and $EA^{\mathcal{A}}/a$ are in S.

Semantics for DM2

We now turn to the model-theoretic interpretation of DM2-languages L. By an *original* DM2-*model* for L we shall understand an ordered triple $M = \langle D, \langle d_0, d_0 \rangle, V \rangle$ where

(i) $D \neq \emptyset$ (a non-empty set of individuals)

(ii) $\langle d_0, d_0 \rangle \in D \times D$ (a designated ordered pair)

(iii) V is a *valuation* of L *on* the domain D

in the sense of a one-place assignment-function satisfying conditions (a)–(c) in clause (iii) in the definition of a QT2-model, with the sole difference that V is now defined for all members of the categories $\mathrm{Cons_L}$ and $\mathrm{Pred_L^n}$ ($n = 0, 1, 2$) of the relevant DM2-*language* L.

Let $M = \langle D, \langle d_0, d_0 \rangle, V \rangle$ be any original DM2-model for some language L of DM2. For any $d, d' \in D$, let M^a/d' be the structure $\langle D, \langle d, d' \rangle, V \rangle$, which is exactly like M except that the ordered pair $\langle d, d' \rangle$ replaces $\langle d_0, d_0 \rangle$ as the designated element of $D \times D$. Given any original DM2-model M as above, then, the *doubly indexed family* of structures $\{M^a/d'\}_{a,a' \in D}$ is thus determined. By a DM2-*model* for L we then mean any member of such a doubly-indexed family determined by some original DM2-model M. Note that M itself is a DM2-model and, in effect, $= M^{d_0}/d_0$.

Next, for any DM2-model M^a/d' and for any member of Tm_L, we define the following function val:

(i) $\text{val}^{M^a/d'}(a) = V(a)$,   for each $a \in \text{Cons}_L$

(ii) $\text{val}^{M^a/d'}(\delta) = d'$

(iii) $\text{val}^{M^a/d'}(\wp) = d$

Here, for any $b \in \text{Tm}_L$, $\text{val}^{M^a/d'}(b)$ is to be understood as the value (or denotation) of b in the model M^a/d'.

We now proceed to the definition of *truth in* M^a/d' $\left(\left| \dfrac{M^a/d'}{} \right. \right)$ for any member of W_L, any original DM2-model $M = \langle D, \langle d_0, d_0 \rangle, V \rangle$ and any $d, d' \in D$:

(1) $\left| \dfrac{M^a/d'}{} \right.$ P^0 iff $V(P^0) = 1$, where $P^0 \in \text{Pred}_L^0$

(2) $\left| \dfrac{M^a/d'}{} \right.$ $P^n a_1, \ldots, a_n$ iff $\langle \text{val}^{M^a/d'}(a_1), \ldots, \text{val}^{M^a/d'}(a_n) \rangle \in V(P^n)$, where $a_1, \ldots, a_n \in \text{Tm}_L$, $P^n \in \text{Pred}_L^n$, and $n = 1, 2$.

(3) $\left| \dfrac{M^a/d'}{} \right.$ $(a = b)$ iff $\text{val}^{M^a/d'}(a)$ is identical to $\text{val}^{M^a/d'}(b)$, where $a, b \in \text{Tm}_L$.

(4)–(7) As in the corresponding definition in the case of QT2, except that M^a/d' replaces M.

(8) $\left| \dfrac{M^a/d'}{} \right.$ $\boxed{u}A$ iff $\left| \dfrac{M^a/d''}{} \right.$ A for each $d'' \in D$

(9) $\left| \dfrac{M^a/d'}{} \right.$ $\boxed{o}A$ iff $\left| \dfrac{M^a/d}{} \right.$ A

(10) $\left| \dfrac{M^a/d'}{} \right.$ $\boxed{X}A$ iff $\left| \dfrac{M d'/a}{} \right.$ A

(11) $\left| \dfrac{M^a/d'}{} \right.$ $\Box A^\delta/a$ iff $\left| \dfrac{M^a/d''}{} \right.$ A^δ/a for each $d'' \in D$

(12) $\left| \dfrac{M^a/d'}{} \right.$ $\Diamond A^\delta/a$ iff $\left| \dfrac{M^a/d''}{} \right.$ A^δ/a for some $d'' \in D$

(13) $\left|\dfrac{M^a/d'}{\rule{1.5cm}{0pt}}\, UA^{\sim\varrho}\,\right/a$ iff $\left|\dfrac{M^{a''}/d'}{\rule{1.5cm}{0pt}}\, A^{\sim\varrho}\,\right/a$ for each $d'' \in D$

(14) $\left|\dfrac{M^a/d'}{\rule{1.5cm}{0pt}}\, EA^{\sim\varrho}\,\right/a$ iff $\left|\dfrac{M^{a''}/d'}{\rule{1.5cm}{0pt}}\, A^{\sim\varrho}\,\right/a$ for some $d'' \in D$

A set S of L-wffs is said to be (*simultaneously*) DM2-*satisfiable* iff there is a DM2-model M^a/d' such that for all wffs A in S: $\left|\dfrac{M^a/d'}{\rule{1.5cm}{0pt}}\right.$ A. Any L-wff A is DM2-satisfiable iff {A} is. A is DM2-*valid* iff —A is not DM2-satisfiable, i.e. iff $\left|\dfrac{M^a/d'}{\rule{1.5cm}{0pt}}\right.$ A for all DM2-models M^a/d'. Moreover, $A \in W_L$ is said to be DM2-d_0-*satisfiable* iff there is some *original* DM2-model M such that $\left|\dfrac{M^{d_0}/d_0(=M)}{\rule{1.5cm}{0pt}}\right.$ A; and A is DM2-d_0-*valid* iff $\left|\dfrac{M^{d_0}/d_0}{\rule{1.5cm}{0pt}}\right.$ A for all *original* DM2-models M.

Axiomatics for DM2

The deductive system DM2 is determined by the following axiom schemata and rules of inference. (The symbol ↔ for material equivalence is defined in the usual way.) We suggest that A0–A15 and R0–R2 be compared with schemata and rules which figure already in the axiomatisation of the calculus Ä given in the Appendix of Åqvist (1973).

A0. All tautologies

A1. $\boxed{u}(A \to B) \to (\boxed{u}A \to \boxed{u}B)$

A2. $\boxed{u}A \to A$

A3. $\boxed{u}A \to \boxed{u}\boxed{u}A$

A4. $\Diamond\!\!\!\!\Diamond\,\boxed{u}A \to A$

A5. $\boxed{u}A \to \boxed{o}A$

A6. $\boxed{o}(A \to B) \to (\boxed{o}A \to \boxed{o}B)$

A7. $\boxed{o}A \leftrightarrow \Diamond\!\!\!\!\Diamond A$

A8. $\boxed{o}A \to \boxed{u}\boxed{o}A$

A9. $\boxtimes(A \to B) \to (\boxtimes A \to \boxtimes B)$

A10. $\boxtimes A \leftrightarrow \langle\!\langle x \rangle\!\rangle A$

A11. $\boxtimes\boxtimes A \to A$

A12. $\boxed{o}(\boxtimes A \to A)$

A13. $\boxed{u}\,\boxed{xox}\,A \leftrightarrow \boxed{xox}\,\boxed{u}A$

A14. $\langle\!\langle xux \rangle\!\rangle \boxed{u} A \to \boxed{u} \langle\!\langle xux \rangle\!\rangle A$

A15. $\boxed{X}A \leftrightarrow \boxed{0}A$, provided that (a) all occurrences of $\delta/\mathscr{D}/$ in A, if any, are in the scope of some $\square$ or $\diamond$ $/U$ or $E/$ in A, and (b) there are no occurrences of $\boxed{u}$, $\boxed{0}$, or $\boxed{X}$ in A.

A16. $A \leftrightarrow \boxed{0}A$, with the same provisos (a) and (b) as under A15.

A17. $\square A \leftrightarrow \boxed{u} A$

A18. $\diamond A \leftrightarrow \boxed{\diamond} A$

A19. $UA \leftrightarrow \boxed{xux} A$

A20. $EA \leftrightarrow \langle\!\langle xux \rangle\!\rangle A$

A21. $\square A \to A^a/\delta$ for any $a \in \mathrm{Cons_L}$

A22. $A^a/\delta \to \diamond A$ for any $a \in \mathrm{Cons_L}$

A23. $UA \to A^a/\mathscr{D}$ for any $a \in \mathrm{Cons_L}$

A24. $A^a/\mathscr{D} \to EA$ for any $a \in \mathrm{Cons_L}$

A25. $a = a$ where $a \in \mathrm{Tm_L}$

A26. $a = b \to (A \to A^a//b)$ provided that $a, b \in \mathrm{Cons_L}$

A27. $a = b \to (A \to A^a//b)$ where $a, b \in \mathrm{Tm_L}$ and provided that no occurrence of b in A that is replaced by a falls within the scope of any quantificational modality or other modal operator in A. (In the presence of A26, this schema A27 is of interest only when at least one of a, b is δ or $\mathscr{D}$.)

A28. $\boxed{u}\boxed{X}\boxed{0}(\delta = \mathscr{D})$

R0. $\dfrac{A,\, A \to B}{B}$ R1. $\dfrac{A}{\boxed{u}A}$ R2. $\dfrac{A}{\boxed{X}A}$

R3. $\dfrac{A \to B^a/\delta}{A \to \square B}$ provided that $a \in \mathrm{Cons_L}$ occurs neither in A nor in B

R4. $\dfrac{B^a/\delta \to A}{\diamond B \to A}$ with the same proviso

R5. $\dfrac{A \to B^a/\mathscr{D}}{A \to UB}$ with the same proviso

R6. $\dfrac{B^a/\mathscr{D} \to A}{EB \to A}$ with the same proviso

In A13, A14, A19 and A20, we have written $\boxed{xux}$ and $\langle\!\langle xux \rangle\!\rangle$ as short for $\boxed{X}\boxed{u}\boxed{X}$ and $\langle x \rangle \boxed{\diamond} \langle x \rangle$, respectively.

Again, the set of DM2-*provable* L-wffs is the smallest set S such that (i) every instance of A0–A28 is in S, and (ii) S is closed under R0–R6. Notions of DM2-*derivability* and DM2-*consistency* are defined as in the case of QT2.

Without proof we now assert that the given axiomatics for DM2 is *sound* relatively to its semantics in the sense that for all A ∈ W$_L$: if A is DM2-provable, then A is SM2-valid. The question as to whether the converse result (*completeness* of DM2) holds is left open for the time being—one seemingly relevant problem in the context is whether proviso (b) to A15 and A16 can be dropped.

We have already pointed out that the deductive system DM2 contains Ä of Åqvist (1973), which calculus was a purely propositional modal logic, of course; therefore, theorem schemata T1–T9 stated in section 18 of that paper are provable in DM2; one also obtains the following fresh schema:

$$\text{T10.} \quad \left\{ \begin{array}{l} A \leftrightarrow \boxed{uXu}\, A \\ A \leftrightarrow \langle\!\langle uXu \rangle\!\rangle\, A \end{array} \right\} \text{provided that A satisfies (a) and (b) in A15–A16.}$$

Hint: use A15 and A16 (*inter alia*) to prove T10 in DM2!

4. *Translation of QT2 into DM2*

Let L be any QT2-language and let L be any DM2-language such that Cons$_L$ = Cons$_L$ and Pred$_L^n$ = Pred$_L^n$ for each n = 0, 1, 2. We now define a translation function ϕ from the basic syntactic categories of L into those of L as follows:

(1) $\phi(x) = \delta$ and $\phi(y) = \mathscr{A}^{\mathscr{y}}$, where $\{x, y\}$ = Var$_L$

(2) $\phi(a) = a$, for each $a \in$ Cons$_L$

(3) $\phi(P^n) = P^n$, for each $P^n \in$ Pred$_L^n$ for n = 0, 1, 2.

Next, we recursively extend the definition of ϕ in such a way that it will translate any wff of L into one of L (map W$_L$ into W$_L$, if you prefer):

(i) $\phi(P^n a_1, \ldots, a_n) = \phi(P^n)\phi(a_1), \ldots, \phi(a_n)$, where n = 0, 1, 2 and where $a_i \in$ Cons$_L$.

(ii) $\phi(a = b) = (\phi(a) = \phi(b))$, where $a, b \in$ Cons$_L$

(iii) $\phi(-A) = -\phi(A)$

(iv) $\phi(A \& B) = (\phi(A) \& \phi(B))$

(v) $\phi(A \lor B) = (\phi(A) \lor \phi(B))$

(vi) $\phi(A \rightarrow B) = (\phi(A) \rightarrow \phi(B))$

$$\text{(vii) } \phi(\forall x A^x/a) = \begin{cases} \Box\phi(A)^\delta/a, \text{ if } x = x \text{ (in which case } \delta = \phi(x) \text{ and} \\ \qquad\qquad a = \phi(a)) \\ U\phi(A)^{\wp}/a, \text{ if } x = y \text{ (in which case } \wp = \phi(x) \text{ and} \\ \qquad\qquad a = \phi(a)) \end{cases}$$

$$\text{(viii) } \phi(\exists x A^x/a) = \begin{cases} \Diamond\phi(A)^\delta/a, \text{ if } x = x \\ E\phi(A)^{\wp}/a, \text{ if } x = y \end{cases}$$

The only clauses in the above definition of ϕ that are non-trivial are (1) together with (vii) and (viii). In the sequel we shall often write simply ϕA instead of $\phi(A)$.

5. *Proof of the adequacy of the translation ϕ*

In this section we want to demonstrate the adequacy of our just defined function ϕ in the precise sense of the following theorem:

Translation Theorem for QT2 and DM2

Let L, L be any pair of a QT2-language and a DM2 one such that $\text{Cons}_L = \text{Cons}_L$ and $\text{Pred}_L^n = \text{Pred}_L^n$ for $n = 0, 1, 2$. Let A be any member of W_L. Then, for all QT2-models $M = \langle D, d_0, V \rangle$ for L we have that:

$$\Big|\overset{M}{=\!=}A \text{ iff } \Big|\overset{M^{d_0}/d_0}{=\!=\!=} \phi(A)$$

where $\phi(A) \in W_L$, and where $M^{d_0}/d_0 = \langle D, \langle d_0, d_0 \rangle, V \rangle$ is *that original DM2-model* which is obtained from the QT2-model $M = \langle D, d_0, V \rangle$ by replacing its designated element $d_0 \in D$ by the 'reflexive' ordered pair $\langle d_0, d_0 \rangle \in D \times D$.

Proof. By induction on the complexity of $A \in W_L$.

I. *Basis.* $A \in AtW_L$. The desired results

$$\text{(i) } \Big|\overset{M}{=\!=}P^n a_1, \ldots, a_n \text{ iff } \Big|\overset{M^{d_0}/d_0}{=\!=\!=} \phi(P^n a_1, \ldots, a_n)$$

$$\text{(ii) } \Big|\overset{M}{=\!=}(a = b) \text{ iff } \Big|\overset{M^{d_0}/d_0}{=\!=\!=} \phi(a = b),$$

where $a, b, a_1, \ldots, a_n \in \text{Cons}_L$ and $n = 0, 1, 2$, are of course immediate by the definition of ϕ and by the relevant truth-conditions.

II. *Induction Step.* In the cases where A has any of the forms $-B$, (B & C), (B ∨ C), or (B → C), the theorem is seen to hold by virtue of the respective clauses (iii)–(vi) in the definition of ϕ and by virtue of the relevant truth-conditions. Consider next the much more interesting

Case $A = \forall x B^x/a$, for some $B \in W_L$ containing $a \in \text{Cons}_L$ but not $x \in \text{Var}_L$. We split the case into two subcases, viz. (i) the one where $x = x$, and (ii) the one where $x = y$.

Subcase (i). We are to show that for all QT2-models M:

$$\left|\underset{\text{M}}{=\!=\!=}\forall x B^x/a \text{ iff } \right|\underset{M^{d_0}/d_0}{=\!=\!=}\Box(\phi B)^\delta/a$$

where, by the definition of ϕ, $\Box(\phi B)^\delta/a = \phi(\forall x B^x/a)$, $\delta = \phi(x)$ and $a = \phi(a)$. Furthermore, by the hypothesis of induction, all QT2-models M are such that:

$$\left|\underset{\text{M}}{=\!=\!=}B \text{ iff } \right|\underset{M^{d_0}/d_0}{=\!=\!=}\phi B.$$

'*Only if*' *part:* Assume for *reductio ad absurdum* that for some QT2-model $M = \langle D, d_0, V\rangle$ we have:

(I) $\left|\underset{\text{M}}{=\!=\!=}\forall x B^x/a\right.$

as well as

(II)   not $\left|\underset{M^{d_0}/d_0}{=\!=\!=}\Box(\phi B)^\delta/a\right.$

By the relevant truth-conditions, (I) and (II) respectively amount to:

(I') For all valuations V' on D with $V' =_a V$: $\left|\underset{\langle D, d_0, V'\rangle}{=\!=\!=}B\right.$ (where $B = (B^x/a)^a/x$ and $a \in \text{Cons}_L$ obviously does not occur in B^x/a).

(II') For some $d \in D$: not $\left|\underset{\langle D, \langle d_0, d\rangle, V\rangle}{=\!=\!=}(\phi B)^\delta/a\right.$

Consider then 'this' $d \in D$, and define V^+ as the valuation of L on D, such that:

   $V^+(a) = d$,
   $V^+(b) = V(b)$ for each $b \in \text{Cons}_L$ distinct from a,
   $V^+(P^n) = V(P^n)$ for all $P^n \in \text{Pred}_L^n$ with $n = 0, 1, 2$.

Clearly, then, we have that $V^+ =_a V$ (our above definition of this relationship applies automatically to DM2-languages L as well). From that result together with Part I of our Substitution Lemma for DM2 (to be stated and proved in the next section, 6, below) we can conclude:

(III) $\left|\underset{\langle D, \langle d_0, d_0\rangle V^+\rangle}{=\!=\!=}\phi B \text{ iff } \right|\underset{\langle D, \langle d_0, V^+(a)\rangle, V\rangle}{=\!=\!=}(\phi B)^\delta/a.$

Again, since $\langle D, d_0, V^+\rangle$ is obviously a QT2-model (because $\mathrm{Cons}_L = \mathrm{Cons}_L$ and $\mathrm{Pred}_L^n = \mathrm{Pred}_L^n$), we obtain by the inductive hypothesis:

(IV) $\left|\overline{\underset{\langle D,\, d_0,\, V^+\rangle}{}}\,\right.$ B iff $\left|\overline{\underset{\langle D,\, \langle d_0,\, d_0\rangle,\, V^+\rangle}{}}\,\right.$ ϕB.

Now, since $V^+(a) = d$, we use (II′), (III) and (IV) to infer

(V) not $\left|\overline{\underset{\langle D,\, d_0,\, V^+\rangle}{}}\,\right.$ B.

On the other hand, since $V^+ =_a V$, (I′) gives us

(VI) $\left|\overline{\underset{\langle D,\, d_0,\, V^+\rangle}{}}\,\right.$ B.

But (VI) contradicts (V), whence the 'only if' part of our desired result is established in subcase (i).

'If' part: Assume for *reductio* that some QT2-model $M = \langle D, d_0, V\rangle$ be such that:

(I) $\left|\overline{\underset{M^{d_0}/d_0}{}}\,\right.$ $\square(\phi B)^\delta/a$, and

(II) not $\left|\overline{\underset{M}{}}\,\right.$ $\forall x B^x/a$.

Here, by the relevant truth-conditions, (I) and (II) respectively amount to:

(I′) For each $d \in D$: $\left|\overline{\underset{\langle D,\, \langle d_0,\, d\rangle,\, V\rangle}{}}\,\right.$ $\phi B^\delta/a$.

(II′) For some V' on D with $V' =_a V$: not $\left|\overline{\underset{\langle D,\, d_0,\, V'\rangle}{}}\,\right.$ B.

Consider 'this' V'; the hypothesis of induction then gives us:

(III) $\left|\overline{\underset{\langle D,\, d_0,\, V'\rangle}{}}\,\right.$ B iff $\left|\overline{\underset{\langle D,\, \langle d_0,\, d_0\rangle,\, V'\rangle}{}}\,\right.$ ϕB.

Again, since $V' =_a V$, we use Part I of the Substitution Lemma for DM2 to infer

(IV) $\left|\overline{\underset{\langle D,\, \langle d_0,\, d_0\rangle,\, V'\rangle}{}}\,\right.$ ϕB iff $\left|\overline{\underset{\langle D,\, \langle d_0,\, V'(a)\rangle,\, V\rangle}{}}\,\right.$ $(\phi B)^\delta/a$.

Now, (II′), (III) and (IV) together imply:

(V) not $\left|\overline{\underset{\langle D,\, \langle d_0,\, V'(a)\rangle,\, V\rangle}{}}\,\right.$ $(\phi B)^\delta/a$.

However, since $V'(a) \in D$, (I′) yields

(VI) $\left|\overline{\underset{\langle D,\, \langle d_0,\, V'(a)\rangle,\, V\rangle}{}}\,\right.$ $(\phi B)^\delta/a$, which result contradicts (V) and establishes the 'if' part of our desired result in subcase (i).

Subcase (ii). The desired result is to the effect that for all QT2-models M:

$$\left|\!\!\frac{\mathrm{M}}{=\!=\!=}\forall yB^y/a \text{ iff } \right|\!\!\frac{M^{d_0}/d_0}{=\!=\!=}\mathrm{U}(\phi B)^{\curlyvee^{\mathscr{Q}}}/a,$$

where, by the definition of ϕ, $\mathrm{U}(\phi B)^{\curlyvee^{\mathscr{Q}}}/a = \phi(\forall yB^y/a)$, $\curlyvee^{\mathscr{Q}} = \phi(y)$ and $a = \phi(a)$.

The 'only if' and 'if' sections here are proved in much the same way as in subcase (i), except that one appeals to Part II of our Substitution Lemma for DM2 at the crucial stages of the demonstration (see section 6 below).

Finally, we consider

Case A = $\exists xB^x/a$, for some B, a, and x as in the previous case. The desired results in our new subcases (i) and (ii), viz. to the effect that for all QT2-models M = $\langle D, d_0, V \rangle$:

$$\left|\!\!\frac{\mathrm{M}}{=\!=\!=}\exists xB^x/a \text{ iff } \right|\!\!\frac{M^{d_0}/d_0}{=\!=\!=}\Diamond\phi B^\delta/a$$

and

$$\left|\!\!\frac{\mathrm{M}}{=\!=\!=}\exists yB^y/a \text{ iff } \right|\!\!\frac{M^{d_0}/d_0}{=\!=\!=}\mathrm{E}\phi B^{\curlyvee^{\mathscr{Q}}}/a,$$

are obtained in an almost automatic fashion, given the proofs so far presented. This completes the inductive proof of our Translation Theorem for QT2 and DM2.

As we have appealed to the Substitution Lemma for DM2 already a number of times, we are now urgently called upon to state it exactly and to establish it.

6. *The Substitution Lemma for DM2*

The Lemma involves two parts, viz. the following ones.

Part I

Let A ∈ W_L and a ∈ $Cons_L$ be such that:

   (a) A contains a,
   (b) A does not contain δ (and hence neither $\square$ nor $\Diamond$),
   (c) A does not contain $\boxed{\mathrm{u}}$, $\boxed{\mathrm{o}}$ or $\boxed{\mathrm{X}}$.

Moreover, let M = $\langle D, \langle d_0, d_0 \rangle, V \rangle$ be any original DM2-model for L, and let V^+ be any valuation of L on D. Assume that $V^+ =_a V$. *Then*, for all $d, d' \in D$:

$$\overline{\overline{\langle D, \langle d, d'\rangle, V^+\rangle}} \; A \; \text{iff} \; \overline{\overline{\langle D, \langle d, V^+(a)\rangle, V\rangle}} \; A^\delta/a.$$

Part II

Let $A \in W_L$ and $a \in \text{Cons}_L$ be such that:

(a) A contains a,

(b) A does not contain $\mathscr{S}$ (and hence neither U nor E),

(c) A does not contain $\boxed{\text{u}}$, $\boxed{\text{o}}$ or $\boxed{\text{X}}$.

Furthermore, let $M = \langle D, \langle d_0, d_0\rangle, V\rangle$ be any original DM2-model for L, and let V^+ be any valuation of L on D. Assume that $V^+ =_a V$. *Then*, for all $d, d' \in D$:

$$\overline{\overline{\langle D, \langle d, d'\rangle, V^+\rangle}} \; A \; \text{iff} \; \overline{\overline{\langle D, \langle V^+(a), d'\rangle, V\rangle}} \; A^{\mathscr{S}}/a.$$

Proof of Part I: By induction on the length of A.

I. *Basis:* $A \in \text{AtW}_L$.

Case $A = P^0$ ($\in \text{Pred}_L^0$). Here the desired result goes through both because $V^+(P^0) = V(P^0)$ and (vacuously) because P^0 fails to contain a.

Case $A = P^1 a$, with $a \in \text{Cons}_L$ by the hypothesis of the Lemma. Now, since $V^+ =_a V$, we have $V^+(P^1) = V(P^1)$, as well as, for all $d, d' \in D$, $\text{val}^{\langle D, \langle d, d'\rangle, V^+\rangle}(a) = V^+(a) = \text{val}^{\langle D, \langle d, V^+(a)\rangle, V\rangle}(\delta)$, by the definition of val. Hence, the desired result is immediate by the relevant truth-condition.

Case $A = P^2 ab$, for some $P^2 \in \text{Pred}_L^2$ and some $b \in \text{Cons}_L \cup \{\mathscr{S}\}$. There are three subcases, (i)–(iii).

(i) b is $\mathscr{S}$. Again, we have $V^+(P^2) = V(P^2)$, and for all $d, d' \in D$: $\text{val}^{\langle D, \langle d, d'\rangle, V^+\rangle}(a) = V^+(a) = \text{val}^{\langle D, \langle d, V^+(a)\rangle, V\rangle}(\delta)$ as well as $\text{val}^{\langle D, \langle d, d'\rangle, V^+\rangle}(\mathscr{S}) = d = \text{val}^{\langle D, \langle d, V^+(a)\rangle, V\rangle}(\mathscr{S})$. By the relevant truth-condition, the desired result is immediate, as both sides of the requisite equivalence assert that $\langle V^+(a), d\rangle \in V(P^2)$.

(ii) $b \in \text{Cons}_L$ and b is a. The desired result follows from the facts pointed out in (i).

(iii) $b \in \text{Cons}_L$ and b is distinct from a. The only additional fact to which we must appeal here is this: since $V^+ =_a V$, $V^+(b) = V(b)$, whence $\text{val}^{\langle D, \langle d, d'\rangle, V^+\rangle}(b) = V^+(b) = \text{val}^{\langle D, \langle d, V^+(a)\rangle, V\rangle}(b)$.

Case $A = P^2 ba$, with the same subcases as in the preceding case, according to the nature of $b \in \text{Cons}_L \cup \{\mathscr{S}\}$. The same facts appealed to in those subcases suffice to establish the Lemma in the present ones as well.

Case A is $(a = b)$, for some $b \in \text{Cons}_L \cup \{\mathscr{S}\}$, with the same subcases as above. The desired result follows unproblematically from the relevant truth-condition and the aforementioned facts.

Case A is $(b = a)$, with the same subcases as above. No problems.

II. *Induction Step:* In the cases where A has one or other of the forms $-B$, (B & C), (B ∨ C), (B → C), Part I of the Lemma is readily seen to hold by virtue of the inductive hypothesis, the relevant truth-conditions, and the fact that our syntactic substitution operation / commutes with $-$ and is distributive with respect to &, ∨, and →, so that the following identities obtain: $(-B)^\delta/a = -(B^\delta/a)$, $(B \& C)^\delta/a = (B^\delta/a \& C^\delta/a)$, and similarly for ∨ and →. See e.g. Hintikka (1955), appendix, p. 53.

Case A = UB, for some B ∈ W_L such that B contains some occurrence(s) of $\wp$ and B satisfies (a)–(c) in the hypothesis of the Lemma, Part I; whence A will satisfy (a)–(c) as well.

We are to show that, on the hypothesis of the Lemma, Part I:

$$\left\|\frac{\langle D, \langle d, d'\rangle, V^+\rangle}{}\right. \text{ UB iff } \left\|\frac{\langle D, \langle d, V^+(a)\rangle, V\rangle}{}\right. \text{ UB}^\delta/a$$

for all $d, d' \in D$.

'*Only if*' *part:* Assume for *reductio ad absurdum* that some $d, d' \in D$ be such such that:

(I) $\left\|\dfrac{\langle D, \langle d, d'\rangle, V^+\rangle}{}\right.$ UB

(II) not $\left\|\dfrac{\langle D, \langle d, V^+(a)\rangle, V\rangle}{}\right.$ UB$^\delta/a$.

By the relevant truth-condition, (I) and (II) respectively amount to:

(I′) For each $d'' \in D$: $\left\|\dfrac{\langle D, \langle d'', d'\rangle, V^+\rangle}{}\right.$ B

(II′) For some $\underline{d} \in D$: not $\left\|\dfrac{\langle D, \langle \underline{d}, V^+(a)\rangle, V\rangle}{}\right.$ B$^\delta/a$.

With respect to 'that' $\underline{d}$, we obtain by virtue of the inductive hypothesis:

(III) $\left\|\dfrac{\langle D, \langle \underline{d}, d'\rangle, V^+\rangle}{}\right.$ B iff $\left\|\dfrac{\langle D, \langle \underline{d}, V^+(a)\rangle, V\rangle}{}\right.$ B$^\delta/a$.

(II′) and (III) together yield

(IV) not $\left\|\dfrac{\langle D, \langle \underline{d}, d'\rangle, V^+\rangle}{}\right.$ B.

However, since $\underline{d} \in D$, we obtain from (I′):

(V) $\left\|\dfrac{\langle D, \langle \underline{d}, d'\rangle, V^+\rangle}{}\right.$ B.

This contradiction proves the 'only if' part.

12

'*If*' *part:* Assume for *reductio* that some $d, d' \in D$ be such that:

(I) $\left|\underline{}\dfrac{\langle D, \langle d, V^+(a)\rangle, V\rangle}{}}\right. UB^\delta/a$

(II) not $\left|\underline{}\dfrac{\langle D, \langle d, d'\rangle, V^+\rangle}{}}\right. UB.$

By the relevant truth-condition, (I) and (II) respectively amount to:

(I') $\left|\underline{}\dfrac{\langle D, \langle d'', V^+(a)\rangle, V\rangle}{}}\right. B^\delta/a$ for all $d'' \in D$

(II') not $\left|\underline{}\dfrac{\langle D, \langle \underline{d}, d'\rangle, V^+\rangle}{}}\right. B,$ for some $\underline{d} \in D.$

With respect to 'that' $\underline{d}$, the inductive hypothesis again gives us the result (III) above, which together with our present (II') yields:

(IV) not $\left|\underline{}\dfrac{\langle D, \langle \underline{d}, V^+(a)\rangle, V\rangle}{}}\right. B^\delta/a.$

On the other hand, since $\underline{d} \in D$, we derive the negation of (IV) from our present (I'), whence the desired 'if' part. The proof of *Case* A = UB is complete.

Case A = EB, for some $B \in W_L$ as in the previous case. The proof technique presents no novelties and is left to the reader.

The induction is complete, and Part I is established.

Most details in the inductive proof of Part II of the Lemma can again be left to the reader; let us only make the following comments on its behalf. In the induction basis, one observes in the last four cases that $b \in Cons_L \cup \{\delta\}$; for the rest, one appeals to such facts as $V^+(a) = val^{\langle D, \langle d, d'\rangle, V^+\rangle}(a) = val^{\langle D, \langle V^+(a), d'\rangle, V\rangle}(\alpha^{\mathscr{G}})$, $V^+(P^n) = V(P^n)$ for $n = 0, 1, 2$; and so on. The crucial cases in the induction step are of course A = $\square$B and A = $\diamondsuit$B.

As a final exercise to the reader, we suggest that he check the applications of the Substitution Lemma for DM2 made in our above (section 5) proof of the adequacy of the translation ϕ.

7. *Some corollaries to the Translation Theorem for QT2 and DM2*

Let L, L be any pair of a QT2-language with a DM2-language such that $Cons_L = Cons_L$ and $Pred_L^n = Pred_L^n$ for $n = 0, 1, 2$. We then have the following two corollaries to our Translation Theorem for QT2 and DM2:

Corollary 1. For any $A \in W_L$: A is QT2-valid iff $\phi A (\in W_L)$ is DM2-d_0-valid.

Corollary 2. For any $A \in W_L$: A is QT2-satisfiable iff $\phi(A) (\in W_L)$ is DM2-d_0-satisfiable.

Proof: These results are immediate from the Translation Theorem and our above definitions of the relevant notions involved.

At this juncture one may ask whether the two corollaries remain true when the notions of DM2-d_0-validity and DM2-d_0-satisfiability are replaced by the 'plain', or more general ones of DM2-validity and DM2-satisfiability *simpliciter*. The answer is affirmative—we draw attention to the following additional results:

Lemma 1. For any A ∈ W_L: ϕA (∈ W_L) is DM2-d_0-valid iff ϕA is DM2-valid.

Lemma 2. For any A ∈ W_L: ϕA (∈ W_L) is DM2-d_0-satisfiable iff ϕA is DM2-satisfiable.

Proof: For any A ∈ W_L, ϕA satisfies provisos (a) and (b) of A15, A16 and T10. Therefore, by T10, the schemata

(i) $\phi A \leftrightarrow \boxed{uX_u} \Box \phi A$

(ii) $\phi A \leftrightarrow \langle\!\langle uX_u \rangle\!\rangle \Diamond \phi A$

are DM2-provable, for any A ∈ W_L. By the soundness result for DM2, then, (i) and (ii) are DM2-valid, and hence DM2-d_0-valid, yielding Lemmata 1 and 2 respectively.

Again, by these two Lemmata, we are entitled to make the desired substitutions in Corollaries 1 and 2.

8. *Definite and indefinite descriptions in QT2 and DM2*

Essentially for reasons adduced already in Carnap (1947) section 8, we favour a Fregean treatment of descriptive phrases (descriptions), using a designated element d_0 ('null-entity') in the domain of any model to serve as *descriptum* for improper descriptions, whether the definite or the indefinite ones to be considered below. Our QT2- and DM2-languages will then possess a *fixed name*, *o*, which denotes d_0 relatively to any model. We apologize for the presentation being somewhat sketchy, as we are more concerned about indicating an idea rather than working it out in a completely detailed fashion.

First, we add to the stock of *logical constants* of any QT2-language *L* the two variable-binding term-forming operators ι and η for *definite* and *indefinite* descriptions, respectively. ι is to be read as 'the', and η as 'a' (or 'an'); they are thus intended as formal counterparts to the *definite* as well as the *indefinite* article of English, then. The fixed name, *o*, of the 'null-entity' is also added to the logical symbols of *L*.

Next, the set Tm_L of L-terms is then defined *simultaneously with* W_L by our adding recursive rules like the following to our earlier rules for L:

(I) $\text{Cons}_L \subseteq \text{Tm}_L$

(II) $o \in \text{TM}_L$

(III) If $x \in \text{Var}_L$, $a \in \text{Cons}_L$, if A is in W_L and contains a but not x, then $\iota x A^x/a$ and $\eta x A^x/a$ are in Tm_L.

Turning to the semantics for our extended system QT2, then, we construct *extended* QT2-*models* for L as ordered quintuples $M = \langle D, d_0, V, c_\iota, c_\eta \rangle$, where c_ι and c_η are functions from $\mathscr{P}D$ (the power-set of D) into D, satisfying the following conditions, respectively, for any $K \subseteq D$:

(IV) $c_\iota K = \begin{cases} \text{the sole member of K, if K is the unit set of an element of D} \\ d_0, \text{ otherwise} \end{cases}$

(V) $c_\eta K = \begin{cases} \text{a 'chosen' member of K, if } K \neq \varnothing \\ d_0, \text{ otherwise} \end{cases}$

Again, let $M = \langle D, d_0, V, c_\iota, c_\eta \rangle$ be an extended QT2-model. For any member of Tm_L, we now define the function val relatively to M by the following conditions:

(i) $\text{val}^M(a) = V(a)$, for $a \in \text{Cons}_L$

(ii) $\text{val}^M(o) = d_0$

(iii) $\text{val}^M(\iota x A^x/a) = c_\iota |A|^M$

(iv) $\text{val}^M(\eta x A^x/a) = c_\eta |A|^M$

where, in (iii)–(iv), $|A|^M = \{d \in D : d = V'(a)$ and $\overline{\overline{}}^{\langle D, d_0, V', c_\iota, c_\eta \rangle} A,$ for some V' on D with $V' =_a V\}$. It is then clear from this definition of $|A|^M$ that val^M is really defined together with $\overline{\overline{}}^{M}$ by *simultaneous recursion*; indeed, val^M shows up in the following conditions of truth in M:

(2) $\overline{\overline{}}^{M} P^n a_1, \ldots, a_n$ iff $\langle \text{val}^M(a_1), \ldots, \text{val}^M(a_n) \rangle \in V(P^n)$,
where $a_1, \ldots, a_n \in \text{Tm}_L$ and $n = 0, 1, 2$.

(3) $\overline{\overline{}}^{M}(a = b)$ iff $\text{val}^M(a)$ is identical to $\text{val}^M(b)$,
where $a, b \in \text{Tm}_L$.

Remark: Our semantics for ι- and η-terms of L exemplifies a general technique for handling variable bound terms, due to Corcoran, Hatcher & Herring (1972).

How is the deductive system QT2 to be modified and extended in our present setting where definite and indefinite descriptions are forthcoming? Without attempting any proof, we suggest the following:

The proviso to Q_1 and Q_2 is this: 'where $a \in Tm_L$ and is such that $A^a/x \in W_L$'. The proviso to Q_3 is simply 'for any $a \in Tm_L$', and in the case of Q_4: 'where $a, b \in Tm_L$ and are such that $A^a//b \in W_L$'. Again, in the cases of r_1 and r_2, the proviso now reads: 'where $a \in Tm_L$ occurs neither in A nor in B and is such that $B^a/x \in W_L$'.

Furthermore, the following schemata are valid in our extended QT2, whence they could be stipulated axiomatically:

$Q_{5.1}$. $\iota xA^x/a = \iota yA^y/a$, where x, y are distinct members of Var_L, $a \in Cons_L$, $A \in W_L$, and where A contains a but neither x nor y.

$Q_{5.2}$. $\eta xA^x/a = \eta yA^y/a$, with the same proviso.

Q_6. $\exists x(A^x/a \ \& \ \forall y(A^y/a \to y = x)) \to A^{(\iota xA^x/a)}/a$, with the same proviso.

Q_7. $-\exists x(A^x/a \ \& \ \forall y(A^y/a \to y = x)) \to (\iota xA^x/a = o)$, with the same proviso.

Q_8. $\exists xA^x/a \to A^{(\eta xA^x/a)}/a$, where $A \in W_L$ contains $a \in Cons_L$ but not $x \in Var_L$.

Q_9. $-\exists xA^x/a \to (\eta xA^x/a = o)$, with the same proviso.

$Q_{10.1}$. $\forall x(A^x/a \leftrightarrow B^x/a) \to (\iota xA^x/a = \iota xB^x/a)$, where A, B $\in W_L$ contain $a \in Cons_L$ but not $x \in Var_L$.

$Q_{10.2}$. $\forall x(A^x/a \leftrightarrow B^x/a) \to (\eta xA^x/a = \eta xB^x/a)$, with the same proviso.

Remark: Here, $Q_{5.1}$–2 and $Q_{10.1}$–2 should be compared with 2.2 and 2.3 on p. 179 of Corcoran *et al.* (1972). Also, the antecedent of Q_6 has the familiar reading: 'there is *exactly one* x such that A^x/a'.

Before leaving our extended QT2, let us add a quick comment on definite descriptions in ordinary language. Obviously, phrases of the grammatical form '*the* so-and-so' run a greater risk of being doomed improper than those of the form '*a*(n) so-and-so'; for, given that there are so-and-so's, this at once guarantees the propriety of the latter, *in*definite descriptive phrase, whereas that of the former requires *uniqueness* as well (there mustn't be more than one so-and-so). An advantage of studying systems like our extended QT2, where both definite and indefinite descriptions are forthcoming, is now that one can easily define a definite description-operator, say $\mathscr{I}$, which is, so to speak, *immune to failure of uniqueness*:

$\mathscr{I}xA^x/a = df \ \iota x(x = \eta yA^y/a)$, where $A \in W_L$ contains $a \in Cons_L$ but neither x nor y $\in$ Var$_L$. With respect to $\mathscr{Y}$, the result $\mathscr{Y}$xA^x/a = ηyA^y/a is readily seen to be valid in our extended QT2, and to be provable in the deductive system given above. $\mathscr{Y}$ may also be helpful from a linguistic point of view, e.g. in explaining the shift from 'a' to 'the' in examples like these: 'A new procedure for electing presidents was adopted last month. The new procedure is to the following effect: . . .'

Let us now pass to consideration of an extended version of DM2, which is to match our enriched QT2 in relevant respects.

We add to the logical constants of any DM2-language L two pairs τ, σ and α, β of term-forming operators, where τ, σ are both to be read as 'the individual such that', and where α, β are both read as 'an individual such that'. Contrast these readings with those adopted for ι and η! The 'null-symbol' o is still with us, too. By simultaneous induction we then define the sets Tm$_L$ and W$_L$ by adding to our earlier L-rules the following:

(I) Cons$_L$ $\cup$ {δ, $\mathscr{Y}$} $\subseteq$ Tm$_L$

(II) o $\in$ Tm$_L$

(III) If a $\in$ Cons$_L$, if A $\in$ W$_L$ contains no occurrences of $\boxed{\text{u}}$, $\boxed{\text{o}}$, or $\boxed{\text{X}}$, and if A contains a but not δ, *then* τA$^\delta$/a and αA$^\delta$/a $\in$ Tm$_L$.

(IV) If a $\in$ Cons$_L$, if A $\in$ W$_L$ contains no occurrences of $\boxed{\text{u}}$, $\boxed{\text{o}}$, or $\boxed{\text{X}}$ and if A contains a but not $\mathscr{Y}$, *then* σA$^{\mathscr{Y}}$/a and βA$^{\mathscr{Y}}$/a $\in$ Tm$_L$.

Thus, by (III) and (IV), τ and α both 'go together with' δ (like $\square$ and $\Diamond$); similarly, σ and β both go together with $\mathscr{Y}$ (like U and E). Note also that, as a piece of terminology, although all four are admittedly term-forming operators, they are not *variable-binding* ones in the same sense as are ι and η.

Now, let L be any QT2-language extended with ι, η and o, let L be any DM2-language enriched by τ, σ, α, β, and o. Again, assume L, L to be such that Cons$_L$ = Cons$_L$ as well as Pred$_L^n$ = Pred$_L^n$ for n = o, 1, 2. We want to extend the translation function ϕ from L into L, and make the following fresh stipulations:

(4) $\phi(o)$ = o

(ix) $\phi(\iota$xA^x/a) = $\begin{cases} \tau(\phi A)^\delta/a, & \text{if x} = x \text{ so that } \delta = \phi(x) \\ \sigma(\phi A)^{\mathscr{Y}}/a, & \text{if x} = y \text{ so that } \mathscr{Y} = \phi(x) \end{cases}$

(x) $\phi(\eta$xA^x/a) = $\begin{cases} \alpha(\phi A)^\delta/a, & \text{if x} = x \\ \beta(\phi A)^{\mathscr{Y}}/a, & \text{if x} = y \end{cases}$

For spatio-temporal reasons, we decide to close the paper at this juncture, just making a few obvious comments.

(i) Using ϕ as now defined, the reader should check the results of translating our extended deductive system QT2 into an appropriate extension of DM2, and consider what additional schemata and rules are to go into the latter.

(ii) Extended DM2-*models* for L will be construed as ordered quintuples $M = \langle D, \langle d_0, d_0 \rangle, V, c_\iota, c_\eta \rangle = M^{d_0}/d_0$ (in the case of *original* models) and, in general, as structures $M^d/d' = \langle D, \langle d, d' \rangle, V, c_\iota, c_\eta \rangle$. One then defines $\mathrm{val}^{M^d/d'}$ for any member of our extended Tm_L and $\left| \underline{\underline{\quad M^d/d' \quad}} \right.$ for our extended W_L by simultaneous recursion. Exactly how? This question is left to the reader. Given a correct answer, one is then in the position to deal with the adequacy of ϕ as extended above.

Bibliography

Åqvist, L.
(1973) 'Modal logic with subjunctive conditionals and dispositional predicates', *Journal of Philosophical Logic*, 2.
(1976) 'Formal semantics for verb tenses as analyzed by Reichenbach', *in* (ed.) T. van Dijk, *Pragmatics of Language and Literature*, Amsterdam.

Åqvist, L. and Guenthner, F.
(1975) 'Fundamentals of a theory of verb aspect and events within the setting of an improved tense-logic', forthcoming *in* (eds.) F. Guenthner and Chr. Rohrer, *Studies in Formal Semantics*, Amsterdam.

Bach, E. and Cooper, R.
(forthcoming) 'A squib concerning a semantics for the NP S analysis of relative clauses within Montague's theory'.

Bar-Hillel, Y.
(1971) 'Out of the pragmatic wastebasket', *Linguistic Inquiry*, 2.

Bellugi-Klima, U. and Klima, E.
(1975) 'Two faces of sign: iconic and abstract', Conference on Origins and Evolution of Language and Speech, New York Academy of Sciences.

Bennett, M.
(1974) 'Some extensions of a Montague fragment of English', Ph.D. diss., U.C.L.A.

Block, N.
(1971) 'Physicalism and theoretical identity', Ph.D. diss., Harvard University.

Bloomfield, L.
(1933) *Language*, New York.
(1936) 'Language and ideas', *Language*, 12.
(1955) 'Linguistic aspects of science', *International Encyclopedia of Unified Science*, Chicago.

Bolinger, D.
(1974) 'Truth is a linguistic question', *Language*, 49.

Burge, Tyler
(1973) 'Reference and proper names', *Journal of Philosophy*, 70.
(1974) 'Demonstrative constructions, reference and truth', *Journal of Philosophy*, 71.

Carnap, R.
(1947) *Meaning and Necessity*, Chicago.

Chateaubriant, O.
(to appear) 'Mathematical reality.'

Chomsky, N.
(1957) *Syntactic Structures*, The Hague.
(1962) 'Explanatory models in linguistics', *in* (eds.) E. Nagel, P. Suppes and A. Tarski, *Logic, Methodology and Philosophy of Science*, Stanford.
(1964) 'Current issues in linguistic theory', *in* (eds.) J. A. Fodor and J. J. Katz,

The Structure of Language: Readings in the Philosophy of Language, Englewood Cliffs.

(1965) *Aspects of the Theory of Syntax*, Cambridge, Mass.

(1966) *Cartesian Linguistics*, New York.

(1967) 'Recent contributions to the theory of innate ideas', *Synthese*, 17.

(1968a) *Language and Mind*, New York.

(1968b) 'Quine's empirical assumptions', *Synthese*, 19. 1/2.

(1971) 'Deep structure, surface structure and semantic interpretation', *in* (eds.) D. D. Steinberg and L. A. Jakobovits, *Semantics, An Interdisciplinary Reader in Philosophy, Linguistics and Psychology*, Cambridge.

(1972) 'Some empirical issues in the theory of transformational grammar', *Studies on Semantics in Generative Grammar*, The Hague.

Church, A.

(1950) 'On Carnap's analysis of statements of assertion and belief', *Analysis*, 10.

(1951a) 'The need for abstract entities in semantic analysis', *Proceedings of the American Academy of Arts and Letters*, 80.

(1951b) 'A formulation of the logic of sense and denotation,' *in* (eds.) P. Henle, H. Kallen and S. Langer, *Structure, Method and Meaning: Essays in Honor of H. M. Scheffer*, New York.

(1956) *Introduction to Mathematical Logic*, Princeton.

Cooper, R.

(1975a) 'Montague's semantic theory of adverbs and the VSO Hypothesis', *Papers from the Fifth Annual Meeting, North Eastern Linguistic Society*, Cambridge, Mass.

(1975b) 'Montague's semantic theory and transformational syntax', Ph.D. diss., University of Massachusetts.

Cooper, R. and Parsons, T.

(1975) 'Montague grammar, generative semantics and interpretive semantics', *in* (ed.) B. Partee, *Montague Grammar*, New York.

Corcoran, J., Hatcher, W. and Herring, J.

(1972) 'Variable binding term operators', *Zeitschrift für Mathematische Logik und Grundlagen der Mathematik*, 18.

Cresswell, M. J.

(1972) 'Intensional logics and logical truth', *Journal of Philosophical Logic*, 1.

(1973) *Logics and Languages*, London.

(1974) 'Adverbs and events', *Synthese*, 28.

(1975a) 'Semantic deviance', *Linguistische Berichte*, 35.

(1975b) 'Hyperintensional logic', *Studia Logica*, 34.

Davidson, D.

(1967) 'Truth and meaning', *Synthese*, 17.

(1968) 'On saying that', *Synthese*, 19.

(1970) 'Mental events', *in* (eds.) L. Foster and J. Swanson, *Experience and Theory*, Amherst.

(1973) 'Radical interpretation', *Dialectica*, 27.

(1974a) 'On the very idea of a conceptual scheme', *Proceedings and Addresses of the American Philosophical Association*, xlvii, (1973–4).

(1974b) 'Belief and the basis of meaning', *Synthese*, 27.

Dixon, R.
(1972) *The Dyirbal Language of North Queensland*, Cambridge.
Dummett, M.
(1976) 'What is a theory of meaning?' (II), *in* (eds.) G. Evans and J. McDowell, *Truth and Meaning*, Oxford.
Edmonds, J.
(1970) 'Root and structure preserving transformations', Ph.D. diss., M.I.T.
Evans, G.
(1975) 'Identity and predication', *Journal of Philosophy*, 12.
Fine, K.
(1975) 'Vagueness, truth and logic', *Synthese*, 30.
Fodor, J. A.
(1968) *Psychological Explanation*, New York.
(1970) 'Troubles about actions', *Synthese*, 21.
Fodor, J., Bever, T. and Garrett, M.
(1975) *The Psychology of Language*, New York.
Fraassen, B. C. van
(1971) *Formal Semantics and Logic*, New York.
Frege, G.
(1956) 'The thought', *Mind*, lxv.
(1960) 'Über Sinn und Bedeutung', *Zeitschrift für Philosophie und philosophische Kritik*, 100 (1892) (translated as 'On Sense and Reference' *in* (eds.) P. T. Geach and M. Black, *Translations from the Philosophical Writings of Gottlob Frege*, Oxford.
(1963) 'Compound thoughts', *Mind*, 72.
(1966) 'On concept and object', *in* (eds.) P. T. Geach and M. Black, *Translations from the Philosophical Writings of Gottlob Frege*, Oxford.
Fung Yu-Lan
(1948) *A Short History of Chinese Philosophy*, New York and London.
Geach, P. T.
(1963) 'Quantification theory and the problem of identifying objects of reference', *Acta Philosophica Fennica*, 16.
Givón, T.
(1973) 'Opacity and reference in language: an inquiry into the role of modalities', *in* (ed.) J. Kimball, *Syntax and Semantics*, ii, New York.
(1974) 'Toward a discourse definition of syntax' (manuscript), U.C.L.A.
(1975a) 'The presupposition of negation in language: pragmatics, function, ontology' (manuscript), U.C.L.A.
(1975b) 'Topic, pronoun and grammatical agreement', *in* (ed.) C. Li, *Subject and Topic*, Austin.
Gödel, K.
(1931) 'Über formal unentscheidbare Sätze der *Principa Mathematica* und verwandter Systeme I', *Monatsheft Math. Phys.*, 38. (Translation *in* (ed.) J. van Heijenoort, *From Frege to Gödel: A Source Book in Mathematical Logic*, 1879–1931, Cambridge, Mass.)
Goodman, N.
(1967) 'The epistemological argument', *Synthese*, 17.
(1974) 'On some questions concerning quotation', *Monist*, 58.

Grice, H. P.
(1968) 'Utterer's meaning, sentence-meaning and word-meaning', *Foundations of Language*, 4.
Hale, Ken
(1971) 'Gaps in grammars and cultures' (manuscript).
Halmos, P. R.
(1962) *Algebraic Logic*, New York.
Harrison, B.
(1974) Critical notice of Katz, *Mind*, 83.
Hart, W. D.
(1970) 'On self-reference', *Philosophical Review*, 79.
Hempel, C. G.
(1965) *Aspects of Scientific Explanation*, New York.
Hermes, H.
(1965) *Enumerability, Decidability, Computability*, Berlin.
Hetzron, R.
(1974) 'The presentative movement, or why the ideal word order is VSOP', in (ed.) C. Li, *Word Order and Word Change*, Austin.
Hintikka, K. J. J.
(1955) 'Form and content in quantification theory', *Acta Philosophica Fennica*, viii.
(1969) *Models for Modalities*, New York.
Hooper, J.
(1974) 'On assertive predicates', *UCLS Papers in Syntax*, 5.
Hooper, J. and Thompson, S.
(1973) 'On the applicability of root transformations', *Linguistic Inquiry*, 4.
Horn, L.
(1975) 'Neg-raising verbs', *Stanford Language Universals Project* (manuscript).
Horne, E.
(1961) *Beginning Javanese*, New Haven.
Jackendoff, R.
(1971) 'Modal structures in semantic representation', *Linguistic Inquiry*, 2.
(1972) *Semantic Interpretation in Generative Grammar*, Cambridge, Mass.
(1975) 'On belief contexts', *Linguistic Inquiry*, 60.
Kalish, D. and Montague, R.
(1964) *Logic*, New York.
Kamp, H.
(1975) 'Two theories about adjectives', in (ed.) E. L. Keenan, *Formal Semantics of Natural Language*, Cambridge.
Kant, I.
(1951) *Prolegomena to Any Future Metaphysic*. New York.
Kaplan, D.
(1968) 'Quantifying in', *Synthese*, 19.
Katz, F. and Katz, J. J.
(1977) 'Is necessity the mother of intension?', *Philosophical Review*, 1.
Katz, J. J.
(1966) *The Philosophy of Language*, New York.
(1967) 'Some remarks of Quine on analyticy', *Journal of Philosophy*, 64.

(1972) *Semantic Theory*, New York.

(1974) 'Where things stand now with the analytic-synthetic distinction', *Synthese*, 28.

(1975) 'Logic and language: an examination of recent criticisms of intensionalism', *in* (ed.) K. Gunderson, *Minnesota Studies in the Philosophy of Science*, VII, Minneapolis.

(1976) 'The dilemma between orthodoxy and identity', *in* (ed.) A. Kasher, *Language in Focus*, Dordrecht.

(1977a) *Propositional Structure and Illocutionary Force*, New York.

(1977b) 'A Proper Theory of Names', *Philosophical Studies*, 1.

Katz, J. J.

(in preparation) *What a Grammar is a Theory of.*

Katz, J. J. and Fodor, J. A.

(1963) 'The structure of a semantic theory', *Language*, 39.

Katz, J. J. and Nagel, R. I.

(1974) 'Meaning postulates and semantic theory', *Foundations of Language*, 11.

Katz, J. J. and Postal, P. M.

(1964) *An Integrated Theory of Linguistic Description*, Cambridge, Mass.

Keenan, E. L.

(1972a) 'On semantically based grammar', *Linguistic Inquiry*, 3.

(1972b) 'Relative clause formation in Malagasy and some related and some not so related languages', *The Chicago Which Hunt*, Chicago Linguistic Society.

(1974) 'Logic and language', *in* (eds.) M. Bloomfield and E. Haugen, *Language as a Human Problem*, New York.

(1975a) 'Toward a universal definition of "subject of"', *in* (ed.) C. Li, *Subject and Topic*, Austin.

(1975b) 'The logical diversity of natural languages', Conference on Origins and Evolution of Language and Speech, New York Academy of Sciences.

(1975c) 'Remarkable subjects in Malagasy', to appear *in* (ed.) C. Li, *Subject and Topic*, Austin.

(1975d) 'Logical expressive power and syntactic variation in natural language', *in* (ed.) E. L. Keenan, *Formal Semantics of Natural Language*, Cambridge.

Keenan, E. and Ebert, K.

(1973) 'A note on marking transparency and opacity', *Linguistic Inquiry*, 4.

Keenan, E. O.

(1974) 'Conversation and oratory in Vakinankaratra', Ph.D. diss., University of Pennsylvania.

Kirsner, R.

(1973) 'Natural focus and agentive interpretation: on the semantics of the Dutch expletive *er*', *Stanford Occasional Papers in Linguistics*, 3.

Kleene, S. C.

(1950) *Introduction to Metamathematics*, Princeton (Garrido, M. (tr.), *Introducción a la Metamatematica*, Madrid, 1974).

Kripke, S.

(1972) 'Naming and necessity', *in* (eds.) D. Davidson and G. Harman, *Semantics of Natural Languages*, Dordrecht.

Kuno, S.

(1974) *The Structure of the Japanese Language*, Cambridge, Mass.

Kuroda, S.-Y.

(1972) 'The categorical and thetic judgement', *Foundations of Language*, 9.

Lakoff, G.

(1971) 'On generative semantics', *in* (eds.) D. Steinberg and L. Jakobovits, *Semantics: an Interdisciplinary Reader in Philosophy, Linguistics and Psychology*, Cambridge.

(1972) 'Linguistics and natural logic', *in* (eds.) D. Davidson and G. Harman, *Semantics of Natural Languages*, Dordrecht.

Lakoff, R.

(1974) 'Remarks on *this* and *that*', *Papers from the Chicago Linguistic Society Meeting*, 10.

Langacker, R.

(1969) 'On pronominalization and the chain of command', *in* (eds.) D. Reibel and S. Schane, *Modern Studies in English*, Englewood Cliffs.

Langford, C. H.

(1937) *Journal of Symbolic Logic*, 2.

Lees, R. B.

(1957) 'Review of syntactic structures', *Language*, 33.

Lewis, C. I.

(1946) *An Analysis of Knowledge and Valuation*, La Salle, Ill.

Lewis, D.

(1969) *Convention: A Philosophical Study*, Cambridge, Mass.

(1972) 'General semantics', *in* (eds.) D. Davidson and G. Harman, *Semantics of Natural Language*, Dordrecht.

(1975) 'Languages and language', *in* (ed.) K. Gunderson, *Minnesota Studies in the Philosophy of Science*, VII, Minneapolis.

Li, C. and S. Thompson

(1974) 'The semantic function of word order', *in* (ed.) C. Li, *Word Order and Word Order Change*, Austin.

(1975a) 'Topic prominent languages', LSA Winter (manuscript).

(1975b) 'Subject and topic: a new typology of language', *in* (ed.) C. Li, *Subject and Topic*, Austin.

Lindauer, M.

(1961) *Communication among Social Bees*, Cambridge, Mass.

Lindenfeld, J.

(1973) *Yaqui Syntax*, Los Angeles.

McCawley, J.

(1970) 'English as a *VSO* language', *Language*, 46.

(1971) 'Where do noun phrases come from?', *in* (eds.) D. Steinberg and L. Jacobovits, *Semantics, An Interdisciplinary Reader in Philosophy, Linguistics and Psychology*, Cambridge.

Mendelson, E.

(1964) *Introduction to Mathematical Logic*, Princeton.

Montague, R.

(1974a) *Formal Philosophy* (Selected Papers of R. Montague, ed. and with an introduction by Richmond H. Thomason), New Haven.

(1974b) 'Pragmatics and intensional logic', *in* Montague (1974a).

Morton, A.

(1973) 'The possible in the actual', *Noûs*, 7.

Needham, R.

(1972) *Belief, Language, and Experience*, Oxford.

Nida, E.

(1945) 'Linguistics and ethnology in translation problems', *Word*, i.

Partee, B.

(1972) 'Some transformational extensions of Montague grammar', *in* (ed.) R. Rodman, *Papers in Montague Grammar*, Occasional Papers in Linguistics, 2, University of California.

(1973) 'The semantics of belief sentences', *in* (eds.) J. Hintikka, J. Moravcsik and P. Suppes, *Approaches to Natural Language*, Dordrecht.

(1975) 'Montague Grammar and Transformational Grammar', *Linguistic Inquiry*, 6.

(1975) (ed.) *Montague Grammar*, New York.

Postal, P.

(1964) 'Constituent Structure', *International Journal of American Linguistics*, 30, 1.

Premack, D. A.

(1969) 'A functional analysis of language', Invited Address, American Psychological Association (unpublished), Washington, D.C.

(1971) 'Language in chimpanzees', *Science*, 172.

Putnam, H.

(1970) 'Is semantics possible?', *Metaphilosophy*, 1.

(1974) 'The refutation of conventionalism', *Noûs*, 8.

(1975) 'The meaning of meaning', *in* (ed.) K. Gunderson, *Minnesota Studies in the Philosophy of Science*, VII, Minneapolis.

Quine, W. V.

(1953a) 'Two dogmas of empiricism', *in* W. V. Quine, *From a Logical Point of View*, Cambridge, Mass.

(1953b) 'The problem of meaning in linguistics', *in* W. V. Quine, *From a Logical Point of View*, Cambridge, Mass.

(1960) *Word and Object*, Cambridge, Mass.

(1962) *Mathematical Logic*, New York (revised edition, originally published 1951). (Hierro S.-Pescador, Jose (tr.), *Lógica Matemática*, Madrid, 1972.) (Koj, L. (tr.), *Logika matematyczna*, Warszawa, 1974.)

(1966a) 'Necessary truth', *in* W. V. Quine, *The Ways of Paradox*, New York.

(1966b) 'Carnap and logical truth', *in* W. V. Quine, *The Ways of Paradox*, New York.

(1968) 'Reply to Chomsky', *Synthese*, 19.

(1969) *Ontological Relativity and Other Essays*, New York.

Reichenbach, H.

(1947) *Elements of Symbolic Logic*, New York.

Sapir, E.

(1921) *Language*, New York.

Schachter, P.

(1975) 'The subject in Philippine languages: topic, actor, actor-topic, or none of the above', *in* (ed.) C. Li, *Subject and Topic*, Austin.

Schiffer, S.
  (1972) *Meaning*, Oxford.
Scott, D.
  (1970) 'Advice on modal logic', *in* (ed.) K. Lambert, *Philosophical Problems in Logic*, Dordrecht.
Searle, J.
  (1969) *Speech Acts*, Cambridge.
Segerberg, K.
  (1973) 'Two-dimensional modal logic', *Journal of Philosophical Logic*, 2.
Steklis, H. and Harnad, S.
  (1975) 'From hand to mouth: some critical stages in the evolution of language' (to appear) *in Annals of New York Academy of Sciences*, 1976.
Stich, S.
  (1975) (ed.), *Innate Ideas*, Berkeley.
Tarski, A.
  (1956a) 'The semantical conception of truth', *in* (ed.) L. Linsky, *Semantics and the Philosophy of Language*, Urbana, Ill.
  (1956b) 'The concept of truth in formalized languages', *in* A. Tarski, *Logic, Semantics, Metamathematics*, Oxford.
Thomason, R.
  (1974) 'Some complement constructions in Montague', *in* (eds.) M. LaGaly, R. Fox and A. Bruck, *Papers from the Tenth Regional Meeting*, CLS.
Thomason, R. and Stalnaker, R.
  (1973) 'A semantic theory of adverbs', *Linguistic Inquiry*, 4.
Wallace, J.
  (1972a) 'On the frame of reference', *in* (eds.) D. Davidson and G. Harman, *Semantics of Natural Language*, Dordrecht.
  (1972b) 'Belief and satisfaction', *Noûs*, 6.
Weydt, H.
  (1973) 'On G. Lakoff, instrumental adverbs and the concept of deep structure', *Foundations of Language*, 10.
Wheeler, S. C.
  (1975) 'Reference and vagueness', *Synthese*.
Whorf, B. L.
  (1956) *Language, Thought and Reality*, Cambridge, Mass.
Wilson, N. L.
  (1959a) *The Concept of Language*, Toronto.
  (1959b) 'Substances without substrata', *Review of Metaphysics*, 12.
  (1972) 'Color qualities and reference to them', *Canadian Journal of Philosophy*, 2.
  (1973a) 'On semantically relevant whatsits', *in* (eds.) G. Pearce and P. Maynard, *Conceptual Change*, Dordrecht.
  (1973b) 'Individual identity, space and time in the Leibniz–Clarke correspondence', *in* (ed.) I. Leclerc, *The Philosophy of Leibniz and the Modern World*, Nashville.
Wittgenstein, L.
  (1965) *The Blue and the Brown Books*, New York.
  (1967) *Philosophical Investigations*, Oxford.

Index of names